Sources of Anglo-Saxon Literary Culture: A Trial Version

medieval & renaissance texts & studies

VOLUME 74

Sources of Anglo-Saxon Literary Culture: A Trial Version

Edited by

FREDERICK M. BIGGS

THOMAS D. HILL

PAUL E. SZARMACH

with the assistance of

KAREN HAMMOND

Center for Medieval and Early Renaissance Studies
State University of New York at Binghamton
Binghamton, New York
1990

The preparation of this volume was made possible (in part) by a grant from the Division of Research Programs of the National Endowment for the Humanities, an independent federal agency.

Library of Congress Cataloging-in-Publication Data

Sources of Anglo-Saxon literary culture : a trial version /
  edited by Frederick M. Biggs, Thomas D. Hill, Paul E.
  Szarmach, with the assistance of Karen Hammond.
     p. cm. — (Medieval & Renaissance texts & studies ;
v. 74)
    ISBN 0-86698-084-9
    1. English literature — Old English, ca. 450-1100 —
Bibliography.   2. Civilization, Anglo-Saxon — Sources —
Bibliography.   I. Biggs, Frederick M.   II. Hill,
Thomas D., 1940- . III. Szarmach, Paul E., 1941- .
IV. State University of New York at Binghamton. Center for
Medieval and Early Renaissance Studies.   V. Series.
Z2012.S58   1990
[PR173]
016.829 — dc20   89-13621
                                         CIP

This book is made to last.
It is set in Baskerville, smythe-sewn,
and printed on acid-free paper
to library specifications.

Printed in the United States of America

Table of Contents

Foreword

The *Sources of Anglo-Saxon Literary Culture* (*SASLC*) is a collaborative project that aims to produce a reference work summarizing current scholarship concerning the knowledge and use of literary sources in Anglo-Saxon England. Departing from J.D.A. Ogilvy's *Books Known to the English, 597–1066* and incorporating more recent scholarship, the *SASLC* volume will include contributions from specialists in the various sub-fields of Old English studies. The book is intended to complement other research tools that are either completed or in progress, viz. the *Dictionary of Old English*, the Greenfield-Robinson *Bibliography of Publications on Old English Literature to 1972*, and the *Fontes Anglo-Saxonici*. When completed, the work of *SASLC* will exist in multiple forms: codex book, diskette, and loose-leaf binder. The rationale for these different forms is to encourage a continuing process of revision and correction.

This volume is a *Trial Version* of the final work. Since the usefulness of a "partial" reference tool could be questioned, it might be appropriate to stress the several purposes here intended. As a preliminary publication in anticipation of the complete volume, this version seeks to serve these set purposes: 1) a test-run for editorial procedures, including input, layout and design; 2) a public document released to solicit even wider field criticism than the project committee has already sought; 3) an efficient sample of the project that will stimulate wider participation from scholars working in Anglo-Saxon studies and related fields; 4) a partial record of work done in the first two years of the project; 5) a publication for many who have successfully participated in the project thus far. There is a sixth and more general aim, which will naturally be more fully realized by the complete volume: to stimulate source work in the field by calling attention to what has been accomplished thus far and to the vast amount of work still remaining to be done. Furthermore, in reviewing the various entries submitted to *SASLC* so far, the members of the Advisory Committee and the editors of this volume have had privileged access to several up-to-date scholarly summaries of what is known about books and authors known to the English. It seems to be in the best tradition of scholarship to share this work at the earliest opportunity within the practical limits imposed by funding constraints. The entries here published for *Apocrypha* and *Hiberno-Latin* . . . are clear and evident examples of such work, which supersede any earlier attempts to collect and present similar information regarding the works or authors concerned. The emphasis in this *Trial Version* is, therefore, on *process*, i.e., the notion that publication of source work is never definitive and final, but rather a continuing process, requiring not rigid dogmatism but rather an openness to new possibilities. The word processor is accordingly both a practical aid supporting this research tool and a metaphor signaling that the next revision is at hand. The committee is aware that this volume is incomplete and that readers will find this *Trial Version* inconvenient in several regards; readers should rest assured, however, that the system of cross-referencing will be expanded in the final, complete volume and that the final volume will include extensive indices.

In the Introduction immediately following this Foreword, Thomas D. Hill presents the intellectual rationale and methodology behind the project. Here I seek only to sketch the administrative history to date and projected future plans.

History of the Project

SASLC is a direct outcome of the 1983 Symposium on the Sources of Anglo-Saxon Culture, held at the Medieval Institute, Western Michigan University, which was co-sponsored by the Center for Medieval and Early Renaissance Studies (CEMERS), State University of New York at Binghamton, and granted major funding by the National Endowment for the Humanities, Division of Research Programs. The proceedings of this first Symposium appear as *Sources of Anglo-Saxon Culture*, Studies in Medieval Culture 20 (Kalamazoo, MI, 1986). The Symposium, now continuing into its eighth year (1990), sought at its inaugural meeting to focus on three subfields in Anglo-Saxon Studies, namely literary culture, iconography, and archaeology, and to consider new directions. Discussions in literary culture, which is by far the dominant area of interest in North America, focussed on questions of methodology, the usefulness and availability of research tools, and advances in manuscript studies. While a transcript of the open discussion and a record of many informal meetings would reveal specific points of interchange and several new ideas, a strong consensus developed that under the right conditions the development of a successor volume to Ogilvy's *Books Known* would meet the apparent greatest need.

This first Symposium stimulated activity in Great Britain, serving as the forerunner for a Conference at Leeds University in March, 1984 organized by Joyce Hill and J.E. Cross. Before long the British initiative took a different direction, viz., towards a very large scale, multi-volume project encompassing all vernacular and Latin works, organized on a different principle, i.e., that of identifying, listing, and excerpting for a database all the sources used in the creation of works produced in Anglo-Saxon England. Thus, in contrast to *SASLC*, which works forward from classical, patristic, and medieval sources seeking to summarize the most convincing evidence for their being known or used in Anglo-Saxon England, the British-based *Fontes Anglo-Saxonici* will work backwards from each Anglo-Saxon text, establishing wherever possible the immediate source of each passage. *SASLC* and *Fontes* are thus in inverse relation. Unlike *SASLC*, *Fontes* aims to establish new source relationships. The scale envisioned by the *Fontes* initiative will require two or three decades of work and many scholars committed to specific volumes. At this writing, *Fontes* is well under way with an incipient data base at Manchester University. In organizational parallel with *SASLC*, the *Fontes* group meets annually in March at a rotating site for a public meeting and conference to discuss the progress of the project. There are annual fall meetings for the *Fontes* Executive Committee, in which *SASLC* Administrative Committee members have actively participated. One happy and tangible piece of evidence for the spirit of cooperation is the joint sponsorship of the publication of Michael Lapidge's *Abbreviations for Sources and Specification of Standard Editions for Sources* (1988), which has served as a working document assisting both projects. The Lapidge list has served as the basis for this volume's Bibliography Part I.

To support the first two years of *SASLC* (1987–89), the National Endowment for the Humanities, Division of Resarch, awarded a major grant. As the project committee began to work out the practicalities of the project and to refine specifics of its original plan, issuing invitations to participate to a broad base of scholars and soliciting criticism of various ideas, it also saw how *SASLC* could evolve into a considerably more useful tool than had originally been proposed. The project committee instituted several major design changes; the most thoroughgoing change was the addition of a headnote for each entry, consisting of five distinct categories of basic information about a work's currency among the Anglo-Saxons, i.e., manuscripts, Anglo-Saxon booklists, Anglo-Saxon versions, quotations/citations/echoes, and references. The gathering and weighing of information to be provided under these headings have naturally complicated the work of the contributors and extended the life of the project. The grand strategy for the *SASLC* volume has concomitantly changed. In almost all cases *SASLC* entries have become new creations rather than mere corrections of Ogilvy's *Books Known*.

All these changes were welcomed by the full Advisory Committee at successive meetings, and likewise endorsed by colleagues in the *Fontes Anglo-Saxonici*. The committee hopes that the revised format will elicit a similar positive reaction from students, scholars in general, and Anglo-Saxonists who will use this *Trial Version* and the ultimate volume. As indicated above, a major purpose of this *Trial Version* is to solicit the reactions of reader-users to the usefulness of the entries, as now designed.

Present and Future Plans

The current academic year (1989–90) is the third year of the project. Operating under a no-cost extension of the original NEH grant and receiving further incidental support from the Center for Medieval and Early Renaissance Studies at SUNY-Binghamton, *SASLC* should come by year's end to the completion of all major entries and to almost all minor entries. For the completion of the core of the project, *SASLC* will rely heavily on committees of research supervised by Thomas D. Hill (Cornell) and Charles Wright (Univ. of Illinois at Urbana-Champaign), whose home departments will offer support. The current revised plan calls for a fourth and fifth year of the project to present a reasonably comprehensive treatment of saints' lives and liturgy, two special areas in the study of Anglo-Saxon literary culture that offer daunting complexities. Particularly problematic for Anglo-Saxonists is the reality that most reference works in the field of hagiography, including the Bollandists' guides to hagiographical texts and manuscripts, are keyed to continental sources and collections. One result of this situation is that Anglo-Saxonists have been forced to rely, for Latin sources of Old English texts, on misleading editions based on non-insular manuscripts. *SASLC*'s *Acta Sanctorum* will constitute the first effort to produce a comprehensive survey of the versions and manuscripts the Anglo-Saxons possessed and used in their study and composition of hagiographical texts. Already the *Acta Sanctorum* database set up by Gordon Whatley contains provisions for 330 entries on the basis of a preliminary survey of the most accessible large-scale sources of evidence. It is expected that the *SASLC* format, by virtue of its rigor, its general design, and the information it provides can inspire and facilitate a new understanding of early medieval hagiography from the Anglo-Saxon perspective. This *Trial Version* offers thirteen sample entries treating saints' lives.

The Liturgy in the Anglo-Saxon period offers its own complexities. In this area of study *SASLC* cannot simply rely on what has survived, but rather it will have to exercise an informed imagination controlled by such facts as can be established in order to present in full dimension the variety of matters gathered under the heading "Liturgy." For Richard Pfaff and the research team he will assemble for this last major task for *SASLC*, the challenge will be to establish an adequate framework for understanding the dimensions of possible liturgical influence during the whole of the period.

An Invitation

At this time more than 60 scholars from the international community have contributed or promised to contribute entries for *SASLC*. While a large, collaborative project poses many practical problems of administration and coordination, such a design nevertheless has the great advantage of employing specialist contributors for individual authors, works, or genres. The end result for the volume should be the best work by the best qualified scholars. Even with the many willing hands now working for *SASLC* out of a common, sustained, and shared purpose, the project can still benefit from more scholars interested in sources. Thus, the committee invites those interested to write for further information. There are still minor entries awaiting their writers. Clearly, the project needs contributors to its major sections on Saints' Lives and Liturgy. Appendices B and C, which give a List of Entries and a List of Saints respectively, suggest the scope of work. Now, as always, the project can use expert criticism and reading of entries that are in hand.

For further information on *SASLC* write to:

Prof. Paul E. Szarmach
Project Director, *SASLC*
CEMERS; SUNY-Binghamton
P.O. Box 6000
Binghamton, NY 13902–6000

PHONE: 607–777–2730

Acknowledgments

As Project Director I have the very happy task to acknowledge the many colleagues who have made various contributions to *SASLC*. It was J.E. Cross who first mobilized Anglo-Saxonists in North America to consider creat-ing a successor volume to Ogilvy's *Books Known*; his enthusiasm, his vision, and his power to persuade others to take on this work form the true beginning. J.D.A. Ogilvy himself gave the project his blessing with that same openness and warmth that one can still see in his pioneering book. Certainly the original 1983 Symposium and its continuation, which have served in parallel to sustain and advance *SASLC*, has been possible through the generosity of Otto Gründler, Director of the Medieval Institute at Western Michigan University. Mario A. DiCesare, Director and General Editor of Medieval and Renaissance Texts and Studies, willingly took *SASLC* on with that same spirited devotion to traditional scholarship in its newer form that has inspired his colleagues and ever furnished me with personal example. While noting some in the *SASLC* network with special praise, I mean not to slight others, but I must thank Thomas D. Hill and Frederick M. Biggs. The former has on countless occasions offered sane and sensible advice for the large and the small of this enterprise, while the latter has been the real dynamo behind it. *SASLC* would have remained only an idea without them. The National Endowment for the Humanities, Division of Research, has been our support and our patron, demonstrating through its staff a sympathy and understanding of our goals and needs. At Binghamton the CEMERS Secretary Ann DiStefano and graduate assistants Deborah Mitchell and Cheryl Gravis have greatly advanced the day-to-day details of the project. There are many scholars who have contributed entries to *SASLC*, not all of whose work, given the funding and the timing, can receive the credit due. George H. Brown, Joseph F. Kelly, and Vivien Law, whose three contributions on (respectively) Bede, Augustine, and Grammar (Grammatical Writings) could easily have formed a book, are, among others, represented only in part here because of technical limitations. To these and to the many whose contributions we could not include in full or in any form, I and my co-editors owe a debt of thanks.

Paul E. Szarmach

PROJECT COMMITTEE MEMBERS

Administrative Committee:

Frederick M. Biggs (Univ. of Connecticut)
Thomas D. Hill (Cornell Univ.)
Thomas Mackay (Brigham Young Univ.)
Paul E. Szarmach (SUNY-Binghamton)
E. Gordon Whatley (Queens College, CUNY)

Advisory Committee:

> Janet M. Bately (Univ. of London King's College)
> Carl T. Berkhout (Univ. of Arizona)
> J.E. Cross (Univ. of Liverpool)
> Antonette di Paolo Healey (Univ. of Toronto)
> Michael Lapidge (Univ. of Cambridge)
> Mary P. Richards (Auburn Univ.)
> Donald G. Scragg (Manchester Univ.)
> Joseph Wittig (Univ. of North Carolina-Chapel Hill)
> David Yerkes (Columbia University)

Special Consultants:

> Richard W. Pfaff (Univ. of North Carolina-Chapel Hill)
> Charles D. Wright (Univ. of Illinois at Urbana-Champaign)

The Administrative Committee has general responsibility for the implementation of the plan of work, while the Advisory Committee reviews and comments on various aspects of the new reference tool with the assistance of the Special Consultants.

Introduction

The predecessor and inspiration for our present volume is J.D.A. Ogilvy's *Books Known to the English, 597–1066,* whose title neatly synopsized the
aims of his collection. Our title is vaguer and more amorphous — in part
because it was composed by a committee and in part because our goals
are less easily defined. Ogilvy was concerned simply with "books" — with
Latin texts transcribed and transmitted in the Anglo-Saxon period —
whereas we are interested more broadly in "sources," including oral traditional literature as well as written texts, and in written texts such as char-
ters, medical recipes, and charms which can only be loosely described as
books. These concerns necessitated a new, somewhat more inclusive title,
and it was necessary to distinguish our project from his in any case; but
we have lost something in the change. Since our title no longer speaks for
itself with the brisk assurance of Ogilvy's, and since the user of the Guide
needs some general orientation in any case, this essay is intended to serve
as an introduction to the entries gathered here. The present reference
volume is a collaborative endeavor; it consists of a collection of single entries by numerous scholars and obviously reflects diverse scholarly opinion. This introduction, in contrast, is written by one individual; and it
should be emphasized that the views expressed in the introduction — to the
degree that they are not merely platitudes — are those of a single individual, who has, however, received enough commentary and criticism over a
period of time that he feels it is appropriate to use the editorial first person
plural. What we hope to accomplish in this introduction is a definition of
certain key terms, a guide and warning to users, and a prospectus concerning the objectives of this particular kind of scholarly inquiry — to put
it simply, why we think source scholarship is valid and worth consolidat-
ing in a reference work of this kind.

Methodology

Since the terms "source" and "influence" are used with a good deal of freedom in literary scholarship, let us begin by defining a literary source and its derivative as a particular mode of textual relationship. The first step in establishing such a relationship is to demonstrate parallels between two texts which are so striking that to assume they were fortuitous would "outrage probability," to use R.E. Kaske's phrase. Once such parallels have been established, the next step is to evaluate the historical relationship of the two texts and to determine the kind and direction of influence that these parallels imply. In principle, at least, it might be possible to distinguish between a source and a text derived from it on the basis of careful analysis of the idiom, style, and structure of the two texts. But in practice scholars rely on such analyses only when external historical evidence is not available. And our assumptions about the larger historical context in which a given text was composed can affect our interpretation of apparently straightforward evidence. Thus, given textual parallels between some of the homilies of Augustine's *Tractatus in evangelium Ioannis* and certain of Ælfric's homilies, the conclusion that Augustine is the source and Ælfric derivative is determined not by analysis of the texts themselves, but by our knowledge of the historical relationship of the two texts. This example is obviously a very simple one. No one has yet proposed that Ælfric influenced Augustine. But it is important to emphasize at the outset that defining source relationships is not as simple as it might seem; one must always consider questions of historical and literary context. To take a suppositious example, parallels of exactly the same sort as those between Augustine and Ælfric which involved an Anglo-Saxon and a Greek text would not necessarily be accepted as proof that the latter was the source of the former. The probability of some Latin intermediary would seem a more plausible way of accounting for the parallels than the assumption that an Anglo-Saxon author knew Greek. But at the same time the assumption that the Anglo-Saxons were Greekless can become a self-fulfilling prophecy if all parallels between Anglo-Saxon and Greek texts are explained away by hypothesizing lost Latin intermediaries. For a variety of reasons, the current working assumption of most Anglo-Saxonists that the Anglo-Saxons were generally ignorant of Greek seems to us plausible, but source-scholars must be sensitive to the fact that this is an assumption, and an assumption that shapes the way they understand the "raw" data of textual relationships.

We have referred to "striking textual parallels," but must concede that defining such parallels is a matter of intuitive judgment and that the range of potential ambiguity and subjectivity is wide. The fact remains, however, that many thousands of such textual relationships have been adduced in the fields of Old and Middle English scholarship alone, and have never seriously been questioned. The appeal to the *consensus omnium* may not be an elegant or sophisticated mode of scholarly argument, but it has its force. If we were asked to define our working methodology, we would respond that source scholarship involves a kind of dialectical process in which individual scholars propose source relationships on the basis of intuitive judgment, and these judgments are then either confirmed or denied by the consensus of scholars who take the trouble to evaluate the argument and the supporting evidence. Such a consensus may not be reached quickly if the source relationship is difficult for one reason or another, or if the text involved is obscure. But in principle, once a number of scholars who have no immediate reason to be prejudiced have examined the evidence, a consensus, or at the least an agenda for further research, can be reached.

Implicit in this methodology is the assumption that a "true" definition of a given source relationship is both desirable and in principle attainable, but it must also be clearly acknowledged, that given the limitations of documentation during this period, even the best-established and most secure examples of source-relationships are provisional and open to correction and modification. If Ælfric drew on Augustine's *Tractatus in evangelium Ioannis*, there remains the question of what version of the text of those homilies was accessible to him, or whether Ælfric's choice of available synonyms in translation was influenced by a previous tradition of glossing; and this list of hypothetical discoveries, which might complicate the apparently simple literary-historical fact that Ælfric used Augustine on John, could be extended almost indefinitely. Scholars may believe that in certain areas of Anglo-Saxon literary source scholarship the work has been pretty thoroughly done, but there is always the possibility of surprising new finds.

Terminology

Apart from the provisional character of source scholarship in the field of Old English and Anglo-Latin literature, another immediate problem that must concern us is that there is no established terminology to distinguish among the many possible modes of relationship between two or more texts which may obtain in any given case. For practical purposes we propose to stipulate some working definitions. In literary-historical discourse a source can consist of as little as one word or as much as thousands of lines of text. Indeed, many Anglo-Saxon texts are wholly dependent on one specific source and are conventionally defined as translations or versions of an original. But in ordinary usage the term "source" generally refers to a text that provides the antecedent for some significant portion of a derivative text, while the terms "citation," "quotation," "allusion," or "echo" refer to smaller and more limited instances of similar textual relationships. These less-extended verbal parallels are sometimes indicated in some explicit fashion comparable to the modern device of using quotation marks. But in both vernacular and Christian-Latin literary tradition the concept of authorial proprietorship was less clearly defined than it is in the modern English literary tradition, and authors would often draw passages from antecedent texts without such acknowledgment. For present purposes a "citation" is defined as a passage which is prefaced or concluded by a reference to the author or text from which the quotation is drawn. A "quotation" by contrast need not include such a reference. Even briefer instances of parallel textual relationships are "allusions" or "echoes," the former consisting of words, phrases or larger units of discourse that purposefully recall some particular antecedent text, and the latter consisting of such parallels that occur simply because one author is so thoroughly familiar with some antecedent text that he echoes it unconsciously and inadvertently. In principle it might be possible to distinguish clearly between these various modes of textual relationship, but in practice it can be very difficult to distinguish between a deliberate allusion, intended to call to mind some particular antecedent text, and an echo. For the immediate purposes of this study and in the context of literary-historical discourse, the distinction is not as important as it might seem, since either allusions or echoes reflect the fact that a given author was familiar with a specific source, but readers who consult the various editions and literary handbooks must be aware that there is a good deal of editorial judgment involved in such discriminations.

Problems of Textual Identity

A further problem involving definition concerns the question of the definition of the text itself, or textual identity. In the modern world the question is a comparatively simple one. An individual author writes a specific text and ultimately "authorizes" its publication in a particular form. The specific form of the text presumably reflects the author's intention — a useful if much debated term — and this particular form of the text is reproduced mechanically and disseminated as widely as the economics of publication permit. Anglo-Saxon literary culture reflects the influence of two originally quite discrete literary traditions — Germanic and Christian-Latin — and the concept of textual identity was rather different from the modern one in both traditions. Germanic literary tradition was in large part an oral one, and without prejudicing the much-discussed question of the character and nature of this tradition, it is clear that a "text" that exists in oral tradition exists in a radically different context than in contemporary "literate" tradition.

As far as the Christian-Latin tradition is concerned, the tradition with which we are for the most part concerned in this study, the issue of textual identity is more immediately apprehensible but still raises problems. The Anglo-Saxons knew and understood the concept of textual identity as we understand it — the concept of a text fixed and determined by the intention of an individual author — but the vagaries of early medieval book production, along with scribal practice and the particular circumstances of both vernacular and Anglo-Latin literary culture, frequently complicate the issue of textual identity enormously. A conscientious scholar such as Bede was aware of the problem of textual variation and corruption, and such scholars attempted to correct and correctly identify the texts with which they were dealing. But lesser scholars were less conscientious, and in any case it was necessary to have both good texts and good judgment to correct the faults of one's exemplar. Textual corruption was as a result endemic, and confusion about attribution and canonicity was simply part of the intellectual culture of the period. It could indeed be argued that modern scholarship is still affected by errors deriving from this period. Migne's *Patrologia Latina* is in large part a reprint of sixteenth and seventeenth century editions of Christian-Latin authors, and these editions in turn were often simply based on "old," i.e., early medieval manuscripts. The misattributions and textual confusions that have plagued scholars attempting to work with that monumental collection are in part a direct heritage of the scholarship of the Anglo-Saxon period.

Thus when one is faced with an apparently simple problem of source-scholarship — whether a given Anglo-Saxon author knew a particular classical or patristic text — the first question which must be raised is in what form the text in question might have been circulated. To take a specific example that illustrates something of the complexity of these issues, the Bible was, as it still is, a central text in Catholic Christian culture. Biblical influence is pervasive in the Christian literature of this period. But as one also might expect in a manuscript culture in which every text had to be copied out by hand, there are relatively few manuscripts of the Bible as we would define it — the full text of the Old and New Testaments from beginning to end. Psalters and Gospels, however — texts that could be used in the liturgy — are relatively abundant, and there is a good deal of evidence that Anglo-Saxons would have been especially familiar with the Bible in the form in which it was read in the services. There is also some evidence of the study of specific biblical texts both in Latin and in the vernacular, and interest in the Bible as a historical text, particularly as a record of the earliest events of human history. Again, there is a good deal of biblical legal material transcribed into Anglo-Saxon law. And, finally, there are biblical texts included in sapiential collections, in contexts in which it is very difficult to know whether the collector or scribe recognized the fact that a given maxim or "sentence" was in fact biblical. Certainly the reader would have no way of knowing the difference between a biblical maxim and one drawn from the Fathers or some similar source in such collections. The text of the Bible thus existed not only in formal monumental codices, but also in a variety of other forms as well, and the fact that a given text has a biblical source does not fully answer the more specific question of what particular kind of text a given poet or homilist might have had in front of him.

In one way or another the problem of textual identity has arisen in virtually every entry in this handbook. The problem may be as simple as when and where a given text begins and ends, or it may involve such virtually unresolvable issues as at what point the process of abridgment, alteration, and scribal error creates a "new" text rather than a "version" of a given exemplar. In such matters the authors of specific entries have simply exercised their best judgment; when appropriate they have attempted to warn users of such problems in the body of their entries. In some genres in particular, the problem of textual identity has been particularly difficult. Texts in the wisdom literature tradition, for example, which consist of a series of "wise" and often enigmatic sayings or homilies — particularly the loosely structured homilies of the anonymous tradition — can sometimes be very hard to define in terms of their specific textual identity. In fact it could be argued that such texts should be viewed as improvisations on a theme rather than fixed textual discourse with a clearly defined beginning and end. But for practical purposes the authors of the various entries have had to treat all of these various literary forms as if they were fixed textual entities comparable to a modern text. As long as it is clearly recognized that this is simply a convenient working assumption — that texts such as the *De duodecim abusivis sæculi* or the *Apocalypse of Thomas* did not circulate in a single authorized version, and that an edition of a single version of these texts would misrepresent the way in which most medieval readers had access to them — then the readers of these entries can use the information gathered without serious misapprehension. But it must be emphasized that even in the Christian-Latin tradition various texts existed in quite different modes of textual identity, and that while some of these texts were indeed "books" in Ogilvy's sense and ours, some were not.

Limitations of Evidence

A question that must be faced is how the readers of this volume may make use of the evidence that the authors of the various entries have gathered together. The answer is a simple one: with great caution. This caution must extend both to the evidence itself and to what significance to attach to it. As editors and authors, we have made every effort to be accurate, but errors are inevitable in these entries—particularly errors of omission. Ideally the author of any given entry should review the corpus of Anglo-Saxon and Anglo-Latin literature in order to verify that the list of references provided in the entry is as inclusive as possible. In practice we have not been able to accomplish any such effort at verification; and indeed the editorial decision not to include newly discovered source findings has meant that even if a contributor were able to add to our current knowledge of source relationships, he or she could not ordinarily do so in the entry prepared for this volume. Thus errors of omission are inevitable and inevitably common in these entries; in fact one of the goals of this project is to indicate where the lacunae are by presenting the available evidence in summary form. To take a specific example, there is evidence for the availability of the political and sapiential text, De duodecim abusivis sæculi, before the Viking invasions because Alcuin quoted from it, and evidence that it was known in the later period because Ælfric quoted from it and either Ælfric or someone in Ælfric's circle translated an abbreviated version of this treatise. But one naturally wonders whether the text was known in the intervening years—whether the Anglo-Saxons were reading it in the generations between Alcuin and Ælfric. At present we have no clearcut evidence of the currency of this treatise during this period, and this lacuna is evident in the presentation of our evidence. But the text in question was a popular one, and we expect that further evidence of its use will turn up, and that whoever discovers this evidence will be alerted to its significance by the lacunae in our entry.

"New" Source Scholarship

A related issue that requires some discussion is the editorial decision not to include unpublished source discoveries in our entries. In part this decision is motivated by the editorial concern that if we accept and implicitly sanction original source scholarship by our authors, the project may be extended indefinitely. For better or worse all of the entries completed so far have suggested significant new lines of research to their authors and one logical extension of this development is a project without a clearcut terminus. Another somewhat more principled reason for not including new research is that source scholarship, like any other branch of scholarship, requires a process of review and assimilation. To encourage contributors to present the results of their own scholarship in a reference work without the benefit of this process would weaken rather than strengthen scholarship in this area. There are many journals that publish source scholarship in Anglo-Saxon and Anglo-Latin literature, and we therefore see no need to make the present volume a vehicle for new research. While this principle governs the guidelines for authors of entries, we have made exceptions on occasion, and scholars have been generous in communicating to us the results of research which have been accepted for publication but are not yet in print.

Paleography

Another problem which the users of this volume must consider is that while the format of the entries we have chosen gives a certain prominence to the manuscript evidence, a very important kind of evidence, to be sure there are certain immediate problems with the witness of the manuscripts in themselves. The first is that interpreting it depends upon the judgment of paleographers, a judgment which is ultimately as subjective and fallible as that of scholars in any other discipline. In the present volume we have simply accepted the dating and and locations suggested by the paleographers and catalogers of the major collections. It is important to bear in mind that while we have reproduced this information and have in some instances based our discussions upon it, we have not ordinarily independently verified it. Although all of the members of the editorial board have at least some experience of working with manuscripts, no member is a paleographer in terms of scholarly specialization. Here as elsewhere we have been concerned not with attempting to provide new information for the present volume, but rather with codifying and gathering received scholarly opinion as of the time of publication. What this means in practical terms is that when users of this volume notice that the evidence for the currency of a certain work is dependent on limited or ambiguous paleographical evidence, then it is important that they examine the evidence and the argumentation for themselves. Error or unwarranted dogmatism on the part of the paleographers we have quoted are, of course, obvious problems; but a more subtle source of confusion is that scholarly qualifications and hesitations tend to be suppressed in transition from one scholarly work to another. If a paleographer discusses a problem of dating at some length and in the end with some reluctance opts for a particular date, the hesitations and in particular the degree of hesitation he or she may have about assigning a particular date are not adequately expressed in the conventional notation we have accepted from our predecessors. Thus a notation like "10c Worcester?" can mean anything from "this is the paleographer's opinon but he is not absolutely certain" to "if forced to hazard an opinion, the paleographer would desperately offer the above-mentioned." As in other areas of scholarship, part of the object of the present volume is to focus attention on possible areas of fruitful scholarly investigation, and the numerous occasions of reticence and the question-marks that adorn our entries can at least illustrate the limitations of our knowledge with graphic clarity.

Literary History

Even when the paleographers agree about the place and the date — or, as more often happens, about a range of possible places and dates which would accord with the evidence of a manuscript — it is still necessary to interpret the evidence of the manuscript in specifically literary terms. If we have, for example, a manuscript of Vergil's *Aeneid* which appears to have been copied by an Anglo-Saxon scribe, does the format and the presentation of the text suggest that the scribe understood what he was copying? Is there evidence that the text was read? And if so, by whom? Such issues might seem narrowly codicological, but as soon as one raises the question of who ordered a manuscript to be written, for whom, and for what purpose, one is dealing with issues that pertain to literary and intellectual history. And once a scholar is dealing with these issues, he or she is very quickly involved with issues of literary criticism as well. For example, if the putative Vergil manuscript was glossed by an Anglo-Saxon scribe, these glosses would provide evidence that some Anglo-Saxon was concerned enough to attempt to read and gloss Vergil's poetry. This inference, however, would depend upon the assumption that these glosses were in fact available in Anglo-Saxon England or at least were an intelligent copy of some continental or Irish precursor. To say the least, these are not simple and straightforward questions, and the answer one arrives at would depend upon one's own interpretation of Vergil's poetry and one's knowledge and understanding of the tradition of commentary on the *Aeneid*. Even if the glosses in question were clearly wrong and inappropriate, the kind of error they reflected might tell us something about the study of classical texts during this period and the level of education of the scribe or scholar who was responsible for them. The point is that there is no escaping the necessity of literary and historical judgment.

One final warning for the user of this volume concerns the complexity of the issues related to source relationships. When one considers the relationship of a given Anglo-Saxon or Anglo-Latin text to its sources, the more closely one examines the relevant texts, the more problems of detail emerge. Even if certain broad patterns can be discerned and clarified, there remain anomalies of detail, problems concerning word-choice, omissions, relevant aspects of textual criticism, and so on. One of the ongoing problems in this field is that scholarly attention has focussed on certain texts almost to the exclusion of others. And those texts which have been studied in detail are the monuments of the native Germanic literary tradition whose sources must be reconstructed. Detailed source study of those texts which actually draw on known Christian-Latin literary sources is very much an ongoing project in modern Anglo-Saxon scholarship. As a result there are relatively few texts from this period which have been studied in detail in terms of their sources, and none that might not be profitably studied further. As this mode of study proceeds, it opens up new questions even as it resolves outstanding ones.

The Scope of the Entries

Given these various warnings and qualifications, it might seem that we have qualified our project out of existence; some positive statement of our goals may therefore be appropriate. The first point to emphasize is that each entry is the work of an individual scholar who is ultimately responsible for its content, and that therefore each entry is to a significant degree an individual statement. But while we emphasize the individual responsibility of our contributors and have allowed them to shape their entries in many ways, the definition of our common purpose is that each entry is intended to provide a succinct and authoritative summary of what evidence exists for the currency of a given text in Anglo-Saxon literary culture as a whole. Each contributor has had to balance the demand for a comprehensive and judicious presentation of the evidence on the one hand and the necessity for succinctness and clarity on the other. In the present volume our aim has been to be relatively brief. Our model has been Ogilvy's volume of approximately 300 pages, and we are very much aware of the larger project based in England, the *Fontes Anglo-Saxonici*, a project that will not merely summarize the evidence as ours does, but will present the evidence itself in some detail. The existence of this project has freed us from the responsibility of presenting evidence or from reviewing in any detail argumentation concerning the currency and use of a given source. We do hope, however, that the bibliographical information we have gathered will permit the users to review the argumentation and available evidence for themselves relatively quickly.

We have construed "literary culture" broadly to include legal, historical, and religious literature as well as the imaginative literature with which literary scholars are conventionally concerned. In this field such a broad definition of literature is a necessary response to the fact that the literary culture of the Anglo-Saxons is fragmentarily preserved; and in any case the distinction between "imaginative" literature and other modes of literature is one which is very much a product of modern literary fashion. Even in the context of contemporary literary culture, the distinction is hard to draw, and in the literature of the Anglo-Saxon period, the distinction between literary and extra-literary genres and works would be both pointless and destructive. This is not to say that esthetic and literary discriminations cannot and should not be made, but simply that for the literary historian or the historian concerned with intellectual or religious culture, all of the available evidence is precious.

In the present volume the range of our concerns is quite wide. We are potentially concerned with the entire corpus of Anglo-Saxon and Anglo-Latin written literature and with oral literature and oral genres as well. Our treatment of some of the larger topics is very succinct indeed, and one problem which does not admit of any easy solution is that it is much easier to present the evidence for the knowledge of an obscure or little-known work than for a much-used text. Here again, the authors of individual entries have exercised their best judgment and have indicated the scope of their discussion in their articles.

Apologia

In the final portion of this essay we would like to offer a prospectus concerning this kind of research and to try to make explicit the rationale for source-work in the field of Anglo-Saxon literary culture. The first point to emphasize is that Old English is a deciphered language. The ability to read Old English accurately was lost for a long time, and the ability to read it with philological accuracy was not fully recovered until the nineteenth century. The process of recovery took place over a period of centuries and was immensely facilitated by the fact that a significant portion of the corpus of Old English literature is based upon readily accessible Latin sources.

These texts remain the most important source of information about what Old English words mean and about what given syntactical devices imply; and the task of Anglo-Saxon lexicography was begun by Anglo-Saxon scribes who glossed difficult Latin words with vernacular equivalents. Any extended study of Old English language or literature which does not consider the problem of sources is in a sense rootless, since our knowledge of the language is so heavily dependent on the cultural interweaving of Latin and Anglo-Saxon in this period. From the perspective of the literary critic and the literary historian, those texts that are most heavily dependent on Latin sources are usually of least intellectual and esthetic merit; but from that of the linguist or the Anglo-Saxonist of any scholarly persuasion who is attempting to explain a difficult word or locution, those Anglo-Saxon texts that have a known Latin source are a crucial linguistic resource without which our knowledge of the language would be much less assured than it is. And obviously the linguist or historian who cites the Latin *Vorlage* of a given Old English text is using either the source scholarship of some predecessor, or offering his or her own.

If the most immediate value of source scholarship is to enable us to understand Old English as a language, the further value of such scholarship for the intellectual and literary historian is no less fundamental. The immediate questions of literary and intellectual history—what the Anglo-Saxons knew and believed about themselves and their world—can best be addressed by detailed study of those texts which the Anglo-Saxons composed or compiled or copied. And in studying such texts it is impossible to proceed very far without facing issues of source scholarship. Tracing the filiations of one text with another is often laborious, but it can be very enlightening. Even the disjunctions, the gaps where one might expect a relationship, can be suggestive, and the larger patterns that emerge when one traces the relationship of one text with its sources can be strikingly revealing. J.E. Cross has spoken of "going close" to one's text, and there are moments in source study when one has the eerie sense of almost eavesdropping on the thoughts and hesitations of an author who may be nameless and has been dead for many hundred years, but whose characteristic voice and intellectual preferences are gradually becoming clear.

In considering scholarly and critical discourse about Anglo-Saxon literary culture in relationship to its sources, it is possible to discern two positions which, with some polemical exaggeration, we will call "maximalist" and "minimalist." The maximalists tend to accentuate the depth and the breadth of Anglo-Saxon literary culture, to take for granted a relatively wide degree of literary Christian-Latin culture and acquaintance with Classical culture. For better or worse, Ogilvy with his concern for libraries and Latin manuscripts was a maximalist, and many of the great Anglo-Saxonists of the first generations of Old English literary scholarship tended toward this position. One thinks of A.S. Cook or Fr. Klaeber, who never hesitated in their belief that the Anglo-Saxons were a deeply literate and literary people. By contrast (and in part in reaction to such assumptions) other scholars have emphasized the enormous obstacles which the Anglo-Saxons faced in attempting to perpetuate a literary culture and have focussed on the very substantial evidence that exists to show the sharp limitations on Anglo-Saxon learning. One eminent and authoritative contemporary Anglo-Saxonist has recently argued, for example, that we must take Alfred quite literally when he says that there were no literate persons, lay or clergy, in large portions of Anglo-Saxon England in his youth. This "minimalism" is, for the literary scholar at least, a less congenial view of the literary culture of the period, but precisely because it is less congenial its implications must be faced directly.

The debate between these two perspectives is an ongoing one, and there is no reason to believe it will be concluded any time in the immediate future. At the risk of seeming to lack zeal for controversy, we would like to suggest a *via media* that grants a certain cogency to both perspectives, and that we would call "particularist." We would begin by granting the enormous problems which the Anglo-Saxons faced in acquiring, disseminating, and transmitting literary culture whether in Latin or the vernacular. The Anglo-Saxons were presumably generally illiterate before they were converted to Christianity; there is some truth in the old and nationalistic saying that the Irish taught the English to write. After the conversion, the Anglo-Saxons could acquire literary skills and literary culture, but it is difficult to know how many of them chose to do so. The literacy rate in Anglo-Saxon England is unknown and unknowable; but lay literacy is often associated with mercantile culture, and the urban population of Anglo-Saxon England was relatively small. The presumption must be that only a minority of Anglo-Saxons were ever literate even in their own language. And if Latin was a learned language everywhere in Europe, Anglo-Saxons were handicapped in comparison with the speakers of the various romance vernaculars in that their mother tongue was quite different from Latin. In addition to the immediate practical difficulties of learning Latin and copying and disseminating Latin manuscripts in the Anglo-Saxon speaking world, Anglo-Saxons concerned with literary culture faced an even larger problem in that learning was threatened by constant internal warfare and after 793 by the threat of pagan Viking raiders, who had no scruples about destroying churches and monasteries.

The list of potential threats to Anglo-Saxon literary culture could be prolonged, and it is certainly easy to find evidence for ignorance and barbarism in the written records of the Anglo-Saxons. There is, however, one immediate counter-argument so salient that it is sometimes overlooked. Christianity is for better or worse a religion of the book. Without a certain degree of literary culture, Christianity, at least Latin Catholic Christianity, could not continue to exist. It is possible to imagine an illiterate or semiliterate priest who fulfilled the functions expected of him by memorizing the Latin words of the canon of the mass and the other most important liturgical texts by rote with only a minimal understanding of what he was saying. But is is very difficult to imagine how such a priest could train a successor. It would therefore follow that an aspirant to the clergy would have good reason to seek out a more learned cleric for his education. It is of course true that a priest or monk need not be an intellectual or a particularly learned man in order to fulfill his office. But Christian education and the continual necessity of training younger generations of clergy demanded a certain degree of Latin and vernacular literary culture. Christianity did not take root everywhere in the early Middle Ages; there were numerous missions which failed, and it is perfectly imaginable that the pagan Anglo-Saxons newly converted to Christianity might have relapsed into the non-literate pagan Germanic culture which they traditionally had practiced. But for the most part they did not. Anglo-Saxon England converted to Christianity and remained Christian, and the consequence was that there existed a milieu, clerical for the most part but to some degree lay, in which literary culture could exist and in which, at the least, there was a tradition of respect for learning and an interest in the transmission of texts. In considering barbarian Anglo-Saxon England from such a perspective, the continued existence of any native literary culture at all either in Latin or Old English represents a substantial achievement, and instances of error and naive ignorance are much more understandable. The Anglo-Saxons, however, did not simply acquire sufficient literacy for a native Christian tradition to exist and perpetuate itself. Within three generations of the conversion there were Anglo-Saxon Christians whose learning and knowledge of Latin were comparable to those of any scholar in Europe. The achievement of Bede would be remarkable in any age, but when one remembers that his grandparents were probably born before the coming of Christianity to Northumbria, it brings his achievement into sharper focus. It is thus a matter of historical fact that some Anglo-Saxons attained a very high level of Latin literary culture in places and times in which one might not have expected it. It is also of course true that the Anglo-Saxons faced formidable problems in acquiring and transmitting literary culture; and we, as particularists, would argue that every Anglo-Saxon text be approached individually and as far as possible without preconceptions either maximalist or minimalist. As a practical matter, Anglo-Saxonists will have to be practicing maximalists when they first approach an Anglo-Saxon literary text, in that one must test every possible hypothesis about sources and influence before dismissing it; but in deference to the minimalist position we must remind readers that no single library in Anglo-Saxon England possessed all of the books listed in our present volume. Indeed, the fact that an author is mentioned and an entry listed in the present volume does not necessarily mean that "this book was known to the Anglo-Saxons," but rather that there is evidence of at least one Anglo-Saxon's having known it, either directly or indirectly— a much more limited and localized proposition. It may also be mentioned in passing that our silence does not prove a given text was not known, but simply that we did not know of any evidence for it.

A prospectus ordinarily includes an invitation to scholars at large, and we would like to make such an invitation in pointing out that the work of tracing the sources of Anglo-Saxon literary culture is very much in progress and that there is much to be done. We hope to be able to publish ongoing revisions of these entries under the auspices of the *Old English Newsletter,* and we hope the more obvious deficiencies of our volume will be corrected in an ongoing process of correction and revision that will extend beyond the date of formal publication.

A question that historians enjoy debating is whether the advent of the Norman conquest involved a radical break with Anglo-Saxon culture and political institutions and whether one defines the relationship between the Anglo-Saxon and Anglo-Norman eras in terms of rupture or continuity. Even accepting the most radical account of the changes which William and his successors worked, however, these changes are trivial in comparison with those that had already occurred in the development of Anglo-Saxon culture and the Anglo-Saxon polity. A scattered and fragmented group of tribes had been joined together to form one nation; these Germanic peoples had become Christian and as a result literate. Any story must have a beginning, and the beginning of the history of England and the English-speaking nations begins with the Anglo-Saxons. For better or worse, "England" became inhabited by the "English," the "English" became Christian during our period, and the consequences of these events are still being felt. The study of the sources of Anglo-Saxon literary culture may sometimes seem pedestrian and it is often difficult, but this kind of scholarship can provide genuine insight into the intelligence and aspirations of men and women who lived a millennium ago, spoke our language, and created the foundations of our culture. And this is no small reward.

Thomas D. Hill

Guide for Readers

The *Sources of Anglo-Saxon Literary Culture* follows its immediate predecessor, J.D.A. Ogilvy's *Books Known to the English, 597–1066 [BKE]*, in organizing its material primarily as an alphabetical list of authors, accepting current scholarly usage for the forms of the names rather than changing all to either Latin or English. Bede's hagiographical works, for example, are found under Bede and not in the *Acta Sanctorum* entry. Major entries on writers such as Bede that include more than one work may treat each title as a separate entry under the author. Works that modern scholars conventionally identify as by, for example, "pseudo-Bede" follow the author in question, and are in turn followed, when there is significant evidence, by entries on the Old English translations of an author—see, for example, the entry on the Old English translation of Bede's *Ecclesiastical History*. Anonymous works are either grouped under generic entries, or are included alphabetically by the first word—other than a preposition—of the title in the list of authors. Generic entries may also include a single work by a named author if this is the only one work by the author known in Anglo-Saxon England: in these cases cross-references will be provided.

The *Sources of Anglo-Saxon Literary Culture*, unlike Ogilvy's volume, is the work of many scholars who have their own ways of presenting material. Some flexibility is necessary since entries on Augustine and Ephraem, or on hymns and the *Heliand* obviously present different problems. Writers, particularly of major entries, often provide introductory remarks calling attention to any peculiar features of their task. Recent scholarship, however, makes it possible to present systematically in a headnote some basic information about the knowledge or use of certain sources in Anglo-Saxon England. An abbreviation immediately following the author and/or title makes it unnecessary to repeat bibliographical information about the best edition of a work. For Latin texts, the abbreviation is from Michael Lapidge's *Abbreviations for Sources and Specification of Standard Editions for Sources*, the relevant parts of which appear in alphabetical order by abbreviation in Part I of the Bibliography at the end of this volume. For Old English texts, the abbreviation is from the system devised for the Toronto *Dictionary of Old English* as listed in the *Microfiche Concordance to Old English* [*MCOE*], a refinement of the system designed by Angus Cameron [AC]; see, however, Appendix A for the Old English *Martyrology*. Similarly references to standard research tools, such as the *Clavis Patrum Latinorum* [*CPL*], often make it unnecessary to provide much information about the source itself. Moreover, it is usually possible to present in a headnote five kinds of information that indicate that a work was available in Anglo-Saxon England:

MSS   *Manuscripts.* The inclusion of a work in a relevant manuscript provides firm physical evidence for its presence in Anglo-Saxon England. Helmut Gneuss' "Preliminary List of Manuscripts Written or Owned in England up to 1100" [HG] provides the basis for this source of information: all contributors have been asked to use it fully, and to query Professor Gneuss when they notice potential discrepancies. We are grateful to Professor Gneuss for allowing us to use his work and for bearing with our questions. In two areas, however, his concerns do not exactly match our needs. First, the list does not yet fully identify the contents of each manuscript, and so writers have sometimes gone back to the catalogs — and occasionally to microfilms or to the manuscripts themselves — in order to develop this evidence. Second, there are some continental manuscripts that either by their script or by some other feature show that a work may have been known in Anglo-Saxon circles.

Lists   *Booklists.* Although less informative than a surviving manuscript, the mention of a work in wills, lists of donations, or inventories of libraries from our period provides a good indication that it was known. In "Surviving Booklists from Anglo-Saxon England" [ML] Michael Lapidge edits the remaining catalogs of manuscripts from our period, and identifies, whenever possible, the work in question. The following shortened titles are used to refer to these lists: 1. Alcuin; 2. King Athelstan; 3. Athelstan (grammarian); 4. Æthelwold; 5. Ælfwold; 6. Sherburn-in-Elmet; 7. Bury St Edmunds I; 8. Sæwold; 9. Worcester I; 10. Leofric; 11. Worcester II; 12. Bury St Edmunds II; and 13. Peterborough. For a discussion of these lists — and specifically of difficulties of localizing the second list associated with Worcester and the Peterborough list — see ML.

A-S Vers   *Anglo-Saxon Versions.* Like the manuscript evidence, an Anglo-Saxon version, either in Old English or in Latin, indicates that the source was known to the English at this time. The *MCOE* provides the basis for identifying the Old English texts. Anglo-Latin texts are identified by the abbreviations in Part I of the Bibliography. Writers of individual entries have, of course, exercised judgment in how to represent the information when a translation or adaptation is quite loose, or when the use of a source is so limited that it is better considered a quotation.

Quots/Cits   *Quotations or Citations*. The source notes of modern critical editions can make it clear that Anglo-Saxon writers knew a work in full or in some shortened form. A citation, including both the name and the words of an author, is sometimes significant since it shows the knowledge of the origin of an idea or phrase. Writers of entries have used their judgment in determining which quotations and citations significantly further the evidence for the knowledge of a work during our period. For example, listing each use by Bede of Augustine's *De genesi ad litteram* may well be less significant for our purposes than indicating a single, anonymous use of a more obscure work. If the quotation or citation is noted in the edition specified in Part I of the Bibliography, or in the *MCOE*, only the primary references — using the system for citing texts described later under *Standard Editions* — to the Anglo-Saxon writer and to the source are provided. If the quotation or citation is not noted in the specified edition, the primary references are noted in the same way in the headnote, and the secondary source will be mentioned in the narrative body of the entry. In order not to overlap with the developing database of the *Fontes Anglo-Saxonici*, this volume will not ordinarily include source identifications published after 1987.

Refs   *References*. Although always open to interpretation, a specific reference by an Anglo-Saxon writer to the author or work may indicate its presence in England during our period. The letters of Boniface and his circle provide good examples of this kind of evidence. Editions are referred to in the same way as quots/cits.

Although schematic, the information in the headnote summarizes much of the strongest evidence for the knowledge of a specific author or work in Anglo-Saxon England.

The body of the entry discusses any information in the headnote that requires clarification or amplification, and then introduces other kinds of evidence for the knowledge of a work in Anglo-Saxon England, such as allusions in literary texts or distinctive iconographic motifs from the visual arts. One kind of evidence that may be considered in this section — and that requires some specific comment here — is the presence of echoes in hexametrical poetry. Within this poetic tradition, the terms "quotation" and "citation" are restricted either to entire lines taken from a previous work, or to situations in which the Anglo-Saxon author calls attention to the source with a phrase such as "as the poet says": these quotations and citations are included in the headnote. In contrast, an "echo" in hexametrical poetry consists of at least two words occurring in the same metrical feet (but not necessarily in the same grammatical form) in both the source and the Anglo-Saxon text: these are discussed in the body. A similar distinction between "quotations and citations" and "echoes" may be preserved in the case of some prose writers. Finally, the body of an entry may consider other questions, such as the temporal and geographical extent of the use of a work. Readers are directed to other entries in the volume — and through these entries to information about the standard edition in Part I of the Bibliography — by names in small capitals.

Entries may conclude with a discussion of bibliography, which attempts to be complete through 1987 but which may include later works other than source identifications (see Quots/Cits above). If for some reason the edition of the work in question cannot be included in Part I of the Bibliography, or if other editions need to be considered, references by editor and date are recorded here, and can be expanded by turning to Part II of the Bibliography. Part II of the Bibliography also includes relevant secondary material mentioned in the entries by author and date. GR numbers can be expanded by consulting Stanley B. Greenfield and Fred C. Robinson, *A Bibliography of Publications on Old English Literature to the end of 1972* (Toronto 1980). The bibliography may conclude with any relevant comments and suggestions about work in progress or desiderata.

Thus, most entries use the following format:

AUTHOR and/or TITLE [abbreviation]: references to research tools; cross references to other entries.

(introductory remarks)

TITLE of individual work [abbreviation]: references to research tools; cross references to other entries.

MSS   Manuscripts: by city, library and MS number, but keyed to a secondary source, usually HG.

Lists   Booklists: by the name or place associated with the list, with reference to the list and item numbers in ML.

A-S Vers   Anglo-Saxon Versions: Old English by the abbreviation in the *MCOE*, with the full AC number; Anglo-Latin by the abbreviation in Part I of the Bibliography.

Quots/Cits   Significant Quotations or Citations: Old English by the abbreviation in the *MCOE*, with the full AC number; Anglo-Latin by the abbreviation in Part I of the Bibliography. The source follows the reference to the Anglo-Saxon writer, and the system for citing texts is described below under *Standard Editions*.

Refs   Significant References: Old English by the abbreviation in the *MCOE*, with the full AC number; Anglo-Latin by the abbreviation in Part I of the Bibliography.

Body

Bibliographical discussion

The system of cross-referencing by using small capitals is complicated enough to require some comment here. In the case of a work by a known author, this system should provide little difficulty: both the name of the author and the title of the work (possibly in a shortened form) will be in small capitals the first time that they appear in an entry (including entries under either a major author or a generic gathering). References to anonymous works gathered into generic entries present greater problems: In these situations, the title of the work will appear in small capitals, and a reference to the name of the generic gathering will accompany the first mention of the work in each entry (but *not necessarily* including individual entries under either a major author or a generic gathering). Thus the first time one encounters a reference in the "Acta Sanctorum" to the "Cotton-Corpus Legendary," COTTON-CORPUS LEGENDARY will be in small capitals, and will be followed with the direction to "see LEGENDARIES," where in the final volume there will be an entry on this collection; in subsequent entries in the "Acta Sanctorum," COTTON-CORPUS LEGENDARY will be in small capitals the first time it appears, but there may be no further direction to "see LEGENDARIES." If the title of a work provides little information about the generic entry under which it can be found, the reference to the gathering may always be kept. The most difficult problem in cross-referencing that has arisen in this trial volume, however, is presented by the evidence from the VERCELLI and BLICKLING collections of anonymous homilies. Donald Scragg discusses both in his entry on ANONYMOUS OLD ENGLISH HOMILIES (see HOMILIARIES), and goes into some detail about a number of items from each, and so the reader should be directed to this information; however, in many entries references to items in either collection are limited to abbreviations from the *MCOE*, and in these cases it seems unnecessarily cumbersome to follow each with "see ANONYMOUS OLD ENGLISH HOMILIES under HOMILIARIES."

Therefore the reader should remember that an abbreviation such as *HomS* 4 (*VercHom* 9) can be pursued further in the volume by turning to Scragg's work.

Standard Research Tools

The following abbreviations are used throughout the volume. When items are individually numbered in these works, references are to items (or to volume and item; e.g. *CLA* 2.139); otherwise, references are to pages (or to volume and page; e.g. *OTP* 2.249–95).

AC = Angus Cameron "A List of Old English Texts" in *A Plan for the Dictionary of Old English* ed. Roberta Frank and Cameron (Toronto, 1973) 27–306.

BCLL = *Bibliography of Celtic-Latin Literature 400–1200* Michael Lapidge and Richard Sharpe (Dublin, 1985).

BEH = *Bibliography of English History to 1485* ed. Edgar B. Graves (Oxford, 1975).

BHG = *Bibliotheca Hagiographica Graeca* 3rd ed., François Halkin (Brussels, 1951; *Subsidia hagiographica* 8a).

BHG[a] = *Auctarium Bibliothecae Hagiographicae Graecae* François Halkin (Brussels, 1969; *Subsidia hagiographica* 47).

BHG[na] = *Novum Auctarium Bibliothecae Hagiographicae Graecae* François Halkin (Brussels, 1984; *Subsidia hagiographica* 65).

BHL = *Bibliotheca Hagiographica Latina* 2 vols. (Brussels 1898–1901; *Subsidia hagiographica* 6); with supplements in 1911 (*Subsidia hagiographica* 12) and 1986 (*Subsidia hagiographica* 70).

BHM = *Bibliotheca Hieronymiana Manuscripta* 4 vols. in 7 parts, Instrumenta Patristica 4, Bernard Lambert (Steenbrugge, 1969–72).

BKE = *Books Known to the English, 597–1066* J.D.A. Ogilvy (Cambridge, MA, 1967); and addenda and corrigenda in *Mediaevalia* 7 (1984 for 1981) 281–325; also available as *Old English Newsletter* Subsidia 11 (1985).

BLS = *Butler's Lives of the Saints* 4 vols., ed. Herbert Thurston and Donald Attwater (New York, 1963).

BSS = *Bibliotheca Sanctorum* 13 vols. (Rome, 1961–70).

CLA = *Codices Latini Antiquiores* 11 vols., E.A. Lowe (Oxford, 1934–66); with a supplement (1971); 2nd ed. of vol. 2 (1972).

CPG = *Clavis Patrum Graecorum* 4 vols., M. Geerard (Turnhout, 1974–83).

CPL = *Clavis Patrum Latinorum* 2nd ed., E. Dekkers and A. Gaar (Steenbrugge, 1961).

DACL = *Dictionnaire d'archéologie chrétienne et de liturgie* 15 vols., ed. F. Cabrol (Paris, 1907–53).

DB = *Dictionary of the Bible* 4 vols. and an extra vol., ed. James Hastings (New York, 1900–05).

DHGE = *Dictionnaire d'histoire et de géographie ecclésiastiques* ed. A. Baudrillart, A. de Meyer, É. Van Cauwenbergh, and R. Aubert (Paris, 1912–).

DMA = *Dictionary of the Middle Ages* 12 vols., ed. Joseph R. Strayer (New York, 1982–89).

DS = *Dictionnaire de spiritualité* ed. M. Viller and others (Paris, 1932–).

DTC = *Dictionnaire de théologie catholique* 15 vols., ed. A. Vacant, E. Mangenot and É. Amann (Paris, 1908–50).

DTC^tg = *Dictionnaire de théologie catholique. Tables générales* ed. B. Loth and A. Michel (Paris, 1953–72).

EHD = *English Historical Documents: Volume 1 c. 500–1042* 2nd ed., ed. Dorothy Whitelock (London, 1979).

GR = Stanley B. Greenfield and Fred C. Robinson *A Bibliography of Publications on Old English Literature to the end of 1972* (Toronto, 1980).

HG = Helmut Gneuss "A Preliminary List of Manuscripts Written or Owned in England up to 1100" *Anglo-Saxon England* 9 (1981) 1–60.

IASIM = *Insular and Anglo-Saxon Illuminated Manuscripts. An Iconographic Catalogue* Thomas H. Ohlgren (New York, 1986).

ICL = *Initia Carminum Latinorum Saeculo Undecimo Antiquiorum* D. Schaller and E. Könsgen (Göttingen, 1977).

ICVL = *Initia Carminum Ac Versuum Medii Aevi Posterioris Latinorum* Hans Walther (Göttingen, 1959).

ISLMAH = *Index Scriptorum Latinorum Medii Aevi Hispanorum* Manuel C. Díaz y Díaz (Madrid, 1959).

KVS = *Kirchenschriftsteller. Verzeichnis und Sigel Vetus Latina* 1/1, Hermann Josef Frede (Freiburg, 1981); *Kirchenschriftsteller. Aktualisierungsheft 1984* (Freiburg, 1984); and *Kirchenschriftsteller. Aktualisierungsheft 1988* (Freiburg, 1988).

LTK = *Lexikon für Theologie und Kirche* 2nd ed., 10 vols. and an index, ed. Josef Höfer and Karl Rahner (Freiburg i.B., 1957–67).

MCOE = *A Microfiche Concordance to Old English: The List of Texts and Index of Editions* compiled by Antonette diPaolo Healey and Richard L. Venezky (Toronto, 1980).

ML = Michael Lapidge "Surviving Booklists from Anglo-Saxon England" in *Learning and Literature in Anglo-Saxon England* ed. Lapidge and Helmut Gneuss (Cambridge, 1985).

NCE = *New Catholic Encyclopedia* 17 vols., ed. William J. McDonald and others (New York, 1967–79).

NRK = N.R. Ker *Catalogue of Manuscripts Containing Anglo-Saxon* (Oxford, 1957); with a supplement in *Anglo-Saxon England* 5 (1976) 121–31; and addenda and corrigenda by Mary Blockley in *Notes & Queries* ns 29 (1982) 1–3.

NTA = Edgar Hennecke *New Testament Apocrypha* 2 vols., ed. Wilhelm Schneemelcher and trans. R. McL. Wilson (Philadelphia, 1963–65).

OCD = *Oxford Classical Dictionary* 2nd ed., N.G.L. Hammond and H.H. Scullard (Oxford, 1970).

ODCC = *Oxford Dictionary of the Christian Church* 2nd ed., F.L. Cross and E.A. Livingstone (London, 1974).

OTP = *Old Testament Pseudepigrapha* 2 vols., ed. James H. Charlesworth (London, 1983–85).

RBMA = *Repertorium Biblicum Medii Aevi* 11 vols., F. Stegmüller (Madrid, 1950–   ).

SC = *A Summary Catalogue of Western Manuscripts in the Bodleian Library at Oxford* 7 vols., Falconer Madan and H.H.E. Craster (Oxford, 1895–1953).

SEHI = *Sources for the Early History of Ireland: Ecclesiastical* James F. Kenney (1929; rpt New York, 1966 with addenda by L. Bieler).

Standard Editions

Unless otherwise noted, the following system for citing texts is used:

1. Old English poetic texts are referred to by the abbreviation in the *MCOE* and AC with line numbers from the *ASPR*.

2. References to Old English prose texts are to the edition specified in the *MCOE*. For a text which is line numbered as a unit in the edition cited, only line numbers follow the abbreviation. For a text in which sections (e.g. books or chapters) are line numbered separately, sectional divisions are in roman (upper case for larger divisions, e.g. books, lower case for smaller ones, e.g. chapters) followed by line numbers (e.g. II.xx.3–4). For a text line numbered by page (or column) or not provided with line numbers in the edition cited, page (or column) and line numbers are used (e.g. 26.1–15 or 37.6–42.4).

3. The headnote refers to Latin editions by the abbreviations expanded in Part I of the Bibliography. The system for citing sections, pages, and lines is the same as used for Old English prose texts (above).

4. References to the Bible are to the *Biblia sacra iuxta vulgatam versionem* 2nd ed., ed. R. Weber (Stuttgart, 1975).

The following abbreviations for standard series are also used; these abbreviations may be followed by volume and page (or column) numbers (e.g. *PL* 33.45).

AH = *Analecta Hymnica Medii Aevi* 55 vols., ed. Guido Maria Dreves and Clemens Blume (Leipzig, 1886–1922).

AS = *Acta Sanctorum* 3rd ed., by the Bollandists (Paris, 1863–   ).

ASPR = *Anglo-Saxon Poetic Records* 6 vols., ed. G.P. Krapp and E.V.K. Dobbie (New York, 1931–53).

BaP = *Bibliothek der angelsächsischen Prosa* 13 vols., Christian W.M. Grein, Richard P. Wülker, and Hans Hecht, eds (Kassel, 1872–1933).

CCCM = *Corpus Christianorum, Continuatio Mediaevalis* (Turnhout, 1966–   ).

CCSA = *Corpus Christianorum, Series Apocryphorum* (Turnhout, 1983–   ).

CCSL = *Corpus Christianorum, Series Latina* (Turnhout, 1953–   ).

CSEL = *Corpus Scriptorum Ecclesiasticorum Latinorum* (Vienna, 1866–   ).

EEMF = *Early English Manuscripts in Facsimile* (Copenhagen, 1951–   ).

EETS = *Early English Texts Society.*
ES = Extra Series.
OS = Original Series.
SS = Supplementary Series.

GCS = *Die griechischen christlichen Schriftsteller der ersten drei Jahrhunderte* (Leipzig, 1897–   ).

GL = *Grammatici Latini* 8 vols., ed. H. Keil (Leipzig, 1857–80).

HBS = *Henry Bradshaw Society* (London, 1891–   ).

MGH = *Monumenta Germaniae Historica.*
AA = Auctores antiquissimi.
CAC = Concilia aeui carolini.
ECA = Epistolae carolini aeui.
ES = Epistolae selectae.
PLAC = Poetae latini aeui carolini.
SRM = Scriptores rerum merovingicarum.

PG = *Patrologia Graeca* 161 vols., ed. J.P. Migne (Paris, 1857–66).

PL = *Patrologia Latina* 221 vols., ed. J.P. Migne (Paris, 1844–64).

PLS = *Patrologiae Latinae Supplementum* 5 vols., ed. A. Hamman (Paris, 1958–74).

RS = "Rolls Series"; *Rerum Britannicarum Medii Aevi Scriptores* (London, 1858–96).

SChr = *Sources chrétiennes* (Paris, 1940–).

SS = *The Publications of the Surtees Society* (London, 1835–).

TU = *Texte und Untersuchungen zur Geschichte der altchristlichen Literatur. Archiv für die griechisch-christlichen Schriftsteller der ersten drei Jahrhunderte* (Leipzig/Berlin, 1882–).

Frederick M. Biggs

ACTA SANCTORUM

Hagiography was clearly an important genre in Anglo-Saxon England. In the early period BEDE, ALDHELM, and ALCUIN, and later ÆLFRIC, devoted much of their energy and output to one or another form of hagiographical writing or study. A substantial part of the surviving corpus of Old English narrative poetry (including three of the poems of "Cynewulf") is likewise hagiographical, as is much of the anonymous Old English prose. Yet most of the scholarly analysis of the hagiographical compositions of Anglo-Saxon England has been produced in a kind of vacuum, without a thorough knowledge of the Latin hagiographical texts and contexts that Anglo-Saxons knew and by which they might be influenced. Although much valuable work has been done on individual works and authors, there is as yet no thorough treatment of Anglo-Saxon hagiographical *composition*, vernacular or Latin, or of the Anglo-Saxons' *reception* of the hagiographical texts produced on the Continent. The materials for such studies have not been readily available. It is only in recent years, for example, that the Latin manuscript legendaries of Anglo-Saxon provenance have begun to be studied with the attention they deserve. The *Sources of Anglo-Saxon Literary Culture* hopes to facilitate the more sophisticated study of hagiography in Anglo-Saxon England by presenting all the currently available information about the hagiographical texts — *vitae, passiones, miracula* — known to the Anglo-Saxons. We have not, however, attempted to incorporate most of the evidence as to *cults*, such as is to be gleaned from calendars, litanies, etc.

The entries below (one by Frederick M. Biggs, five by Hugh Magennis, and the rest by E. Gordon Whatley) are a representative sample of the 330 or so entries that will comprise the hagiography section of the final volume in which all the works of Latin hagiography known to the English up to 1100, listed alphabetically *by saint*, are to be treated. For the most part, these entries will deal with anonymous texts concerning both native English and foreign saints, the latter far outnumbering the former. In most cases also, the texts to be dealt with are those that were considered by the scribes as distinct works, as opposed to the lives, deaths, and miracles of those saints who were known mainly through their inclusion in "collective biographies" such as GREGORY THE GREAT'S DIALOGUES or the HISTORIA MONACHORUM of RUFINUS, which will be treated elsewhere in the final volume.

Works of hagiography by a known author will be listed under the saint's name here, but the proper entry for each work will appear as part of the main entry for the author. Occasionally, however, the author of a given hagiographical text may be known solely by that one work: in such cases the proper entry for the work will appear here in this section, not as an author entry. For example, Felix of Crowland, the eighth-century author of the *Vita S. Guthlaci*, will be listed in the alphabetical author sequence of the volume, but the reader will be referred to this section, under GUTHLAC-US, for the full entry (see below).

Specific hagiographical texts are identified not only by the saint's name and the genre of the work, but also, where possible, by the Bollandists' classification number, as listed in their standard reference guide to Latin hagiographical texts, the *BHL* (*Bibliotheca Hagiographica Latina* 2 vols [Brussels 1898–1901] with supplements in 1911 and 1986). The section also follows the conventions in the *BHL* for ordering works such as the "Seven Sleepers" (under "D" for DORMIENTES) and the INVENTIO SANCTAE CRUCIS (included under the general heading "Iesus Christus").

The sources of information from which the entries are being compiled are many and varied, but the chief are as follows: BEDE'S MARTYROLOGY; ALDHELM'S prose and verse DE VIRGINITATE; the Old English *Martyrology* [*Mart*, B19], especially in the light of source studies by J.E. Cross; ÆLFRIC'S CATHOLIC HOMILIES [*ÆCHom*] and LIVES OF SAINTS [*ÆLS*]; the anonymous Old English *Lives of Saints* [*LS*]; and several manuscripts containing Latin hagiographical texts, including most notably, the surviving eleventh-century copies of the COTTON-CORPUS LEGENDARY (see LEGENDARIES): London, BL Cotton Nero E.i and Cambridge, Corpus Christi College 9, and the closely related MSS, Salisbury, Cathedral Library 221 and 222 (olim Oxford, Bodleian Library Fell 4 and 1). Patrick Zettel's unpublished Oxford thesis (1979) has been a valuable guide to these MSS. In his opinion they represent a legendary of late-ninth-century continental origin that was in widespread use in later Anglo-Saxon England, where it was introduced most likely at some point during the tenth century.

E. Gordon Whatley

Dormientes (Septem) passio [ANON.Pas.Dorm.sept.]: *BHL* 2316. See also GREGORY OF TOURS, PASSIO SEPTEM DORMIENTIUM (*BHL* 2313) and his LIBER IN GLORIA MARTYRUM (*BHL* 2314).

MSS   1. London, BL Cotton Nero E.i: HG 344.
    2. Salisbury, Cathedral Library 222 (olim Oxford, Bodleian Library Fell 1): HG 623.
Lists   none.
A-S Vers   1. *ÆCHom* II, 32 (B1.2.34) 183–231: see below.
    2. *LS* 34 (B3.3.34).
Quots/Cits   1. *ÆCHom* I, 16 (B1.1.18): see below.
    2. ? ANON.Vit.Aedward.conf.: see below.
Refs   none.

BEDE and his contemporaries do not mention the legend of the Seven Sleepers, and evidence for Anglo-Saxon knowledge of specific versions comes from only late in the period. The legend was known, however, to some of the English community in late-eighth-century Germany. According to the English Huneberc's *Vita Willibaldi* (*MGH* Scriptores 15, part 1, 93.16), St Willibald and his brother visited the spot (near Ephesus) where the remains of the Seven Sleepers lay.

The two main versions of the story were known in the early medieval West, one by GREGORY OF TOURS (*BHL* 2313), the other anonymous (*BHL* 2316); see P. Huber (1910 pp 59–62). They are apparently independent of one another. The earliest MSS of *BHL* 2316, a Frankish translation from Greek according to Siegmund (1949 p 218), are ninth-century; see also P. Huber (1910 p 61) and Magennis (forthcoming in *Leeds Studies in English*). The two English MSS represent the COTTON-CORPUS LEGENDARY.

The anonymous version has been shown (see Ott GR 5351) to be the source of the much-expanded Old English version, *LS* 34 (B3.3.34), surviving in two eleventh-century copies, one complete (London, BL Cotton Julius E.vii), the other fragmentary (London, BL Cotton Otho B.x). Although not written by ÆLFRIC, this version is generally regarded as roughly contemporary with his work. Among extant texts of *BHL* 2316, however, the closest to the Latin source of *LS* 34 is not the Cotton-Corpus recension, but that in the eleventh-century MS London, BL Egerton 2797, of continental provenance and closely related to a later text in London, BL Harley 3037; see P. Huber (1910 p 161), Whitelock (GR 6467), and Magennis (1985). For other MSS of importance for determining the source text of *LS* 34, see Magennis (forthcoming in *Leeds Studies in English*).

Despite the brevity of ÆLFRIC's account of the Seven Sleepers in *ÆCHom* II, it clearly depends on *BHL* 2316, as P. Huber (1910 p 157) first showed. *BHL* 2316 was unknown to Förster (GR 5300), but it corresponds closely to the hypothetical source (containing elements of *BHL* 2313 and the Greek of Simeon Metaphrastes) that he posited (p 40). Zettel (1979 pp 192–94) suggests that the version of *BHL* 2316 ÆLFRIC used is that in the Cotton-

Corpus legendary, but various discrepancies suggest that his source was not identical with Cotton-Corpus, and further that he also drew on the passio written by Gregory of Tours, *BHL* 2313, which is not otherwise known to have been read in Anglo-Saxon England; see Magennis (forthcoming).

Ælfric also briefly mentions the Seven Sleepers, as an exemplum of the resurrection of the body, in a passage he added to *ÆCHom* I, 16 in the period 1002–05, but which is not printed by Thorpe; the passage would occur on p 236 between lines 22 and 23. It appears in six of the eleven extant MSS of the homily (see Gatch 1977 pp 86–87, and Magennis, forthcoming). Here, as in *ÆCHom* II, 32, Ælfric says the length of the sleep is 372 years, which suggests his dependence on a text of *BHL* 2316 different from that in the Cotton-Corpus legendary.

The *Vita Aedwardi regis* (*BHL* 2421), attributed by Barlow to Goscelin of Canterbury, contains Edward the Confessor's vision of the Sleepers' turning over onto their left sides (Barlow 1962 pp 66–71). The authoritative MS (HG 420), however, is deficient at this point and the vision has to be supplied from later revised versions. Barlow (1962 pp xxxix–xli) is suspicious of the episode, but concedes that in truncated form it may well have been in the original version of the life, composed, as many believe, as early as 1067. The details of the legend as presented in the *Vita Aedwardi* are not specific enough to indicate any particular source. Barlow (1962 p 68) sees the figure of 272 years as a harmonization of more than one tradition.

Hugh Magennis

Eulalia Barcinone passio [ANON.Pas.Eulal.Barc.]: *BHL* 2696; *CPL* 2069a; *DHGE* 15.1380–84. See also EULALIA EMERITAE.

MSS Paris, Bibliothèque Nationale lat. 10861: HG 898.
Lists none.
A-S Vers Mart (B19.hi).
Quots/Cits BEDA.Mart. 221.1–5: see below.
Refs none.

Eulalia of Barcelona (feast day Feb. 12), purportedly martyred as a young girl under the prefect Dacian during the Diocletian persecution, is regarded by many (*BLS* 4.530) as a doublet of EULALIA EMERITAE (feast day Dec. 10). But the question is by no means settled, especially in Spain where Fábrega Grau argues that Eulalia of Barcelona's passio (*BHL* 2693) is a mid-seventh-century composition by Bishop Quirinus of Barcelona, based on oral tradition surrounding the saint's authentic local cult, and that it is entirely independent of the cult of Eulalia of Merida (see his summary

of his position, *DHGE* 15.1380–84). The Bollandist de Gaiffier (1959), along
with other scholars outside Spain, does not accept Fábrega Grau's arguments. A more recent Spanish assessment by García Rodríguez (1966 pp
289–90) is unfavorable.

The earliest version known to the English, *BHL* 2696, used by BEDE in
his MARTYROLOGY (see Quentin 1908 p 71), and represented in the Paris
MS, relates the passion of Eulalia of Barcelona, but associates her with
Dec. 10. According to Fábrega Grau, this version was composed in the early
eighth century, outside Spain. The anonymous passio (*BHL* 2696) also lies
behind the entry in the Old English *Martyrology* (Cross 1981a). ALDHELM's
brief effusion in his prose DE VIRGINITATE 300.10–12, indicates only his aware-
ness that she was a virgin martyr, but his source is undetermined, although
a possibility is PERISTEPHANON III, which he uses elsewhere.

                                                E. Gordon Whatley

Eulalia Emeritae passio [ANON.Pas.Eul.Emer.]: *BHL* 2700; *CPL* 2069b;
DHGE 15.1384–85. See also PRUDENTIUS, PERISTEPHANON.

MSS   Cambridge, Corpus Christi College 9: HG 16.
Lists — Refs   none.

The cult of Eulalia, virgin, martyred at Merida, Spain, for her defiant
Christianity under Maximian in the early fourth century, is attested in the
early fifth century by the poet PRUDENTIUS in PERISTEPHANON III (his hymn
on her shrine and martyrdom). *BHL* 2700, according to Fábrega Grau
(*DHGE* 15.1384), was composed in the late seventh century, drawing not
only on Prudentius but also on a lost "texte primitif" which was itself
Prudentius' source. This argument is not completely convincing, since there
is no tangible evidence for the existence of the lost "acta." The passio's non-
Prudentian features need not necessarily derive from a pre-Prudentian
source. Fábrega Grau admits in the end (1385) that all we know for sure
about Eulalia is in Prudentius.

Eulalia of Merida may have been known to ALDHELM (and possibly BEDE),
who echoes Prudentius' *Peristephanon* III. The passio that most clearly squares
with Prudentius' treatment of Eulalia, *BHL* 2700, was adopted by the later
Anglo-Saxons in the eleventh-century COTTON-CORPUS LEGENDARY and its
later affiliates, including the twelfth-century MSS Hereford, Cathedral
Library P.7.vi, and Oxford, Bodleian Library Bodley 354.

For further information on Eulalia, see Roger Collins (1980 pp 189–219)
and García Rodríguez (1966 pp 284–89).

                                                E. Gordon Whatley

Euphrosyna vita [ANON.Vit.Euphros.]: *BHL* 2723.

MSS — Lists none.
A-S Vers *LS* 7 (B3.3.7).
Quots/Cits — Refs none.

Evidence so far adduced for Anglo-Saxon knowledge of this vita (translated into Latin in the eighth century; see Siegmund 1949 p 235) is confined to the existence of the Old English translation, *LS* 7, which occurs in London, BL Cotton Julius E.vii, and in fragmentary form in BL Cotton Otho B.x. The source of *LS* 7 was identified first by Loomis (GR 5358, pp 5–6); see also Magennis (1985 p 299). Loomis had assumed that the Old English text was ÆLFRIC's work. Although this is not the case (Magennis 1986 pp 342–47), the similarity of approach to the Latin source supports the generally accepted view that *LS* 7 is contemporary with Ælfric. Wenisch (1979 pp 57, and 291) finds in its vocabulary occasional traces of Anglian influence.

Further work remains to be done on the Latin vita, of which Rosweyde's edition is reprinted in *PL* 73.643–52, in addition to the *AS* (cited in the Bibliography Part I). The *AS* edition is based on several MSS and collated with Rosweyd's. Neither is satisfactory as a guide to the early medieval state of the text.

Hugh Magennis

Eustachius passio [ANON.Pas.Eust.]: *BHL* 2760.

MSS Cambridge, Corpus Christi College 9: HG 16.
Lists none.
A-S Vers *LS* 8 (B3.3.8).
Quots/Cits — Refs none.

The first mention of Eustachius in the West is considered to be that of John of Damascus, *De Imaginibus* (*PG* 94.1382), a work translated into Latin immediately after its composition in 726 (Heffernan 1973 p 65). A considerable number of Latin versions of the legend of Eustachius were produced from the ninth century, of which at least two were known in Anglo-Saxon England, one prose (*BHL* 2760), the other verse (*BHL* 2767; see next entry). *BHL* 2760 is a reworking of an older text, *BHL* 2761, believed by Siegmund (1949 p 236) to have been translated from the Greek of *BHG* 641, possibly in connection with the introduction of the cult of Eustachius into Rome under Pope Gregory II (715–33).

The date of the composition of *BHL* 2760 is unknown, but the earliest extant MSS are from the tenth century (Monteverdi 1908–11 p 397), and the original may have been composed slightly earlier. It was incorporated into the COTTON-CORPUS LEGENDARY and survives in the Corpus MS, of the mid-eleventh century; another copy is in the twelfth-century MS Oxford, Bodleian Library, Bodley 354 (Zettel 1979 p 28).

As first pointed out by Loomis (GR 5358, pp 4–5), *BHL* 2760 is the source of the Old English prose translation, *LS* 8, surviving in London, BL Cotton Julius E.vii, and, in fragments, in Cotton Vitellius D.xvii. Magennis (1985) shows that the Cotton-Corpus texts of *BHL* 2760 represent the Old English writer's source more closely than the printed editions used by Loomis. Although the Old English version is not ÆLFRIC's work (Magennis 1986 pp 336–42), as Loomis assumed, it is reasonable to date it in Ælfric's time. Examination of the vocabulary has led Wenisch (1979 pp 57, 258, 291, and passim) to suggest Anglian influence on its composition.

In addition to the edition in Mombritius (Bibliography Part I), the text also appears in the *AS* (Sept. 6.127–37).

Hugh Magennis

Eustachius passio metrica [ANON.pas.Eust.metr.]: *BHL* 2767; *ICL* 14237; *ICVL* 16700.

MSS   none.
Lists   1. ? Æthelwold: ML 4.9.
      2. Peterborough: ML 13.60.
A-S Vers — Refs   none.

The "Passio Eustachii Placide uersifice," mentioned in a booklist thought to come from Peterborough around 1100 (ML 13.60), and probably identical to the "Vita Eustachii" donated to Peterborough by Bishop Æthelwold (ML 4.9), must be, according to Lapidge, the hexameter poem, *BHL* 2767. See also Monteverdi (1908–11 p 407). According to Lapidge, "on the evidence of the Aethelwold donation, the poem must have been in existence by the late tenth century, and its style marks it as a Carolingian product."

Hugh Magennis

Felix II passio [ANON.Pas.Fel.II]: *BHL* 2857.

MSS   1. London, BL Cotton Nero E.i: HG 344.
      2. London, BL Harley 3020: HG 433.

3. Salisbury, Cathedral Library 222 (olim Oxford, Bodleian Library Fell 1): HG 623.

Lists — Refs   none.

Pope Felix II (feast day, July 29), actually an Arian anti-pope under the emperor Constantius, was confused in the *Liber pontificalis* with Pope Liberius, and thereafter honored as a martyr for the cause of orthodox Christianity; see Duchesne (1955 vol 1 pp ccxxiv-xxv, and 211) and *BLS* 3.206–07. Cotton Nero E.i and the Salisbury MS are both witnesses of the COTTON-CORPUS LEGENDARY (see Zettel 1979 p 23).

E. Gordon Whatley

Felix Nolanus presbyter. See BEDE and PAULINUS OF NOLA.

The prose and verse lives of Felix of Nola are treated under BEDE and PAULINUS OF NOLA, but his confusing relationship with another Felix (of Rome) requires some comment here.

The earliest literary records concerning this saint of Campania are several poems (*BHL* 2870) by Paulinus of Nola, who adopted Felix as his patron on retiring from public life to Nola in 394 (P. Brown 1981 pp 53–60). Among the score of Felixes in the Roman calendar, two share the feast day Jan. 14: Felix "priest of Nola," and Felix "priest of Rome" ("in Pincis"), martyr (*BHL* 2885). It is generally accepted that Felix of Nola is the authentic original of the two Jan. 14 saints, and that the church "in Pincis" was originally a locus of Roman devotion to the Campanian saint (for the later, spurious Felix of Rome, see below).

Paulinus' poems on Felix of Nola were well known in early Anglo-Saxon England, and are quoted and echoed many times by ALDHELM, BEDE, and ALCUIN. In addition, Bede wrote a prose epitome (*BHL* 2873) of the poems, which he knew to be Paulinus' work (see PAULINUS OF NOLA). But Paulinus' patron was gradually forgotten by later Anglo-Saxons. According to Cross (1985a p 241 note 73), the ninth-century Old English martyrologist, in his entry for Felix, drew on both Bede's MARTYROLOGY and life of Felix, but the vernacular writer already shows the influence of the confusing development of Felix's cult in Rome, since he identifies Felix as "priest of Rome, in the place called Pincis," bypassing Bede's "in Campania." This suggests that the Old English *Martyrology* entry may depend on a calendar or liturgical book, as well as on Bede.

In the later Anglo-Saxon period, the Paulinus-Bede traditions concerning Felix are displaced by the Roman tradition represented in *BHL* 2885.

E. Gordon Whatley

Felix Romanus presbyter vita [ANON.Vit.Fel.Rom.]: *BHL* 2885; *CPL* 2189; *BSS* 5.535, 552; *DHGE* 6.909.

MSS   1. London, BL Cotton Nero E.i: HG 344.
2. Salisbury, Cathedral Library 221 (olim Oxford, Bodleian Library Fell 4): HG 625.
Lists — Refs   none.

Reputed brother of another Felix of Rome (feast day Aug. 30, *BHL* 2878–84), Felix "in Pincis" is believed to be a doublet of Felix of Nola, in whose honor the church on the Pincio was originally built (Delehaye 1897 p 23). *BHL* 2885 was probably composed in the seventh century (or sixth: see *CPL* 2189) by the same author as the passio of Felix and Adauctus (*BHL* 2878). Apparently, the work was not known to BEDE. The entry for Jan. 14 in the ninth-century Old English *Martyrology* (B19.y) speaks of a Felix, "priest of Rome, in the place called Pincis," but the remainder of the brief narrative is drawn word for word from Bede's writings on Felix of Nola (Cross 1985a). *BHL* 2885, therefore, would not appear to have been known to the early Anglo-Saxons.

The mid- and late-eleventh-century English MSS listed above, both examples of the COTTON-CORPUS LEGENDARY (see Zettel 1979 p 16), have not been collated with the printed edition. The *BHL* mistakenly entitles Felix's vita as a passio.

E. Gordon Whatley

Felix Tubzacensis passio [ANON.Pas.Fel.Tub.]: *BHL* 2894 and 2895b; see also *CPL* 2054.

MSS   1. London, BL Cotton Nero E.i: HG 344.
2. Salisbury, Cathedral Library 221 (olim Oxford, Bodleian Library Fell 4): HG 625.
3. Paris, Bibliothèque Nationale lat. 10861: HG 898.
Lists — A-S Vers   none.
Quots/Cits   1. ALDH.Pros.uirg. 264.13–14: see below.
2. BEDA.Mart. 160.9–17: see below.
3. *Mart* (B19.gj): see below.
Refs   none.

Bishop Felix of Thibiuca, near Carthage, apparently suffered martyrdom in the North African city early in the Diocletian persecution (303), for refusing to hand over the Christians' sacred books to the local magistrate. The passio survives in several recensions (see Delehaye 1921), two of which were known in Anglo-Saxon England. One, in which the martyrdom takes place in Nola (*BHL* 2894, designated by Delehaye 1921 as N), appears in the London and Salisbury MSS of the COTTON-CORPUS LEGENDARY (see Zettel 1979 p 16). The other, which moves the martyrdom to Venosa in Apulia (*BHL* 2895, designated by Delehaye 1921 as V), occurs in the Paris MS; see M. Brown (1987 p 122); Quentin (1908 pp 526–27), who edits the text; and Delehaye (1921 pp 247–52), who collates it. It is this second recension that underlies the use by ALDHELM (probably), BEDE (see Quentin 1908 p 74), and the ninth-century Old English *Martyrology* (Kotzor 1981 vol 2 p 343, note).

Although Felix's original feast day was probably July 15 or 16, it was early transferred to Aug. 30, probably owing to confusion with the feast of the martyrs Felix and Adauctus (*BHL* 2878), and later to Oct. 24, its present position in the calendar. The Cotton-Corpus legendary assigns the text to a January date, immediately after FELIX ROMANUS, in apparent confusion with FELIX NOLANUS.

BL Cotton Nero E.i contains another copy of the N type, although in the later (twelfth-century) portion of the MS, not in the Cotton-Corpus legendary proper; Delehaye (1921 p 246) mentions but does not collate it. It is also necessary to note that Delehaye (1921) has chosen London, BL Add. 11880 as his base text for N, and that his alternate readings are apparently from the edition of Baluzius (1678–1715 vol 1 pp 77–81). Bishop Fell (1680), as an appendix to his edition of Lactantius' *De morte persecutorum*, prints the text of Baluzius, but provides readings from the Salisbury MS.

E. Gordon Whatley

Guthlacus vita [FELIX.Vit.Guth.]: *BHL* 3723; *CPL* 2150; *DHGE* 22.1214–18.

MSS 1. Arras, Bibliothèque Municipale 1029: HG 781.
  2. Boulogne, Bibliothèque Municipale 106: HG 804.
  3. Cambridge, Corpus Christi College 307: HG 88.
  4. Cambridge, Corpus Christi College 389: HG 103.
  5. Dublin, Trinity College 174: HG 215.
  6. London, BL Cotton Nero E.i: HG 344.
  7. London, BL Royal 4.A.xiv: HG 456.
  8. London, BL Royal 13.A.xv: HG 484.
Lists 1. Saewold: ML 8.19.
  2. Peterborough: ML 13.16.

A-S Vers   1. ? *GuthA* (A3.2).
   2. *GuthB* (A3.2).
   3. *LS* 10 (B3.3.10).
Quots/Cits   ? *Mart* (B19.bv): see below.
Refs   none.

Although his death seems to have occurred in 714 (feast day April 11), Guthlac, the hermit of the Fens, is not mentioned by BEDE, and the Latin life by the monk Felix is dated by Colgrave to 730–49, that is after the completion of Bede's ECCLESIASTICAL HISTORY. Felix's life of Guthlac, while written in the ornate Insular style, is heavily indebted for its content and structure to Bede's prose VITA CUTHBERTI and to the early classics of monastic hagiography such as EVAGRIUS' VITA ANTONII and SULPICIUS' VITA MARTINI; see Kurtz (GR 3804) and Colgrave (1958).

Guthlac was widely venerated in Anglo-Saxon England and his popularity is reflected in the number of extant pre-Conquest copies of the life, and related vernacular texts. A late-eighth- or early-ninth-century fragment of Felix's life survives as the fly leaves of a tenth-century MS Royal 4.A.xiv, and the complete copy in the Corpus MS 307, of unknown provenance, is dated to the ninth century. The other Latin MSS listed above are of the tenth and eleventh centuries; for descriptions of these and other MSS and for their affiliation, see Colgrave (1956 pp 26–51). Lapidge identifies the item in the Saewold list (ML 8.19) as Arras, Bibliothèque Municipale 1029 (HG 781); and he suggests that the item in the Peterborough list (ML 13.16) may be London, BL Harley 3097.

Guthlac's continuing importance in the period is reflected in vernacular versions in both prose and verse. According to Kotzor (1981 vol 2 p 301), the entry on Guthlac in the ninth-century Old English *Martyrololgy* appears to draw mainly on Felix's life (the short account of Guthlac's sister, Pega, in *Mart* [B19.s] draws on Felix's chapter 53), although J. Roberts (GR 3811, pp 203–04) thinks it more likely that the martyrologist's immediate source for these entries was liturgical. The anonymous homiletic version, *LS* 10, a vernacular prose translation of Felix's life in a late West Saxon MS (London, BL Cotton Vespasian D.xxi, formerly part of Oxford, Bodleian Library Laud Misc. 509; NRK 344), was probably composed in the ninth or early tenth century in Mercia (J. Roberts 1986). A portion of the translation (corresponding to Felix's chapters 28–32, concerning Guthlac and the demons), but independent of the Vespasian text or its immediate exemplar, appears in the VERCELLI BOOK (Homily 23; see ANONYMOUS OLD ENGLISH HOMILIES under HOMILIARIES). Bolton (GR 6454) points to Corpus 389 or Cotton Nero E.i. (or a similar text of Colgrave's group IV type) as the Latin source text of *LS* 10. The Old English glosses in these MSS, however, are apparently not related to the Old English prose translation.

Two vernacular poems, *Guthlac A* and *Guthlac B,* dealing respectively with the saint's encounters with demons in his fenland retreat and with his death, survive in the *Exeter Book. Guthlac B* is widely accepted as a rendering of chapter 50 of Felix's life (J. Roberts 1979 pp 36–43), but while *Guthlac A* corresponds in some respects to the subject matter of Felix's chapters 28–32 (e.g. in both works Guthlac is taken to the gates of hell by demons), the few verbal correspondences formally adduced to indicate the poet's dependence on the Latin are not decisive. The ending of *Vercelli Homily* 23 (which departs from Felix), later iconographic evidence, and *Guthlac A* suggest the existence of some lost literary sources concerning Guthlac's visionary experiences or a flourishing oral tradition, or both (J. Roberts 1979 pp 19–29; also 1988). The dating and provenance of both poems are uncertain, but they are probably no later than the late ninth century; *Guthlac A* may be older than *Guthlac B*; see J. Roberts (1979 pp 70–71). See also J. Roberts (1967) for an edition of both the vernacular prose and poetic versions.

E. Gordon Whatley

Inventio sanctae crucis [ANON.Invent.cru.]: *BHL* 4169.

MSS   1. Cambridge, Pembroke College 24: HG 131.
    2. Cambridge, Trinity College O.10.31: HG 200.
    3. Salisbury, Cathedral Library 221 (olim Oxford, Bodleian Library Fell 4): HG 625.
    4. ? Oxford, Bodleian Library, Laud Misc. 129 (*SC* 1575).
    5. ? Munich, Bayerische Staatsbibliothek clm 22053.
    6. ? Paris, Bibliothèque Nationale lat. 2769: *CLA* 5.550.
    7. ? Paris, Bibliothèque Nationale lat. 5574.
    8. ? St Gall, Stiftsbibliothek 225: *CLA* 7.928.
Lists   none.
A-S Vers   1. *El* (A2.6).
    2. *LS* 6 (B3.3.6).
Quots/Cits   ? *Mart* (B19.ck): see below.
Refs   none.

The *Inventio,* which recounts the discovery of the cross by Helena, is neither a vita nor a passio, which may account for its preservation in MSS that are not primarily hagiographic. Coxe's Catalogue (1858–85, fasc 2, col 129) describes Laud Misc. 129 as "ix, literis Anglo-Saxonicis exaratus." Lowe states that BN lat. 2769 "by the 8th century . . . may have migrated . . . to a center under Anglo-Saxon influence." Citing Levison (GR 512A), who discusses the general indebtedness of Continental libraries to the Anglo-

Saxons, but who does not mention specific manuscripts, Gradon (GR 3563) comments that the St Gall MS "could have derived from an English original" (p 19 note 3); Lowe notes insular abbreviations for *autem* and *est* in this MS. The Munich MS may have been copied from an Anglo-Saxon original, especially in light of the use of runic symbols for "ga" and "enti"; see Waldman (1975 pp 1–2). Avril (1987 p 11) notes that BN lat. 5574 was in England at the beginning of the tenth century.

The Old English *Elene* and the anonymous homily *LS* 6 both use this text, and the details in the Old English *Martyrology* (B19.ck) could also have been drawn from it. The *Inventio* is also cited as a possible source for two passages in the *Dream of the Rood* (*Dream*, A2.5): the vision of the cross in the sky (4–7), and the discovery of the cross (76–78). On the first passage, see in particular Patch (GR 3501), who points out that the wording is somewhat closer to the Latin than to the Old English version in *Elene*, but who also concludes in part, "the episode in the *Dream* may possibly be based on one having nothing to do with the story of the *Inventio*" (p 237).

The liturgical celebration of the Invention of the Cross on May 3 — the date to which *BHL* 4169 is firmly tied in the text — was originally Roman (established by the sixth century), and was introduced into Gaul in the eighth century (see Chavasse 1958 pp 350–57). Willibrord's calendar (edited by Wilson 1918) assigns the feast to May 7, suggesting that the new date had not reached Gaul in his time, and BEDE does not mention the feast, implying that it reached England after the mid eighth century. The *Pontifical of Egbert* (Paris, Bibliothèque Nationale lat. 10575; edited by Greenwell 1853) contains a benediction for the *Inventio* on May 3, but Gneuss (1985 p 132) notes that "the attribution to Egbert is unfounded." Thus *Elene* and the *Dream* may represent some of the earliest evidence for the legend in England.

For bibliography on *Elene*, see GR 3558–3600; on *LS* 6, see Bodden (1987); and on the *Dream*, see GR 3482–3600. For a general discussion of cross lore in Anglo-Saxon England, see Stevens (GR 621) and for more information on the Irish material, see McNamara (1975 pp 78–79).

Frederick M. Biggs

Juliana passio [ANON.Pas.Julianae]: *BHL* 4522/4523; *CPL* 2201.

MSS 1. London, BL Cotton Nero E.i: HG 344.
  2. London, BL Harley 3020: HG 433.
  3. Paris, Bibliothèque Nationale lat. 10861: HG 898.
  4. Salisbury, Cathedral Library 221 (olim Oxford, Bodleian Library Fell 4): HG 625.

5. ? Paris, Bibliothèque Nationale lat. 5574.
Lists   none.
A-S Vers Jul (A3.5).
Quots/Cits   BEDA.Mart. 35.7–17: see below.
Refs   none.

The earliest Latin account (*BHL* 4522–3) of the virgin martyr Juliana
of Nicomedia is believed to be the original form of the legend, despite the
saint's purported Eastern origin (see Siegmund 1949 p 197; and Geith 1965
p 27) and was probably composed in Italy before the putative translation
of the saint's relics from Pozzuoli to Cumae in the mid sixth century (see
Woolf, GR 3880, p 11). The latest opinion of the Bollandists, on the evidence of the early martyrologies, is that Juliana was originally a local Cumae martyr whose cult became general in the Naples area before spreading
elsewhere, and whose martyrdom in Nicomedia is (along with the whole
legend) a fabrication (see *AS* Nov. vol 2 part 2 pp 301–02).

Geith (1965) regards England in the late-seventh- to the early-eighth-
century as an early locus of devotion to Juliana. As evidence he points to
BEDE's use of the passio in his MARTYROLOGY, the eighth-century English
recension of the Hieronymian martyrology (Paris, Bibliothèque Nationale
lat. 10837 — the Epternach MS), and Neapolitan influence through Abbot
Hadrian of Canterbury. He also argues that two of the three main families
of MSS of the passio originated in England (note that Geith's classification
of MSS does not retain the Bollandists' distinctions between *BHL* 4522 and
4523).

Four MSS now known to be of English provenance contain copies of
the passio. BN 10861 was almost certainly written at Christ Church, Canterbury, in the early ninth century (M. Brown 1987), and belongs to Geith's
Würzburg family of MSS, which he links with the Anglo-Saxon mission
to Germany. Harley 3020, however, is a member of Geith's Corbie family,
most of the members of which he associates with Anglo-Saxon influence
on the monastery at Corbie founded by the princess Bathilda. Geith was
unaware that the Paris and Harley MSS are actually of English provenance,
as pointed out by Price (1986) in her recent study of the Middle English
Liflade. None of these scholars, however, seems to have been aware of the
copies in the mid-eleventh-century Worcester legendary, Cotton Nero E.i,
and the somewhat later Salisbury legendary, Salisbury 221, which have not
been classified (Zettel 1979 p 18, simply lists them as examples of *BHL* 4522;
both MSS represent the COTTON-CORPUS LEGENDARY). Avril (1987 p 11) notes
that BN lat. 5574 was in England at the beginning of the tenth century.

The lack of an entry for Juliana in the Old English *Martyrology* (ninth
century) is doubtless due to the loss of most of the February saints.

There is as yet no modern critical edition of the passio: those of Brunöhler (GR 3889), d'Ardenne (1961), and Mombritius (1910), which reproduce specific MSS, are to be preferred to the contaminated text in *AS* Feb. 2.875–78 (see Geith 1965 24–25). Studies of the surviving early medieval MSS, e.g. those of Brunöhler (GR 3889), and Geith, have been done mainly with the German tradition in mind. That of Geith is the most useful and thorough, but not definitive. English source studies of Cynewulf's *Juliana* and the Middle English *Liflade* have tended to rely on the *AS* text, and it is used by Allen and Calder (1976 pp 121–32) for their translation. Despite Geith's opinion that Cynewulf's source was closely related to BN lat. 10861, a detailed study of the Old English poem in relation to this and other extant English copies of the *Passio Julianæ* remains to be undertaken.

For other, earlier studies dealing with the passio in relation to the Old English or other vernacular versions, see GR 3879, 3884, 3886, 3887. For a useful review of Geith's dissertation (1965), see Berschin (1978).

E. Gordon Whatley

Maria Aegyptiaca vita [PAUL.DIAC.NEAP.Vit.Maria.Aeg.]: *BHL* 5415.

MSS   1. London, BL Cotton Claudius A.i: HG 312.
2. London, BL Cotton Nero E.i: HG 344.
3. Salisbury, Cathedral Library 221 (olim Oxford, Bodleian Library Fell 4): HG 625.
Lists   none.
A-S Vers   *LS* 23 (B.33.23).
Quots/Cits — Refs   none.

This text, which was translated from the Greek by Paulus Diaconus "Neapolitanus" in the ninth century (Siegmund 1949 p 269; Kunze 1969 pp 26–28), was known in England in the late Anglo-Saxon period, although it is uncertain when it was first introduced. Of the MSS listed above, Cotton Claudius A.i has been dated mid tenth century, but was written on the Continent. The other two MSS (from Worcester and Salisbury) are copies of the COTTON-CORPUS LEGENDARY, which was known in England by the late tenth century, if not earlier.

The Old English homiletic version, *LS* 23, is a fairly literal translation of *BHL* 5415. Comparative study of the Old English and Latin versions reveals that the translator must have worked from a text very like that in the Cotton-Corpus group, which is also close to Cotton Claudius A.i. *LS* 23 shares with these Latin MSS many features that contrast with what we find in the printed editions; see Magennis (1985 pp 294–97). Chase (1986) argues that despite its close dependence on a Latin source *LS* 23 is nonetheless a distinctive literary document controlled, like other versions of the life, by the presuppositions of the age in which it was written.

The Old English translation is preserved in London, BL Cotton Julius E.vii (NRK 162) a MS containing ÆLFRIC'S LIVES OF SAINTS, and there are also fragments in two other MSS of the first half of the eleventh century (NRK 117A and 177). Although not written by Ælfric himself (see Magennis 1986 pp 332–36), *LS* 23 has generally been regarded as coming from the same period. Elements of its vocabulary, however, have been seen as suggesting an Anglian original (Wenisch 1979 pp 56, 257–58, 291, and *passim*).

Hugh Magennis

ADO OF VIENNE: *LTK* 1.150–51; *NCE* 1.133–134.

De sex aetatibus mundi [ADO.VIENN.Sex.aet.mundi].

MSS 1. London, British Library, Royal 13.A.xxiii: HG 486.
    2. Cambridge, Corpus Christi College 290: HG 84.
Lists — Refs none.

This ninth-century Archbishop of Vienne used the earlier history of BEDE as one of his sources, but his own reciprocal influence on Anglo-Saxon writers appears to have been modest. Both MSS owned in England date from no earlier than the mid eleventh century. The Cambridge text is "in all respects" like the London, including a faulty title: "*incipit cronica Odonis abbatis.*"

Daniel Nodes

ÆLFRIC OF EYNSHAM (c. 950–1010).

Ælfric's numerous writings, in English and in Latin, were extensively copied and circulated in his own time and throughout the next two centuries. His immediate impact is evident from the prefaces and rubrics to individual works. His first major work, the CATHOLIC HOMILIES, was addressed to Sigeric, Archbishop of Canterbury, and apparently encouraged by him.

Other works were commissioned by Wulfsige, Bishop of Sherborne; Eal-dorman Æthelweard and his son Æthelmær; WULFSTAN, Archbishop of York and Bishop of Worcester; and Æthelwold II, Bishop of Winchester. Others are addressed to Cenwulf, Bishop of Winchester; to several individual lay-men, Sigefyrth, Sigeweard, and Wulfgeat; and to the monks of Ælfric's own abbey, Eynsham. His writings were used as sources by his contemporaries Wulfstan of York, and Byrhtferth of Ramsey, and by a host of anonymous writers; in particular, his homiletic works were plundered for telling pas-sages and phrases by subsequent writers of vernacular sermons. Yet the only external references to him as a writer are a colophon in Cambridge, Corpus Christi College 178 (written in the first quarter of the eleventh cen-tury, and at Worcester later in the century) explaining that the homilies in that MS have been taken from the books which "Ælfricus abbas" trans-lated (NRK 62), and a rubric in Oxford, St John's College, 154 (written at the beginning of the eleventh century, and at Durham in the thirteenth century) by ÆLFRIC BATA assigning the COLLOQUY which follows to "Ælfricus abbas who was my teacher" (NRK 436).

For the canon and chronology of Ælfric's works, see Clemoes (GR 5397, pp 136–50). Recent surveys of his work include Hurt (GR 5215), and Greenfield and Calder (1986 pp 68–88). A study of his influence on Anglo-Saxon writers is by Godden (1978 pp 99–117).

[For this *Trial Version*, only the homilies are included.]

Catholic Homilies (*ÆCHom* I and II; B1.1.1–41, and B1.2.1–50).

MSS   see below.
Lists   none.
A-S Vers   see below.
Quots/Cits — Refs none.

There is one surviving MS of the whole collection, Cambridge Univer-sity Library Gg.3.28, dating from Ælfric's lifetime and possibly produced in his own scriptorium. London, BL Royal 7.C.xii (a facsimile is by Elia-son and Clemoes, GR 153) contains the First Series only, with annotations in Ælfric's own hand, and there are two other copies of the First Series from the early eleventh century (London, BL Cotton Vitellius C.v, and Cambridge, Corpus Christi College 188). Some 30 other MSS containing selections or fragments, ranging in date from the end of the tenth century to the early thirteenth century, are listed in NRK pp 511–15, apart from one edited by Fausbøll (1986). Ælfric composed the two Series of *Catholic Homilies* at Cerne Abbas, but sent copies immediately to Archbishop Sige-ric at Canterbury, and it was probably from there that they were mainly disseminated. Christ Church Canterbury, Rochester, the New Minster at

Winchester, Worcester, and Exeter certainly all had copies in the eleventh century, but many copies are so far unlocalized. A note at the end of the preface to the First Series indicates that Ælfric also gave a copy to Ealdorman Æthelweard.

Wulfstan adapted the first piece in the *Catholic Homilies* to form his own homily VI (*WHom* 6, B2.2.1) and drew on other items for his homilies IV, V, VII, and XVIII (*WHom* 4, B2.1.4; *WHom* 5, B2.1.5; *WHom* 7, B2.2.2; and *WHom* 18, B2.3.6; see the notes to these items in Bethurum's edition, GR 6503), and for the INSTITUTES OF POLITY (*WPol*, B13.2; see the notes in Jost's edition, GR 6504). Excerpts also appear in a variety of anonymous composite homilies found in eleventh-century MSS—*HomS* 27, 28, 34, and 41 (B3.2.27, 28, 34, and 41), *HomU* 44 (B3.4.44), *LS* 6 (B3.3.6)—and four others (in three MSS) included unclearly in the AC: Cambridge, University Library Ii.2.11 (NRK 21, article 27; listed only in AC under Ælfric, B1.2.24); London, Lambeth Palace 489 (NRK 283, articles 5 and 6; 5 is listed in AC under B3.4.46; 6 under B3.2.49 and B3.4.23); and Oxford, Bodleian Library Hatton 113, 114 (NRK 331, article 52; in AC under B3.2.30); detailed lists of the borrowings can be found in NRK's descriptions of the relevant MSS, and in Godden (1978) and Godden (1979). Excerpts also appear as marginalia in the only copy of Æthelwold's *Revival of Monasticism* (B17.11; see NRK p 195).

Lives of Saints (*ÆLS*, B1.3.1–35).

MSS   see below.
Lists   ? Peterborough: ML 13.54.
A-S Vers   none.
Quots-Cits   see below.
Refs   none.

The only extant copy of the whole collection is London, BL Cotton Julius E.vii (from the beginning of the eleventh century, later at Bury St Edmunds). Selections appear in 17 other MSS (indexed by NRK pp 530–35). The Peterborough booklist includes a collection of saints' lives in English, which may be this work.

In his preface, Ælfric says that the *Lives* were written at the request of Ealdorman Æthelweard and his son Æthelmær. Excerpts from items in the *Lives* collection appear in three anonymous composite homilies: *HomU* 26 (B3.4.26; see Jost, GR 6528); a text printed in Morris (GR 6214, pp 296–304; not in AC), drawing on Skeat items 13 and 16; and an item in London, Lambeth Palace 489 (NRK 283, article 6; AC under B3.2.49 and B3.4.23).

Other Homilies (*ÆHom* and *ÆHomM*, B1.4.1–31, and B1.5.1–15).

MSS   see below.
Lists   none.
A-S Vers   see below.
Quots/Cits   see below.
Refs   none.

These homilies were composed at various stages in Ælfric's life, mostly for inclusion in collections of homilies drawing on his earlier set, the CATHOLIC HOMILIES. Various selections are to be found in some 26 MSS, listed by Pope (GR 5297) and AC (under B1.5.1–15), usually in association with items from the Catholic Homilies. Wulfstan adapted one of them, *ÆHom* 22 (B1.4.22; Pope's item 21) to form his homily XII (*WHom* 12, B2.2.10); and excerpts from another, *ÆHom* 11 (B1.4.11), appear in an anonymous composite homily in Cambridge, University Library Ii.2.11 (NRK 21.27; listed only in AC under Ælfric, B1.2.24).

M.R. Godden

ALCUIN: *DS* 1.296–99; *DMA* 1.142–43; *ODCC* 31.

[This trial version includes only a selection of Alcuin's works.]

Dialogus Franconis et Saxonis de octo partibus oratonis [ALCVIN.Gramm.].

MSS   none.
Lists   ? Athelstan (grammarian): ML 3.8.
A-S Vers — Refs   none.

This lively grammar, cast in the form of a conversation between two teenage boys with occasional interventions from the teacher, presents information from DONATUS, PHOCAS, and PRISCIAN'S INSTITUTIONES GRAMMATICAE, as well as one or two foretastes of linguistic issues, *secundum dialecticos*. Although it is highly likely that Alcuin's grammar arrived in England along with other grammars popular in Carolingian France, no copies and no borrowings have so far been indentified in the English grammatical tradition. The two references to Alcuin in booklists (the second is in Worcester II: ML 11.41) do not specify which work is meant. That in Athelstan the grammarian's list is probably the grammar, given the context, or possibly Alcuin's DE ORTHOGRAPHIA.

For Alcuin's excerpts from Priscian's *Institutiones grammaticae*, see Priscian. See also Law (1982 p 103), Holtz (1981 p 321), and Holtz (1988).

V. Law

Liber de virtutibus et vitiis [ALCVIN.Virt.uit.].

MSS   1. Avranches, Bibliothèque Municipale 81: HG 783.
   2. London, BL Cotton Vespasian D.vi: HG 389.
   3. Cambridge, Pembroke College 25: HG 131.
Lists   none.
A-S Vers   1. *Alc* (Warn 35, B9.7).
   2. *Alc* 14 (Först, B9.7).
   3. *Alc* 16 (Först, B9.7).
   4. *HomS* 38 (*VercHom* 20, B3.2.38).
Quots/Cits   1. *HomS* 11.2 (*VercHom* 3, B3.2.11): see below.
   2. *HomS* 16 (Ass 12, B3.2.16) 99–103: ALCVIN.Virt.uit. 629.30–34.
   3. *HomS* 16 (Ass 12, B3.2.16) 106–22: ALCVIN.Virt.uit. 629.44–57.
   4. *HomS* 16 (Ass 12, B3.2.16) 140–56: ALCVIN.Virt.uit. 632–32–53.
   5. *HomS* 41 (B3.2.41) 6–12: ALCVIN.Virt.uit. 621.23–29.
   6. *LawIudex* (B14.54): see below.
Refs   none.

The *Liber de virtutibus et vitiis* is a book of biblical and patristic commonplaces meant to help the addressee, Count Wido, attain eternal salvation. Written at Tours after 799 and in Alcuin's (d. 804) last years, the work enjoyed wide popularity in the early Middle Ages (and later), being pillaged and adapted in whole or in part in the Latin tradition. Because of its commonplace nature and the rhetorical tradition of adapting *sententiae*, some of the current attributions to the *Liber*, which are commonly accepted, may not on further analysis prove acceptable. Thus, the theme "the three kinds of alms," present in chapter 17, is not in itself evidence of the *Liber* because the theme enjoyed a wide currency. On the treatise generally see Wallach (1959 pp 231–54) and Szarmach (1981b especially pp 133–34).

The Avranches MS, lacking a list of chapters and the *peroratio*, offers different titles for chapters and otherwise contains different readings from BL or Pembroke. The BL MS contains some 30 Old English interlinear glosses for a Latin text that diverges greatly from the mainline tradition. The Pembroke MS contains a redaction of the work in three homilies (articles 93–95; see the HOMILIARY OF ST PÈRE DE CHARTRES under HOMILIARIES), thus showing transmission through intermediary forms. Cross (1987a pp 52–54) summarizes the use of the treatise elsewhere in Pembroke (also articles 20, 22, 23, 25, 48, and 91); see also his analysis of sources (pp 17–43). *HomS* 38 (included in AC under B9.7), commonly known as VERCELLI 20 (see ANONYMOUS OLD ENGLISH HOMILIES under HOMILIARIES), relies on an earlier version of the Pembroke MS (see Cross 1987a). The other versions are incomplete translations or single chapters. Thus *Alc* (Warn 35) gives the first sixteen chapters (Cambridge, University Library Ii.1.33, not listed in *MCOE*, but included in AC B9.7, offers a variant through thirteen chapters); *Alc* 14 (Först) translates chapter 14; and *Alc* 26 (Först) chapter 26. The relationships of these texts to each other and to the Latin tradition needs further work. Lindström (1988) examines a number of passages for their problematic and defective features, and see also Szarmach (forthcoming, 1989/1986).

The quotations in the Old English texts are noted by the following scholars: for *HomS* 11.2 (commonly VERCELLI 3), Förster (GR 6200, pp 71–72), listing thirteen parallels; for *HomS* 16, Jost (GR 6519, pp 307–12); *HomS* 41, Bazire and Cross (1982 p 90), and with cautions, Lees (1985b pp 177–78); for *LawIudex*, Torkar (1981, 248–55), printing the Latin of chapter 20 opposite the equivalent Old English. For the issues involved in source analysis with particular problematical examples in ÆLFRIC and WULFSTAN see the overview in Torkar (1981, pp 22–35), the discussion focussing on Ælfric's works in Pope (GR 5297, pp 284–85), and Lees (1985b pp 178–83).

Förster (GR 248, and 6200) is incorrect in questioning the authenticity of the *Liber*. Rochais (1951 p 79) has no evidence for his suggestion of the separate existence of chapters 27–34 as a treatise, though clearly these chapters were detached, as in Vatican, Vat. lat. 650. Ogilvy (*BKE* p 56) is right in questioning the provenance of BL Add. 18338 and in questioning the eleventh-century BL Harley 3070. The *CCSL* projects an edition of the *Liber* in the mid-1990s (to be edited by Szarmach).

Paul E. Szarmach

Vita S. Martini [ALCVIN.Vit.Mart.]: BHL 5625.

MSS   1. Cambridge, Pembroke College 25: HG 131.
     2. Salisbury, Cathedral Library 221 (olim Oxford, Bodleian Library Fell 4): HG 625.
Lists—A-S Vers   none.
Quots/Cits   ÆCHom II, 39.1 (B1.2.32): 146–52, 152–54, 219–25, and 239–66: see below.
Refs   none.

Alcuin's life of Martin is a redaction of three works by SULPICIUS SEVER-
US on the Saint, his VITA, DIALOGORUM LIBRI III, and EPISTULAE. The Cambridge MS suggests that the work may have first circulated in England in
the HOMILIARY OF ST PÈRE DE CHARTRES, and was added later to the COTTON-
CORPUS LEGENDARY (see LEGENDARIES) represented by the Salisbury MS.
Zettel (1979 pp 99–110) first noted ÆLFRIC's use of this work in his first life
of St Martin, identifying the four major passages previously thought to
have come from Sulpicius's *Dialogues* as deriving more directly from Alcuin's
redaction. He discusses as well some other correspondences.

For a discussion of Alcuin's sources, see I Deug-Su (1983 pp 167–72);
and for an analysis of Ælfric's change in attitude to this source, see Biggs
(forthcoming).

Frederick M. Biggs

APOCRYPHA

The term "Apocrypha" is used here instead of "Pseudepigrapha" because
the perspective of this volume is not exactly the same as that of modern
scholars who distinguish among three kinds of biblical material: books accepted as canonical by Catholics and Protestants (from the Hebrew canon), additional books accepted by Catholics but not by Protestants (from
the Septuagint canon), and books excluded by both groups. For Anglo-
Saxon England, where the Bible was essentially the Vulgate (see BIBLE),
it is more appropriate to distinguish between the Bible as the canon and
the Apocrypha as the non-canonical books, a distinction suggested by the
contemporary writers ALDHELM (the prose DE VIRGINITATE 313.11–14), BEDE
(RETRACTIO IN ACTUS APOSTOLORUM I.13.56), and FRITHEGOD (BREVILOQUI-
UM VITAE WILFRIDI 1210–11; for patristic uses, see *NTA* 1.25–26). The use
of the term, however, is not meant to imply that the advances in modern
scholarship in dating, placing, and characterizing these texts will be ignored.

Unfortunately, deciding which term to use is less difficult than defining
what it means. While useful, the definitions of modern scholars — in particular Charlesworth (*OTP* 1.xxv) and Hennecke (*NTA* 1.26–28) — are
perhaps too strict for our purposes because they exclude works that would
have appeared to be "Apocrypha" to the Anglo-Saxons. For example, the
REVELATIONES of PS METHODIUS, now dated to the mid seventh century and
so too late for Charlesworth's criteria, is in some ways similar to Daniel.
Thus for practical purposes, this section adopts the inclusive list of

Apocrypha in volume 1—and expanded in volume 8—of the *Repertorium Biblicum Medii Aevi* [*RBMA*]. This list also provides a convenient system of dividing the works into Old Testament Apocrypha, Apocryphal Gospels, Apocryphal Acts, and Apocryphal Apocalypses; the Apocryphal Gospels and the Apocryphal Acts have their own introductory remarks. The section includes a few texts not listed in the *RBMA* but which are often considered with the Apocrypha. An example is the BIBLICAL ANTIQUITIES of PS PHILO, which, following the *OTP*, has been included with the Old Testament Apocrypha even though the *RBMA* treats the work as a biblical commentary. A concluding Miscellaneous section, which has been omitted from this "Trial Version," will include several texts that do not fit neatly into the scheme but that are discussed by Anglo-Saxonists as Apocrypha.

There is considerable overlapping within apocryphal books, which of course increases the difficulty of establishing which were known in Anglo-Saxon England. For example, as Cross (1979b p 17) notes, the PS ABDIAS collection of Apocryphal Acts, which has been cited as a source for works such as the Old English *Martyrology* [*Mart*, B19], draws on earlier lives, and so is often indistinguishable from them. Moreover recent studies of Hiberno-Latin biblical materials (see HIBERNO-LATIN BIBLICAL COMMENTARIES; Bischoff 1976; McNamara 1975; Cross 1986a; and C. Wright 1987a) indicate that many apocryphal motifs circulated in these works, and so an individual motif may not necessarily reflect a direct knowledge of the entire book in question.

Contributors to the Apocrypha have signed their individual entries, but all have read the entire section, and have been generous in offering advice and criticism. The unsigned entries are my own. For further scholarship on the texts themselves, see Charlesworth's bibliographies for works related to the Old Testament (1981) and to the the New Testament (1987).

Frederick M. Biggs

I. OLD TESTAMENT APOCRYPHA

Life of Adam and Eve [ANON.Vit.Adae]: *RBMA* 74; *OTP* 2.249–95.

MSS—Refs   none.

Surviving in distinct Greek (sometimes called the Apocalypse of Moses) and Latin recensions, the Life of Adam and Eve was composed—probably in Hebrew—late in the first century AD, and translated probably before the beginning of the fifth century (*OTP* 2.252). The Latin version relates events in the life of Adam and Eve from the expulsion to their deaths.

Pächt (1961 p 169) suggests that the illumination in the illustrated Old English Hexateuch (BL Cotton Claudius B.iv; *IASIM* 191.17) of an angel instructing Adam and Eve in tilling the earth after the Fall is related to this apocryphon. The other possibility, JUBILEES 3.15, is less likely since here Adam and Eve are instructed before the Fall. The illumination is reproduced in *EEMF* 18, and discussed on pp 19 and 65.

Groos (1983) cites Satan's account of his expulsion from heaven as a possible source for the question of angelic seniority in *Guthlac A* (*GuthA*, A3.2; 4b). Evans (1968 p 146 note 4) suggests that this account may underlie Lucifer's explanation of his rebellion in *Christ and Satan* (*Sat*, A1.4; 84–86).

For a list of the Latin MSS, see Halford (1981). For a discussion of the Hiberno-Latin material, see C. Wright (1987a pp 130–33).

Adam Octipartite and **Adam's Name** [ANON.Adam.comp.]: *RBMA* 75,22.

MSS   1. Cambridge, Corpus Christi College 326: HG 93.
2. Durham, Cathedral Library A.IV.19: HG 223.
Lists   none.
A-S Vers   Sol I (B5.1).
Quots/Cits—Refs   none.

The motif that describes Adam's creation from eight substances may rest ultimately on II Enoch 30.8J (*OTP* 1.150). It is widespread in Insular circles, appearing in the eighth-century LIBER DE NUMERIS (in HIBERNO-LATIN BIBLICAL COMMENTARIES, number 39; see also the QUESTIONS OF BARTHOLOMEW) and later texts. The DURHAM RITUAL (p 192; see LITURGY) has an Old English gloss (*DurRitGlCom*, C13.1). This motif occurs in questions 8 and 9 of the prose *Solomon and Saturn* (*Sol I*); see Cross and Hill (1982, 26.8–18), and their discussion of sources and analogs (pp 68–70).

Along with the description of Adam's material creation in the Cambridge MS is another motif also perhaps derived from II Enoch 30.13–14J (*OTP* 1.152; also mentioned in the SIBYLLINE ORACLES 3.24–26: *OTP* 1.362), the derivation of Adam's name from four stars. This motif underlies questions 6 and 7 of the prose *Solomon and Saturn* (see Cross and Hill 1982 pp 66–67), but does not occur in the Durham Ritual. A version of the motif, which links the names to the four corners of the world but does not mention stars, occurs in BEDE (COMMENTARIUS IN GENESIM II.729–33); Bede apparently follows AUGUSTINE (ENARRATIONES XCV.15.6–12) or AUGUSTINE (TRACTATUS IX.14.9–14 and X.12.2–12). D'Alverny (1976 p 169) notes a trace of this motif in one of the illuminations in Byrhtferth's *Manual* (*ByrM* 1, Crawford, B20.20.1), printed as the frontispiece in *EETS* OS 177: the cardinal points are also given the names that spell out Adam, and reinforced with separate capitals.

In addition to the text specified in the Bibliography Part I, Förster (1907–08) prints other versions. For further references to Hiberno-Latin and Irish texts, see McNally (1957 p 72), McNamara (1975 p 21–23), Tristram (1975), and C. Wright (1987a pp 140–43). Hill (1977a) cites the theme as relevant to the "Æcerbot Charm" (*MCharm* 1, A43.1). See also Cerbelaud (1984) for a general discussion of the theme.

Jubilees [ANON.Jubilees]: *RBMA* 77; *OTP* 2.35–142. See LIFE OF ADAM AND EVE and I ENOCH.

MSS — Quots/Cits   none.
Refs   see below.

Composed in Hebrew in the middle of the second century BC, Jubilees (also known as the "Little Genesis") recounts stories from Genesis and the beginning of Exodus. A single fragmentary Latin MS survives (Milan, Biblioteca Ambrosiana C 73 inf.; *CLA* 3.316), which contains about a fourth of the work. The work is mentioned by JEROME (EPISTOLA AD FABIOLAM [78] 68.14–17), and condemned in the GELASIAN DECREE (286). Bischoff (1976 p 77) notes that it is cited twice in the glosses of THEODORE OF CANTERBURY in Milan, Biblioteca Ambrosiana M. 79 sup., a work being edited by Bischoff and Lapidge.

An English translation, based primarily on the Ethiopic but referring to the Hebrew, Latin, and Syriac fragments, is in *OTP* 2.52–142. Charles' edition (Bibliography Part I) places the Latin fragments opposite the Ethiopic text.

Ps Philo, Biblical Antiquities [ANON.Lib.Antiq./PS.PHILO]: *RBMA* 4.6980,2; *OTP* 2.297–377.

Ogilvy (*BKE* pp 69–73) indirectly refers to this work, which was composed in Hebrew in the first century BC, when he discusses four fragments, the "Prayer of Moses," the "Vision of Kenaz," the "Lamentation of Seila the daughter of Jephthah," and the "Song of David," printed by James (1893 pp 166–85) from Phillipps MS 391; Cohn (1898) recognized the fragments to be from the *Biblical Antiquities*. The MS is listed in the 30 Nov. 1965 sale catalog of Sotheby & Co. (*Bibliotheca Phillippica* 1965), as from the second half of the eleventh century (early twelfth century in Kisch 1949 p 27) and from the Abbey of St Matthias, Trier. Thus there is currently no evidence for the knowledge of this work in Anglo-Saxon England.

I Enoch [ANON.Enoch]: *RBMA* 78,16; *OTP* 1.5–89.

MSS   London, BL Royal 5.E.xiii: HG 459.

Lists—A-S Vers   none.
Quots/Cits   ? BEDA.Comm.epist.cath. 340.226–27: see below.
Refs   BEDA.Comm.epist.cath. 340.220.

This composite work, attributed to Enoch (Gen 5.24) but composed in Hebrew or Aramaic between 200 BC and 100 AD, presents eschatological themes, discussion of the fallen angels, and astronomical lore. The only known Latin fragment is a shortened version of chapter 106 (considered in the *OTP* to be an appendix from an independent work), which describes Moses' miraculous form at birth, and foretells the Flood. Milik (1976 pp 78–81), who argues that "there is no irrefutable evidence for the existence of a Latin version of the Enochic writings," proposes that the fragment and its surrounding passages are "probably some extracts from a chronicle or from a collection of Exempla or of Testimonia." Dumville (1973) identifies the manuscript as Breton from the ninth century, but states that it "was in England (perhaps Worcester) during the next century" (p 331).

According to Kaske (GR 2343), BEDE's discussion in his COMMENTARIUS IN EPISTOLAS of I Enoch "is clearly based on a similar discussion by AUGUSTINE in DE CIVITATE DEI" (XV.23.104–24), but "it does at least raise the question of whether Bede may not have known of the Book of Enoch directly" (p 422). The passage Kaske cites as suggesting independent knowledge by Bede is referred to I Enoch 6–7 in the *CCSL* edition of Bede's commentary, although Augustine may be Bede's only source.

As evidence for the circulation of I Enoch, James (1909–10) has identified a number of early Insular works that include the motif of the seven archangels: Cuthbert's coffin; the DURHAM RITUAL (pp 145, 146, and 198; see LITURGY); the BOOK OF CERNE (p 153; see LITURGY); the ANTIPHONARY OF BANGOR (p 85; see LITURGY); Cambridge, Corpus Christi College 41 (p 326; HG 39); and the *Textus Roffensis* (*EEMF* 7 fol 116v); as well as several other Irish and Continental examples. Hill (1974) adds that some of the names from the list occur in the *Pater Noster Dialogue* (*Sol II*, B5.3; 169.3 and 9) and that BONIFACE condemns a prayer containing the names of eight angels (*MGH.ES* 1.117). Cross (1986a) discusses the possibility of Irish biblical commentaries as intermediaries for such material (see McNally 1959 p 28 for a further Irish example).

Menner (GR 4337) cites I Enoch three times for parallels to the poetic *Solomon and Saturn* (*MSol*, A13; 247a–48b; 253b, and 263–64). The possibility that I Enoch may underlie the depiction of Grendel and Grendel's mother in *Beowulf* (*Beo*, A4.1) has long intrigued critics, with three details commanding the most attention: the monsters' cannibalism, their home in the wasteland, and the "el" ending of Grendel's name; see in particular Bouterwek (GR 2713, p 401), Emerson (GR 623, p 878 note 1); Kaske (GR

2343), Peltola (GR 2353); Mellinkoff (1979 and 1981); and Cross (1986a pp 82–83).

Two of the illuminations of Enoch, one in the Old English Hexateuch (BL, Cotton Claudius B.iv.; *IASIM* 191.35) and another in the Junius MS (Oxford, Bodleian Library Junius 11; *IASIM* 163.35), illustrate Gen 5.24, the translation of Enoch, and show no apparent influence of the apocryphal tradition. A second illustration in the Junius MS, however, is less straight-forward, showing "Enoch, nimbed and holding an open book, trampl[ing] a dragon, while an angel addresses him" (*IASIM* 163.34). Neither the Vulgate, nor *Genesis A* (*GenA*, A1.1; 1195–1217a) accounts for this depiction; Gollancz (GR 136, p xliv) suggests it may represent Enoch as the inventor of writing (JUBILEES 4.18) or as the author of an apocryphal book (see I Enoch 13.6, 14.7, etc.). Similarly, Gollancz suggests that the sign above the family inhabiting the first city earlier in the Hexateuch (*IASIM* 191.22) is the sign of Aries, and can be explained by assuming a confusion of Cain's son Enoch (Gen 4.17) and Jared's son Enoch (Gen 5.19): the latter, according to JUBILEES 4.17 composed an astronomical text. According to Milik (1976 p 11) this passage from Jubilees refers to I Enoch 72–82.

A translation of the entire work, based on the Ethiopic but including references to the Greek and Latin fragments, appears in *OTP* 1.13–89. The Greek fragments are edited by Black (1970 pp 19–44). In addition to editing the Latin fragment, James (Bibliography Part I, pp 146–50), discusses the work.

Oratio Moysis: (*RBMA* 89,7): see PS PHILO, BIBLICAL ANTIQUITIES.

Jamnes and Mambres [ANON.Jamnes]: *RBMA* 89,13; *OTP* 2.427–42.

MSS London, BL Cotton Tiberius B.v: HG 373.
Lists none.
A-S Vers   Mambres (B8.5.7).
Quots/Cits — Refs none.

Legends about Jamnes and Mambres (Greek: Jannes and Jambres), at some point identified as the two Egyptian magicians who compete against Moses and Aaron in Ex 8, are pre-Christian since they are alluded to in the Damascus Document, a text dated around 100 BC (*OTP* 2.427). The *OTP* notes that "most early development of the Jannes and Jambres tale took place in a Greek (and Latin) Christian milieu," with early references to the two including II Tim 3.8. By the third century, ORIGEN refers to an apocryphon devoted to their exploits (Commentary on Mt 27.9, *PG* 13.1769), and a Latin version is condemned by the GELASIAN DECREE (303–04).

The Latin excerpt and Old English translation from the British Library MS were printed by Cockayne (GR 293) and James (GR 5734), and then more carefully edited and discussed by Förster (GR 5735). The Old English translation, amounting to some 15 lines and accompanied by a full page illustration, is the only vernacular version that has yet come to light. In it, Mambres raises the spirit of his dead brother Jamnes from hell with the aid of necromancing spells in Jamnes' magical books. The shade of Jamnes appears and warns Mambres of hell's torments, adjuring him to lead a better life. Comparison with the reconstructed Greek fragments shows this episode to come near the end of the apocryphon (*OTP* 2.440–41). The excerpt has apparently been added on to the MARVELS OF THE EAST.

Three other passages in Old English mention the magicians by name but are not manifestly dependent upon the apocryphon. One of the Old English additions to *Orosius* (*Or*, B9.2; 26.19–22) tells that by means of sorcery, "Geames and Mambres" persuaded the Egyptians to follow the Israelites through the Red Sea. Nothing in the extant Greek fragments agrees with this assertion; see however ISIDORE'S ETYMOLOGIES (VII.vi.44–45) which connects the two names with the sea, and may thus have given rise to the addition. ÆLFRIC makes a similar comment in his piece on auguries (*ÆLS*, Auguries, B1.3.18; 114) where he states that Jamnes and Mambres made many pronouncements through the devil's craft, deceiving Pharaoh with their cunning tricks so that he drowned in the deep sea. Finally, the anonymous Life of St Margaret (*LS* 14 [MargaretAss 15]; B3.3.14; 258) records that when God cast Satan out of paradise, he gave him two lands (presumably to rule), one named Jamnes and the other Mambres. This detail accords with none of the extant Latin lives of St Margaret (*BHL* 5303), which do mention Jamnes and Mambres, but only in a speech in which a demon proclaims, "Satan is our king, who was expelled from paradise. In the books of Jamnes and Mambres you will find our lineage [recorded]" (Mombritius 1910 vol 2 p 194). The precise relationship of these three Old English passages to the apocryphon, or related legends, has yet to be determined.

Jamnes and Mambres also have been identified in three illuminations. The illustrated Old English Hexateuch (BL Cotton Claudius B.iv; *IASIM* 191) depicts the miracle of the rods (Ex 7.12) with two figures between Moses and Aaron and Pharaoh; although the text does not identify them, Ohlgren's (*IASIM* 191.252) suggestion that they are Jamnes and Mambres seems likely. Two similar figures appear in the depiction of the plague of lice (Ex 8.18), and again Ohlgren (191.258) identifies them as Jamnes and Mambres. BL Cotton Tiberius B.v (see above) depicts the scene described in the fragment (*IASIM* 192.62).

For an English translation of the extant fragments in Greek, Latin, and Old English, see *OTP* 2.437–42; on the texts themselves, see the introduction to the translation, with further bibliography in Charlesworth (1981 pp 133–34). The Toronto *Dictionary of Old English* is using Förster's edition (GR 5735). Further discussion of the Old English appears in James (1920 pp 31–38).

Thomas N. Hall

Threnis Seilae Iephthedis in Monte Stelaco: *RBMA* 89,16. See PS PHILO, BIBLICAL ANTIQUITIES.

Visio Zenez: *RBMA* 91,4. See PS PHILO, BIBLICAL ANTIQUITIES.

4 Ezra [ANON.Esdrae.lib.IV]: *RBMA* 95; *OTP* 1.516–59.

MSS — Refs   none.

Composed in the late first century AD, with four chapters added in the third century, 4 Ezra contains seven visions concerning primarily the end of the world. The work circulated in some Latin Bibles (for a list of early manuscripts, see Gry 1938 vol 1 pp xi-xiii); and was certainly known in Irish circles (see McNamara 1975 p 27). Ogilvy concludes too readily from a passage quoted in James' introduction to Bensly's (1895) edition that "the French family of MSS are thought to rest on an English archetype" (*BKE* p 69). According to Bischoff (1968 p 24), the manuscript in question (now Paris, Bibliothèque Nationale lat. 11504 and 11505) is from St Germain in Paris, although the illuminated initials may show the influence of Insular practice. McNamara (1975) indicates that one of the Irish texts dependent on 4 Ezra belongs to the French family.

A number of motifs perhaps derived ultimately from 4 Ezra have been noted in Old English texts, particularly *ChristC* (A3.1; see GR 626, 3265, Hill 1986, Biggs 1986, and Biggs 1989; see also HIBERNO-LATIN COMMENTARIES, NUMBER 1).

For an English translation, see *OTP* 1.525–59. In addition to the text in Bensly and James (1895), the introduction includes a list of patristic and medieval citations of the work. See also Gry's (1938) study and edition, which contains French translations of the Syriac and Ethiopic, and a Latin text with many variants. On the relationship of 4 Ezra to other Ezra material, see Stone (1982).

Revelatio Esdrae [ANON.Rev.Esd.]: *RBMA* 99.

MSS 1. London, BL Cotton Titus D.xxvi: HG 380.
    2. London, BL Cotton Tiberius A.iii: HG 363.
Lists   none.

A-S Vers   1. *Prog* 3.9 (Först; B23.3.3.9).
   2. *Prog* 5.1 (Warner; B23.3.5.1).
   3. *Prog* 6.4 (Cockayne; B23.3.6.4).
Quots/Cits — Refs   none.

The Revelatio Esdrae, which predicts the weather for the coming year on the basis of the weekday on which the new year falls, is closer in genre to the PROGNOSTICA than to the Apocrypha; it is, however, associated with Ezra in the seventh-century *Chronicle* of John of Nikion, and in Latin MSS such as Vatican, Pal. lat. 1449 (Mercati, Bibliography Part I). The two eleventh-century MSS in the BL (printed in Birch 1892 pp 257–58; and Förster, GR 6152, pp 296–97) do not associate the work with Ezra. The work also occurs in Vatican, Pal. lat. 235, but beyond the portion of this manuscript accepted in HG 910.

In addition to the glossed Latin text, Cotton Tiberius A.iii also includes a version only in Old English (*Prog* 3.9). The other two Old English versions are from the twelfth century. *Prog* 6.4, unlike the other versions known in Anglo-Saxon England, associates the predictions with Christmas rather than with the new year; this tradition is also found in London, BL Sloane 475, a MS not included in HG, but dated by Matter (1982 p 389) to the eleventh century.

Matter (1982) pays special attention to the English transmission of the work, and also provides a translation of the Latin. In addition to the Latin texts printed by Mercati (Bibliography Part I), a version appears in *PL* 90.951 among the doubtful works of Bede.

Psalm 151 [ANON.Ps.151]: *RBMA* 105,2; *OTP* 2.610–12.

MSS   1. Florence, Biblioteca Medicea Laurenziana 1 (Amiatinus): HG 825.
   2. Cambridge, Corpus Christi College 272: HG 77.
   3. Cambridge, Corpus Christi College 391: HG 104.
   4. Cambridge, Corpus Christi College 411: HG 106.
   5. London, BL Additional 37517: HG 291.
   6. London, BL Arundel 60: HG 304.
   7. London, BL Cotton Galba A.xviii: HG 334.
   8. London, BL Cotton Vespasian A.1: HG 381.
   9. London, BL Cotton Vitellius E.xviii: HG 407.
   10. London, BL Harley 2904: HG 430.
   11. London, Lambeth Palace Library 427: HG 517.
   12. Salisbury, Cathedral Library 150: HG 740.
   13. Salisbury, Cathedral Library 180: HG 754.
   14. Vatican, Reg. Lat 12: HG 912.
Lists — Refs   none.

Composed originally in Hebrew, and translated in the Septuagint, Psalm 151 draws much of its content from I Sam, purporting to be spoken by David after his fight with Goliath. In the Codex Amiatinus it is introduced "psalmus dauid proprie extra numerum." The psalm is also included in the PSALTERIUM ROMANUM (see LITURGY) — brought to Canterbury by St Augustine (Weber 1953 p ix), but the psalm does not occur in several English MSS of this psalter, including Pierpont Morgan 776 (HG 862), Cambridge University Library Ff.1.23 (HG 4), and East Berlin Deutsche Staatsbibliothek Hamilton 553 (HG 790). It does occur in the Additional MS (the Bosworth Psalter), but without an Old English gloss (Morrell 1965 p 129). The Vespasian Psalter, in its original plan, deliberately omitted this psalm, but it "was added by the 4th hand on an inserted leaf" (*EEMF* 14.46), and has been glossed. NRK (203) suggests that the Latin text is "probably by the same hand" as the Old English glosses, which he dates to the mid ninth century. Morrell (1965 pp 104, 111, 114, 118) records the presence of Psalm 151 in some Gallican Psalters (see LITURGY) with Old English glosses (above, nos 6, 9, 11, and 12), although in these cases the psalm is apparently not glossed. Mearns (1914 pp 94–95) notes simply that this psalm "is in many of the earlier Psalters," and in addition to those already noted, he includes references to two more Gallican Psalters listed in HG (above, nos 7, and 10). James' catalog (1911–12 vol 2) notes the psalm in the three Corpus MSS (the beginning is imperfect in 272); Schenkl (1969, V. Salisbury, p 44) in the second Salisbury MS (above 13); and Wilmart's catalog (1937–45 vol 1) in the Vatican MS.

Citharismus Regis David contra Daemonium Saulis: *RBMA* 105.
See PS PHILO, BIBLICAL ANTIQUITIES.

Interdictio Salomonis [ANON.Inter.Sal.]: *RBMA* 108,15.

MSS — Refs   none.

The GELASIAN DECREE (332) mentions as apocryphal an "Interdictio Salomonis," also called in some manuscripts the "Contradictio Salomonis." Because this work has not yet been identified, its relationship to other Solomon literature, particularly the Testament of Solomon — in which the Old Testament ruler interrogates various demons (*RBMA* 108,3, and *OTP* 1.935–87) — remains uncertain. The work has often been mentioned in connection with poetic *Solomon and Saturn* (*MSol*, A.13); for example, James (1920 p 52) states the Interdictio was the source for the Old English. Menner (GR 4337), following Vincenti (GR 4345), notes that "this sixth-century *Contradictio* could hardly . . . be the immediate and sole source of a poem which contrasted Germanic and Christian wisdom," but he concludes that it "is at least welcome testimony from an obscure period to the continued popularity of the apocryphal literature concerning Solomon, and if really a debate, might well be the ancestor of the medieval dialogues" (p 24).

Sibylline Oracles [ANON.Sibyl.]: *RBMA* 122; *OTP* 1.317–472; *NTA* 2.703–45.

MSS—A-S Vers none.
Quots/Cits ALDH.Metr. 79.24, 93.21, and 93.33: see below.
Refs Æ*Let* 4 (B1.8.4) 712–25: see below.

Surviving primarily in Greek, the Sibylline Oracles span the pagan, Jewish, and Christian traditions, being written between the second century BC and the seventh century AD. According to Collins (*OTP* 1.318), "the most characteristic feature" of these works "is the prediction of woes and disasters to come upon mankind." The Latin tradition, as Bischoff (1966 pp 150–71) has shown, is dominated by the discussions of LACTANTIUS and particularly AUGUSTINE, who in DE CIVITATE DEI XVIII.23 includes a Latin translation of a Greek acrostic poem that begins ΙΗΣΟΥΣ ΧΡΕΙΣΤΟΣ ΘΕΟΥ ΥΙΟΣ ΣΩΤΗΡ, and a collection of oracles drawn from Lactantius. However, Bischoff (1966 pp 164–68) has also edited a Latin text (*RBMA* 124,2.2), identified in one MS as the "prophetia Sibillae magnae," that he has discovered in three MSS, two of which date to the ninth century. Another Latin text (*RBMA* 124) is printed among the "dubia" of BEDE (*PL* 90.1181–86); Bischoff (1966 p 151) dates this work to the eleventh century.

ALDHELM quotes three lines from a Latin translation of the Greek acrostic poem mentioned above, identifying in each case the "Sibillinus versus" as his source. His citations, however, do not correspond with Augustine's translation. Bulst (1938) suggests that Aldhelm may have been the translator of this version; Lapidge (in Lapidge and Rosier 1985 p 265 note 8) considers this unlikely due to Aldhelm's limited knowledge of Greek, but indicates that the translation may have been produced in the school of THEODORE and HADRIAN (p 16).

In his discussion of the Old Testament canon, ÆLFRIC identifies the Sibyls as ten virgins who prophesied Christ to the heathens; he apparently follows traditions about the Sibyls represented in ISIDORE's ETYMOLOGIES VIII.8.

Grau (GR 626, pp 51 and 67) cites Augustine's translation of the acrostic poem, and a passage in the Greek text as possible sources for *ChristC* (A3.1; 964–70a and 1195); neither however is conclusive (see Biggs 1986 pp 13 and 24).

The Greek text is edited by Geffcken (Bibliography Part I). Translations appear in the *OTP* 1.335–472; and the *NTA* 2.709–45 (on pp 741–45 is a translation of Bischoff's "prophetia Sibillae magnae"). For further bibliography, see Charlesworth (1981 pp 184–88).

Ps Methodius, Revelationes [ANON.Rev./PS.METH.]: *CPG* 1830; *RBMA* 124,4–8.

MSS   1. Salisbury, Cathedral Library 165: HG 749.
   2. ? London, BL Royal 5.F.xviii.
   3. ? Oxford, St John's College 128.
   4. ? Oxford, Bodleian Library Bodley 163 (*SC* 2016): HG 555.
Lists—A-S Vers   none.
Quots/Cits   see below.
Refs   see below.

The original version of the Revelationes was a Syriac apocalypse with historical and prophetic sections. It recounts the Creation, Fall, and Flood followed by the succession of empires, the Arab invasions, the eventual triumph of the Last Roman Emperor, the coming of the Antichrist, and the end of the world. It was composed between 644–678, then translated into Greek in the seventh century, and into Latin in the eighth century (and thence into various vernaculars), directly influencing ADSO'S LIBELLUS (Verhelst 1973 pp 94–97), the *Visions of Daniel*, the medieval Alexander legend (Alexander 1985 p 14 etc., p 18 etc.), and the *Liber Aethici dilatus ex cosmographia* (*KVS* p 576).

Although the Revelationes is attested in 22 pre-twelfth-century Latin MSS and in four Latin recensions (Laureys and Verhelst 1988; Prinz 1985 pp 4–5), only Salisbury 165 (not listed in Laureys and Verhelst) is accepted as originating from England before 1100. The three other MSS are queried above because some uncertainty remains about their date and provenance. Royal 5.F.xviii is considered a Salisbury MS of the eleventh or twelfth century (Watson 1987 pp 60–61) or a Continental MS of the second half of the eleventh century (Prinz 1985 p 4 note 16). Bodley 163 is a composite MS, and the folios including the Revelationes are not listed in HG 555. Both parts of the MS are considered from the first quarter of the twelfth century by Madan (Madan, Craster, and Hunt 1895–1953 vol 2.1 p 164); Ker (1964 p 151) lists the MS as eleventh century without distinguishing the parts. D'Evelyn's (1918) text is from St John's College (she selects variants from Bodley 163), which has been dated either to the beginning of the eleventh century (Coxe 1852 vol 2 pp 38–39) or to the second half of the twelfth century (Prinz 1985 p 4 note 17).

BL Cotton Claudius B.iv (Hexateuch) contains Latin and late Old English notes to Genesis (B8.1.4.7) which cite "Methodius." NRK (142) dates the Old English notes to the mid-twelfth century. Crawford (GR 5236, pp

419-22 and GR 5244) transcribes only the Old English notes; see numbers 1, 6, 7, 12, 13, and possibly 18. The Latin notes citing "Methodius" may be found in *EEMF* 18, fols 3v, 8, 12v, and 28. The Kentish characteristics of the Old English notes are cited as partial evidence of Canterbury provenance (*EEMF* 18.16; NRK 142).

Hill (1987) notes that in preserving the tradition of a fourth son of Noah, the Revelationes may be relevant to the West-Saxon royal genealogies.

On the date of the text and translations into Greek and Latin, see Alexander (1985 pp 13-25); for texts of the four Greek recensions, see Lolos (1976); for the first Latin recension, see Sackur (1898 pp 59-96); and for the second Latin recension (found in the 4 MSS listed in A above), see Prinz (Bibliography Part I) — the same recension is in D'Evelyn (1918 pp 191-203).

Michael W. Twomey

II. APOCRYPHAL GOSPELS

The general term "Infancy Gospels" is used by modern scholars (e.g. Cullmann, in *NTA* 1.363-69) to refer to a number of overlapping texts that describe the birth of Mary, her marriage to Joseph, and the birth and childhood of Christ. Because the manuscript evidence is often incomplete, the relationships among these works remains at points unclear, but it seems preferable on the whole to consider them as discrete works; see below the PROTEVANGELIUM OF JAMES, the DE NATIVITATE MARIAE, and the GOSPEL OF PS MATTHEW. ÆLFRIC'S condemnation of this material is discussed under the GOSPEL OF PS MATTHEW, although the details he mentions could have been drawn from the other works.

Gospel of Bartholomew: see the BOOK OF THE RESURRECTION OF CHRIST by Bartholomew; and the QUESTIONS OF BARTHOLOMEW.

Book of the Resurrection of Christ by Bartholomew [ANON.Res. Christ.Bart.]: see *RBMA* 135.

On the relationship between this work and the "Gospel of Bartholomew" see the QUESTIONS OF BARTHOLOMEW.

Heimann (1966 p 41) states that the six dragons springing from the head of Satan/Mors in the Vita-Mors drawing of the Sphaera Apulei in the LEOFRIC MISSAL (Oxford, Bodleian Library Bodley 579, fol 50, *IASIM* 95.4, cf. *IASIM* 203.17; see LITURGY) "are clearly the six sons of Death mentioned

in the apocryphal Coptic Book of the Resurrection of Christ," and proposes the same source for another drawing in the Stuttgart Psalter (p 44).
Deshman (1977 p 167) accepts Heimann's identification, but Jordan (1986
p 293; see also p 314 note 32) dismisses the suggestion with the comment
that "there is no evidence that the work was ever known in the West during
the Middle Ages," referring instead to a cryptic allusion in ALDHELM'S AE-
NIGMATA to Lucifer's "six companions" (comites). It is not necessary to assume direct knowledge of the Book of the Resurrection of Christ, however,
to believe that the motif is ultimately derived from Coptic apocryphal tradition. Coptic apocryphal motifs are known to have found their way into
the West (see Dudley 1911), and the six (or seven) sons of Death or of Satan occur in other sources as well. The motif of the daughters of the Devil
(anywhere from six to ten) is apparently a later medieval development; see
P. Meyer (1900 pp 54-72).

Charles D. Wright

Questions of Bartholomew [ANON.Quaest.Bart.]: RBMA 135; NTA 1.484-508.

MSS — Quots/Cits   none.
Refs   BEDA.Comm.Luc., Prooemium: see below.

JEROME, in the Preface (*Plures fuisse*) to his COMMENTARII IN MATHAEUM,
mentions Bartholomew in a list of authors supposed to have written gospels,
and the GELASIAN DECREE also mentions an *Evangelia nomine Bartholomaei*. Jerome's reference, however, may be from ORIGEN'S first homily on Luke, while
the Gelasian Decree may in turn depend on Jerome. Two surviving works
have been identified with the Gospel of Bartholomew, a Coptic BOOK OF
THE RESURRECTION OF CHRIST by Bartholomew and the Questions of Bartholomew extant in Greek, Slavonic, and Latin. The most recent investigation, by Kaestli (1988) urges that the latter work should be designated
Questions of Bartholomew (as in the Slavonic and in one of the Latin
manuscripts) rather than "Gospel of Bartholomew" (see pp 8-9), and suggests that the Gospel mentioned by Jerome and the Gelasian Decree may
be a different work, perhaps attested in other scattered allusions and citations (p 9, note 14; see also Cherchi 1984). Kaestli concludes that the Coptic work has "only a few motifs in common" with the Questions of
Bartholomew, "and they cannot be two recensions of the same original writing" (English Summary, p 6). Regarding the relationships of the various
versions of the Questions of Bartholomew, Kaestli stresses that the conclusions of Wilmart and Tisserant must be reassessed in light of the evidence

of the complete Latin text published by Moricca. James (1924 pp 166–81) and the *NTA* include eclectic English translations of the Questions of Bartholomew, conflating the various versions; for criticisms see Kaestli (1988 pp 18–21).

Two MSS preserve Latin translations of the Questions of Bartholomew: Vatican, Reg. lat. 1050 (L), which contains three fragments of the text, edited by Wilmart and Tisserant (Bibliography Part I), and Rome, Biblioteca Casanatense 1880 (C), the only complete version, edited by Moricca (Bibliography Part I).

BEDE's reference to a gospel written by Bartholomew (*CCSL* 120.19) depends on Jerome.

Gollancz (GR 136, p civ) suggests that the devils' reference to a "son" of Satan in *Christ and Satan* (*Sat*, A1.4) may depend on the Questions of Bartholomew, in which Satan has a son named Salpsan. However, other more plausible explanations have been offered for the allusion (see Clubb, GR 3344, pp 62–63; Hill 1977c pp 323–35; and Finnegan 1977 p 27).

Grant (1982 pp 43 and 46) cites the "Gospel of Bartholomew" among other apocryphal texts for the archangel Michael's participation in creation and struggle with Satan in *LS* 24 (MichaelTristr, B3.3.24).

Henderson (1986 p 81, note 33) refers to the "Gospel of Bartholomew" (i.e. the Questions of Bartholomew, translated by James 1924 pp 174–75) as a possible source for Bartholomew's power over the devils in *Guthlac A* (*GuthA*, A3.2); but see Hill (1979 p 185, note 1) for another possible source in PS ISIDORE, DE ORTU ET OBITU PATRUM (the section on Bartholomew is dependent on PS ABDIAS according to Dumville 1973 p 314).

C. Wright (1987a pp 142–43) cites a passage from the Questions of Bartholomew (from Moricca's edition, p 512) as a possible source for a description of the creation of Adam (*De plasmatione Adam*, CPL 1155f viii; edited in *PLS* 4.937–41, and C. Wright 1987a pp 140–41; see also ADAM OCTIPARTITE) found in four early manuscripts, including an Anglo-Saxon missionary manuscript known as the *Vocabularius Sancti Galli* (St. Gall, Stiftsbibliothek 913, second half of the eighth century, "by a scribe trained in the Anglo-Saxon tradition," *CLA* 7.976; edited by Baesecke 1933). C. Wright (1987a pp 142–43) draws attention to a similar description of the creation of Adam in the probably Irish Fragmentum Pragense (*CPL* 2255; *KVS* An creat, edited in *PLS* 2.1484–85), where it is accompanied by allusions to the creation of the angels from fire and water and to the prior creation of Satanahel, both motifs also found in the Questions of Bartholomew.

Charles D. Wright

Protevangelium of James [ANON.Proteuang.Iac.]: *RBMA* 141; *BHG* 1046; *NTA* 1.370–88.

MSS Cambridge, Pembroke College 25: HG 131.
Lists — Quots/Cits none.
Refs ? for Ælfric, see under GOSPEL OF PS MATTHEW.

This Greek apocryphon, compiled around 150–200 AD, contains the earliest written account of the Nativity and dedication of Mary, providing the names for her parents. It also recounts the miracles attending the births of John the Baptist and Christ, the flight of John and Elizabeth from Herod, and the murder of Zacharias. Extant Greek manuscripts number over 130, and translations exist in at least eight other Eastern languages. It must have been translated into Latin by the early sixth century when it was condemned in the GELASIAN DECREE (271). The first eight chapters of a Latin version, as noted by Clayton (1986a p 289) and Cross (1987a p 37 item 51), were known in England from their inclusion in a sermon on the Nativity of Mary in Pembroke 25 (see HOMILIARY OF ST PÈRE DE CHARTRES under HOMILIARIES).

Ties with Old English literature are not well established. Hill (GR 3481) proposed the Protevangelium as the source for a passage in the *Descent into Hell* (*Hell*, A3.26; 99–106) on the stasis of the Jordan River, but see Hall (forthcoming in *Traditio*) for an alternative view. Remly (1974) advanced the apocryphon as the source for a passage in *HomS* 40.3 (*VercHom* 10, B3.2.40.6) which contains an obscure allusion to Solomon by "sanctus Iacobus." Her thesis — that the passage confuses a statement in the canonical Iac with the mention in the Protevangelium not of Solomon but of Salome — is not convincing, and the allusion, certainly apocryphal, needs to be reexamined. At one time, influence of the Protevangelium or another "Infancy Gospel" was also suspected for the Joseph-Mary dialogue (lyric 7) in *ChristA* (A3.1); Cook (GR 3265) thus refers to supposed parallels from the Protevangelium, the GOSPEL OF PS MATTHEW, DE NATIVITATE MARIAE, and the *History of Joseph the Carpenter* (*RBMA* 156; at present there is no evidence of this work in Anglo-Saxon England) in the notes to his edition; for further bibliography, see Reinsch (1879 p 124). Any direct debt, however, has since been discounted (see Burlin, GR 3329; and Hill 1977b for a more likely source).

A new edition of the Greek text by A. Frey is forthcoming in the *CCSA*. At the moment, the best edition of the Greek is by de Strycker (1961); other editions include Tischendorf (1876 pp 1–50), Amann (Bibliography Part I), and de Santos Otero (1963 pp 136–76), which includes a Spanish translation, notes on the text, and a bibliography. An English translation appears in *NTA* 1.374–88, prefaced by a brief textual history pp 370–71. On surviving early Latin versions, see Canal-Sánchez (1968) and Vattioni (1977). The Latin Nativity sermon in Pembroke 25 is unedited, but a variant is edited by Vattioni (1977) from a thirteenth-century MS. Other evidence for early circulation of a Latin version in the British Isles is offered by McNamara (1975), who draws attention to several distinctively Insular features of the Protevangelium in Montpellier, École de Médicine 55 (eighth or ninth century), concluding that Ireland in particular was "connected with the transmission, or even the formation of this Latin rendering of the Protevangelium" (p 39; see also pp 42–47 and 49).

Thomas N. Hall

Letters of Abgar and Jesus [ANON.Ep.Sal.]: *RBMA* 147; *NTA* 1.437–44; *DACL* 1.87–97.

MSS London, BL Royal 2.A.xx: HG 450.
Lists none.
A-S Vers *ÆLS* (Abdon & Sennes, B1.3.24) 81–188.
Quots/Cits — Refs none.

Eusebius' *Ecclesiastical History* I.13 — known through RUFINUS' translation — is the first witness to this apocryphal correspondence between Abgar, ruler of Edessa, and Christ. Other Church Fathers noted that Christ left behind no collection of writings (e.g. AUGUSTINE, DE CONSENSU 11.16–18), which may have led to the letters being condemned in the GELASIAN DECREE (328–29).

The Royal MS, which contains only Christ's letter but with additions not found in the *Ecclesiastical History*, is closely related to Irish prayer books; see *SEHI* 576). Loomis (GR 5358) notes that ÆLFRIC's source is Eusebius' *Ecclesiastical History.*

The Royal MS has been printed in the appendix to Kuypers (1902 pp 205–06). An English translation of the relevant part of Eusebius' work is in the *NTA* 1.441–44.

Sunday Letter [ANON.Epist.Sal.Dom.]: *RBMA* 148,3; *DACL* 3.1534–46 and 4.858–994.

MSS — Lists none.
A-S Vers 1. *HomU* 35.1 (Nap 43, B3.4.35.1).
    2. *HomU* 35.2 (Nap 44, B3.4.35.2).
    3. *HomU* 36 (Nap 45, B3.4.36).
    4. *HomU* 46 (Nap 57, B3.4.46).
    5. *HomU* 53 (NapSunEpis, B3.4.53).

6. *HomU* 54 (Priebsch, B3.4.54).
7. *HomM* 6 (KerOthoB 10, B3.5.6).
Quots/Cits   BONIF.Epist. 59, 115.13–28: see below.
Refs   ECGRED.Epist. 21–22.

The Sunday Letter (also known as the "Heavenly Letter" and the Carta Dominica), apparently composed in Greek in the sixth century (*RBMA* 148), became widely disseminated in the West; see Delehaye (1899). The letter purports to be from Christ, and to be written variously in his own blood, with a golden rod, or dictated to an angel, and to have fallen on one of the principal altars of Christendom—often Rome, Jerusalem, or Bethlehem. The work survives in a number of Latin MSS (that have been only generally divided into recensions), but has yet to be identified in MSS known in England during the Anglo-Saxon period.

The Old English versions, however, can be divided into three groups that are related to different recensions of the known Latin tradition. *HomU* 36 and *HomU* 54 are generally agreed to represent the first Latin recension, which survives in Vienna, Österreichische Nationalbibliothek lat. 1355 (edited by Priebsch, Bibliography Part I), and Paris, Bibliothèque Nationale lat. 12270 (edited by Delehaye, Bibliography Part I); see Priebsch (Bibliography Part I), Whitelock (1982 p 54) and Lees (1985a p 132). The Paris MS is recognized as particularly close to *HomU* 54; see Priebsch (1936 p 10), Whitelock (1982 p 62 note 95), and Lees (1985a pp 133–34). Apparently *HomM* 6, destroyed in the 1731 fire, belonged to this group; see Whitelock (1982 p 54 note 51). The second group includes *HomU* 46 and *HomU* 53; Whitelock (1982 p 55) states that these are "independent translations of a text with similarities with [Munich, Bayerische Staatsbibliothek] Clm 9550," (edited by Delehaye, Bibliography Part I). The third group includes *HomU* 35.1 and 35.2. Whitelock (1982 p 51) has discussed these homilies in detail, arguing that they "are variant versions of a lost homily," that in turn was based on "Pehtred's book" mentioned in Ecgred's letter to Wulfsige (see *Refs* above). This letter makes it clear that the book contained a version of the Sunday Letter. Whitelock (1982 pp 52–58) also compares these two Old English homilies with the Irish *Cáin Domnaig* (on the Irish tradition, see McNamara 1975 pp 60–63), and both the Old English and Old Irish texts with Munich, Bayerische Staatsbibliothek clm 9550 (pp 58–59).

Priebsch (1936 pp 4–5) notes that BONIFACE quotes from the beginning of a version of the Letter similar to that printed from the transcription of a now lost MS in the Cathedral Library of Tarragona by Petrus de Marca, archbishop of Paris (d. 1164); the transcription is edited by Priebsch (Bibliography Part I).

Related to the Sunday Letter is a tradition of Sunday Lists, also known as the "Benedictions of Sunday" or the *Dignatio diei dominici* (*DACL* 4.985–86; see also HIBERNO-LATIN BIBLICAL COMMENTARIES, NUMBER *4). Tveitane (GR 6242, p 127) suggests that these lists "developed from a shorter form, agreeing with biblical tradition, towards a much longer, apocryphal version . . ."; see also Lees (1985 pp 136–43). These longer versions appear in three recensions edited by McNally (Bibliography Part I), and include Vatican, Pal. lat. 220 — a ninth-century MS in an Anglo-Saxon hand. Whitelock (1982 p 59) cites McNally's list III as a parallel to *HomU* 35.1. A list also appears in item 33 of Cambridge, Pembroke College MS 25 (see the HOMILIARY OF ST PÈRE DE CHARTRES; Lees 1986 p 142, and Cross 1987a p 32).

Although there are three fifteenth-century Latin MSS in the BL that combine the two works (see Lees 1985a pp 135–36), none have been identified from our period. Whitelock (1982 p 60) argues that they were combined in the Latin text used by Pehtred and by the author of *Cáin Domnaig*. The Old English homilies that contain both a Sunday Letter and a Sunday List are *HomU* 35.1; *HomU* 35.2; *HomU* 36; *HomU* 46; and *HomU* 53. Sunday Lists also occur in *HomS* 27 (B3.2.27; edited by Lees 1986, lines 31–70) and in an early Middle English homily, "In die dominica," preserved in London, Lambeth Palace 487 (edited by Morris, GR 6214, number 14; see Lees 1985a pp 143–46).

In addition to the Latin texts already mentioned, see also editions by Priebsch (1901 pp 400–06; BL Royal 8.F.vi), Röhricht (1890 pp 440–42; Hamburg, Bibliothek der Hansestadt, S. Petri Kirche 30b), and Rivière (1906 pp 602–05; Toulouse, Bibliothèque Publique 208). For the Old English homilies, see also Jost (GR 6528, pp 221–36). A recent overview of the subject can be found in Deletant (1977).

Clare A. Lees

Historia de ligno crucis: *RBMA* 151.

[Thomas N. Hall]

De Nativitate Mariae [ANON.Nat.Mariae]: *RBMA* 160.

MSS 1. Durham, Cathedral Library A.III.29: HG 222.
   2. Salisbury, Cathedral Library 179: HG 753.
   3. ? Worcester, Cathedral Library F.94.
Lists — Quots/Cits none.
Refs ? for Ælfric, see under the GOSPEL OF PS MATTHEW.

De Nativitate Mariae, a revision of the GOSPEL OF PS MATTHEW, dates from the Carolingian period or, more probably, later. It has frequently been attributed to PASCHASIUS RADBERTUS, but Beyers (1980), the most recent editor, has shown that this attribution is improbable. The first proof of the existence of the apocryphon is in a sermon by FULBERT OF CHARTRES (SERMO DE NATIVITATE 6–29). In private communication, J.E. Cross has noted the presence of this work in the Worcester MS, which, although not listed in HG, is a companion to Worcester F.91 (HG 762) and F.92 (HG 763).

De Nativitate Mariae was clearly known in Winchester in the eleventh century. The Durham manuscript, a version of the homiliary of PAUL THE DEACON, has Winchester connections, as it contains texts for the two feasts of St Swithun and for the feasts of St Birinus and St Æthelthryth. The author of the benediction for the feast of the Conception of the Virgin in the Canterbury Benedictional (London, BL Harley 2892: HG 429) seems to have known the text also. The benediction (Woolley 1917 pp 118–19) refers to the angel's announcement of Mary's name before her birth, a detail that seems to depend on the De Nativitate Mariae, the only apocryphon to include it. Prescott (1987) argues that the Canterbury benedictional was probably composed in Winchester.

Amann (Bibliography Part I) has been superseded by the superior but less accessible Beyers (1980), which includes as well a discussion of the history of the text. An earlier edition is by Tischendorf (1876 pp 113–21). For further discussion, see Clayton (forthcoming).

Mary Clayton

De Transitu Mariae [ANON.Trans.Mariae.]: *RBMA* 164.

MSS Cambridge, Pembroke College 25: HG 131.
Lists none.
A-S Vers 1. *LS* 20 (AssumptMor, B3.3.20): see below.
   2. *LS* 21 (AssumptTristr, B3.3.21).
Quots/Cits BEDA.Retract.Act. VIII.1.5–35: see below.
Refs 1. BEDA.Retract.Act. XIII.2.7–19.
   2. ? *ÆCHom* I, 30 (B1.1.32) 436.6–20: see below.
   3. ? *ÆCHom* II, 34 (B1.2.36) 115–33: see below.

Apocryphal texts discussing the death and assumption of the Virgin appear, at the latest, by the fifth century. Because of complex textual histories in several different languages, the versions have yet to be fully sorted out into separate traditions, but the Latin versions relevant to Anglo-Saxonists (Transitus B2 [*RBMA* 164,5.1] and Transitus C [*RBMA* 164,6.1]) apparently both descend from a lost Greek version of the fifth century via a Latin text of the fifth to seventh century (see Clayton 1986b pp 25-26). Transitus B2, which purports to be the work of Melito (thus the attribution to PS MELITO), dates to the fifth century according to Haibach-Reinisch (Bibliography Part I) and is older than the version (B1) published by Tischendorf (1866 pp 124-36). Transitus C, composed according to Wenger (1955 p 66) in the seventh or eighth century, has been edited by Wilmart (Bibliography Part I), but Pembroke 25 (see the HOMILIARY OF ST PÈRE DE CHARTRES) was not collated for this edition. The work is condemned in the GELASIAN DECREE (296).

LS 20 (AssumptMor) combines Transitus C (pp 137-55.19) and Transitus B2 (pp 155.19-57.35); see Willard (GR 6184 and 6185) and Clayton (1986b). The homilist, however, apparently used an abridged version of Transitus C, from which references to the corporal assumption of the Virgin had been eliminated (Clayton 1986b). (The version of C in Pembroke 25 is less close to the Old English than is the one in St Gall, Stiftsbibliothek 732 [Wilmart's G], although even this MS does not correspond to the Old English in all respects.) The homilist then draws on B2 for a detailed account of the assumption. The two accounts may of course have been combined in a source not yet discovered. LS 21 (AssumptTristr), also from B2 (see Clayton 1989), is a more faithful and competent translation of this version than is LS 20.

B2 was known to BEDE, who quotes directly from it and objects to its chronology in his RETRACTIO (the CCSL provides references to PG 5.1233 and 1234, and to Tischendorf 1866 pp 125ff). Haibach-Reinisch suggests that B2 was disseminated in southern Germany by Anglo-Saxon missionaries. This version is probably the basis for the account of the Virgin's assumption given by the Anglo-Saxon nun Huneberc (Vita Willibaldi, MGH Scriptores 15, part 1, 93.16), who wrote in Heidenheim Germany around 780, although it contains details which do not agree with any published apocryphon; her account may be based on hearsay.

In his Assumption homilies in both CATHOLIC HOMILIES I and II, ÆLFRIC objects to the circulation of unauthorized apocryphal accounts: he was presumably referring to B2 or to C, or to both.

The influence of the Transitus texts can also be discerned in Anglo-Saxon art. A carved stone slab in Wirksworth, Derbyshire (published J. Campbell 1982 illustration 136), which Cramp (1977) dates to the first half of the ninth century, includes a representation of the dead Mary on a bier carried by two apostles (Peter and Paul, according to the apocryphal tradition), preceded by another figure carrying a palm (John). Attached by his hands to the bier is the Jew who wished to burn Mary's body and in a circle or cloud above are six heads, presumably angels. The Benedictional of St Æthelwold (London, BL Add. 49598, fol 102v; *IASIM* 111.25), a Winchester manuscript of 971–84, includes a miniature of the feast of Mary's Assumption which depicts nine apostles, while above them Mary lies on a bed, attended by three women, and the hand of God, flanked by four angels, lowers a crown. The scene clearly illustrates the death of Mary as recounted in the apocryphal narratives. Deshman (1970 pp 86–87) and Therel (1984 pp 53–54) argue that the artist was illustrating a scene found only in Transitus A (Wenger 1955 pp 245–56), but there is no evidence that this particular apocryphon was known outside of Reichenau; moreover, the scene can be paralleled in Transitus C (see Clayton, forthcoming). A simplified version of this miniature is found in the Benedictional of Robert of Jumièges (Rouen, Bibliothèque Municipale 369, fol 54v: HG 923)

LS 21 has been edited more recently by Grant (1982). For the knowledge of the Transitu Mariae in Ireland, see McNamara (1975 pp 122–23), and Willard (1937 pp 341–64). For further discussion of Transitus C, see Willard 1939.

Mary Clayton

Gospel of Ps Matthew [ANON.Euang.Ps.Matt.]: *RBMA* 168; *BHL* 5334–42; *NTA* 1.406.

MSS London, BL Cotton Nero E.i: HG 344.
Lists none.
A-S Vers *LS* 18 (B3.3.18).
Quots/Cits 1. *HomU* 10 (*VercHom* 6, B3.4.10): see below.
   2. ? *ANON.OEMart* (B19.gx): see below.
Refs 1. ? *ÆCHom* II, 36.2 (B1.2.39): see below.
  2. ? *ÆHomM* 8 (Ass 3, B1.5.8) 5–7a: see below.

The Gospel of Ps Matthew is a composite Latin apocryphon whose date is difficult to determine; *NTA* 1.406 advises "probably about the eighth or ninth century." Scholars once speculated that PASCHASIUS RADBERTUS compiled the tract in the first half of the ninth century (see Canal-Sánchez 1968 p 473; accepted by *RBMA* vol 8), but the most recent assessment has pushed the date back to 550–700, rendering the text once more anonymous (Gijsel 1981 p 12). J.E. Cross in correspondence notes that chapters 1–6 "with slight variations and omissions" occur in the British Library MS Cotton Nero E.i, Pt. II, fols 116v–18. He continues "thus a section of Ps Matthew is used as an item called 'sermo' in a legendary"; (see further the COTTON-CORPUS LEGENDARY (see LEGENDARIES); and Cross 1985b pp 125–26 who shows that this tract also appears in ninth-century Continental MSS). It is as yet unpublished, and its relationship to other versions of the apocryphon has not been determined.

The text, as printed in Tischendorf (Bibliography Part I), falls into three parts: chapters 1–17 comprise a selective translation of the PROTEVANGELIUM OF JAMES, detailing the early life of Mary but omitting, for instance, any mention of John the Baptist; chapters 18–24 recount the Flight into Egypt; and chapters 25–42, probably based on the Gospel of Thomas (*RBMA* 175,2–23; there is no independent evidence for the knowledge of this work in Anglo-Saxon England), narrate the eccentric childhood miracles of Christ.

One partial translation exists in Old English in an anonymous sermon on the Nativity of Mary (*LS* 18, B3.3.18) found in three MSS: Oxford, Bodleian Library Bodley 343 (B3.3.18.2); Oxford, Bodleian Library Hatton 114 (B3.3.18.3); and imperfectly in Cambridge, Corpus Christi College 367 (B3.3.18.1). Assmann's edition (*BaP* 3.117–37) is based on the Bodley and Hatton MSS. The text translates chapters 1–12 of Ps Matthew beginning with the infertile marriage of Anna and Joachim and continuing through the doubting of Mary.

A series of translated excerpts is also incorporated into *HomU* 10 (*Verc-Hom* 6, B3.4.10). In the notes to his edition, Förster (GR 6200) shows lines 61–90 of the homily to correspond closely to chapters 13, 17–18 and 22–25 of Ps Matthew. The detail from chapter 25, however, depends ultimately on Mt 2.19–20, and so provides little evidence of when the sections from the Gospel of Thomas were incorporated into Ps Matthew. The details from Ps Matthew in the Old English *Martyrology* could have derived from the version in the British Library (MSS above); see Cross (1985a p 248) and for further discussion of this passage, see Herzfeld (GR 6364, p 235) and Kotzor (1981 pp 348–49).

Following the homily for the sixteenth Sunday after Pentecost in the CATHOLIC HOMILIES II, Ælfric includes a brief note on the birth of the Virgin in which he condemns apocryphal traditions (*ÆCHom* II, 36.2), while in fact recording some material from them. Similarly, in his homily for the Nativity of the Blessed Virgin Mary (*ÆHomM* 8), he again states that he will avoid apocrypha.

Elsewhere, two episodes from Ps Matthew (from chapters 23 and 24) are paralleled in a sermon on the Nativity of the Innocents in Pembroke 25 (see Cross 1987a p 23, item 11; Cross 1987b p 64; and the HOMILIARY OF ST PÈRE DE CHARTRES). A Latin gloss to Ps 148.10 in the Vatican, Pal. lat. 68 (HG 909) quotes from Ps Matthew 18.1 (McNamara 1986 p 308). Also relevant is Saxl's argument (GR 4267, pp 4–5) for at least indirect influence of an Infancy Gospel, probably Ps Matthew, on the Flight into Egypt (or out of Egypt) panel on the Ruthwell Cross—a belief affirmed by Swanton (GR 3487, pp 15–16).

Clayton (forthcoming) discusses the two illustrations of Ps Matthew in Cotton Caligula A.xiv, the earliest surviving in a Western MS (see *IASIM* 202.7 and 8).
A new edition of Ps Matthew is in preparation for *CCSA* by J. Gijsel and R. Beyers. In addition to Tischendorf (Bibliography Part I), Amann (1910 pp 272-338) prints chapters 1-17, with a French translation; see also the edition of de Santos Otero (1963 pp 179-242), with a translation. On the textual history, see Gijsel (1971-80), Gijsel (1976), and Gijsel (1981). For early Irish knowledge of this work see McNamara (1975 p 48); note too that the Gospel of Thomas circulated in Ireland. For further discussion of the Old English evidence, see Healey (1985 pp 102-03).

Thomas N. Hall

Gospel of Thomas: *RBMA* 175: see the GOSPEL OF PS MATTHEW.

Gospel of Nicodemus [ANON.Euang.Nic.]: *RBMA* 179,4-27; *NTA* 1.444-84; *DB* 3.544-47.

MSS   London, BL Royal 5.E.xiii: HG 459.
Lists   Exeter: ML 10.14.
A-S Vers   1. *NicA* (B8.5.2.1).
      2. *NicB* (B8.5.2.2).
      3. *NicC* (B8.5.3.1).
Quots/Cits — Refs   none.

The title Gospel of Nicodemus, used in the later Middle Ages (e.g. Vincent of Beauvais, *Speculum historiale* Book 7, chapters 40, 41, 48, 56 etc.), has been variously applied to the four recensions of the work distinguished in the scholarship. Since translations of Greek recension A exist in several oriental languages, scholars generally agree that it is the original version, but disagree on when it was composed; the prologue dates the work to 425 and EPIPHANIUS refers to what might have been something like it in the late fourth century (*NTA* 1.447). This version, known as the "Commentaries" of Nicodemus (a supposed disciple mentioned in Io 3.1-10, 7.50, and 19.39), retells the trial, passion, resurrection and ascension of Christ. The later recensions, one in Greek and two in Latin, add to the narrative the "Descensus Christi ad Inferos" (the Harrowing of Hell), the ostensible account by Karinus and Leucius, two "eyewitnesses" who rose at the Crucifixion (Mt 27.52-53). Of main interest to Anglo-Saxonists is Latin recension A, which contains material from both the "Commentaries" and the "Descensus" and appends a letter from Pilate to the emperor Claudius. A early witness of Latin recension A, which contains only the "Commentaries," is a fifth-century MS (*CLA* 10.1485); O'Ceallaigh's (1963) error in dating this MS to the ninth century (see Philippart 1970 p 396) undermines many of his dates. A later MS of Latin recension A, which contains all three parts, is Einsiedeln Stiftsbibliothek, MS 326 (*RBMA* 179.27; edited by Kim, Bibliography Part I); this recension apparently underlies the Old English versions.

Editors refer to the "Commentaries" as part 1 (prologue and chapters 1–16) and to the "Descensus" as part 2 (chapters 17–27 and the letter). The titles "Acta Pilati" and "Gesta Pilati" are sometimes applied to part 1 and sometimes to the whole work. The *descensus* theme dates to the early patristic period, and part 2 may be earlier than part 1 (*NTA* 1.449), but O'Ceallaigh (1963 p 23) believes that the Gospel of Nicodemus' *descensus* narrative was originally a Latin production (see also Collett 1981 p 30).

The Royal MS (*RBMA* 179,12), "written in several hands of continental type, but with corrections in an English hand of the tenth century" (Warner and Gilson 1921 vol 1 p 116), belongs to Latin recension A. It omits the prologue and the MS ends as a palimpsest shortly before the end of chapter 27. Ker (1964 p 208) lists it as a Worcester manuscript. J.J. Campbell (1982 p 112 note 9) doubts it was the source of the Old English translations.

Each of the three Old English versions "seems to descend independently from the translator's autograph" (J.J. Campbell 1982 p 114), though the possibilities of intermediate versions and of subsequent collations with the Latin complicate matters. *NicA* (Cambridge, Univ. Lib Ii.2.11), in which the Gospel of Nicodemus appears after the four Gospels, is the earliest manuscript. It represents a literal translation except where it omits and "splices" sections together (Allen 1968 p 11). Allen identifies two major omissions from part 1: chapters 5–11 (debate of the Jewish leaders with Nicodemus, scourging, and crucifixion), and chapters 16–17 (reports of Christ's post-resurrection activity). Part 2 omits chapters 27–29 (dialogue between Pilate and Annas and Caiphas). *NicB* (London, BL Cotton Vitellius A.15) lacks at the beginning approximately two printed pages of *NicA*. Although *NicB* contains some details from the Latin not found in *NicA* (and so *NicA* cannot be its sole direct source), it also omits the three major sections omitted by *NicA*, and is otherwise so close verbally to *NicA* that Hulme (GR 5741, p 583) and Förster (GR 5740, p 319) suggest a common original. Allen (1968 p 53) postulates the existence of a version based on *NicA* that *NicB* used while consulting the Latin. *NicC* (London, BL Cotton Vespasian D.xiv) "extends the splicing and abridging technique" (Allen 1968 p 49) of *NicA* and *B* in homiletic form. Again, minor additions lead Allen to postulate collation with the Latin, though he admits that it is not "an absolute necessity" (p 53).

In addition to the direct use of Latin recension A, scholars have often cited the Gospel of Nicodemus when discussing examples of the Harrowing; see GR 3344 p 98; GR 3479 pp 349-52; and Allen and Calder (1976 pp 175-76). The motif is popular in Old English poetry and prose from at least as early as the time of BEDE (see, for example, his IN ASCENSIONE DOMINI). The issue, however, is complicated both by the evolution of orthodox Church doctrine and by popular developments of the theme. Independent of the Gospel of Nicodemus proper, but of particular interest to Anglo-Saxonists, is the PSEUDO AUGUSTINE, HOMILY 160 (PL 39.2059-61) on the Harrowing proposed by Förster (GR 5353) as a source for HomS 26 (BlHom 7; B3.2.26). Building on this argument, Dumville (1972 p 375) postulates a lost Latin homily that drew on homily 160 as a source for the discussion of the Harrowing in the ninth-century section of the BOOK OF CERNE (see LITURGY) and HomS 26 (BlHom 7). This tradition may also underlie the entry on the Harrowing in the Old English Martyrology for March 26 (B19.bn); and it may also be related to an anonymous homily in Oxford, Bodleian Library Junius 121 (HomS 28, B3.2.28; printed by Luiselli Fadda 1972); but J.J. Campbell thinks not (1982 p 140). Similarly, the Harrowing composes the first part of an anonymous homily for Easter preserved in two Cambridge, Corpus Christi College MSS, 41 and 303 (NicD and E [B8.5.3.2; a better title would be HomS 29 B3.2.29.1 and 2]). The immediate source has not yet been found, although the phrase "an þissum bokum" implies that the homilist worked from written sources, and the connection of 41 to the Leofric donation (NRK 32) may indicate some link to NicA (ML 10.14). Moreover, a discussion of the Harrowing appears in Cambridge, Corpus Christi College 162 (HomS 27, B3.2.27; see Lees 1986). Descent loci in Old English poetry include the Descent into Hell (Hell, A3.26); ChristA, B and C (A3.1); Christ and Satan (Sat, A1.4), and GuthB (A3.2).

J.J. Campbell's study (1982) is the most comprehensive for the Old English material although his thesis — that little convincing evidence has been advanced for the knowledge of the Gospel before the translations (NicA, B, and C) — as a negative one leaves the question open. Healey (1985) is more willing to see the direct influence of the Gospel in a variety of texts; see also the bibliographical essay by Pelteret in Woods and Pelteret (1985 pp 164-65). Hulme (GR 5736) prints NicA and NicB; Allen 1968 prints NicA and variants from NicB and C, as well as a Latin text based on Tischendorf (1876). NicA also appears in Crawford (GR 5737) and NicC in Warner (GR 5292). In addition to the text edited by Kim (Bibliography Part I), see Tischendorf (1876) and more recently Collett (1981), who edits an example of recension A in Oxford, Bodleian Library Fairfax 17 (twelfth century) and of recension B in Cambridge, Corpus Christi College 288 (thirteenth century). The exact relationship of the four recensions awaits critical editions of the texts now in progress for the *CCSA*.

James H. Morey

Vindicta Salvatoris: *RBMA* 180.

[Thomas N. Hall]

III. APOCRYPHAL ACTS

From the New Testament, the Anglo-Saxons would have known of the Apostles as the twelve disciples chosen by Christ to spread his message (Mt 10.1–42, Mc 3.13–19, Lc 6.12–16, and Act 1.13–26; for a discussion of the term "apostle" prior to the writing of the Gospels, see *NTA* 2.25–31; and for remarks on discrepancies in the canonical lists, see the *NCE* under "apostle"). In addition to the canonical traditions, apocryphal material also circulated in the early Church, with five early Acts (John, Peter, Paul, Andrew, and Thomas) competing with the canonical Acts of the Apostles. According to Schneemelcher and de Santos (*NTA* 2.571), the "literary 'type' of the apocryphal Acts lingered on and proved effective beyond the third century and then gradually merged with that of sacred legend" (see ACTA SANCTORUM). The Anglo-Saxons would have derived much of their knowledge of the apocryphal traditions from these later texts, referred to as "Passions," which are dated generally between the third and sixth centuries. BEDE (RETRACTIO IN ACTUS APOSTOLORUM I.13) refers to "historiae" containing "passiones apostolorum," which he asserts are held by most to be apocryphal. The detail he cites is referred in the *CCSL* to PS ABDIAS, APOSTOLICAE HISTORIAE, but Bede need not be referring specifically to this work. Similarly the mention of "passiones apostolorum" in the Exeter List (ML 10.42) could refer to the Ps Abdias collection, to the anonymous BREVIARIUM APOSTOLORUM; or to collections such as Würzburg, Universitätsbibliothek, M.p.th.f.78 (*CLA* 9.1425; Anglo-Saxon majuscule and minuscule, written according to Lowe, "in an Anglo-Saxon center on the Continent, perhaps in the Würzburg region") and Brussels, Bibliothèque Royale II 1069 (*CLA* 10.1551; also "written in an Anglo-Saxon center on the Continent"). Apocryphal traditions about the Apostles circulated as well in other works; see in particular the two collections called DE ORTU ET OBITU PATRUM, by ISIDORE and PS ISIDORE.

Following the *RBMA*, this section begins with works that include most of the apostles, and then considers works dealing with one, or sometimes two, apostles, arranged by apostle in alphabetical order. As in the *RBMA*, PS CLEMENS and the apocryphal EPISTLE OF PAUL TO THE LAODICEANS are included in this section. For an overview of research on the Apocryphal Acts, see Bovon and van Esbroeck (1981), MacDonald (1986), and the *DS* under "apocryphes."

Breviarium apostolorum [ANON.Breu.apos.]: *RBMA* 191.1; *BHL* 652.

MSS   none.
Lists   ? see APOCRYPHAL ACTS (above).
A-S Vers — Refs   none.

The Breviarium lists thirteen apostles (including both Paul and Matthias, but excluding Judas Iscariot) and provides in most cases an etymology for the name, a brief biography, and the feastday of each. The first manuscript witness of the work is in the two supplementary quires of the Gelasian Sacramentary (Vatican, Reg. lat. 316) preserved in Paris (Bibliothèque Nationale lat. 7193; see Lowe 1925–26 pp 357–73), a MS that dates to the eighth century. As noted by de Gaiffer (1963), the work also appears in Vatican, Pal. lat. 235, but beyond the folios accepted by HG 910.

The possibility that the Breviarium is a source for Cynewulf's *Fates of the Apostles* (*Fates*, A2.2) has been discussed since Sarrazin (GR 3653; see also 3656, 1446, 1419, 6357A, and 1420), but the problem has remained unresolved because there is much overlap among the possible sources, and no single source has been identified for the entire poem; see, in particular, Cross (1979a passim). Lapidge (in Lapidge and Rosier 1985 p 42) asserts that section 4 of ALDHELM's CARMINA ECCLESIASTICA ("On the Altars of the Twelve Apostles") belongs to a tradition that includes this work.

In addition to Mohlberg (Bibliography Part I), the work is printed in Schermann (1907 pp 207–11), who notes readings from six MSS. It is translated in Allen and Calder (1976 pp 37–39).

Notitia de locis Apostolorum [ANON.Notit.Apost.]: *BHL* 648; not in *RBMA*.

MSS — Refs   none.

Printed in the introductory material to the MARTYROLOGIUM HIERONYMIANUM (see MARTYROLOGIES) in the *PL* (30.435–37), the Notitia lists the feasts of twelve apostles, in most cases a place with which they are associated, and in some cases, additional biographical details.

Brooks (GR 1420, p xxx) comments that the order of Apostles in the *Fates* (A2.2) is closest to that found in this work; see also Cross (1979a).

In addition to the edition in Schermann (Bibliography Part I), the text appears in the *AS* (Nov, vol 2 pars posterior, p 2), from which Allen and Calder (1976 p 37) translate.

Nomina locorum in quo apostoli requiescunt [ANON.Nom.Apost.]: *BHL* 651d; not in *RBMA*.

MSS   Durham, Cathedral Library A.IV.19: HG 223.
Lists — Refs   none.

As the title indicates, this text lists the resting places of the apostles, including John the Baptist and St Stephen. It occurs in the DURHAM RITUAL (see LITURGY; GR 6129, pp 195–97) with an interlinear gloss in Old English (*DurRitGlCom*, C13.1).

Ps Abdias, Historiae Apostolicae [ANON.Hist.Apos./PS.ABD.]: *RBMA* 192.

MSS   none.
Lists   ? see APOCRYPHAL ACTS (above).
A-S Vers   none.
Quots/Cits   see below.
Refs   ? see APOCRYPHAL ACTS (above).

Compiled in Gaul in the sixth century (Kaestli 1981 p 52), the Historiae contains the following sections: 1 Peter; 2 Paul; 3 Andrew; 4 James the Great; 5 John; 6 Simon, Jude, and James the Less; 7 Matthew; 8 Bartholomew; 9 Thomas; and 10 Philip. Some are drawn from Acts (or Passions) that still exist, and so, as Cross (1979b p 17) points out, it is often impossible to determine if this collection has been used. Nor is it certain if the entire collection was known in Anglo-Saxon England (see the headnote above for possible general references), although the possibility that ÆLFRIC consulted it for his CATHOLIC HOMILIES was suggested by Förster (GR 5300, pp 43–45; see also Zettel 1979 p 4).

If a passio that has been discussed as a possible source for an Anglo-Saxon text exists independently of the Historiae, it is discussed later in this section (with a cross-reference at this point). Some relevant versions, however, are unique to the Historiae.

Andrew (see *BHL* 430): Herzfeld (GR 6364, p xlii) identifies the account of Andrew's passion (502–15) as the source for the Old English *Martyrology* entry on Andrew (B19.hf). Cross (1979b pp 27–28), who notes that this entry in the Martyrology also draws on the PASSIO ANDREAE, adds specific details drawn from Ps Abdias that do not occur in the Passio. Cross (1979a pp 170–71) also considers Ps Abdias a possible source for details about

Andrew in the *Fates* (A2.2; 16–22), but none of these details are restricted to this source. See also ACTA ANDREAE ET MATTHIAE.

Bartholomew: see PASSIO BARTOLOMAEI and the QUESTIONS OF BARTHOLOMEW.

James the Great: Herzfeld (GR 6364 p xl) cites this account in relation to the Old English *Martyrology* entry (B19.ex), but Cross (1979b pp 32–34; following Cockayne, GR 296) notes that the Bible is the primary source. Cross (1979a p 172) mentions this work as a possible source for details about James in Cynewulf's *Fates of the Apostles* (*Fates*, A2.2; 33b–37a), but here, too, most are biblical. See also the PASSIO JACOBI MAIORIS.

James the Less (*BHL* 4089): Cross (1979b pp 29–31) notes that this account relies on EUSEBIUS-RUFINUS HISTORIA ECCLESIASTICA, and so is a possible source for the Old English *Martyrology* entry (B19.ds); similarly Cross (1979a p 174) considers this account a possible source for material on James in Cynewulf's *Fates* (A2.2; 70–74). See also the PASSIO JACOBI MAIORIS.

John (*BHL* 4316): item 10 of Cambridge, Pembroke College MS 25 (see the HOMILIARY OF ST PÈRE DE CHARTRES, and Cross 1987a p 22) is largely drawn from the account of John's death in the Historiae (581.3–589.14). Herzfeld (GR 6364 p xxxvi) cites this work as the source for the entry in the Old English *Martyrology* (B19.e), but Cross (1979b pp 34–37) qualifies this suggestion. See also PS MELLITUS, PASSIO JOHANNIS.

Matthew: see the PASSIO MATTHAEI.

Paul: see the PASSIO PAULI.

Peter: see the PASSIO PETRI.

Philip: see the PASSIO PHILIPPI.

Simon and Jude: see the PASSIO SIMONIS ET JUDAE.

Thomas (*BHL* 8140): apparently not used in Anglo-Saxon England, but see the PASSIO THOMAE.

According to Kaestli (1981 p 52), Fabricius (Bibliography Part I) reprints the edition of Lazius (1551); however, the edition of Nausea (1531) is closer to the manuscripts.

Acta Andreae: *RBMA* 198.

Ogilvy (*BKE* p 68) incorrectly states that Förster (GR 6173, pp 202–06) identified this work as the source of Blickling 19 (*LS* 1.1): Förster in fact showed that ACTA ANDREAE ET MATTHIAE is the source of this homily. The case of Worcester Cathedral Library F.91 is less easily resolved: Floyer (1906 p 46), the catalog from which Ogilvy apparently worked, comments on this MS: "Bound up at the end of the volume are three folios of a treatise (Acts of St. Andrew?) eleventh century, or earlier." This MS is in HG 762.

Acta Andreae et Matthiae [ANON.Act.Andr.Matt.]: *RBMA* 201 (*And* is incorrectly listed in vol 8 [198,9.1]); *NTA* 2.576.

MSS—Lists none.
A-S Vers 1. *And* (A2.1).
    2. *LS* 1.1 (AndrewBright, B3.3.1.1).
    3. *LS* 1.2 (AndrewMor, B3.3.1.2).
Quots/Cits—Refs none.

This originally Greek legend (written according to the *RBMA* in Egypt around the turn of the fifth century, but dated perhaps to the sixth century in the *NTA*) relates the adventures of the two apostles among a race of cannibals. On the relationship of this work to the *Acta Andreae* (with implications for dating), see Flamion (1911) and the recent exchange between MacDonald (1986) and Prieur (1986).

In a study of the sources of the Old English *Andreas*, Schaar (GR 3404) distinguishes two main traditions of the legend, the "detailed and fantastic" and the "shorter and less miraculous" (p 15). He includes the Greek versions, the Latin prose version in the Casanatense Library, and the Old English *Andreas* (*And*) in the former group, and the Latin poetic version and the Old English prose versions (*LS* 1.1 and 1.2) in the latter. He also notes that the Greek versions sometimes contain details relevant to *Andreas* not found in the Latin versions (p 23). Brooks (GR 1420) asserts that the Latin poetic version "is in fact so free a rendering that it cannot be considered the source of any of the existing Old English versions" (p xvii), although he acknowledges that in using the proper names Achaia, Mirmidonia, and Plato it contains details not found in either the Greek versions or in the Casanatense. Baumler (1985) adds further general similarities between the Latin poetic version and *Andreas*.

The introduction in *Bright's Old English Grammar and Reader* (GR 314) to the Old English prose version found in Cambridge, Corpus Christi College 198 (*LS* 1.1) notes that this version is "a very lightly abridged form of the text" in the Blickling collection (*LS* 1.2), but it "cannot be derived" directly from the earlier manuscript (p 205). The editors also assert that the "Bonnet Fragment" is closer to their text than is the Latin version in the Casanatense, and they print this version, with one omission, in the apparatus of the text. Baumler (1985 p 71) suggests that there may have been "more than one model" for the Cambridge and Blickling versions.

The surviving Greek versions have been edited by Tischendorf (1851 pp 132-66) and by Bonnet (1898); Tischendorf's text has been translated by Walker (1873). Blatt has edited two Latin versions: one in prose is found in the twelfth-century MS, Rome, Biblioteca Casanatense 1104 (Bibliography Part I; translated by Allen and Calder 1976 pp 15-34); and the other in verse is found in the eleventh-century MS, Vatican, Vat. lat. 1274. The "Bonnet Fragment" (Rome, Biblioteca Vallicelliana, plut. I, tom. iii), an eleventh-century palimpsest, is also in prose; Blatt prints it opposite the Casanatense text (pp 13-15). A shorter Latin prose account occurs in the University of Bologna MS 1576; it has been edited by Baumler (1985 pp 90-112), who dates the MS to the eleventh century. Finally, much-condensed Latin versions occur in the PS ABDIAS (Fabricius 1719 vol 2 pp 457-59) and in GREGORY OF TOURS' *Liber de miraculis beati Andreae Apostoli* (*MGH*.SRM 1.827-28). For further discussions of *Andreas'* relationship to its sources, see Hill (GR 1468); Szittya (1973); M.M. Walsh (1977 and 1981); Earl (1980); and Biggs (1988).

Passio Andreae [ANON.Pas.Andr.]: *RBMA* 199,6; *BHL* 428.

MSS—Lists   none.
A-S Vers   ÆCHom I, 38 (B1.1.40) Thorpe 586.29-598.32.
Quots/Cits—Refs   none.

The Passio recounts the conflict between Andrew and Aegeas, the ruler in Achaia who attempts to force the Christians to worship idols; Andrew is eventually put to death on a cross. Zettel (1979 p 32) lists the Passio as item 139 in his reconstructed COTTON-CORPUS LEGENDARY. Although it does not occur in either the Cotton or the Corpus manuscript, it is included in Oxford, Bodleian Library Bodley 354 (twelfth century), and in the table of Salisbury, Cathedral Library 222 (olim Oxford, Bodleian Library Fell 1; HG 623). Förster (GR 5300, pp 21-22) notes that ÆLFRIC uses it in his homily for the Nativity of Andrew (*ÆCHom* I, 38); see also Zettel (1979 pp 166-71, and 244-46). Cross (1979b pp 27-28) cites it as a source for details about Andrew in the Old English *Martyrology* (B19.hg) not found in PS ABDIAS. Cross (1979a pp 170-71) also identifies it as a possible source for Cynewulf's comments about Andrew in *Fates* (A2.2; 16-22).

Item 66 from the BOOK OF CERNE (161.4-15; see LITURGY) is taken with minor changes from the Passio (24.8-26.1); see Kuypers (1902 p 233).

In addition to the text printed in Bonnet (Bibliography Part I), see also Fábrega Grau (1955 vol 2 pp 59-64).

Passio Bartholomaei [ANON.Pas.Bart.]: *RBMA* 207,1; *BHL* 1002; *NTA* 2.577.

MSS   1. London, BL Cotton Nero E.i: HG 344.
2. Salisbury, Cathedral Library 222 (olim Oxford, Bodleian Library Fell 1): HG 623.
Lists   none.
A-S Vers   ÆCHom I, 31 (B1.1.33).
Quots/Cits — Refs   none.

The Passio tells how, by overthrowing idols in India, Bartholomew is able to convert one king, Polymius, before his brother, Astriges, has the apostle martyred. Zettel (1979 p 24) identified this work as item 89 in his reconstructed COTTON-CORPUS LEGENDARY: it occurs in both the London and Salisbury MSS. Förster (GR 5300, p 21) notes ÆLFRIC's use of this work for the first part of his homily on Bartholomew (*ÆCHom* I, 31) and Zettel (1979 pp 181-82) indicates several passages where readings from the Cotton MS are closer to Ælfric's version than the text in Mombritius. Herzfeld (GR 6364, p xl) points out that the entry on Bartholomew in the Old English *Martyrology* (B19.gb) draws on this account; see also Cross (1979b pp 19-20). Cross (1979a pp 172-74) considers this work as a possible source for details concerning Bartholomew in Cynewulf's *Fates* (A2.2; 42-49).

In addition to the text in Bonnet (Bibliography Part I), see also Mombritius (1910 vol 1 pp 140-44), and PS ABDIAS (Fabricius 1719 vol 2 pp 669-87).

Ps Clemens, Recognitiones [ANON.Recog./PS CLEMENS]: *RBMA* 208,3; *BHL* 6644-45; *CPG* 1015.5; *ODCC* 304; *NTA* 2.532-70.

MSS   1. Oxford, New College s.n.: HG 679.
2. Salisbury, Cath Lib 11: HG 701
3. ? Oxford, Trinity College 60.
4. ? London, BL Royal 6 B xiv.
Lists — A-S Vers   none.
Quots/Cits   1. ALDH.Pros.uirg. 257.7-8: ANON.Recog. 6.2-3.
2. BEDA.Exp.Act.apost. V.xxxiv.71-73: ANON.Recog. 45.1-3.
3. BEDA.Retract.Act. V.xxxiv.37-40: ANON.Recog. 45.1-3.
4. BEDA.Comm.Gen. I.309-22: ANON.Recog. 23.21-24.9.
5. BEDA.Temp.rat V.61-69: ANON.Recog. 191.4-11.
Refs   1. ALDH.Pros.uirg. 257.13-15.

2. ALDH.Epist. 482.29.

The Anglo-Saxons would have known the Recognitiones through RUFI-
NUS' translation of a lost Greek text dated to the third century (*ODCC* 304).
The work relates the story of Clement, who is separated from his family
early in life; who travels to meet Peter, becoming his disciple and witness-
ing his encounter with Simon Magus; and who finally is reunited with his
family. But as Irmscher comments, the story is secondary to the didactic
aim of the work, which attempts "to communicate the Christian doctrine
or certain outward forms of it apologetically and systematically" (*NTA*
2.532). The narrative is adapted by various heretical groups (the Recognitiones is posited to be a reaction to heretical expansions of the earlier *Homilies*
[*CPG* 1015.4]), and although Rufinus' translation omits unorthodox passages, a version is still condemned by the GELASIAN DECREE (263–64).

The Oxford, New College MS is listed in HG as a fragment; and the
Salisbury MS is considered by Rehm (1965 p lxxvii) to be twelfth century.
Ker (1976 p 25) includes it among group 6 of his breakdown of the MSS
from Salisbury Cathedral, which he suggests are later than the first 5 groups.
Rehm lists both the Oxford, Trinity College MS and the Royal MS as
eleventh century, but neither appears in HG. Ogilvy (*BKE* p 117) notes
one other MS, BL Add. 18400, but it is included by Rehm among the German MSS (1965 p xxii), and is not in HG.

Ogilvy (*BKE* p 116; corrected in 1984 p 296) states that the "Clemens"
mentioned by ALCUIN in his VERSUS DE PARTIBUS, REGIBUS ET SANCTIS EU-
BORICENSIS ECCLESIAE (1552) is the author of this work; Lapidge (ML 1.12)
identifies the reference as to Aurelius PRUDENTIUS Clemens, and the context of the name among Christian Latin poets supports his assertion; see
also Godman (1982 p 125) who translates "Prudentius."

In both his commentary and retraction on the Acts of the Apostles, BEDE
cites "Clemens" as his source for information. In addition to the two other
uses listed above, Bede may draw on the Recognitiones elsewhere in his
didactic works; see the *CCSL* 123.734. See also PS CLEMENS, EPISTULA AD
JACOBUM.

In addition to Rehm (Bibliography Part I), the work also appears in *PG*
1.1207–1454.

Ps Clemens, Epistula ad Jacobum [ANON.Epist.Iac./PS CLEMENS]:
RBMA 209,1; *BHL* 6647; *CPG* 1015.3; *ODCC* 304; *NTA* 2.532-70.

Ogilvy suggests that this work "may have been used by Bede" (*BKE* p
116) in explaining the succession of Laurence to Augustine as archbishop
of Canterbury by recalling Peter's designation of Clement as his successor
in Rome (ECCLESIASTICAL HISTORY II.iv, 144.16-22). Ogilvy notes, however,

that Plummer (1896 vol 2 p 82) adduces other sources including Rufinus' preface to the PS CLEMENS REGONITIONES (4.29–5.10), and the LIBER PONTIFICALIS (123.5–8), both works that Bede is known to have used elsewhere. On the role of the Epistle in shaping this tradition, see Ullmann (1960), who mentions Bede's remarks and adds that ALDHELM also identifies Clement as the first pope in his prose DE VIRGINITATE (257.3–5).

Passio Jacobi Maioris [ANON.Pas.Iac.Mai.]: *RBMA* 213,11; *BHL* 4057.

MSS 1. London, BL Cotton Nero E.i: HG 344.
2. Salisbury, Cathedral Library 222 (olim Oxford, Bodleian Library Fell 1): HG 623.
3. Paris, Bibliothèque Nationale 10861: HG 898.
Lists none.
A-S Vers *ÆCHom* II, 31–32 (B1.2.34).
Quots/Cits — Refs none.

In this Passio, James the Great preaching in Judea overcomes a magician named Hermogenes, but eventually is decapitated by king Herod. Zettel (1979 p 23) identifies it as item 74 in his reconstructed COTTON-CORPUS LEGENDARY: it occurs in the London and Salisbury MSS. Förster (GR 5300, p 23) notes that it is ÆLFRIC's source for his homily on James (*ÆCHom* II, 31–32).

In addition to the edition in Fábrega Grau (Bibliography Part I), the work also appears in Mombritius (1910 vol 2 pp 37–40); and in PS ABDIAS (Fabricius 1719 vol 2 pp 516–31).

Passio Jacobi Minoris [ANON.Pas.Iac.Min.]: *BHL* 4093; not in *RBMA*.
See also PS ABDIAS, and RUFINUS-EUSEBIUS, HISTORIA ECCLESIASTICA.

MSS 1. London, BL Cotton Nero E.i: HG 344.
2. Salisbury, Cathedral Library 221 (olim Oxford, Bodleian Library Fell 4): HG 625.
Lists — Refs none.

James the Less' martyrdom, as this brief Passio relates, is brought about by the Pharisees who want the apostle to speak out against Christ; James uses the occasion to preach the Gospel. Zettel (1979 p 19) lists it as item 45 of his reconstructed COTTON-CORPUS LEGENDARY: it occurs in the London and Salisbury MSS. Cross (1979b pp 29–31) cites it, among others, for details in the Old English *Martyrology* on James (B19.ds).

In addition to the text in Fábrega Grau (Bibliography Part I), see also de Smedt, de Backer, van Ortroy, and van den Gheyn (1889 pp 136–37).

Ps Mellitus, Passio Johannis [ANON.Pas.Ioh./PS.MEL.]: *RBMA* 221; *BHL* 4320; see also *NTA* 2.204–06.

MSS   Cambridge, Pembroke College 25: HG 131.
Lists   none.
A-S Vers   *ÆCHom* I, 4 (B1.1.5).
Quots/Cits   ALDH.Pros.uirg.: see below.
Refs   none.

Item 9 of the Pembroke MS (see the HOMILIARY OF ST PÈRE DE CHARTRES; and Cross 1987a p 22) includes, in a slightly shortened form with a homiletic introduction and conclusion, the opening miracles from this work (1241.18–1243.22). The following homily, on John's assumption, is drawn largely from the account in PS ABDIAS, and opens with a passage that overlaps with the Passio (1249.28–39).

Zettel (1979 p 33) lists this work as item 150 in his reconstructed COTTON-CORPUS LEGENDARY; it occurs only in Oxford, Bodleian Library Bodley 354 (twelfth century). Förster (GR 5300, pp 17–18) notes ÆLFRIC's use of it in his homily on John's Assumption (*ÆCHom* I, 4); see also Zettel (1979 pp 160–62, 164–66, and 238–241) for further correspondences between Ælfric's homily and this version.

In the prose DE VIRGINITATE, ALDHELM recounts the incidents of John restoring shattered gems (254.15–17), resurrecting a woman (254.17–255.3), and drinking poison (255.3–8), all recounted in the Passio (1242.20–1243.15, 1241.33–17, and 1248.5–23). Cross (1979a p 165) asserts that BEDE "had available, and disliked, the pseudo-Melitus account of John the Evangelist," but the exact comments in his RETRACTIO (I.48–85 and VIII.13–14) appear to be too general to support this claim.

In addition to the edition in the *PG* (Bibliography Part I), the work is also printed in Fabricius (1719 vol 3 pp 606–23), and in Fábrega Grau (1955 vol 2 pp 102–10).

Passio Marci [ANON.Pas.Marci]: *RBMA* 224,2; *BHL* 5276.

MSS   1. London, BL Cotton Nero E.i: HG 344.
2. Salisbury, Cathedral Library 221 (olim Oxford, Bodleian Library Fell 4): HG 625.
Lists   none.
A-S Vers   *ÆLS* (Mark, B1.3.16).
Quots/Cits   BEDA.Mart.: see below.
Refs   none.

The Passio describes how Mark establishes the faith in Egypt, particularly in Alexandria, before he is martyred by being dragged through the streets of the city. Zettel (1979 p 19) identifies this work as item 43 of his reconstructed COTTON-CORPUS LEGENDARY: it occurs in the London and Salisbury MSS. Ott (GR 5351, pp 40–41) recognizes it as the source for ÆLFRIC's account of Mark's death (*ÆLS* Mark); see also Zettel (1979 pp 224–26). Quentin (1908 pp 85–86) shows the passio to be the source for BEDE's entry on Mark in his MARTYROLOGY.

In addition to Mombritius (Bibliography Part I), the work is also printed in the *AS* (April, vol 3 pp 350–51).

Passio Matthaei [ANON.Pas.Mattaei]: *RBMA* 225,17; *BHL* 5690.

MSS   1. London, BL Cotton Nero E.i: HG 344.
      2. Salisbury, Cathedral Library 222 (olim Oxford, Bodleian Library Fell 1): HG 623.
Lists   none.
A-S Vers   ÆCHom II, 37 (B1.2.40) 80–225.
Quots/Cits — Refs   none.

After converting Ethiopia by driving out dragons and resurrecting the king's son, Matthew is eventually martyred at the altar when he attempts to prevent a succeeding king's marriage. Zettel (1979 p 26) identifies this work as item 104 of his reconstructed COTTON-CORPUS LEGENDARY: it appears in the London and Salisbury MSS. Förster (GR 5300, p 24) notes that it is the source for ÆLFRIC's discussion of Matthew's passion (*ÆCHom* II, 37). Herzfeld (GR 6364, p xli) cites it in discussing the entry on Matthew in the Old English *Martyrology* (B19.hf); see also Cross (1979b pp 23–25). Cross (1979a p 169) identifies this passio as a source for details about Matthew in Cynewulf's *Fates* (A2.2; 63–69).

In addition to Talamo Atenolfi's work (Bibliography Part I), a version of the work appears in the PS ABDIAS (Fabricius 1719 vol 2 pp 636–68).

Ps Linus, Passio Pauli [ANON.Pas.Paul./PS LINUS]: *RBMA* 230,4; *BHL* 6570.

MSS   1. ? London, BL Cotton Nero E.i: HG 344.
      2. ? Salisbury, Cathedral Library 222 (olim Oxford, Bodleian Library Fell 1): HG 623.
Lists — Refs   none.

Zettel (1979 p 22) lists a "Passio S. Pauli apostoli" as item 68 in his reconstructed COTTON-CORPUS LEGENDARY, and he identifies this text as similar to *BHL* 6570 and 6574, the version that occurs in PS ABDIAS (Fabricius 1719 vol 2 pp 441–56).

The editors of BEDE's DE ORTHOGRAPHIA (600) refer to chapter 8, line

14 (31.15?) of this work, but the correspondence appears to be a single word.

Epistle of Paul to the Laodiceans [ANON.Epist.Laod.]: *RBMA* 233; *NTA* 2.128-32.

MSS   1. London, BL Royal 1.E.viii: HG 449.
  2. ? Cambridge, Trinity College B.5.2 (148): HG 169.
Lists — Quots/Cits   none.
Refs   *ÆLet* 4 (Sigeweard, B1.8.4) 948.

This short apocryphal letter is largely a tissue of quotations from the other Pauline epistles. In his catalog, James (1900-04 vol 1 p 186) asserts that the MS B.5.2 "must have contained the Epistle to the Laodiceans," apparently basing his judgment on the explicit following the Epistle to the Hebrews at the end of the MS: "epistole Pauli numero xvcim expl."

In his letter to Sigeweard concerning the Old and New Testament, ÆLFRIC attributes fifteen epistles to Paul, listing this work.

Lightfoot (1879 pp 282-84) provides a list of MS including this epistle. It was known in Ireland, appearing in the Book of Armagh; see McNamara (1975 pp 103-04).

Ps Marcellus, Passio Petri et Pauli [ANON.Pas.Pet.Paul./PS MAR-CEL.]: *RBMA* 251,3; *BHL* 6657-59.

MSS — Lists   none.
A-S Vers   1. *LS* 32 (Peter & Paul, B3.3.32).
  2. *ÆCHom* I, 26 (B1.1.28), Thorpe 374.12-384.19.
Quots/Cits — Refs   none.

In this account, Peter and Paul oppose Simon Magus before Nero, and after a number of other exchanges, end his magic flight through their prayers; the two are then martyred — Peter hanged head down on a cross, and Paul beheaded. Förster (GR 6173, pp 185-93) notes that BLICKLING HOMILY 15 (*LS* 32) is a translation of this work. Förster (GR 5300, pp 18-20) also points out that ÆLFRIC uses this work in the second half of his homily on the passion of Peter and Paul (*ÆCHom* I, 26). Cross (GR 691, pp 90-92 and 97-100) shows that Ælfric used this work to structure his homily for Rogation Monday (*ÆCHom* II, 21, B1.2.24). Cross (1979a p 170) notes that the pairing of the two in Cynewulf's *Fates* (A2.2; 11b-15) may "hint" at the use of this account.

Item 62 in the BOOK OF CERNE (158.10-15; see LITURGY) corresponds to a passage from this text (173.3-8); see Kuypers (1902 p 233).

In addition to Lipsius (Bibliography Part I), the work is also printed in

Fábrega Grau (1955 vol 2 pp 283-93). For the knowledge of this work in Ireland, see McNamara (1975 pp 99-101).

Ps Marcellus, Epistolae I et II ad Fratres Nerei et Achillem [ANON.Epist.Ner.Achil.]: *BHL* 6060; not in *RBMA*.

see ACTA SANCTORUM.

Conflictio apostolorum Petri et Pauli cum Simone Mago et Passiones eorundem.

Ogilvy (*BKE* p 72) takes this title from a list of books supposedly given by Gregory to St Augustine's, Canterbury. The list is recorded in the fifteenth century *Historia monasterii S. Augustini Cantuariensis* by Thomas of Elmham (*BEH* 2158; *RS* 8.96-99), but Ogilvy offers no evidence that it reflects books from the Anglo-Saxon period.

Actus Petri cum Simone [ANON.Acta.Pet.]: *RBMA* 235,1; *BHL* 6656; *NTA* 2.259-322.

MSS — Refs none.

This work, which is preserved in its most complete form in a Latin MS, Vercelli, Biblioteca Capitolare CLVIII (sixth-seventh century), was composed in Greek at the end of the second century; see *NTA* 2.275. Schneemelcher (*NTA* 2.262) considers the Acts of Peter to be a more appropriate title, and he discusses its relationship to other early acts, including the PS CLEMENTINE RECOGNITIONES. The Latin text focusses primarily on Peter's confrontation with Simon Magus (chapters 2-29) and his martyrdom (chapters 30-39); the second part circulated also independently (*RBMA* 245,1).

Lapidge (in Lapidge and Rosier 1985 p 239 note 42) suggests that ALDHELM may have drawn the details from this work in the section on Peter in the CARMINA ECCLESIASTICA.

Passio Petri [ANON.Pas.Petri]: *BHL* 6664.

MSS 1. ? London, BL Cotton Nero E.i: HG 344.
2. ? Salisbury, Cathedral Library 222 (olim Oxford, Bodleian Library Fell 1): HG 623.
Lists — Refs none.

Zettel (1979 p 22) lists a "Passio S. Petri apostoli" as item 67 in his reconstructed COTTON-CORPUS LEGENDARY, and he identifies this text as similar to *BHL* 6664. Förster (GR 5300, pp 18-21) links ÆLFRIC's Latin interjections opposing other traditions concerning Paul's and Peter's passion

(CATHOLIC HOMILIES I, 26, B1.1.26; Thorpe 374.25–27 and 382.28–29) to this text and to the PASSIO PAULI. See also Zettel (1979 pp 177–78).

In addition to Mombritius (Bibliography Part I), a version of the work appears in PS ABDIAS (Fabricius 1719 vol 2 pp 390–92 and 402–41).

Passio Philippi [ANON.Pas.Phil.]: *RBMA* 254; *BHL* 6814.

MSS   1. London, BL Cotton Nero E.i: HG 344.
   2. Salisbury, Cathedral Library 221 (olim Oxford, Bodleian Library Fell 4): HG 635.
   3. Paris, Bibliothèque Nationale 10861: HG 898.
Lists   none.
A-S Vers   *ÆCHom* II, 18 (B1.2.21) 1–60.
Quots/Cits — Refs   none.

In this brief passio, Philip converts the people of Scythia by driving out a dragon and resurrecting the people it has killed, and then travels to Asia where he is martyred. Zettel (1979 p 19) identifies the work as item 46 in his reconstructed COTTON-CORPUS LEGENDARY: it appears in the London and Salisbury MSS. Förster (GR 5300, p 22) notes that the material on Philip in ÆLFRIC's homily on Philip and James (*ÆCHom* II, 18) is from this account; see also Zettel (1979 pp 186–87).

Herzfeld (GR 6364, p xxxviii) discusses this account as the source for details about Philip in the Old English *Martyrology* (B19.ch); see also Cross (1979b pp 28–29). Cross (1979a pp 166–67) cites this work as a source for the *Fates* (A2.2; 37b–41), and mentions one detail — that Philip was crucified — which occurs in Mombritius (Bibliography Part I; 385.41–42), but not in PS ABDIAS (Fabricius vol 2 1719 pp 738–42). Lapidge (in Lapidge and Rosier 1985 p 241 note 64) notes that in the section on Philip in his CARMINA ECCLESIASTICA, ALDHELM departs from his main source (ISIDORE's DE ORTU) in claiming that Philip preaches in Scythia; Lapidge identifies PS ABDIAS as a possible source.

Passio Simonis et Judae [ANON.Pas.Sim.Iud.]: *BHL* 7749–50; see *RBMA* 255,14.

MSS — Lists   none.
A-S Vers   *ÆCHom* II, 38 (B1.2.41).
Quots/Cits — Refs   none.

Simon and Jude convert Persia by overcoming two magicians, and performing other miracles; they are eventually martyred when they travel to the provinces to continue their missionary work. Zettel (1979 p 28) includes the Passio as item 121 in his reconstructed COTTON-CORPUS LEGENDARY.

Although it does not occur in either the Cotton or the Corpus MSS, it is included in Oxford, Bodleian Library Bodley 354 (twelfth century), and in the table of Salisbury, Cathedral Library 222 (olim Oxford, Bodleian Fell 1: HG 623). Förster (GR 5300, pp 24–25) notes that it is ÆLFRIC's source for his homily on Simon and Jude (*ÆCHom* II, 38). See also Zettel (1979 pp 195–98). Herzfeld (GR 6364, p xli) identifies it as relevant to the entry in the Old English *Martyrology* (B19.ih); see also Cross (1979b pp 25–27). Cross (1979a pp 169–70) considers it a source for Cynewulf's *Fates* (A2.2; 75–84).

In addition to Mombritius (Bibliography Part I), a version of this work appears in PS ABDIAS (Fabricius 1719 vol 2 pp 608–36).

Acta Thomae: *RBMA* 259: see PASSIO THOMAE.

Passio Thomae [ANON.Pas.Thom.]: *RBMA* 259,8; *BHL* 8136; see *NTA* 2.425–42.

MSS — Lists   none.
A-S Vers   *ÆLS* (Thomas, B1.3.34; 13–424).
Quots/Cits   none.
Refs   ? *ÆCHom* II, 39.2 (B1.2.43) 7–9.

The original Acta Thomae, composed in Syriac and surviving also in Greek, are closely linked to Gnostic sects (see *NTA* 2.429–41). Two Latin adaptations, the Passio and the *De miraculis beati Thomae apostoli* (also printed in Zelzer 1977, but previously known from PS ABDIAS vol 2 pp 687–736), have been largely stripped of their overt gnostic content (Zelzer 1977 pp xi-xxiii). Zelzer dates the two to the fourth century (p xxv).

Zettel (1979 p 33) lists this work as item 146 in his reconstructed COTTON-CORPUS LEGENDARY. Although it does not occur in either the Cotton or the Corpus manuscript, it is included in Oxford, Bodleian Library Bodley 354 (twelfth century), Hereford, Cathedral Library P 7 vi (twelfth century; see Bannister 1927 p 172) and in the table of Salisbury, Cathedral Library 222 (olim Oxford, Bodleian Library Fell 1: HG 623).

As Loomis (GR 5358, p 7) notes, ÆLFRIC adapts this work in his LIVES OF SAINTS (*ÆLS* Thomas), shortening and omitting some sections. Ælfric's possible reference to this work in his "Apology" in his CATHOLIC HOMILIES II—"the Passion of Thomas we leave unwritten because it was long ago translated from Latin into English, in verse"—is further linked to this text by the reference to an exchange between the saint and a cupbearer, an account that Augustine condemns; Ælfric again mentions this incident at the beginning of the version in the Lives of Saints. See also Zettel (1979 pp 259–62).

Cross (1979a pp 167–69) concludes that the *Fates* (A2.2; 50–62) probably draws on the passio. Herzfeld (GR 6364, p 240) identifies it as the source for the entry on Thomas in the Old English *Martyrology* (B19.jn); Cross (1979b pp 21–23) agrees, and notes further that the PS ABDIAS account does not include many relevant details.

In the prose DE VIRGINITATE (255.20–23), ALDHELM quotes a speech by Thomas concerning virginity, but his source has not yet been located (see Lapidge and Herren 1979 pp 194–95).

There is some evidence that the Irish knew the original Acta Thomae; see McNamara (1975 pp 118–19).

IV. APOCRYPHAL APOCALYPSES

Shepherd of Hermas [ANON.Past.Herm.]: *RBMA* 267; *CPG* 1052; *GCS* 86–87; *DACL* 6.2265–90; see also *NTA* 2.629–42; *ODCC* 641–42; *KVS* HER.

MSS   1. Düsseldorf, Landes- und Stadtbibliothek B. 215 + C. 118 + Staatsarchiv Fragm. 20: HG 819 (Staatsarchiv fragment is not in HG).
2. Cambridge, Corpus Christi College 265: HG 73.
Lists — A-S Vers   none.
Quots/Cits   see below.
Refs   BEDA.Exp.Act.apost. 12.15: Past.Hermas Mand. VI.ii.2–5: see below.

The Shepherd of Hermas was composed in Greek at Rome in the second century, or perhaps as early as the late first century. The *NTA* describes the work as a "Pseudo-Apocalypse," "since it includes no disclosures of the eschatological future or of the world beyond" (p 630; see also pp 634–38), but its apocalyptic intent has been reasserted by other scholars (Bauckham 1974 pp 29–30; Hellholm 1980; and Osiek 1986). Hermas, who describes himself as a freed Christian slave who became a merchant and who later suffered persecution, is identified as the brother of the bishop of Rome in the Muratorian Canon and other sources, but scholars are not agreed on how much of the work can be attributed to Hermas himself. The Shepherd is traditionally divided into 5 Visions, 12 Mandates, and 10 Similitudes, and is thought to have been combined from two originally independent books (Visions 1–4; and Visions 5–Similitudes 8, supplemented by Similitudes 9–10; see *NTA* pp 633–34 and Barnard 1968 p 32), or according to Giet (1963) three different works (Visions 1–4; Similitude 9; and the Mandates and Similitudes 1–8).

The Shepherd was regarded as Scripture in the early Greek Church (*ODCC* 641). JEROME, in DE VIRIS ILLUSTRIBUS, says that it was virtually unknown in the West (*PL* 23.626), but the Shepherd is cited or mentioned by various early Latin authors (see De Gebhardt and Harnack, Bibliography Part I pp lxi-lxx; *DS* 7.332–33; Courcelle 1969 pp 91, 94–95, and 228), not always favorably, although a favorable judgment by ORIGEN was repeated by SEDULIUS SCOTTUS (see De Gebhardt and Harnack pp lxiv-lxv, note 1). Dronke (1981 pp 37–38) argues that St Patrick knew the work.

Two Latin versions have survived: the Vulgata (V or L[1], dating from the second century, surviving in several manuscripts and fragments) and the Palatina (P or L[2], dating from the fourth or fifth century, surviving in two fifteenth-century MSS and in the Düsseldorf fragment). The Vulgata includes the end of the book, lacking in the Greek manuscripts. On the relationship between the Latin and Greek versions see Carlini (1983). On the Latin versions see Mazzini and Lorenzini (1981); on the Palatina version see also Mazzini (1980). For lists of the Latin manuscripts see *GCS* and De Gebhardt and Harnack (Bibliography Part I, pp xiv ff). On the Düsseldorf MS see *CLA* 8.1187 and Coens (1956 pp 90–91), who identifies the fragment (apparently in the 2 leaves in C.118) as mandata in the Palatina version. I have not been able to confirm Ogilvy's statement (*BKE* p 157) that St Gall, Stiftsbibliothek 151, pt 3 "may go back to an English exemplar."

The brief extract (Mand. IV.1) in the Cambridge MS apparently corresponds to the COLLECTIO CANONUM HIBERNENSIS 46.15 (see Bateson 1895 p 720); the *Hibernensis* also has other extracts from Hermas; this particular extract occurs in related canonical collections, including Orléans, Bibliothèque Municipale 221 (193) and Paris, Bibliothèque Nationale 3182. Another extract (Sim. II) occurs in Paris, Bibliothèque Nationale nouv. acq. lat. 763 (see Omont 1906 pp 355–57).

BEDE, commenting on the reference to guardian angels in Acts 12.15, states "quod unusquisque nostrum habeat angelos et in libro Pastoris et in multis sanctae scripturae locis inuenitur" (*CCSL* 121.159). The reference is probably to Mandate 6, as Laistner indicates in the apparatus of his edition (Bibliography Part I), rather than to Vision 5, as Laistner (1933 p 83) had earlier suggested. Laistner (1933 p 83) states that "it was undoubtedly [the Vulgata version] to which Bede had access," but the Düsseldorf MS suggests that if Bede did know the work at first hand, it might well have been in the Palatina version. According to Jenkins (1966 p 182), however, "we may doubt if he knew the book except at second hand," since he does not refer to it on the significance of the stones of the Temple in DE TEMPLO. Ogilvy (*BKE* p 157) thinks it "likely" that Bede knew the work first hand, in view of the Düsseldorf fragments, which Lowe considers to have been written probably in the north of England. But the passage to which Bede refers on the guardian angels was cited or paraphrased in several patristic works, including ORIGEN, DE PRINCIPIIS III.ii.4 (in RUFINUS' translation; *PG*

11.309 and *GCS* 22.251) with attribution to "Pastoris liber" (cf. Daniélou
1976 pp 80-81), and CASSIAN, CONLATIONES VIII.xvii.2 (*CSEL* 13.233) with
attribution to "liber Pastoris" and in reference to Acts 12.15 (see Courcelle
1969 p 228). De Gebhardt and Harnack (Bibliography Part I p LXVII
and note 4) already suggested that Bede's reference, as well as one in the
Visio Wettini, was taken over from Cassian. The passage also appears as a
separate extract (but attributed to Jerome) in London, BL Cotton Nero
A.ii folio 35 (*CLA* 2.186; beyond the part listed in HG; see *BHM* vol 4A,
p 21 which does not identify the source of the excerpt).

The same passage on the guardian angels has been cited by Menner
(GR 4337, p 143) as an early example of the conception of the good and
bad angels appearing in the poetic *Solomon and Saturn* (*MSol*, A13) with reference to similar descriptions in *HomU* 9 (*VercHom* 4; B3.4.9) and *GuthA* (A3.2).

For the Greek text, in addition to Whittaker (Bibliography Part I), see
the edition by R. Joly (1958), which replaces the traditional divisions with
consecutively numbered chapters. For English translations see Crombie
(1905) and Snyder (1968).

                                                    Charles D. Wright

Apocalypse of the Virgin [ANON.Apoc.Mariae]: *RBMA* 273.

MSS—A-S Vers   none.
Quots/Cits   see below.
Refs   none.

The Apocalypse of the Virgin, probably composed in Greek in the second half of the fourth century (W. Wright 1865 p 7) exists in numerous
Eastern languages. Although *RBMA* does not include any Latin version,
a short Latin recension has been edited by Wenger (Bibliography Part I).

One detail—Mary's role in aiding condemned souls—in two Old English homilies—*HomU* 6 (*VercHom* 15, B3.4.6) and *NicD* and *NicE* (B8.5.3.2
and B8.5.3.3—but see GOSPEL OF NICODEMUS) may go back to this work.
In the Apocalypse, Mary is taken to hell with the apostles after her death
so that they can view its torments; they plead with Christ, and He eventually grants a respite for the suffering souls. In the Anglo-Saxon texts, Mary,
Michael, and Peter plead for the damned after the Judgment, and each
is granted a third of the condemned souls. For further details, see Clayton
(1986c).

ÆLFRIC was presumably familiar with this vernacular version, and ob-
jected that neither Mary nor any other saint could save those condemned
by Christ (*ÆCHom* II, 44, B1.2.48; 184-95).

For the knowledge of this text in Ireland, see Donahue (1942 p 9).

Mary Clayton

Visio Sancti Pauli [ANON.Vis.Pauli]: *RBMA* 275–76; *BHL* 6580–82; *NTA* 2.755–98.

MSS ? Vatican, Pal. lat. 220.
Lists none.
A-S Vers *HomM* 1 (B3.5.1).
Quots/Cits none.
Refs 1. ALDH.Pros.uirg. 256.7–14: see below.
 2. *ÆCHom* II 22 (B1.2.26) 14–16: see below.

Although the *NTA* calls this work the "Apocalypse of Paul" to emphasize its close filiations with other apocalypses such as the Apocalypse of Peter, the title Visio Sancti Pauli, here accepted, is more common among Anglo-Saxonists. The Latin tradition, which contains long versions and eleven redactions, has been largely established by Silverstein (1935, 1959, and 1976); see also the *NTA* 2.755–59. The Vatican MS, in an Anglo-Saxon hand of the ninth century, has recently been published by Dwyer (1988 pp 121–38), who identifies it as redaction XI. According to Silverstein (1959 p 212) redaction IV has "has special currency in England (perhaps even its origin there)"; the known MSS of this redaction, however, are later than our period (see Silverstein 1935 pp 220–21 for a list of MSS).

The Visio, translated into Latin somewhere between the fourth and sixth centuries, was popular in Anglo-Saxon England as an accessible and instructive guide to the fate of the soul at the moment of death. One clear indication of its popularity is the vigor with which it was condemned by two of the most articulate voices of the period: ALDHELM, writing around the turn of the eighth century, spurns the work by categorizing it with "other absurdities of the apocrypha"; and ÆLFRIC, writing three centuries later, repudiates it as "a false composition."

Only the first part of the Visio was actually translated into Old English, existing in a unique copy, *HomM* 1. Luiselli Fadda (1974) has concluded that the translation follows a Long Latin Version, and Healey (1978) has argued that none of the extant Long Latin Versions is its source. Matter found in the Old English, but lacking in the Long Latin and yet confirmed as original by the Russian and Syriac versions establishes in a positive way the existence of another Latin recension, the source of the Old English.

A number of Old English texts are indebted to the Visio Sancti Pauli for significant motifs as well as several minor themes. The incident of the going-out of souls can be found in *Bede* 5 (B9.6.7; pp 436–42), *GuthA* (A3.2; 1–29), *HomM* 5 (B3.5.5), *HomS* 5 (B3.2.5), and *HomS* 31 (B3.2.31); most recently Acker (1986) has analyzed this motif in *HomS* 14 (*BlHom* 4, B3.2.14). The address of the soul to the body can be found in *HomM* 8 (B3.5.8), *HomM* 14.1 (B3.5.14.1), *HomM* 14.2 (B3.5.14.2), *HomS* 6 (Ass 14, B3.2.6), *HomU* 9 (*VercHom* 4, B3.4.9), *HomU* 26 (Nap 29, B3.4.26), *HomU* 55 (B3.4.55), and *Soul I* and *II* (A2.3 and 3.19). The respite of the damned, which is the climax of Paul's journey to hell in the Visio, appears domesticated in *GuthA* (A3.2; 205–14), *HomM* 8, *HomM* 14.2, *HomU* 35.1 (Nap 43, B3.4.35.1), *HomU* 35.2 (Nap 44, B3.4.35.2), *HomU* 55, and *Soul* I and II. The correspondence of punishment to sin, which conveys a straightforward justice in the Visio Sancti Pauli, is appropriated by Old English writers in *HomS* 14, *HomS* 42 (B3.2.42), *HomU* 37 (Nap 46, B3.4.37), *Let* 1 (B6.1), and *LS* 25 (Michael-Mor, B3.3.25). Moreover, minor influences of the Visio may be seen in the detail of men with tongues of iron in *HomS* 4 (*VercHom* 9, B3.2.4), *HomU* 35.1, *HomU* 12.2 (Willard, B3.4.12.2). And, as Hill (GR 3778) has suggested, the *Visio* is a possible source for the northwest direction of hell in *GenB* (A1.1; 275). Despite its censure by Aldhelm and Ælfric, Anglo-Saxon homilists and poets drew upon the Visio Sancti Pauli to articulate the direct relationship between human deeds and the fate of the soul.

Finally, the vexed question of the relationship of the hell scene in the Visio with the hell scene in the Blickling Homily on the dedication of St Michael's church (*LS* 25) and with the description of Grendel's mere in *Beowulf* (*Beo*, A4.1; 1367–76) has been opened once again by R.L. Collins (1984) who observes that the vocabulary of the Blickling homilist here is closer to the Visio than to *Beowulf*. He cautiously concludes that if there is any influence, it may be from the homilist to *Beowulf*, the reverse of what has usually been thought.

For bibliography on the Old English Visio Sancti Pauli, see GR 4365, 6235, 6239, 6240; and Healey (1978 pp 96–98). The most complete Long Latin Version is published by James from Paris, Bibliothèque Nationale nouv. acq. lat. 1631 (Bibliography Part I). Silverstein (Bibliography Part I) publishes a second fragment of this version from St Gall, Stadtbibliothek 317; and a related fragment from Vienna, Österreichische Nationalbibliothek 362. The Latin redactions have been discussed and published by Silverstein (1935, 1959, 1962, and 1976); see also his review (1981) of Healey (1978). As noted above, redaction eleven is published by Dwyer from the Vatican MS (Bibliography Part I). The work was also known to the Irish; see McNamara (1975 pp 108–09). A new edition of the Armenian version is *CCSA* 3.

A. diPaolo Healey

Apocalypse of Thomas [ANON.Apoc.Thom.]: *RBMA* 280; *CPL* 796a; *NTA* 2.798–803. See also COLLECTANEA BEDAE.

MSS ? Vatican, Pal. Lat. 220.
Lists none.
A-S Vers 1. *HomU* 12 (B3.4.12).
      2. *HomU* 6 (*VercHom* 22, B3.4.6).
      3. *HomS* 26 (*BlHom* 7, B3.2.26).
      4. *HomS* 44 (B3.2.44).
      5. *HomS* 33 (B3.2.33).
Quots/Cits — Refs none.

This Apocalypse, which purports to be a revelation to the apostle concerning the end of the world, survives in two recensions. The longer recension alludes to fifth-century events as contemporary, and the earliest witness of the shorter recension is in a MS also dated to this century (Vienna, Österreichische Nationalbibliothek Lat. 16; *CLA* 3.396). The Vatican MS, in a ninth-century Anglo-Saxon hand (McNally 1979 pp 121–22), represents the longer version. The work is condemned in the GELASIAN DECREE (293).

Förster (GR 6224) reached several conclusions about the relationship of the Old English translations of the Apocalypse to the two main Latin recensions: 1) the five homilies represent four independent versions (Förster considers *HomS* 33 and 44 as one version); 2) 1, 2, and 3 follow the longer Latin recension closely enough to be called translations; 3) 1 and 2 incorporate almost the entire apocalypse whereas 3, 4, and 5 use only the signs of Doomsday; 4) 4 and 5 show no trace of the interpolated Latin recension.

Probably related to the Apocalypse is the tradition of the Fifteen Signs before Judgment (*Notes* 22, B24.22). Although the Apocalypse lists signs for only seven days before Judgment, the use of a numbered sequence and the similarity in many of the signs suggest that the Fifteen Signs developed from this work. Heist (1952) specifically argues that the early Middle Irish poem *Saltair na Rann* provides the transition; however, the question remains open to new evidence such as the discovery of manuscripts of the COLLECTANEA BEDAE in which a Latin version of the work appears (*PL* 94.555).

Evidence for an earlier knowledge of these works is difficult to establish. *ChristC* (A3.1), often ascribed to the ninth century, does not list signs for the days preceding Judgment, but it contains in its description of the destruction of the world details found in these traditions. The difficulty in identifying exclusive echoes of either Apocalypse or the Fifteen signs in poetic texts arises because the signs often have some basis in biblical passages such as Mt 24.30. See, however, the suggestion by Cross (1982 p 105 note

10) that the Apocalypse may be the ultimate source for the phrase "mare siccabitur" in PS AUGUSTINE HOMILY 251.

Förster (GR 2224, p 10) states that the Latin MSS in Vienna, Österreichische Nationalbibliothek Lat. 16 (fragment) and Munich, Bayerische Staatsbibliothek clm 4563 (both in Bibliography Part I) represent the uninterpolated tradition; and that Verona, Biblioteca Capitolare 1 (fragment), and Munich, Bayerische Staatsbibliothek clm 4585 (both in Bibliography Part I) represent the interpolated tradition. James (1953 pp 556–62) translates these versions. For other MSS, see Förster (GR 2224, pp 9–10). For bibliography on the Old English versions of the Apocalypse, see GR 248, 923, 3343, 5300, and 6239; and on the Old English version of the Fifteen Signs, see GR 626. For further information on the Irish evidence, see McNamara (1975 pp 119–21).

Apocrypha Priscillianistica [ANON.Apoc.Pris.]: *RBMA* 283; *CPL* 790–95; *BCLL* 1252; *KVS* AN Bruyne.

MSS   1. London, BL Royal 5.E.xiii: HG 459.
2. Salisbury, Cathedral Library 9: HG 699.
Lists—A-S Vers   none.
Quots/Cits   HomS 44 (B3.2.44, ed. Bazire and Cross 1982) 51.91–96: see below.
Refs   none.

The Apocrypha Priscillianistica consist of six texts published by De Bruyne (1907) from Karlsruhe, Badische Landesbibliothek Aug. CCLIV (*CLA* 8.1100), the first six items in a larger compilation headed in the manuscript "incipit collectario de diversis sententiis." The Royal MS includes the beginning of De Bruyne's item 6 (*Liber "canon in ebreica" Hieronimi presbiteri*, *CPL* 795; see also *BHM* 403 and Bischoff 1976 p 159 note 126) in an expanded version, before breaking off; see Warner and Gilson (1921 vol 1 p 116). The Salisbury MS includes item 4 (*Homilia de die iudicii*, *CPL* 793); see Schenkl (1969 V. Salisbury, p 5).

De Bruyne's theory of Priscillianist origins for these pieces has since been abandoned (see Vollmann 1965 p 48), but M.R. James (1918–19 p 16) remarked that they "appear to be from a Celtic workshop," an opinion supported by many other scholars; for details, see C. Wright (1987a pp 135–36), and Frede (*KVS* 1981 p 78). C. Wright (forthcoming in *Cambridge Medieval Celtic Studies*) outlines the parallels with Irish traditions, including the seven heavens apocryphon, extracts from HIBERNO-LATIN COMMENTARIES (first remarked by Dumville 1973 p 327), and other themes and enumerations paralleled in Hiberno-Latin compilations, including the LIBER DE NUMERIS, the FLORILEGIUM FRISINGENSE, the CATACHESIS CELTICA, and the homilies IN NOMINE DEI SUMMI.

Item 2 is an epitome of the so-called Seven Heavens apocryphon, which describes (in broken and confused fashion) the journey and purgation of the soul through a series of seven heavens, assigning names to each heaven as well as to the doors of each (for other lists of the seven heavens in Hiberno-Latin texts, see Cross 1986a pp 78–79 and 90–91). The apocryphon survives in variant forms in three Irish texts (Vision of Adamnan, Evernew Tongue, and an excerpt in the Liber Flavus Fergusiorum, ed. Mac Niocaill 1956) and in Old English in *HomU* 12.2 (Willard; B3.4.12.2; this homily also contains an Old English version of the APOCALYPSE OF THOMAS). The relationship between the Irish texts and the Latin fragment has been studied by James (1918, with suggested emendations for the Latin fragment), Seymour (1923, with a translation of the Latin, pp 22–23; see also Seymour 1927 and 1930 pp 112–20), Dando (1972), Dumville (1977/78) and Stevenson (1982). Willard (GR 6235, pp 1–30) provides a detailed examination of the relationship between these versions and *HomU* 12.2, in addition to a passage in *HomS* 5 (B3.2.5) on the descent of the soul through 12 dragons and 12 circles of hell (see pp 24–28).

C. Wright (forthcoming in *Neuphilologische Mitteilungen*) shows that a Judgment theme in item 4 — in which Christ demands a pledge for each man's thoughts, words, and deeds, and each responds that he has nothing to pledge but his soul — is the ultimate source for a closely similar passage in *HomS* 44 (B3.2.44, ed. Bazire and Cross 1982; 51.91–96), where the Old English term *wed* corresponds to the Latin *area* (= *arrha*). A similar idea occurs in several other Old English homilies. Luiselli Fadda (1977 p 101) printed part of the theme from item 4 opposite a passage from *HomS* 32 (B3.2.32), but here there are no close verbal parallels with the Latin, and only one other homily, *HomS* 25 (B3.2.25, ed. Evans 1981; 142.351–53) uses the distinctive term *wed*. C. Wright points out, however, that Cynewulf's *Elene* (*El*, A2.6; 1281b–86a) echoes the theme with the phrase *wed gesyllan* and the "thought, word, deed" triad.

J.E. Cross, who noted item 4 in the Salisbury MS, has also noted its occurrence in Munich, Bayerische Staatsbibliothek clm 19410. C. Wright (1988b pp 228–29) points out that substantial portions of the Apocrypha Priscillianistica (including part of item 4, but not the Judgment passage) also occur in Einsiedeln, Stiftsbibliothek 199 (*CLA* 7.875). Item 3 includes parallels with the APOCALYPSE OF THOMAS (see under Apocrypha). The Karlsruhe MS also contains a text of the THREE UTTERANCES apocryphon (see under MISCELLANEOUS).

Charles D. Wright

AUGUSTINE

[Only one work has been included in this *Trial Version*.]

Confessiones [AVG.Confess.]: *CPL* 251.

MSS   1. Cambridge, Corpus Christi College, 253: HG 71.
  2. Cambridge, Trinity College, B.3.25 (104): HG 163.
  3. London, BL, Harley 3080: HG 434.
  4. London, Lambeth Palace Library 414 (excerpts): HG 516.
  5. Oxford, Bodleian Library, Bodley 815 (*SC* 2759): HG 603.
  6. Salisbury, Cathedral Library 6: HG 697.
  7. Salisbury, Cathedral Library 118: HG 723.

Lists—A-S vers   none.

Quots/Cits   1. BEDA.Orthogr.746: AVG.Confess. I.ix.15.
  2. BEDA.Temp.rat. V.45–48: AVG.Confess. XII.20–29.
  3. BEDA.Nat.rer. I.1: AVG.Confess. XII.7–8.
  4. BEDA.Nat.rer. II.1: AVG.Confess. XII.8.
  5. BEDA.Comm.Gen.: see below.

Refs   ANON.Lib.precum.Cerne: see below.

This is clearly Augustine's most popular and widely read work, although its popularity stems largely from the Renaissance after Petrarch took it along on his famous climb of Mount Ventoux. Moderns prize the work for its ruthless psychological investigation of a sinner redeemed and for its abundant spirituality; scholars use it for its valuable biographical data. This fascination with the work is, however, rather late.

Augustine wrote the *Confessiones* between 397 and 400. Books 1–9 contain his spiritual autobiography; book 10 describes his moral and spiritual state at the time he wrote the book; and books 11–13 contain a meditation on time and eternity and the relation of God to the created world. It is a testimony to how the book was regarded that its most extensive use by BEDE in his COMMENTARY ON GENESIS (see *CCSL* 118A. 254 for a list of eight quotations) and all of his citations are from books 12–13. Indeed, only the references in Bede's DE ORTHOGRAPHIA are from Books 1–9. The reference in the BOOK OF CERNE (see LITURGY) appears on p 122 therein.

Joseph F. Kelly

BEDE

Bede, Anglo-Saxon England's foremost Anglo-Latin author, "father of English scholarship," "father of English history," "teacher of the whole Middle Ages," produced works in every discipline of the monastic school system. His educational treatises—basic schoolbooks and reference works—gave the Anglo-Saxons access to classical authorities and provided early medieval supplements to late antique manuals. His scientific writings on computus and chronology established a new norm. His commentaries on the Bible offered Anglo-Saxon readers a carefully edited and annotated synthesis of patristic sources, particularly the four Fathers of the Western Church. His historical writings formed a model for later historiographers and are still the principal sources, along with the ANGLO-SAXON CHRONICLE, for information on England before the Conquest. By including a fairly complete bibliography of his works at the end of the HISTORIA ECCLESIASTICA (V.xxiv), Bede furnished a list to his readers of writings available for use.

Teacher, exegete, historian, and saintly monk, Bede was cited as "magister," "nostrae cathegita terrae," "se snotera lareow," "breoma bocera," "se trahtnere," "se halga Beda"; both in England and on the Continent he was ranked on a footing with the Fathers of the Church; see BONIFACE (*EHD* 180), CUTHBERT (*EHD* 185), LUL (*EHD* 188), ALCUIN (*MGH* ECA 337.5, 360.16–20, 443.8) and ÆLFRIC (in the Preface to the FIRST SERIES OF CATHOLIC HOMILIES, and in his letters to Wulfsige [*ÆLet* 1, B1.8.1; 16] and to Sigefyrth [*ÆLet* 5, B1.8.5; 209]). Wherever Bede's name was associated with a work, scribes gave the work special attention; see *CCSL* 123A.xv and 185, and *CCSL* 123B.242.

Continental MSS of Bede's works are numerous, but, despite his primary importance for Anglo-Saxon culture, his undoubted influence on writers such as Alfred and Ælfric, and the honor they paid him, insular MSS of his works (except for the HISTORIA ECCLESIASTICA and the VITA CUTHBERTI) are relatively few. Bede's work suffered the same fate as many other pre-1100 insular MSS. The Viking invasions and cultural decay brought about general destruction; in addition, his school texts were particularly vulnerable to abuse, hard wear, and eventual discard. Manuscript evidence suggests that most of Bede's works were re-imported into England after the Conquest.

Bede's influence generally permeates the writings of the educated class in Anglo-Saxon England, but it is difficult to establish always when authors are borrowing from him, since sometimes Bede is the intermediary source for a late antique or patristic idea or quotation which they may have gotten directly or from another intermediary, and sometimes authors incorporate material from him in a reworked fashion that conceals the full extent of indebtedness to him. As a rule, if an Anglo-Saxon author undertakes a topic Bede has written on, Bede is a likely source for at least some of it; it is fruitless to seek Bede in treatments of non-canonical and pseudepigraphal topics.

For a detailed treatment of Bede's life, see G. Brown (1987).

[For this *Trial Version*, only the headnote for one of Bede's didactic works has been included.]

De orthographia [BEDA.Orthogr.]: *CPL* 1566.

MSS   1. Cambridge, Corpus Christi College 221: HG 69.
    2. London, BL Harley 3826: HG 438.
Lists   none.
A-S Vers   none.
Quots/Cits   1. ALCVIN.Orthogr.: see below.
    2. ? BONIF.Gramm.: see below.
Refs   none.

George H. Brown

OLD ENGLISH BEDE   (*Bede*, B9.6).

MSS   1. Cambridge, University Library Kk.3.18: HG 22.
    2. Cambridge, Corpus Christi College 41: HG 39.
    3. London, BL, Cotton Otho B.xi: HG 357.
    4. London, BL, Cotton Domitian ix, fol. 11: HG 330.
    5. Oxford, Bodleian Library, Tanner 10 (*SC* 9830): HG 668.
    6. Oxford, Corpus Christi College 279 part ii: HG 673.
Lists — A-S Vers   none.
Quots/Cits   1. *ÆCHom* II.9 (B1.2.10) 57–58: *Bede* 96.10–11.
    2. *ÆCHom* II.9 (B1.2.10) 77–78: *Bede* 96.31–32.
Refs   *ÆCHom* II.9 (B1.2.10) 7–8.

The Old English *Bede* is a shortened vernacular version of BEDE'S HISTORIA ECCLESIASTICA: the translator edits Bede's work, consistently omitting most epitaphs, poems, letters, and other documents, many geographical details, and much historical information about the Church which does not directly affect England; see Whitelock (GR 5587, pp 61–62). Excerpts were copied into MS Cotton Domitian ix, fol 11 around 900 (NRK 151). The Tanner MS is from the first quarter of the tenth century (NRK 351). Cot-

ton Otho B.xi, which was later badly burned in the fire of 1731, dates from
the mid tenth century (NRK 180); in 1562, Laurence Nowell made a transcription (BL Additional 43703) of the MS. The three other MSS date from
the eleventh century. See Whitelock (GR 5587, pp 80-81) for a stemma
which implies at least three lost MSS.

Whitelock (GR 5587, p 79 note 10) notes the specific quotations of the
Old English translation by ÆLFRIC in his homily on Gregory, and she provides a number of other verbal parallels as well. She asserts that in other
places where Ælfric uses Bede's *Historia* the verbal parallels are not convincing enough to claim that he follows the Old English rather than the
Latin (p 80 note 18).

At the start of this same homily, Ælfric claims King Alfred translated
Bede into the vernacular: "and eac historia anglorum ða ðe Ælfred cyning
of ledene on englisc awende" (see Refs above). Although the dates of the
surviving MSS do not contradict this theory, Miller's (GR 5549 p xxxiii)
assertions about the Mercian dialect — and hence origin — of the work complicate matters considerably. After reassessing the evidence, Whitelock (GR
5587, p 77) concludes that, while there is "no evidence that Alfred took
part in the actual translation of Bede," it "remains a probability" that "the
work was undertaken at Alfred's instigation." In contrast, Kuhn (GR 5591,
pp 172-80) has again argued that Alfred translated the work using "an older
Mercian interlinear gloss" late in his career "when renewed invasions of
England and the task of carrying out his ambitious domestic programs left
the king little leisure for polishing his work" (pp 179-80). The problem
of the dialect is apparently again discussed in Waite (1985), a work not
yet seen.

Emily Cooney

BOETHIUS

Anicius Manlius Severinus Boethius (c. 480-524), member of the Italian
senatorial class and, after his father's death, protégé of Quintus Aurelius
Memmius Symmachus, rose to the rank of consul (510) and reached the
peak of his public career in 522 when his two sons were named consuls
and he himself became "Master of the Offices." While in this latter post,
he became somehow entangled in the political feuding between Theoderic
and Justin, emperor in the East (Boethius gives his own account of this
in the first Book of the CONSOLATIO); in late 523 or early 524 he was ac-

cused of treason by Theoderic, imprisoned at Pavia, and subsequently executed (524/525).

His class and the interests of his patron Symmachus provided him with a milieu suited to his scholarly interests. Adept at Greek, and thoroughly conversant with the then prestigious Neoplatonic schools of Alexandria and Athens, he had absorbed and understood their teaching and educational programs; through an industrious career as translator, commentator and adaptor, he preserved for the Latin West much of the Greek culture and learning of his age, producing works on mathematics, logic and theology and his masterpiece, the *Consolatio philosophiae*. Introductions to his life and works, along with bibliography, can be found in Chadwick (1981) and Gibson (1981).

As is typical in the case of secular texts, evidence that Boethius' works circulated widely begins to appear only in the Carolingian Renaissance. The entire range of Boethius' output had at least some circulation in Anglo-Saxon England; knowledge of the individual works is discussed under four headings: Mathematical, Logical, and Theological Works, and the Consolation of Philosophy. [Only a selection has been included in this *Trial Version.*]

Mathematical Works

De institutione arithmetica [BOETH.Arith.]: *CPL* 879.

MSS 1. Cambridge, Corpus Christi College 352: HG 97.
2. Paris, Bibliothèque Nationale lat. 6401: HG 795.
Lists — Refs none.

De institutione arithmetica, an expanding translation of the Greek work by Nichomachus, became a standard text from the time of ALCUIN and was studied by scholars connected with the Carolingian court especially in northern France but also in Germany, France in general, and the Low countries; see White 1981 pp 164–68; Masi's (1983 pp 58–63) very provisional survey of MSS lists 38 copies dating from the ninth through the tenth centuries. The Irish, however, knew the work and quoted it in their computistical texts from the seventh century; see Jones (1939 p 49), and Walsh and Ó Cróinín (1988 p 122). The oldest St Gall catalog (841–72) lists, among some 30 "libri scottice scripti," an "Arithmetica Boetii, volumen I" (Lehmann 1918 p 71); this copy, which does not survive, is likely to have been an early one, belonging to the pre-Benedictine cell, that is pre–750 (Clark 1926 p 25). The knowledge of this work among the Irish, the apparently early copy at St Gall, and the fact that St Gall was a foundation with close ties to

the Columban communities and on the route between Bangor and Bobbio, all make it especially interesting that the earliest fragment of *De institutione arithmetica* known (Turin Bibl. Naz. F.IV.1, an Italian uncial MS
from the turn of the seventh century, *CLA* 4.450) was at Bobbio. It is thus
possible that the interest of the Irish in computistical questions, sparked
by the Paschal controversies, was instrumental in bringing this work to light
and that it circulated along the routes of the Irish missionaries of the seventh
century.

But there is no direct evidence for Anglo-Saxon knowledge of *De institutione arithmetica* until the two MSS copies listed above (both from the tenth
century). Despite the fact that Bede used Irish sources as a basis for his
own computistical works, he does not use Boethian material; Jones states
categorically that he "definitely did not use Boethius' mathematical works"
(1939 p 49). The Corpus MS suggests that both Celtic and Continental
influences were active when this copy was made and that the work was then
studied seriously. Bishop (1967 pp 259–62) has argued that the Corpus MS
was copied in the mid tenth century, probably at St Augustine's Canterbury, from a Celtic, perhaps a Welsh, exemplar. The MS was laid out for
glosses, some of which were copied from the exemplar, some of which were
added by various later hands, and its text was collated with at least one
and probably several Continental MSS. The Paris MS (from the end of
the tenth century) is a more ornamental book and contains also CONSOLA-
TIO PHILOSOPHIAE and illustrations but few glosses; it was at at St Benoît-
sur-Loire (Fleury) and was perhaps written there by an English scribe
(White 1981 p 174 and note 67).

De institutione musica [BOETH.Mus.]: *CPL* 880.

MSS   1. Avranches, Bibliothèque Municipale 236 (49): HG 784
        2. Cambridge, Corpus Christi College 260: HG 72
Lists — Refs   none.

Like the ARITHMETICA, *De institutione musica* became a standard text beginning with the Carolingian revival and was first studied in the same
milieu: northern France, then France generally, Germany and the Low
Countries (Caldwell 1981 p 143, White 1981 pp 164–68).

Bower's (1988) survey of the extant MSS shows it very well represented
in England in the twelfth century (nine MSS, five before around 1160),
but extant in only two copies before 1100. The Avranches MS (from the end
of the tenth century) was perhaps written by an insular scribe working at
Mont Saint Michel; it also contains excerpts from BEDE on computus (Bower
1988 p 211). The Cambridge MS (tenth century, Christ Church Canterbury) contains excerpts only of the *Musica* (fols 1–2v, 17–19) along with the

COMMEMORATIO BREVIS DE TONIS ET PSALMIS MODULANDIS and the MUSICA ET SCOLIA ENCHIRIADIS (Bower 1988 p 214). Nevertheless Bower's study of the textual tradition of the *Musica* leads him to posit a significant "pre-conquest insular tradition" for this work (p 214).

Geometria: see *CPL* 895; see PS BOETHIUS, ARS GEOMETRIAE ET ARITH-METICAE.

Although CASSIODORUS testifies that Boethius wrote a geometry, the work does not survive in its original form. Rather, portions of a presumably Boethian translation of Books I-V of Euclid's Elements are preserved in four different classes of works: in the third recension of Cassiodorus' IN-STITUTIONES; in a recension of the Roman *Corpus agrimensorum* (gromatic, or land surveying, texts) which adapted it as a mathematical school book; and in two "geometries," now referred to as Geom1 (see PS BOETHIUS, ARS GEOMETRIAE ET ARITHMETICAE) and Geom2, which were widely attributed to Boethius in the MSS. The third recension of Cassiodorus, the adaptation of the Roman gromatic corpus, and Geom1 have been associated with Corbie and date from the late eighth or ninth century. Geom2 is dated 1025–50 and originated in Lorraine. (See Folkerts 1970, 1981 and 1982.) All four of these traditions thus contain some material which is apparently genuine Boethius (the Latin translation of Euclid), combined with material from other sources. It is Geom1 which is preserved in two English MSS of our period.

Consolatio Philosophiae

Consolatio Philosophiae [Cons.Phil.]: *CPL* 878.

MSS   1. Antwerp, Museum Plantin-Moretus M.16.8: HG 776.
2. Cambridge, Corpus Christi College 214: HG 68.
3. Cambridge, Trinity College O.3.7: HG 193.
4. Cambridge, University Library Gg.5.35: HG 12.
5. Cambridge, University Library Kk.3.21: HG 23.
6. El Escorial, Real Biblioteca e.II.1: HG 823.
7. Geneva, Bibliotheca Bodmeriana Cod. 175: HG 829.
8. London, BL Egerton 267: HG 408.
9. Oxford, Bodleian Library Auct. F.1.15 (*SC* 2455): HG 533.
10. Oxford, Corpus Christi College E.74: HG 671.
11. Oxford, Merton College 3.12: HG 678.
12. Paris, Bibliothèque Nationale lat. 6401: HG 886.
13. Paris, Bibliothèque Nationale lat. 6401A: HG 887.

14. Paris, Bibliothèque Nationale lat. 14380: HG 899.
15. Paris, Bibliothèque Nationale lat. 17814: HG 901.
16. Vatican, Vat. lat. 3363: HG 908.
Lists 1. Leofric: ML 10.31 (= MS 9 above).
2. ? Worcester II: ML 11.12.
A-S Vers 1. Bo (B9.3.2).
2. *Met* (A6).
3. *BoGl* (C9.1).
Quots/Cits none: see below.
Refs ? *Deor* (A3.20): see below.

The *Consolatio*, written c. 524, first appears in extant MSS of the ninth century, the earliest copy dating from the first quarter of this century (Orléans Bibliothèque Municipale 270, Fleury). Thereafter it was widely copied and circulated; but although it was obviously known in Anglo-Saxon England by Alfred's time, his prose translation (*Bo*) is the earliest certain evidence for knowledge of the work there. ALCUIN knew it and quoted from it (Wallach 1959 pp 64, and 66; and Courcelle 1967 especially pp 39–46), but only in works written after he had left England for the Continent; his VERSUS DE SANCTIS EUBORICENSIS ECCLESIAE do not quote from or allude to it, and the books written by Boethius mentioned there (line 1548) probably do not include the *Consolatio* (Godmann 1982 p 124; ML 1.8). As Lapidge says, "it has yet to be demonstrated that the *De consolatione Philosophiae* was known in England before the late ninth century" (ML p 47). According to Lapidge, the Worcester list "presumably (but not necessarily)" refers to the *Consolatio*.

One of the earliest MS copies of the *Consolatio* now extant did make its way to Anglo-Saxon England and may have been there by Alfred's time. The Vatican MS, written in the Loire region in the mid ninth century, has Latin glosses added from the end of the ninth or the beginning of the tenth century by several insular hands. The earliest hand is Welsh, Cornish or Southwest English (although it could conceivably have been written on the Continent). Troncarelli (1981 p 204) has suggested that this MS was used by Alfred for his translation and that some of the glosses it contains were written by ASSER; but there is no firm evidence to support this hypothesis (Wittig 1983 p 163 note 20). The MS was almost certainly in southern England by the mid tenth century along with other copies of the *Consolatio*: among several tenth-century glossing hands is one identified as St Dunstan's, and a gloss by this hand indicates that Dunstan was comparing the text of 3363 with that of other copies of the *Consolatio* available to him (Parkes 1981).

Because it is generally agreed that the Old English metrical version of the meters (*Met*), whether by Alfred or not, was based on the Alfredian prose translation rather than on the Latin *Consolatio*, it does not attest to independent knowledge of the Latin text.

The fifteen surviving MSS of the *Consolatio* written in Anglo-Saxon England amply demonstrate knowledge of the text in the later tenth and eleventh centuries: two are from the second half of the tenth century, nine from around the turn of the eleventh century, and four from the eleventh century. Canterbury has been identified as the source of seven of them (at least two from St Augustine's, two from Christ Church), and two were written at Abingdon. Failure to identify the MS of the *Consolatio* used by Alfred, together with the chance survival of two MS copies in very fragmentary form (BL Egerton and Oxford Merton) and the migration of other MSS from England (Antwerp, El Escorial, Paris), indicate the likelihood that other copies of the *Consolatio* owned or made in Anglo-Saxon England have not survived.

As Glauche (1970) has shown, the *Consolatio* became a "school text," and the surviving English copies argue that this must have been the case in Anglo-Saxon England as well. With one exception (Paris 6401), they all contain at least part of the (Latin) Remigian commentary, some with distinctively English revisions indicating an active process of grappling with the text (see D. Bolton 1978 and see REMIGIUS OF AUXERRE), a process further illustrated by Corpus Christi College, Cambridge 214 which has, in addition to Remigian glosses, interlinear lexical glosses in late West Saxon (*BoGl*).

Markland and W.F. Bolton (GR 3469,5439) have argued that the *Consolatio* 2 (especially Prose 3.34–45) underlies *Deor*. The date of the poem is problematical and the similarities are those of thought rather than obvious verbal echoes; consequently these similarities may have arisen through familiarity with the ideas expressed in the *Consolatio* (e.g. via the prose *Boethius*) rather than from knowledge of the Latin itself.

Joseph S. Wittig

PS BOETHIUS

Ars geometriae et arithmeticae [ANON.Geom.1/PS.BOETH]: *CPL* 895; see also BOETHIUS, GEOMETRIA.

MSS   1. Cambridge, Trinity College R.15.3 (939): HG 185.

2. Oxford, Bodleian Library Douce 125 (*SC* 21699): HG 615.
Lists—Refs   none.

The *Ars geometriae et arithmeticae* (Geom1), a treatise in five books, is generally attributed to BOETHIUS in the MSS. As preserved in the 26 extant copies (see Folkerts 1982 pp 95–102), it is an unskillful and sometimes uncomprehending compilation which draws on the gromatic corpus adapted for school use and on the Latin translation of Euclid's Elements, combining these with extracts from Boethius' ARITHMETICA, ISIDORE'S ETYMOLOGIAE, CASSIODORUS' INSTITUTIONES, and the Roman Columella (Folkerts 1981 p 190, and 1982 p 87). It served as a geometry textbook for studying this aspect of the quadrivium.

There is no modern edition of the whole treatise. Migne (*PL* 63.1352D–1364) printed the first two books of Geom1 immediately after Geom2, apparently from the Basel edition of 1546 or 1570, without clear indication that a new work was beginning. *CPL* 895 refers the reader to Bubnov (1899), whose outline of all five books allows one to reconstruct the entire work by page references to Migne and the gromatic and Euclidian texts as printed by Lachmann (1848). Folkerts (1982 pp 88–90) provides a similar outline and reconstruction which also relies on Lachmann for the gromatic texts, but which refers the reader to his own critical editions of the Euclidian translation (Folkerts 1970 pp 173–217) and the "altercatio duorum geometricorum" (Folkerts 1982 pp 103–13).

In the Trinity College copy (tenth century, St Augustine's Canterbury), Geom1 (fols 3–43v) is followed by extracts of other gromatic-geometric material, including excepts from Isidore and Cassiodorus; the Douce MS (eleventh century, Old Minster Winchester) contains just Geom1. Moreover as Folkerts reconstructs the transmission of Geom1 (1982 p 102), the two copies belong to two separate branches of the textual tradition and so were made quite independently of one another.

Joseph S. Wittig

CYPRIANUS GALLUS

Virtually nothing is known about the composer of the most expansive versification of the Old Testament from Late Antiquity. Scholars judging from internal evidence generally maintain that the poet was from Gaul and wrote during the first quarter of the fifth century, but even these details have been disputed. This uncertainty notwithstanding, numerous quotations by early English writers are extant.

Heptateuchos [CYPR.GALL.Hept.]: *CPL* 1423.

MSS Cambridge, Trinity College B.1.42 (40): HG 159.
Lists—A-S Vers none.
Quots/Cits 1. ALDH.Metr. 92.12: CYPR.GALL.Hept. Iudicum 18.
  2. ALDH.Ped.reg. 158.3-5; 189.32: CYPR.GALL.Hept. Iudicum 679-81; Numeri 503.
  3. BEDA.Art.Metr. I.17.8-22: CYPR.GALL.Hept. Exodus 507-21.
  4. Alcuin.Epist. 260.36-40: CYPR.GALL.Hept. Exodus 129-30.
Refs none.

The attribution of the *Heptateuchos* to a Cyprianus does not appear to have been made before the end of the ninth century. ALDHELM and BEDE, for example, cite the work but do not make the attribution. Aldhelm refers to the poet once but only as *ille versificus* (*MGH* AA 15.157). The library catalog of St Riquier, dating from the early ninth century, retains this anonymity. The poem is connected with the name Cyprianus, however, in the catalog of the library at Lorsch dating from the ninth century and in later MSS, including the eleventh-century MS of Canterbury. Herzog (1975 pp 53-60) therefore believes that the name was added in order to give the work greater respectability through association with St Cyprian.

In his metrical VITA CUTHBERTI, BEDE echoes this work in the following lines: 152 (Genesis 308); 189 (Genesis 522); 236 (Genesis 286); 516 (Iudicum 469); and 828 (Deuteronomium 54). He also draws on it in lines 62, 439, 545, 662, 729, 736, and 921. Æthelwulf also echoes this work in his *De abbatibus*: 147 (Genesis 327); 280-81 (Genesis 189-90); 413-14 (Exodus 1312-13); 418 (Exodus 1309); 419-20 (Exodus 1317-18); and 646-47 (Exodus 1082-83); see Traube (1888 pp 17-24). Strecker, the editor of the anonymous *Miracula Nynie episcopi*, cites Exodus (827 and 881) for the usage "clepantes" (*MGH* PLAC 4.210).

M. Roberts (1985 pp 94-95) presents a useful summary of the textual history of the *Heptateuchos* in Medieval England as well as on the Continent.

Deperditorum carminum reliquiae [CYPR.GALL.Carm.rel.]: *CPL* 1424.

MSS—A-S Vers none.
Quots/Cits ALDH.Metr.80.12: see below.
Refs none.

The so-named HEPTATEUCHOS originally treated all the historical

books of the Old Testament. The library catalog of Lorsch, dating from
the tenth century, lists the poem of Cyprian on the Heptateuch as well as
on Kings, Esther, Judith, and Machabees. The twelfth-century Cluny catalog attributes the *Heptateuchos* to Alchimus and also lists versifications of
Kings, Paralipomenon, Esther, Judith, and Machabees.

ALDHELM provides the sole quotation from Regum IIII; and the *CSEL*
edition of Cyprian also refers to DE METRIS (64.1) for a line from Iob (211.2).

Daniel Nodes

BLOSSIUS AEMELIUS DRACONTIUS: *DS* 3.1706–11; see also ALCUIN, FLORILEGIUM; ANTHOLOGIA LATINA; and EUGENIUS OF TOLEDO, HEX- AEMERON.

Dracontius was a North African poet of the late fifth century. He received
a literary education, then studied and practiced law in Carthage. One of
his poems from this early period, addressed to a foreign ruler, brought upon
him the disfavor of Gunthamund, king of the Vandals in North Africa
(484–96). His release came with the help of friends but not before he was
interned long enough to write his two Christian poems, the SATISFACTIO
and the LAUDES DEI.

These works were well known to English writers. Additionally, in the
seventh century a 635-line portion of the first book of the *Laudes Dei* was
detached from the work and published separately by EUGENIUS OF TOLEDO
in a version showing numerous alterations of the original. In the Middle
Ages, this recension became more popular than the original on which it
was based and was widely used in the European schools.

Columban, the sixth-century Irish abbot and missionary, also knew
Dracontius and quotes amply from his works; see Moussy and Camus (1985
pp 102–03).

Satisfactio [DRACONT.Satisfact.]: *CPL* 1511.

MSS—A-S Vers   none.
Quots/Cits ANON.Mir.Nin. 131: DRACONT.Satisfact. 53.
Refs   none.

Dracontius wrote the *Satisfactio ad Gunthamundum* as a reparation for the offense he committed against the Vandal king. In the work the poet explains that what caused the offense was Dracontius' celebration of a foreign lord in another poem.

In addition to the quotation of a full line in the anonymous *Miracula S. Nyniae*, ALDHELM echoes two lines of this work (5 and 9) in his CARMEN DE VIRGINITATE (2874–75). Camus (Moussy and Camus 1985 pp 103–04 note 3) notes that line 5 of the *Satistactio* imitated by Aldhelm is omitted in Eugenius' recension of that work. The *CCSL* edition of HWÆTBERHT also provides a cross-reference to the *Satisfactio* (5) for AENIGMATA 4.4 (p 214).

Laudes Dei [DRACONT.Laud.Dei]: *CPL* 1509.

MSS — Refs   none.

The *Laudes Dei* is a didactic poem in three books totalling over 2,200 hexameters. It treats of God's goodness and merciful forbearance, drawing examples from the Creation, the Incarnation, and God's dealings with the human race.

ALDHELM and BEDE appear to have imitated the *Laudes Dei* frequently. Vollmer's edition (*MGH* AA 14) connects Aldhelm's CARMEN ECCLESIASTICA IV.vi.7 with *Laudes Dei* II.554. The *CCSL* edition (vol 133) of Aldhelm's ENIGMATA lists echoes of *Laudes Dei* III.200, and III.137 in ENIGMATA XXXIX.1, and XCI.1

Among Bede's works the metrical VITA CUTHBERTI (201, 246, 389, 582, and 874) contains echoes of the *Laudes Dei* (II.326, I.516, III.631, I.650, and II.652). DE NATURA RERUM (20.4) echoes *Laudes Dei* II.232. Also, according to Vollmer (p 9 note 14), in Bede's HYMN 14 (*De die iudicii*) verses 49, 115, 133, and 134 echo *Laudes Dei* II.559, I.14, I.7, and I.16. Romano (1959 p 92 notes 243–44) endorses these identifications.

Evans (1968 p 140) cites the listing of *Laudes Dei* in a catalog of the monastic library at Reichenau as evidence of the accessibility of this work to the Continental author of the Old Saxon original of *Genesis B* (*GenB*, A1.1).

Vollmer also connects *Laudes Dei* III.1 with ALCUIN, CARMINA CXXI.1, and *Laudes Dei* III.20 with a letter from Coena (Ethelbert) archbishop of York to Lul (*MGH* ES 1.262 line 5; see *EHD* 188). Alcuin composed a florilegium, preserved in Bamberg, Staatsbibliothek, Misc. Patr. 17 (B.II.10), which presents excerpts from books 2 and 3 of *Laudes Dei*. Glauche (1970 p 11) notes the importance of Alcuin's anthology for our knowledge of the use of Dracontius' poems in medieval schools.

Romulea [DRACONT.Romul.]: *CPL* 1513.

MSS — Refs   none.

The *Romulea* in Vollmer's *MGH* edition (AA 14) is a collection of ten separate poems on mythological themes. The collective name is derived from a reference to fragments of these poems contained in the Florilegium Veronense (Biblioteca Capitolare CLXVIII [155]). The ten poems are extant together only in this one MS; it is not generally held that Dracontius himself considered the poems as a unit.

BEDE's metrical VITA CUTHBERTI (57) echoes *Romulea* VIII.401. The *CCSL* edition of ALDHELM's ENIGMATA cites echoes of *Romulea* VII.154 in four places: XVI.2-3, XXVI.2, XLII.3, and XLVIII.6

Orestis tragoedia [DRACONT.Orest.Trag.]: *CPL* 1514.

MSS — Refs none.

The *Orestis tragoedia* is a series of short epic pieces, totalling 974 hexameters, on the theme of Orestes' revenge against Clytemnestra for the murder of Agamemnon.

BEDE's metrical VITA CUTHBERTI (302, and 584) echoes *Orestis tragoedia* (639, and 158).

Daniel Nodes

GRAMMARIANS

[This generic entry provides a general introduction to grammatical writings in Anglo-Saxon England, and in the final version will include entries on anonymous grammatical works. In this *Trial Version*, only the entries under ALCUIN and PRISCIAN have been included S.N.]

The evidence for the use of Latin grammars in Anglo-Saxon England falls into two distinct periods: an earlier one, coinciding with the first flowering of Anglo-Latin literature around 700, and a later one which commences with the Benedictine reform movement and covers the latter part of the tenth and the eleventh centuries. In the earlier period our chief source of information is the writings of Anglo-Latin teachers — ALDHELM, TATWINE, BONIFACE, and BEDE. In the later period the evidence is more varied, including manuscripts and booklists as well as grammars by Anglo-Saxon authors. For the intervening period, extending from the second third of the eighth century to the opening of the tenth, source material is scarce. ALCUIN's writings are an uncertain guide, for they may well have been compiled on the Continent (as his DIALOGUS FRANCONIS ET SAXONIS DE OCTO PARTIBUS ORATIONIS almost certainly was), and are more likely to reflect

the resources of Frankish rather than those of Anglo-Saxon libraries. (ABBO
OF FLEURY'S QUAESTIONES GRAMMATICALES raise similar difficulties, for Abbo
spent only two years at Ramsey, and his replies to the questions put him
by the monks are likely to depend upon knowledge he acquired at home.
Or are we to imagine that he walked into the library at Ramsey and looked
up answers to the questions in books the monks could have consulted for
themselves?) It is to be hoped that work on the *fontes* of Anglo-Latin works
from this period on subjects other than grammar will help to fill in this gap.

The following discussion surveys the distribution of works dealing with
grammar narrowly defined, i.e. with the eight parts of speech. It does not
take into account texts on metrics, orthography, or rhetoric.

The introduction of Christianity brought with it the need to learn Latin, the language of the Church. Although the grammars written under the
later Roman Empire were themselves diverse and varied, they provided
nothing directly designed to help beginners master Latin morphology, a
lacuna which medieval teachers filled in many ways. Only a few grammars
were widely available in Anglo-Saxon England during the earlier period:
DONATUS' ARS MINOR and ARS MAIOR, PRISCIAN'S INSTITUTIO DE NOMINE, and
the first book of ISIDORE'S ETYMOLOGIAE. Various combinations of works
by the following authors could be found at individual centers: ASPER/
ASPORIOS, AUDAX, CHARISIUS, CONSENTIUS, DIOMEDES, EUTYCHES, MARTIANUS
CAPELLA (Book III), PHOCAS, POMPEIUS, PRISCIAN'S INSTITUTIONES GRAMMAT-
ICAE and PARTITIONES, SERGIUS (PS CASSIODORUS), SERGIUS (DE LITTERA), VIC-
TORINUS, VIRGILIUS MARO GRAMMATICUS, the ANONYMUS BOBIENSIS, and a lost
grammar ascribed to JEROME. To provide a more straightforward introduction to Latin declension and conjugation, Anglo-Saxon teachers made use
of compilations of noun and verb paradigms accompanied by copious lists
of examples (*Declinationes nominum*) and composed their own introductory
grammars (Tatwine, Boniface). Taken to the Continent during the eighth
century, these works and most of the ancient grammars studied by the
Anglo-Saxons enjoyed a brief vogue until a few decades into the ninth century. The Carolingian renaissance brought with it a change in grammatical and pedagogical fashion. Of the ancient texts, those which were based
on material similar to Donatus' grammars, the so-called *Schulgrammatik*
genre — Audax, Charisius, Consentius, Diomedes, Victorinus, *Anonymus
Bobiensis* — dropped out of favor, as did the commentaries by Pompeius and
Sergius (Ps Cassiodorus), along with early medieval attempts at providing
instructional material better suited to beginners (Asper/Asporius, *Declinationes nominum*, the elementary grammars). Grammars of *regulae* type (that
is, works which set out rules for the identification of particular grammatical forms) like those by Phocas and Eutyches, pseudo-Palaemon and pseudo-
Augustine, retained or increased their popularity. But the biggest change

was the dissemination of several works by Priscian which had not previously been widely available, notably the *Institutiones grammaticae* and the *Partitiones*. Much pedagogical activity from the ninth century on was devoted to the problem of making the doctrine of the *Institutiones* accessible, whether by explicit comparision between it and Donatus, or by incorporating material from it into commentaries on Donatus, or by preparing abridged versions. At a lower level a new genre, the parsing grammar, permitted the teacher greater flexibility, whilst the commentaries by SMARAGDUS, the *Scotti peregrini*, and REMIGIUS OF AUXERRE elucidated the text of currently fashionable grammarians—Donatus, Eutyches, Priscian. The evidence from tenth- and eleventh-century England corresponds closely to the Continental pattern, implying that English grammatical instruction was heavily influenced by imports from the Continent in the wake of the Benedictine reform movement. Parsing grammars and abridgements of Priscian's *Institutiones grammaticae* (as well as the real thing) are well attested, along with works by Donatus, Eutyches, and Remigius. ÆLFRIC's grammar breaks with the Carolingian tradition, substituting a textbook in the vernacular for the Latin-medium intermediate grammars in circulation previously.

The reader should note the following outstanding problems and warnings:

(a) Several texts preserved in English MSS (*Anonymus ad Cuimnanum* [edition in preparation by B. Bischoff], *Anima quae pars*, *Iustus quae pars*) or mentioned in an English booklist (*Terra quae pars*) have not yet been definitively localized, nor have their sources been studied. Data from them is not included in these entries. Note also that only a little information from Alcuin's grammars and *Beatus quid est* has been included at this stage, and none at all from the *Quaestiones grammaticales* of Abbo of Fleury.

(b) Given that every Anglo-Latin writer had by definition a training in Latin grammar, it is very likely that grammarians are mentioned or quoted in texts on subjects other than grammar. I have not attempted to locate such passages, but would be glad to receive notification of them, and/or to help in their identification. Evidence of this kind is needed most urgently for the period between roughly 750 and 950, for which direct sources are few.

(c) As stated above, I have tried to cover only those ancient works which deal with the parts of speech. In the case of most authors this is unproblematical; with Bede, however, difficulties have arisen. He used a large number of sources, including not only the ancient *grammatici*, but also *metrici*, *orthographici*, *rhetorici*, and glossaries. Without checking all these possible sources one cannot always ascertain whether a grammarian rather than a writer on rhetoric, say, was the source for a particular passage. Consequently, my policy has for practical reasons been as follows: in the *De orthographia* I have checked all the passages attributed to the grammarians (and checked them against other possible sources, except for glossaries); thus, where BEDA.Orthogr. is included under Quots/Cits in the entry for a particular grammarian, this means that that grammarian was in my opinion known to Bede. Where reference to BEDA.Orthogr. is lacking, this means that (again in my judgment) that grammarian was not used by Bede. (Thus, the absence of this entry under Priscian's *Institutiones grammaticae* is not accidental.) I have not, however, attempted to draw up entries for sources used by Bede other than the *grammatici* narrowly defined. In the case of *De schematibus et tropis*, except for a few obvious cases it seemed best to leave this text to a specialist in metrics.

For further discussion, see Holtz (1981), Law (1982), Law (1983), Law (1985), Law (1986), and Law (1987).

V. Law

HIBERNO-LATIN AND IRISH-INFLUENCED BIBLICAL COMMENTARIES, FLORILEGIA, AND HOMILY COLLECTIONS

Under this heading are grouped three kinds of texts. The first group includes the mostly anonymous or pseudonymous biblical commentaries identified by Bischoff (1976) as Irish or Irish-influenced. Certain major Hiberno-Latin exegetes, notably JOHN SCOTTUS ERIUGENA and SEDULIUS SCOTTUS, are not included here but will be found as separate entries under each author's name. Several commentaries not in Bischoff's list are included: one (number 13) was too late for Bischoff's ninth-century limit; and several others (numbers 2, *3, *5, *14, 15, *27, *28, *33, *37) have been identified by other scholars as possibly Irish in origin. Two items which are mostly in Irish (numbers 12 and 23) are included for reasons explained in each entry.

The second group includes a number of anonymous catechetical dialogues and florilegia of biblical and moral extracts that have been identified by Bischoff and other scholars as Hiberno-Latin or Irish-influenced. Penitential and canonical collections, such as the POENITENTIALE CUMMEANI, the COLLECTIO CANONUM HIBERNENSIS, and the LIBER EX LEGE MOYSI, are not included here. Nor are such unified ethical or theological treatises such as PS CYPRIAN, DE DUODECIM ABUSIVIS SAECULI, PS ISIDORE, DE ORDINE CREATURARUM, or AUGUSTINUS HIBERNICUS, DE MIRABILIBUS SACRAE SCRIP-TURAE. The COLLECTANEA BEDAE, considered Irish by many scholars, will be found under PS BEDE. For the COLLECTANEUM of SEDULIUS SCOTTUS, see under that author's name.

The third group includes five Latin homily collections or catecheses whose contents are partially or largely if not wholly Hiberno-Latin, one homily collection (number *49) in a Continental Anglo-Saxon MS with contacts with other Irish collections, and one Irish vernacular homiliary (number 50) that contains extensive passages in Latin and some Latin items. The so-called APOCRYPHA PRISCILLIANISTICA, a collection of homiletic and exegetical pieces considered Irish by many scholars, will be found under APOCRYPHA.

The reader should be aware that Bischoff's method of identification of anonymous works as Irish or Irish-influenced by way of Irish "symptoms" has been criticized by Coccia (1967 pp 328–49) and Stancliffe (1975). Stancliffe's article, however, makes only limited objections to certain of Bischoff's arguments, and his conclusions have on the whole been corroborated by subsequent research. Stancliffe herself agrees that "we can allow the main picture to stand" (p 366), and in a later article (1982) she accepts without argument the Irish character of several of the commentaries in Bischoff's catalog. For a balanced statement of the problem, see Herren (1981 pp 8–10). However, the difficulty of distinguishing between "Irish" and "Irish-influenced" commentaries remains, and Bischoff is not always explicit on this point for individual items in his catalog. In Stancliffe's words, "there is a hard core of commentaries which are definitely Irish, but outside this we have a gradual shading off through probabilities to possibilities; through compilations in which an Irishman had a hand to ones in which some Irish influence is discernible" (1975 p 366). It must also be remembered that "Hiberno-Latin" does not necessarily mean "written in Ireland," since many of these works are believed to have been written by Irish peregrini on the Continent. The BCLL accordingly distributes these commentaries among three different sections: Ireland; Celtic Peregrini on the Continent; and Authors and Works of Possible or Arguable Celtic Origin (two items, numbers *4 and *44, are included in the section for Brittany). In the following list, works included in the third category (as well as doubtful works not in Bischoff or the BCLL) are marked by an asterisk; in these cases I also record the opinion of Frede (KVS, including the 1984 and 1988 supplements) when he offers one. Titles of individual works generally follow the BCLL, but with modifications to conform to the style of the present volume, and to accommodate the system of abbreviations suggested by Lapidge (1988 pp 51–52). The reader is referred to the BCLL for additional bibliography for each item.

Many of these Hiberno-Latin texts are still unedited, but several commentaries have appeared in *CCSL* 108B and 108C (for detailed reviews of these volumes see Bieler 1978a pp 86–91 and 1987b pp 264–67 and Duke et al. 1977). A project is currently underway to edit the remaining commentaries for the *CCSL*. For a description of this project, see the *Hiberno-Latin Newsletter* 1 (1986/87 pp 3–4) and 2 (1987 p 2); some editions in progress have been listed in volumes 1 (1986/87 pp 10–12) and 2 (1987 pp 16–18). Excerpts from several Hiberno-Latin gospel commentaries are printed in W. Huber (1969 see pp 90–95). A full catalog of Irish exegetical texts by Joseph F. Kelly is scheduled to appear in a forthcoming volume of *Traditio*. Surveys of the field include McNally (1969), McNamara (1972, 1973b, 1984, and 1989) and Kelly (1981b and 1982b).

Few of these works survive in MSS written or owned in England, and few have been proven to be direct sources for Anglo-Saxon texts, but many have been cited for parallels or analogues for specific themes and ideas which were especially popular with, if not unique to, both Irish and Anglo-Saxon authors. The evidence for the Irish contribution to Anglo-Saxon literary culture is thus not limited to specific Hiberno-Latin works which were direct sources for an Anglo-Saxon text, but includes themes and ideas which can be identified as characteristically Irish (or better, "Insular") in formulation or dissemination if not in origin. However, as Biggs has pointed out, "work in this area remains somewhat problematic both because much of the evidence is not readily available and because what is available has not always been adequately compared with the larger Christian Latin tradition" (1986 p 4). Since there is no comprehensive survey of the subject, in order to consolidate recent work, and to facilitate future study, I have included not only those Hiberno-Latin commentaries, florilegia, and homily collections that were clearly known to the Anglo-Saxons by evidence of the categories of the headnote, but also those that have been cited by scholars for parallels of themes and ideas which may have been disseminated to the Anglo-Saxons through Irish compilations. In such cases I have made no entry in the headnote for Quots/Cits, but mention in body of the entry the themes and ideas for which the work has been cited in connection with an Anglo-Saxon text. (I have generally omitted references when the work is cited merely as a representative example of a widespread patristic theme.) Although the HOMILIARY OF ST PÈRE DE CHARTRES or "Pembroke Homiliary" (see HOMILIARIES) is probably of Continental origin, it has definable Insular connections, and was an important source for Anglo-Saxon homilists, so I have included references to motifs in this work. I also include three recently-discovered texts (numbers *28, *43, and *48) so far cited only in connection with this homiliary. The reader is therefore cautioned not to assume that a Hiberno-Latin text in the following list was known in Anglo-

1982; see pp 58 and 61, note 13). On this theme, which occurs also in the LIBER DE NUMERIS (number 39), see Willard (GR 6235, pp 1–30), Stevenson (1982), and the APOCRYPHA PRISCILLIANISTICA (under APOCRYPHA). Reynolds (1983 p 126 and note 172) notes that an Anglo-Saxon MS, London, BL Royal 8.C.iii [HG 475], fol 62v, has a Latin dialogue on the seven heavens beginning "De septem spatiis celorum Virgilius dixit. . . ." This may be an extract from a version of the Reference Bible, which introduces the list of seven heavens with the words "non sunt septem celi ut alii dicunt sed septem spacia celorum. Virgilius dicit . . ." (Paris, Bibliothèque Nationale lat. 11561, fol 8v col 2).

2. The age of Adam, in the prose *Solomon and Saturn* (*Sol I*, B5.1), *Notes* 10.2 (B24.10.2), and *HeptNotes* (B8.1.4.7); see also Cross and Hill (1982 pp 70–72).

3. Eve's creation from Adam's left side, in *Adrian and Ritheus* (*Ad*; B5.2); *HomS* 34 (*VercHom* 19, B3.2.34); see Bazire and Cross (1982 p 8), Cross and Hill (1982 pp 129–30) and Cross (1987a p 99).

4. The Tree of Knowledge as a fig tree, in *Sol I* (B5.1) and *HomS* 34 (*VercHom* 19, B3.2.34; see Bazire and Cross 1982 p 8; this information is omitted in the VERCELLI BOOK text of the sermon, but is included in the other three witnesses); see also Cross and Hill (1982 pp 127–29). The idea occurs also in the Hiberno-Latin PS ISIDORE, LIBER DE ORDINE CREATURARUM.

5. The speaking ox in Rome, in the Old English *Martyrology* (*Mart*; B19.a); see also Cross (GR 6368, pp 248–54) and Cross (1987a p 21).

Some of this information, as Cross noted (1986a p 79; see also Bazire and Cross 1982 p 8), occurs also in the ST GALL COMMENTARY ON THE CREATION AND FALL, number *8. For further discussion of several of these themes see C. Wright (1987a pp 128–29). Cross concludes that "the common factor" for these ideas "is *The Irish Reference Bible*, which now becomes important to Anglo-Saxonists" (p 80). Cross also cites the Reference Bible as a possible source of dissemination for the conception of the descent of monsters from Cain in *Beowulf* (*Beo*, A4.1; see Cross 1986a pp 82–83, with an edition of the relevant section of the commentary in an Appendix, pp 92–100).

Cross elsewhere (1987b p 65, and 1987a p 69; see also Cross 1985b p 110) cites the Reference Bible (number 1C) as one of several (but not the closest) Irish analogs for the number of the Innocents in item 11 of the HOMILIARY OF ST PÈRE DE CHARTRES; the number of the Innocents is specified also in numbers *20, 21, 24, *48 and 50.

O'Neill (1981 pp 29–30) cites the comment on Ps 1 from the Reference Bible, together with other Irish works on the Psalter (see numbers *10, 12, and *14) to show that the author of the Old English Introductions to the prose translations of Psalms 2–50 in the *Paris Psalter* (B8.2.1) "derived the basic fourfold structure of his Introductions, with their second historical interpretation, from an Irish plan for psalm commentaries. . . ."

Biggs (1986 p 6 and forthcoming in *Traditio*) cites the Reference Bible as one of several Irish analogs (including numbers 18, 21, 24, 25, 42, *44, and 45) for the motif of Judgment occuring at midnight in *ChristC* (A3.1). Biggs (*Traditio*) also cites the Reference Bible for the motif of Mt. Sion as the place of the congregation of the saints and of Judgment (cf. number 18).

C. Wright (1987a pp 129-30; cf. C. Wright 1984 pp 159-61) cites the Reference Bible and other Hiberno-Latin commentaries (numbers *6, *7, and *8) for analogs of a geographical conception concerning the ratio of dry land to water (based on IV Esr 6.42) in the "Theban Anchorite" legend in *HomS* 4 (*VercHom* 9, B.3.2.4), *HomU* 15 (Robinson, B3.4.15) and *HomU* 27 (Nap 30, B3.4.27).

C. Wright (forthcoming in *Cambridge Medieval Celtic Studies*) also cites a parallel from the Reference Bible for the enumeration of three characteristics of the Caesarian tax in *HomS* 1 (*VercHom* 5, B3.2.1); cf. *46.

2. Questiones sancti Hysidori tam de nouo quam de uetere testamento [ANON.Quaest.nou.uet.test./PS.ISID.]: *RBMA* 5232; *CPL* 1194; *ISLMAH* 134; *BCLL* 779; *KVS* IS test.

MSS   none.
Lists   ? Leofric: ML 10.46.
A-S Vers — Refs   none.

Lapidge remarks that the entry in the Exeter booklist, "Liber Isidori De nouo et uetere testamento," may refer either to ISIDORE'S PROOEMIA to the books of the Old and New Testaments, or to this text.

Cross and Hill (1982) cite the work for a parallel for a question on the number of canonical books in the prose *Solomon and Saturn* (*Sol I*, B5.1, see p 123), and for a question asking "who first prophesied" in *Adrian and Ritheus* (*Ad*, B5.2; see p 140).

*3 Inuentiones nominum [ANON.Inuent.nom.]: *CPL* 1155d and Addenda; *KVS* AN inv.

MSS   ? St Gall, Stiftsbibliothek 913: see below.
Lists — Refs   none.

The purpose of this work is "to collect, for the convenience of students of the Bible, instances of persons mentioned in various parts of the Scriptures, who bore the same name, and to discriminate between them" (James, Bibliography Part I p 218; an earlier edition by Amelli 1897a pp 9-16 is reprinted in *PLS* 4.907-15). Of the four surviving MSS, St Gall 913, the so-called *Vocabularius Sancti Galli*, containing a fragment of the work, is an Anglo-Saxon missionary MS from the second half of the eighth century, and "by a scribe trained in the Anglo-Saxon tradition," (*CLA* 7.976; cf. Baesecke 1933). James (pp 239–40) noted that at two points the text agrees with the Spanish text of IV Esr, as well as a prologue to IV Esr in a Leon MS, in making the author of that work the son of Chusi. Dumville (1973 p 317), who discusses the work in connection with Irish transmission of apocrypha, concurs with James' conclusion that it is not possible to determine the date or origin of the work, but Dumville points out that three of these MSS "contain works with Insular connections," and states that "one is bound to point to the evidence indicating Spanish and Insular influences." In another of the MSS (St Gall, Stiftsbibliothek 133, *CLA* 7.911) the work is followed by a pair of Hiberno-Latin texts, *Virtutes Heliae* and *Virtutes Helisei* (*CPL* 1155e and Addenda; *KVS* AN Hel I-II), which are also incorporated in the REFERENCE BIBLE (number 1).

The Albi BM 29 MS of *Inuentiones nominum* (*CLA* 6.705) contains additional notes on the identity of persons in the Bible, assigning names to some of the nameless. James (p 243) points out that the names given to the two thieves are similar to those in *Notes* 12.1 (Nap, B24.12.1) and PS BEDE, COLLECTANEA; on these names see further C. Wright (1987a p 139 note 85). Names are also given to the wives of Noah and his sons, but these do not agree with the names in *Solomon and Saturn* (*Sol I*, B5.1) or in *HeptNotes* (B8.1.4.7); cf. LIBER DE NUMERIS, number 39.

*4. Dies dominica [ANON.Dies.dom.(Rec.I-III)]: Bischoff (1976 number 39); *RBMA* 9.10060,1 (Recension I), 9419 and 9.11560,1 (Rec. II), and 9.11562,1 (Rec. III); *BCLL* 903–05; cf. *CPL* Addenda 1155e.

MSS   ? Vatican, Pal. lat. 220; see below.
Lists — Refs   none.

McNally (Bibliography Part I pp 177–79) distinguishes three recensions of this text, which lists biblical and apocryphal events that occurred on a Sunday. McNamara (1975 p 63, number 52C) follows McNally in designating them Hiberno-Latin; the *BCLL* assigns them to Brittany, since the MSS of two of the three recensions come from there. The Vatican MS (first half of the ninth century, Rhineland), written in Anglo-Saxon script, contains Recension II (as well as the longer version of APOCALYPSE OF THOMAS and a unique redaction of VISIO SANCTI PAULI; cf. C. Wright 1987b p 453 note 15). Other copies of Recension II, unknown to McNally, occur in Karlsruhe, Aug. CCLV, fol 8 (ninth century; for the incipit and explicit, see *RBMA* 9419 [not cross-referenced at *RBMA* 9.11560,1]) and St Gall, Stiftsbibliothek 682, pp 330–34.

Lees (1985a pp 146–50) discusses the *Dies dominica* as examples of the "Sunday Lists" or "Benedictions of Sunday" (*Dignatio diei dominici*), including examples in Irish vernacular texts and Old English "Sunday Letter" homilies (for details see SUNDAY LETTER, under APOCRYPHA). See also Lees (1986 pp 130-33), Whitelock (1982 p 59), and Tveitane (GR 6242, p 127).

Biblical Commentaries — Old Testament

*5. Ps Bede, In Pentateuchum commentarii, expositio in primum librum Mosis [ANON.Pent.comm.exp.Gen./PS.BEDA]: *RBMA* 9.1647.

MSS—Refs   none.

The commentary on Genesis has been very tentatively considered Irish by McNally (1969 p 15, 1970 pp 676-77, and 1973 p 199 note) and Ó Cróinín (1976 p 353). A remark by Laistner (1957 p 188 note 16) that "its author sometimes copies Hrabanus" is termed "misleading" by Gorman (1982 p 178 note 27). Cross (1987a p 76) suggests independently that the commentary "certainly includes ideas found elsewhere in anonymous texts with definable insular influences" (cf. also Cross 1987b p 62 note 26). For a further Irish symptom in the commentary, see C. Wright (1987a pp 142-43, note 94).

MacLean (GR 5217) cites a number of general parallels from the Genesis commentary for ALCUIN'S IN GENESIM, but see O'Keeffe (1978/79 p 464 note 2).

Doane (1978) cites the Genesis commentary at several points in his notes on *Genesis A* (*GenA*, A1.1), mostly illustrating commonplace interpretations, but also (p 244) for the Jewish legend that the serpent was created with feet, which may be reflected in *GenA* 908a.

Cross (1987a pp 76-77) cites several parallels from the commentary for passages in the HOMILIARY OF ST PÈRE DE CHARTRES item 30.

*6. Munich Commentary on Genesis (1–34) (Bayerische Staatsbibliothek clm 6302) [ANON.Comm.Gen.(Mun.6302)]: Bischoff (1976 number 2); *BCLL* 1258.

MSS-Refs   none.

On this commentary's use of AUGUSTINE, DE GENESI AD LITTERAM, see Kelly (1977 p 147 note 39). An edition is in preparation by Michael Gorman.

The commentary has been cited by C. Wright (1984 p 158; cf. C. Wright 1987a pp 129-30) for an analog for a geographical conception concerning the ratio of dry land to water (for details, see number 1).

*7. Commemoratio Geneseos [ANON.Comm.Gen.(BN.10457+10616)]:
Bischoff (1976 number 3); *RBMA* 10404; *BCLL* 1259.

MSS — Refs   none.

On this commentary Bischoff remarks: "Perhaps of continental origin,
it was certainly formed under Irish influence" (p 104; cf. Bischoff 1961, rpt
1966-81, p 185 and note 94; cf. also Cross 1987a pp 11 and 77). A commentary with the same title and incipit was in Chartres, Bibliothèque
Municipale 63 (125), fols 50-67 (destroyed in 1944). An edition is in preparation by Thomas O'Loughlin. For another possibly Hiberno-Latin text
in the second part of the two-part MSS (Paris, Bibliothèque Nationale lat.
10457 + lat. 10616), see the INTERROGATIO DE SINGULAS QUAESTIONES, number *43.

The commentary has been cited by C. Wright (1984 pp 159-60; cf. C.
Wright 1987a pp 129-30) for an analog for a geographical conception concerning the ratio of dry land to water (for details, see number 1), here combined with the cosmological theme of the earth as a point as in the "Theban
Anchorite" legend.

*8. St Gall Commentary on the Creation and Fall (Stiftsbibliothek
908) [ANON.Comm.Gen.(StGall.908)]: Bischoff (1976 number 4); *RBMA*
11054; *BCLL* 1260.

MSS — Refs   none.

For the Irish character of this commentary see also Kelly (1983a pp 80ff),
and C. Wright (1987a pp 124-25). An edition is in preparation by Wright
and Michael Gorman.

The commentary has been cited by Cross (1986a) and C. Wright (1987a)
for analogs of certain "distinct ideas" in Old English texts: the age of Adam;
Eve's creation from Adam's left side; the Tree of Knowledge as a fig tree;
and the ratio of dry land to water (for details, see number 1). The information concerning the Tree of Knowledge is part of a citation from a lost
"Sedulius in tractatu Mathei," for which see Bischoff (1976 number 19 pp
119-20) and *BCLL* 646. C. Wright (1987a) shows that other texts in the
same MS transmit apocryphal lore known in Ireland and Anglo-Saxon
England.

9. Laidcenn Mac Baith, Egloga de Moralibus in Iob
[LAIDC.Egl.Mor.Iob]: Bischoff (1976 number 5); *RBMA* 5265,1, 5384; *CPL*
1716; *BCLL* 293; *KVS* LATH. See also LAIDCENN, LORICA.

MSS   Cambridge, Pembroke College 88: HG 135.
Lists — Refs   none.

For the Cambridge MS, from Bury St Edmunds, see Thomson (1972 p 623, note 27). The commentary is an abbreviation of GREGORY's MORAL-IA. In addition to the studies cited in the *BCLL*, see McNamara (1973c).

*10. Glossa in psalmos (39.11-151) [ANON.Gloss.psalm.(Pal.lat.68)]: Bischoff (1976 number 6A); *BCLL* 1261; *SEHI* 465.

MSS Vatican, Pal. lat. 68: HG 909.
Lists — Refs none.

The Vatican MS (*CLA* 1.78) was written by the Northumbrian scribe Edilbericht. McNamara (Bibliography Part I) argues that "the work originated in an area where there were both Irish and Northumbrian scholars i.e. either in Ireland or Northumbria," and that it "belongs to the Irish (and Irish-Northumbrian) tradition of exegesis . . ." (pp 73-74; cf. McNamara 1979 and Stancliffe 1975 p 365). The MS contains several scholia in Old English and Old Irish; for the Old English glosses (*PsScholia*, B8.3) see McNamara (pp 24-26) and the literature cited there. The so-called Psalter of Charlemagne (edition in preparation by Pádraig P. Ó Néill) "contains introductory material to each psalm, closely related to that of Vat. Pal. lat. 68" (*Hiberno-Latin Newsletter* 2 p 16).

O'Neill (1981 p 30) cites the gloss on Ps 1 as a further witness to (but not the actual source of) the "Irish fourfold scheme" of psalm exegesis adapted by the author of the Introductions to Ps 2-50 in *Ps* (B8.2.1); cf. numbers 1, 12, and *14.

For a full survey of Irish Psalter texts and commentaries see McNamara (1973a; see pp 218-19 for the *Glossa*); see also McNamara (1984b).

11. Eclogae tractatorum in psalterium [ANON.Ecl.tract.psalt.]: Bischoff (1976 number 6B); *BCLL* 783.

MSS — Refs none.

McNamara (1973a p 255) states that for the sections he examined "virtually the sole source" is the Milan commentary in Milan, Biblioteca Ambrosiana C 301 inf. (for which see McNamara 1973a pp 221-25). An edition is in preparation by McNamara; for extracts see McNamara (1973a pp 285-90).

The commentary is cited by Thomas Hall (forthcoming in *Medium Ævum*) for an analog of the twelve-fold division of the Red Sea in *HomU* 53 (Nap-SunEpis, B3.4.53) and *Orosius* (*Or*, B9.2; book 1); cf. numbers 13 and *20.

12. Old-Irish Treatise on the Psalter [ANON.OIr.Treat.psalt.]: *SEHI* 516.

MSS—A-S Vers none.
Quots/Cits ? Introductions to Ps 2–50 in *Ps* (B8.2.1): see below.
Refs none.

Only the introduction to the psalter and part of the comment on Ps. 1.1 survives from the treatise. O'Neill (1979), who examines the relationship of the Old Irish treatise and other Irish commentaries (especially the Reference Bible, number 1), dates the text early ninth century. See also McNamara (1973a pp 229–30). For a verse rendering of the introduction of the treatise by Airbertach Mac Coisse, see O'Neill (1977) and McNamara (1973a pp 238–39).

Ramsay (1912a and 1912b) believed that the treatise is a translation of a Hiberno-Latin original used also by the glossator of the SOUTHAMPTON PSALTER (see following entry), and that it was used by the author of the Introductions to Ps 2–50 in *Ps* (B8.2.1); see also Bright and Ramsay (1912). O'Neill (1981), however, shows that the Old Irish treatise is but one of several witnesses to "the Irish fourfold scheme" of psalm interpretation (cf. numbers 1, *10, and *14).

13. The Southampton Psalter [ANON.Gloss.psalt.South.]: *BCLL* 509; *SEHI* 476.

MSS Cambridge, St. John's College C.9: HG 148.
Lists—Refs none.

Ramsay (1912b p 471) believed that the Latin glosses in this Psalter derived from a Hiberno-Latin commentary translated in the OLD-IRISH TREATISE ON THE PSALTER (see preceding entry). On this Psalter see also McNamara (1973a pp 241–42). Only the Irish glosses (in Stokes and Strachan 1901–03 vol 1 pp xiv, 4–6) and a few Latin glosses (in Ramsay 1912b pp 472–73) have been published. An edition is in preparation by Pádraig P. Ó Néill.

A Latin gloss from the Psalter has been cited by Thomas Hall (forthcoming in *Medium Ævum*) for an analog of the twelve-fold division of the Red Sea in *HomU* 53 (NapSunEpis, B3.4.53) and *Orosius* (*Or*, B9.2; book 1); cf. numbers 11 and *20.

*14. Ps Bede, De titulis psalmorum, Argumenta [ANON.Arg. psalm./PS.BEDA]: *RBMA* 1665; *CPL* 1384, cf. 607a.

MSS—A-S Vers none.
Quots/Cits Introductions to Ps 2–50 in *Ps* (B8.2.1): see below.
Refs none.

According to Fischer (1971 p 93) the *argumentum* for each psalm consists of three sections: a comment on the historical situation of the Psalm, mostly based on THEODORUS MOPSUESTENUS; series I of the *Tituli psalmorum*; and a brief moral interpretation, frequently based on JEROME'S COMMENTARIO-LI, or on ARNOBIUS. He suggests that the *Argumenta* sections of this composite work may be associated with an Irish milieu (p 107). See also McNamara (1973a pp 216–18).

O'Neill (1981 pp 30ff) accepts Ramsay's (1912a and 1912b) and Bright and Ramsay's (1912) evidence that the *Argumenta* (together with the *Explanationes* from the same composite text, which Bright and Ramsay call *In Psalmorum Librum Exegesis*) were a source for the author of the Introductions to Ps 2–50 in *Ps* (B8.2.1). Ramsay thought that the influence was indirect, through the Irish commentary represented by the OLD IRISH TREATISE ON THE PSALTER (number 12). O'Neill concludes that the Old English paraphrast "followed a structure of fourfold interpretation developed and used by the Irish commentaries on the Psalms [numbers 1, *10, and 12]; for the matter of this scheme he drew mainly on the *Argumenta* and *Explanationes*, though not nearly to the extent proposed by Bright and Ramsay" (p 38). See also Whitelock (1966 pp 94–95).

Dempsey (1987) provides a detailed examination of the dependence of the Introductions upon the *Argumenta*, and the dependence of the latter upon THEODORUS MOPSUESTENUS, EXPOSITIO IN PSALMOS. Dempsey (who seems to have overlooked O'Neill's study) argues that the Anglo-Saxon author "had access to a fuller Theodorean commentary" than the *Argumenta* (p 375), or at least a "more ample" form of the *Argumenta* than survives in *De titulis psalmorum* (p 384). He suggests further that that source may have been an Irish work (though not the Theodorean commentary in Milan, Biblioteca Ambrosiana C. 301 inf., formerly attributed to Columbanus). Following a tenuous chain of associations concerning the cultivation of Antiochene exegesis by the Irish and by THEODORE OF CANTERBURY, Dempsey ultimately speculates that Theodore and ALDHELM may have had a hand in the putative source.

15. Ps Jerome, Breuiarium in psalmos [ANON.Breu.psalm./PS. HIER.]: *RBMA* 3333; *CPL* 629; *BCLL* 343; *BHM* 427; *KVS* PS-HI bre.

MSS   1. London, BL Royal 2.E.xiii and 2.E.xiv: HG 453.
   2. Vatican, Reg. lat. 338: HG 914.
   3. London, BL Royal 4.A.xiv: HG 455: see below.
   4. ? Cambridge, Pembroke College 91: HG 136.
Lists — A-S Vers   none.
Quots/Cits   1. ? ALDH.Epist.4.482: see below.

2. ALCVIN.Exp.psalm.: see below.
Refs none.

For the Irish origin (seventh-eighth century).of this work see McNamara (1973 p 225 note 39, citing Fischer 1971 p 93 and Frede 1961 p 76, note 4; cf. *KVS* p 371). On the Vatican MS see Gneuss (GR 6248 p 44 note 13). There has been considerable confusion regarding two other MSS. Gneuss (HG 455) lists the *Breuiarium* among the contents of Royal 4.A.xiv (cf. *CLA* 2.216), but Ogilvy (*BKE* 1984 p 304) notes that Stegmüller lists it under JEROME, TRACTATUS IN PSALMOS (*RBMA* 3325; *CPL* 592; *BHM* 220), dated to the eighth century (although Stegmüller also lists it, as tenth century, under the spurious *Breuiarium*). The MS in fact contains Jerome's *Tractatus* (*BHM* vol 2, p 304) from Ps 109–49, but with interpolations from the *Breuiarium*; see Morin (*CCSL* 78.xvi-xvii) and Warner and Gilson (1921 vol 1, p 81). Ogilvy (*BKE* p 181) says that the selections in Cambridge, Pembroke College 91 "may be from either" Jerome or Ps Jerome; Gneuss (HG 136) lists the work as *Breuiarium in Psalmos*, but Lambert lists this MS under Jerome's *Tractatus* (*BHM* vol 2, p 303). Lambert's index also lists entry number "437" for this MS, but there is no such number in Lambert's catalog, and one suspects a misprint for 427, the number of the *Breuiarium*; but Lambert does not list the Pembroke MS there, either in the main entry or in the Addenda.

The parallel cited by Ehwald in the apparatus to his edition of ALDHELM, EPISTOLA 4.482 (cf. *PL* 26.1026) is slight (both works identify the *domus* of Ps 67.7 as the Church, an interpretation that occurs elsewhere).

Ogilvy (*BKE* p 183) states that the work was "much used by ALCUIN in his commentary on the gradual psalms and elsewhere," but Alcuin used the *Breuiarium* in his commentary on the penitential psalms (*RBMA* 1089), and not in the commentary on the gradual psalms (*RBMA* 1090); I do not know what works are meant by "elsewhere."

Jenkins (1966 p 189) doubts that Bede knew the *Breuiarium*.

*16. Marburg Commentary on the Song of Songs (fragment) [ANON.Comm.Ct.(Marb.Hr2,11)]: Bischoff (1976 number 7); *BCLL* 1262.

MSS ? Marburg, Staatsarchiv, Hr 2, 11, mutilated double leaf.
Lists — Refs none.

The Marburg MS (beginning of the ninth century, "perhaps from Fulda," Bischoff 1976 p 106), is written in Anglo-Saxon script, but from an Irish original according to Bischoff.

17. Josephus Scottus, Abbreuiatio commentarii Hieronimi in Isaiam [IOS.SCOT.Abbreu.HIER.Comm.Isai.]: Bischoff (1976 number

8); *RBMA* 5146; cf. *CPL* 1354; *BCLL* 649. See also JOSEPHUS SCOTTUS, CARMINA.

MSS—Quots/Cits none.
Refs Alcuin: see below.

The commentary was compiled from JEROME, COMMENTARII IN ISAIAM at the request of ALCUIN: "Haec brevi, prout potui, sermone in Isaiam de lacinioso Hieronimi tractatu, sicut, dilectissime magister Albine, iussisti, devotus excerpsi" (*MGH* PLAC 1.151). On the commentary itself see Kelly (1980).

Biblical Commentaries — New Testament

In his catalog, Bischoff (1976 number 18, p 119) refers to a compilation *Quaestiones super Euangelium ex dictis Augustini* [ANON.Quaest.euang.dict.AVG.] (*RBMA* 9377 and 9945) found in several MSS, including Brussels, Bibliothèque Royale 8654–72, fols 1–98v, which includes two Anglo-Saxon glosses, *CollGl* 33 (Ker, D33; see NRK 1957 p 476). Bischoff concludes, however, that "it is probably early Carolingian."

18. Ps Jerome, Expositio quatuor euangeliorum [ANON.Expos.quat.euang./PS.HIER.]: Bischoff (1976 number 11A-C); *RBMA* 3424–27 (Recension I), 3428–31 (Recension II), 3433, 3435 (Recension III); *CPL* 631; *BCLL* 341; *BHM* 470–72; *KVS* PS-HI Ev.

MSS—A-S Vers none.
Quots/Cits 1. ? BEDA.Comm.Luc.: see below.
2. ? *Or* 5 (B9.2.6): see below.
3. ? *Solil* 3 (B9.4.4): see below.
Refs none.

Ogilvy (*BKE* p 183) states that St Gall, Stiftsbibliothek 125 "may have English connections," but Lowe (*CLA* 7.909) makes no such suggestion. Beeson (1913 p 103) merely says that the abbreviations "zeigen insulare Einflüsse."

Kelly (1986 pp 68–69, cf. Kelly 1981b p 60) adduces two parallels with BEDE, IN LUCAM which suggest "that Bede knew either the *Expositio* or the Irish tradition which stood behind it."

The commentary on Luke may have been used in *Orosius* (*Or*, B9.2; ed. Bately 1980, 130.30–131.21) on the portents in Augustus' reign, specifically the allusion to the golden ring around the sun (*PL* 30.587–88); see Bately

(1971 p 249), citing Whitelock (1966 p 91); on these portents see also Cross (1973) and the CATACHESIS CELTICA (number *44).

Whitelock (1966 p 88) suggests that Alfred's statement in *Solil* 3 (B9.4.4, ed. Endter 67.31ff) that the wicked will see God after death "may be influenced by Jerome's [recte Ps Jerome's] words [on Lk 16.23] that from hell the wicked *videbunt regnum Dei ut majorem poenam habeant*" (*PL* 30.575). A similar idea occurs also in IV Esr 7.83, cf. Biggs (1986 pp 26–27) in connection with *ChristC* (A3.1).

Hill (1977a pp 215–18) cites Ps Jerome, along with PS BEDE, COLLECTANEA and the REFERENCE BIBLE (number 1) for the association of the four evangelists with other quaternities in connection with the "Æcerbot Charm" (*MCharm* 1, A43.1; cf. McNally 1971).

Cross (1987a p 82) refers to Ps Jerome among other commentaries, both Irish and non-Irish, on the interpretation of the gifts of Magi in the HOMILIARY OF ST PÈRE DE CHARTRES item 13 (cf. numbers 24 and *48).

The commentary is cited by C. Wright (1988a pp 135–36) for parallels for two passages in *HomS* 10 (*BlHom3*, B3.2.10); see also numbers 21, 24–26, 31, *44, and 50.

Biggs (forthcoming in *Traditio*; cf. Biggs 1986 p 6) cites the commentary for the motif of Judgment occuring at midnight in *ChristC* (A3.1; cf. numbers 1, 24, 25, 42, *44, and 45). Biggs (*Traditio*) also cites the commentary for the motif of Mt. Sion as the place of the congregation of the saints and of Judgment (cf. number 1). (A reference by Hill 1986 p 22 to Ps Jerome on Matthew is properly to another Hiberno-Latin commentary on Mark, number 29.)

19. Aileran Sapiens, Kanon euangeliorum rhythmica ("Quam in primo speciosa quadriga") [AIL.Kan.euang.]: Bischoff (1976 number 12): *RBMA* 843; *CPL* 1121; *BCLL* 300; *SEHI* 107 (ii); *KVS* AIL Eus.

MSS ? Augsburg, Universitätsbibliothek (olim Harburg, Fürstlich Oettingen-Wallersteinsche Bibliothek) I.2.4o.2.
Lists – Refs none.

Aileran's poem on the Eusebian canons is included among the prefatory matter in the Augsburg MS (Maihingen Gospels, eighth century, *CLA* 8.1216), written in Anglo-Saxon script. See McGurk (1961 pp 68–70), who gives the origin as "Echternach-Trier/Northumbria"; Bischoff says "saec IX, West-German" (1976 p 160, note 138). The MS contains Old-English scratched glosses, *OccGl* 51.3 (Hofmann, C51.2; see NRK 287*). Bischoff notes that fol 1 contains another poem, *In primo certe canone/quattuor concordant ordine* (*RBMA* 848), which "may also be an Irish production . . ." (p 160, note 138).

Schönbach (1903 p 78) remarks that Aileran's *Interpretatio mystica progenitorum Christi* and *Interpretatio moralis progenitorum Christi* (Bischoff 1976 number 25; *CPL* 1120; *BCLL* 299; ed. *PL* 80.327–42 with *PLS* 4.1612–13) corresponds closely to ALCUIN's *Interpretationes nominum Hebraicorum progenitorum . . . Christi* (*PL* 100.723–34), but declines to draw any conclusions concerning the relationship of these works to each other and to the interpretations in HRABANUS MAURUS' COMMENTARY ON MATTHEW. Kelly (1975 p 45) argues that "Alcuin follows Aileran . . . in choosing the progenitors according to Matthew rather than Luke" and perhaps also in his selection of certain biblical passages.

In addition to the text in Meyer (Bibliography Part I), the poem is also edited in De Bruyne (1920 p 185) and *PL* 101.729.

*20. Gospel Commentary of Máel Brigte [MAEL.Comm.euang.]: *SEHI* 483; see *BCLL* 350 and 531.

MSS — Refs none.

Rittmueller (1981, 1982, 1983, 1984) argues that the interlinear and marginal glosses (mostly on Matthew 1–27) in London, BL Harley 1802, written by Máel Brigte at Armagh in AD 1138, are based upon both patristic and Hiberno-Latin sources (especially numbers 1, 21, and 24), "dating back at least to the eighth century" (1983 p 186). Imbedded within the commentary are several glosses ascribed to "M," "Man," or "Manchanus," an Irish exegete Rittmueller would place in the seventh century. Bischoff (1976, Appendix, pp 145–49) argues for a later date for the "Man" glosses, ninth or tenth century. *BCLL* 350 assigns them to the tenth or eleventh century. On the MS see also Flower (1926 pp 428–32). Glunz (1933 pp 328–41) prints extracts from the glosses.

Cross (1987a p 69; cf. also Cross 1987b pp 62–64) cites from James (1927 p 100) a gloss from this MS on the number of Innocents as a parallel for the HOMILIARY OF ST PÈRE DE CHARTRES item 11 (cf numbers 1, 21, 24, *48, and 50).

Biggs (1986 p 20) cites a "Man" gloss on the appearance of the Cross in the sky at Judgment in *ChristC* (A3.1).

Thomas Hall (forthcoming in *Medium Ævum*) cites a gloss for an analog of the twelve-fold division of the Red Sea in *HomU* 53 (NapSunEpis, B3.4.53) and *Orosius* (*Or*, B9.2; book 1); cf. numbers 11 and 13.

21. Ps Alcuin, Liber questionum in euangeliis [ANON.Lib.quaest. euang./PS.ALCVIN]: Bischoff (1976 number 16I); *RBMA* 1100, and 9.10348,1; *CPL* 1168; *BCLL* 764; *KVS* PS-ALC Mt.

MSS ? Fulda, Priesterseminar, s.n. + Dresden, S.L., HS R52um.

Lists—A-S Vers   none.
Quots/Cits   ? *HomS* 10 (*BlHom* 3, B3.2.10): see below.
Refs   none.

The Fulda MS (dated to the end of the eighth century, *CLA* 8.1181), a fragment, is written in German-Anglo-Saxon script (for a fragment of another recension of the same commentary in an English MS, see following entry).

C. Wright (1988a pp 134–36) points out that portions of the commentary on the Temptation correspond to the CATACHESIS CELTICA (number *44). Bischoff (1976 number 20, pp 122–23) also noted similarities to a then lost Matthew commentary by a Hiberno-Latin exegete named "Frigulus" (known through quotations in SMARAGDUS, EXPOSITIO LIBRI COMITIS (*KVS* 1988 FRI ap Smaragdum, see p 58: "Ungesichert ist die mögliche Identität mit VIR-S [Virgil of Salzburg]"). On its connections with the present commentary see further Kelly (1981a pp 367–72) and Cross (1987a p 12). Kelly raises but dismisses as "[a] decidedly lesser argument" the possibility of Anglo-Saxon connections for Frigulus. Frigulus' commentary has recently been discovered by Bischoff (see *BCLL* 645). An edition of the Frigulus commentary is in progress by Jutta Fliege. An edition of the *Liber questionum in euangeliis* is in preparation by Jean Rittmueller. For printed excerpts and fragments see Bischoff (1976).

The commentary has been cited by C. Wright (1988a pp 133–36), together with closely parallel comments from CATACHESIS CELTICA (number *44) as a possible source for several brief passages in *HomS* 10 (*BlHom* 3); cf. numbers 18, 24–26, 31, and 50.

Cross (1987a) cites this commentary in connection with the HOMILIARY OF ST PÈRE DE CHARTRES item 11 on the fall of the idols during the flight into Egypt (pp 23, 74–76; cf. number 24, and compare GOSPEL OF PS MATTHEW under APOCRYPHA), and on the number of the Innocents (p 69; cf. also Cross 1987b pp 62–64, and numbers 1, *20, 24, *48, and 50).

Biggs (1986 p 6, and forthcoming in *Traditio*) also cites the commentary as one of several Irish analogs (numbers 1, 18, 24, 25, 42, *44 and 45) for the motif of Judgment occuring at midnight in *ChristC* (A3.1), and also (1986 p 25) for the description in the poem of the biblical "goats" as "foul."

*22. Ps Alcuin, Liber questionum in euangeliis (Recensio altera) [ANON.Lib.quaest.euang.2/PS.ALCVIN]: Bischoff (1976 number 16II); *BCLL* 1267.

MSS   Hereford, Cathedral Library, P.II.10, fly-leaves: HG 268.
Lists—Refs   none.

On the Hereford MS, written in Northumbrian uncials, see *CLA* 2.158. This fragmentary commentary shows "extensive verbal agreement" (Bischoff 1976 p 114) with PS ALCUIN, LIBER QUESTIONUM IN EVANGELIIS (see preceding entry). Rittmueller (1986 p 6) states that it represents "a separate recension" of the Ps Alcuin commentary. Ogilvy (*BKE* p 201, under the heading "IN MATTHAEUM") wonders whether this fragmentary commentary is related to the glosses on Matthew in Oxford, Bodleian Library Laud Misc. 520 (SC 1194; apparently not, to judge by the incipit and explicit given by Coxe 1858–85 fasc 2, col 376); or to the fragmentary commentaries in Dresden R52um and Paris Bibliothèque Nationale lat. 12292 (the latter is *CLA* 5.642, not *CLA* 8.1181, which is rather the Dresden fragment); or perhaps to the Ps Alcuin commentary. The last two shots in the dark somehow hit the same mark: the Dresden and Paris fragments are in fact both from Ps Alcuin—the other recension of the present commentary!

23. Lambeth Commentary on the Sermon on the Mount
[ANON.Comm.serm.Dom.mont.]: *BCLL* 347.

MSS ? London, Lambeth Palace 119, flyleaves (now "Fragments 1229," fols 7 and 8).
Lists—Refs none.

These fragments, from the tenth century, were used as fly-leaves for a late twelfth-century English MS, but there is no evidence for their place of origin. The fragmentary commentary, mostly in Irish with some Latin, is considered early eighth-century by its editors (Bibliography Part I).

24. Vienna Commentary on Matthew (Österreichische Nationalbibliothek 940) [ANON.Comm.Matth.(Vien.940)]: Bischoff (1976 number 17I); *BCLL* 772.

MSS—Refs none.

On the Vienna MS, see Cross (1987a p 13); the commentary is unedited.
Cross (1985b pp 121–22) cites a simile applied to Mary's conception through the Holy Spirit "sicut in arbores et terram descendit ut florsecat terra ut fructificent arbores" as a rough parallel for a simile in *Mart* (B19.bm): "swa þás treowa ðonne hi blostmiað þurh þæs windes blæd." C. Wright (in a forthcoming study) notes a similar comment in the LINZ HOMILY COLLECTION (number *46).
Cross (1987a) cites this commentary for parallels for the HOMILIARY OF ST PÈRE DE CHARTRES item 11 on the apocryphal story of the fall of the idols during the flight into Egypt (pp 23, 73–74; cf. number 21, and compare GOSPEL OF PS MATTHEW, under APOCRYPHA), and on the number of the In-

nocents (p 69; cf. also Cross 1987b pp 62–63, and cf. numbers 1, *21, 20, *48, and 40), as well as for echoes of comments on the Magi in item 13 (p 245; cf. numbers 18 and *48).

C. Wright (1988a pp 132, note 7; 133, note 12; and 135–36) cites parallels in the commentary for brief passages in *HomS* 10 (*BlHom* 3, B3.2.10); cf. numbers 18, 21, 25–26, 31, *44, and 50.

Biggs (forthcoming in *Traditio*) cites the commentary for eschatological motifs in *ChristC* (A3.1), including the saints and angels in the company of Christ at Judgment and Judgment occurring at midnight (cf. Biggs 1986 p 6, and numbers 1, 18, 21, 25, 42, *44, and 45).

25. Würzburg Commentary and Glosses on Matthew (Universitäts-bibliothek M.p.th.f. 61) [ANON.Comm.Gloss.Matth.(Würzb.61)]: Bischoff (1976 number 22A-B); *RBMA* 11756–11768; *BCLL* 768; *SEHI* 462.

MSS—Refs none.

The commentary (with longer explanations on Mt 1–27, and interlinear glosses on Mt 1.1–16.18) has been cited by C. Wright (1988a pp 133, note 12, and 135 note 20) for parallels for brief passages in *HomS* 10 (*BlHom* 3, B3.2.10; cf. numbers 18, 21, 24, 26, 31, *44, and 50).

Biggs (forthcoming in *Traditio*; cf. Biggs 1986 p 6) cites the commentary for the motif of Judgment occuring at midnight in *ChristC* (A3.1; cf. numbers 1, 18, 21, 24, 42, *44, and 45).

26. Munich Commentary on Matthew [ANON.Comm.Matth. (Mun.6233)]: Bischoff (1976 number 23); *RBMA* 9913; *BCLL* 769.

MSS ? Munich, Bayerische Staatsbibliothek clm 6233.
Lists—Refs none.

The Munich MS (second half of the eighth century, South Bavaria) has corrections in a contemporary Anglo-Saxon hand; see *CLA* 9.1252 and Cross (1987b pp 62–63). For possibly Irish homilies in the same MS, cited by Cross for extensive parallels with several homilies in the HOMILIARY OF ST PÈRE DE CHARTRES, see number *48. According to Bischoff (1976 p 127) the commentary "probably did not originate in Ireland." An edition of the commentary is in preparation by Denis Brearley.

The Munich commentary is cited by C. Wright (1988a pp 131–32, note 7) for a minor parallel for a phrase in *HomS* 10 (*BlHom* 3, B3.2.10; cf. numbers 18, 21, 24, 25, 31, *44, and 50).

*27. Ps Bede, Expositio in Matthei euangelium [ANON.Ex-pos.Matth./PS.BEDA]: *RBMA* 1678 and 7061; *BCLL* 1269.

MSS—Refs none.

On the commentary see Schönbach (1903 pp 19–34). McNally (1969 p 17 and 1970 pp 676–77) states that this commentary "reflects the Irish tradition." The commentary has been cited by Payne (see Biggs 1986 p 22) as a parallel for the theme of Christ's display of his wounds at Judgment in *ChristC* (A3.1).

*28. Paris Commentary on Matthew (BN lat. 12021) [ANON.Comm. Matth.(BN.12021)]: *RBMA* 10457.

MSS—Refs none.

Cross (1987a p 81) states that the commentary "has not yet been considered by Hiberno-Latin scholars, but its phraseology often has correspondences with that in Pseudo-Jerome" (number 18). The possibility of Irish connections is supported by its context in the MS, which also contains the COLLECTIO CANONUM HIBERNENSIS, as Cross pointed out. It should be added that the sermons immediately following the commentary correspond to items in the reputedly Irish CATACHESIS CRACOVIENSIS (number 45). The MS is tenth-century and Breton, according to Bischoff (private communication reported by Cross, p 11). The commentary is unedited.

Cross (1987a pp 31 and 81) cites this commentary for a parallel of the theme of the *quatuor mortes* in the HOMILIARY OF ST PÈRE DE CHARTRES item 30 (cf. numbers 33 and 42 for the related theme of the three deaths).

29. Ps Jerome, Commentarius in euangelium Marci [ANON. Comm.Marc./PS.HIER.]: Bischoff (1976 number 27); *RBMA* 3436; *CPL* 632; *BCLL* 345; *BHM* 473; *KVS* CU-D Mc.

MSS—A-S Vers none.
Quots/Cits BEDA.Comm.Marc.: see below.
Refs none.

The provenance of London, BL Harley 3213 (continental script, tenth century; see *BHM* vol 3B, p 378), mentioned by Ogilvy (*BKE* p 179) is unknown; it is not listed in HG. A Worcester MS of this commentary, dated to tenth century by Turner (1916 p 50, cf. *CPL*), and to the beginning of the eleventh century by Glunz (1933 p 313) is from the second half of the twelfth century according to Lambert (*BHM* vol 3B, p 381). Bischoff's attribution of the commentary to CUMMIAN, author of the letter DE CONTROVERSIA PASCHALI (paschal letter to Ségéne), disputed by Stancliffe (1975 pp 361–70), has been supported recently by M. Walsh (1987 pp. 225–29) and in greater detail by Walsh and Ó Cróinín (1988 pp 217–21); it is accepted by Frede (*KVS* p 284). For an earlier suggestion that it is by REMIGIUS OF AUXERRE, under Irish influence, see Glunz (1933 pp 314–15).

Hill (1986 p 22) cites the commentary on Mark (inadvertently identified as Ps Jerome on Matthew) for an analog for the motif of the bleeding trees at Christ's Crucifixion in *ChristC* (A3.1). The commentary is here quoting 4 Esr 5.5, but the application of the motif to the Crucifixion instead of the more common use as one of the "Fifteeen Signs of Judgment" (see APOCALYPSE OF THOMAS under APOCRYPHA) is apparently attested only in *ChristC*, Ps Jerome on Mark, and an Old Irish poem of Blathmac. See Hill (pp 16–18) and Biggs (1986 p 24).

Kelly (1986 p 69) suggests on circumstantial grounds that the commentary "would have been an attractive source" for BEDE's commentary on the gospel.

30. Praefacio secundum Marcum [ANON.Praef.Marc.]: Bischoff (1976 number 28); *RBMA* 9.9916,2; *BCLL* 775.

MSS — Refs   none.

Cross (1981b p 189; cf. Walsh and Ó Cróinín 1988 pp 219–20) cites this text, along with PS JEROME, COMMENTARIUS IN EVANGELIUM MARCI (see preceding entry) for an additional parallel for the distinctive phrase *furtum laudabile* in *Mart* (B19.cc). In the *Praefacio*, as in the more immediate source (PS ISIDORE, DE ORTU ET OBITU PATRUM), but not in Ps Jerome on Mark, the phrase refers to Mark as in *Mart*.

Cross and Hill (1982 pp 113–14) cite the work, along with the KARLSRUHE COMMENTARY ON THE CATHOLIC EPISTLES (number 34) for a parallel for the question "Who first named the name of God" in *Solomon and Saturn* (*Sol I*, B5.1) and *Adrian and Ritheus* (*Ad*, B5.2). The motif also occurs in the Reference Bible (number 1).

31. Vienna Commentary on Luke (Österreichische Nationalbibliothek 997) [ANON.Comm.Luc.(Vien.997)]: Bischoff (1976 number 30); *RBMA* 9.11646,1; *BCLL* 773; *KVS* PS-BED Lc.

MSS — Refs   none.

According to Cross (1987a pp 23, 25, and 70–73), passages in the HOMILIARY OF ST PÈRE DE CHARTRES, items 12 and 15, "have close verbal parallels with sections of the Vienna 997 Commentary on Luke" (p 71).

The commentary has also been cited by C. Wright (1988a pp 132, note 7; 133, at note 12; and 135–37) for parallels for several brief passages in *HomS* 10 (*BlHom* 3, B3.2.10; cf. numbers 18, 21, 24–26, *44, and 50).

*32. Expositio Iohannis iuxta Hieronimum [ANON.Expos.Iohan./PS.HIER.]: Bischoff (1976 number 32); *BCLL* 1268; *BHM* 474.

MSS—A-S Vers   none.
Quots/Cits   ?   ALCVIN.Comm.Iohan.:   see below.
Refs   none.

According to Brearley (Bibliography Part I p 152) the two MSS listed by Lambert (*BHM* 474) in addition to Angers, Bibliothèque Municipale 275 (olim 266) "contain separate commentaries unrelated beyond their incipits." On the commentary see also Brearley (1986). Brearley (Bibliography Part I p 157) states that there are similarities between this commentary and two other Hiberno-Latin commentaries (number 18 and the Vienna commentary on John, Bischoff 1976 number 31; *BCLL* 774), but that "there are surprisingly few parallel discussions . . . and the three writers have often selected different lemmata for comment."

Brearley (Bibliography Part I p 159) states that ALCUIN "may have read this commentary along with the more widely circulated" PS JEROME, EXPOSITIO QUATUOR EVANGELIORUM (number 18); but Brearley goes on to say that Alcuin's commentary "was of a quite different character," and his footnote (52) gives only a parallel between Alcuin's commentary and PS BEDE, IN S. IOHANNIS EVANGELIUM EXPOSITIO, with reference to Michel and Schwarz (1978 pp 16ff).

*33. De questione apostoli [ANON.Quaest.apost.].

MSS   Oxford, Bodleian Library Auctarium F.4.32 (*SC* 2176): HG 538.
Lists—Refs   none.

The *Quaestio* on Col 2.14 occupies fol 21v in part III (the so-called "Liber Commonei") of the composite Oxford MS, which was owned by St Dunstan. The text is unedited but can be consulted in the facsimile edition by R. W. Hunt (1961). According to Hunt (p ix), "the treatment of the 'chyrographum' as a document to be divided into two parts suggests that the piece belongs to the Irish exegetical tradition brought to light by B. Bischoff" (citing Bischoff 1955 p 299 [= 1966–81, I, p 120] and 1954 p 268 [= 1976 p 139]; Hunt also compares the title with Bischoff number 26, *De questione porcorum*). Bischoff traces the custom of the Chirographum document, which first appears in England in the ninth century, to Irish exegesis of Col 2.14, as attested in a Hiberno-Latin commentary on the Pauline epistles (Bischoff 1976 number 33) and a commentary on Luke (Bischoff 1976 number 29).

C. Wright (forthcoming in *Cambridge Medieval Celtic Studies*) cites the *Quaestio* for an analog of the theme of the three deaths in *HomS* 4 (*VercHom* 9, B3.2.4), which appears in other Hiberno-Latin compilations, including the PS BEDE, COLLECTANEA and the PREBIARUM DE MULTORIUM EXEMPLARIBUS (number 42).

34. Karlsruhe Commentary on the Catholic Epistles (Badische Landesbibliothek Aug. CCXXXIII) [ANON.Comm.epist.cath.(Karlsr. 233)]: Bischoff (1976 number 35); *RBMA* 9381-87; *BCLL* 340; *SEHI* 105; *KVS* AN cath.

MSS — Refs   none.

On the date and provenance of this commentary, and its relationship to number 35, see Breen (1984).

According to Kelly (1986 p 68), McNally (Bibliography Part I) concluded that BEDE used this work in his COMMENTARIUS IN EPISTOLAS SEPTEM CATHOLICAS. However, although McNally does state that both Bede and another Hiberno-Latin commentary on the Catholic Epistles, that of PS HILARY, "depend upon" the anonymous Irish commentary (p x), his argument seems to be that the influence upon Bede is through Ps Hilary (see following entry). The parallels McNally adduces between this anonymous commentary and Bede's work (p xiii) are in fact all mediated through Ps Hilary. McNally's conclusion is rather that "the Reichenau commentary of the anonymous Scottus is basic to Pseudo-Hilary's work and reflects an older exegetical tradition, while Bede's Expositio, later in origin, depends at least partially on Pseudo-Hilary . . ." (p xvi). Thus by his earlier (unfortunately ambiguous) statements about Bede's dependence McNally appears to have meant that the anonymous commentary influenced Bede through Ps Hilary, not that Bede knew the earlier work directly. In any case he cites no parallel between Bede and the anonymous work that is not present in Ps Hilary.

Cross and Hill (1982 pp 113-14) cite the work, along with the PRAEFACIO SECUNDUM MARCUM (number 30) for a parallel for the question "Who first named the name of God" in *Solomon and Saturn* (*Sol I*, B5.1) and *Adrian and Ritheus* (*Ad*, B5.2). The motif also occurs in the REFERENCE BIBLE (number 1).

Biggs (1986 p 13) cites this commentary and the following for parallels for the motif of the destruction of the heaven, earth, and sea in *ChristC* (A3.1).

35. Ps Hilary, Expositio in VII epistolas catholicas [ANON.Expos.epist.cath./PS.HIL.ARELAT.]: Bischoff (1976 number 36); *RBMA* 3525-31; *CPL* 508; *BCLL* 346; *KVS* PS-HIL-A.

MSS   Salisbury, Cathedral Library 124: HG 724.
Lists — A-S Vers   none.
Quots/Cits ÆCHom I,21 (B1.1.23) 304.1-15: ANON.Expos.epist.cath. 65.444-48.
Refs ? BEDA.Comm.epist.cath. 267.260ff: ANON.Expos.epist.cath. 102.136-37: see below.

On the date and provenance of the Ps Hilary commentary and its relationship to number 34, see Breen (1984).

Cross (forthcoming in *Hiberno-Latin Newsletter* 3) reports the discovery of Tessa Webber, in an Oxford D.Phil. thesis on the MSS of Salisbury Library, that MS 124 contains on fols 42v–49r the beginning of the commentary of Ps Hilary (corresponding to *CCSL* 108B.53–78/55). For extracts of another Hiberno-Latin commentary in a Salisbury MS, see number 1. For the Irish character of the work, see McNally (Bibliography Part I pp x–xvii).

Bischoff (1976 p 143) states that BEDE, in his COMMENTARIUS IN EPISTOLAS SEPTEM CATHOLICAS "must have had this commentary (or in any case, one very like it) before him . . . since with the words *ridicule quidam . . . interpretantur* he criticises the attempt of the Irishman to render inspiration through the Holy Spirit intelligible by means of the comparison *more fistulae* (on II Peter 1:21)". McNally (Bibliography Part I p xiv) says that Bede's commentary was written "partially under the influence" of Ps Hilary. He cites textual parallels between the two works (pp xiv–xv), and cites Bede's commentary for other parallels in his notes at various points. See further Kelly (1986 pp 67–68) and Bieler (1976 pp 217–18). For Bede's indirect dependence, through Ps Hilary, upon an anonymous Hiberno-Latin KARLSRUHE COMMENTARY ON THE CATHOLIC EPISTLES, see the preceding entry.

ÆLFRIC translates the comment on James 2.19 in *ÆCHom* I,21 (B1.1.23); the Latin text is also quoted in one MS (Cambridge, University Library Gg.3.28: HG 11). For the identification see Cross (GR 5332, pp 77–78), citing the text of Amelli (1897b pp 207–60 at p 216, rpt in *PLS* 3.59–131). Ælfric introduces the quotation with a remark expressing doubt as to the work's authenticity ("In quodam tractu, qui aestimatur Sancti Hilarii fuisse . . . ").

Biggs (1986 p 13) cites this commentary and the preceding for parallels for the motif of the destruction of heaven, earth, and sea in *ChristC* (A3.1).

36. Ps Jerome (Ps Isidore), Commentarius in Apocalypsin

[ANON.Comm.Apc./PS.HIER.]: Bischoff (1976 number 37); *RBMA* 5271 [= 3461]; *CPL* 1221; *ISLMAH* 134; *BCLL* 781; *BHM* 491; *KVS* AN Apc.

MSS—A-S Vers none.
Quots/Cits ? BEDA.Comm.Apc.: see below.
Refs none.

On this commentary see also Frede's revised comment (*KVS* 1984 p 23): "von einem Iren Mitte des 8.Jh, oder eher um 600 in Vivarium von einem Schüler des CAr [Cassiodorus]?"

Kelly (1982a pp 402–06) notes "fourteen passages where the Irish commentary and Bede agree with one another but do not depend on an earlier patristic source." He admits that six of these parallels are slight, but argues that taken together they "indicate the existence of a common, if limited, insular tradition of Apocalypse exegesis" (p 405). Because the priority of the Irish commentary cannot be firmly established, Kelly prefers to believe that "both drew from a third, possibly oral, source or tradition which was probably Irish . . . ."

The edition specified in the Bibliography, Part I is reprinted from G. Lo Menzo Rapisarda (1967); the work is also printed in Hartung (1904).

*37. Ps Alcuin, De septem sigillis [ANON.Sept.sig./PS.ALCVIN]: *BHM* 492; *KVS* (1984) AN sig.

MSS — Refs   none.

This short treatise associates the seven seals of Apoc 5.1–5 with seven events in Christ's life, each of which is associated with one of the seven gifts of the Holy Spirit; the seven gifts are in turn associated with seven patriarchs. In a recent edition of this work, Matter (Bibliography Part I; also edited in *PL* 101.1169–70) dismisses the possibility that ALCUIN wrote the treatise and suggests on stylistic and other grounds that it could either be a sixth-century Visigothic work or an eighth-century Irish one (p 132). She concludes in favor of Spanish origin, however, largely on the basis of the liturgical linking of the seven seals with the ministry of Christ in the Mozarabic fraction at Easter (pp 119–22, 137). The problem of a Visigothic or an Irish origin for the treatise may require reconsideration, since Matter was unaware of the many parallels in Irish and Insular sources for the linking of the seven seals with the events of Christ's life and for the association of the seven gifts of the Holy Spirit with the seven patriarchs. Both themes are found in the LIBER DE NUMERIS (number 39), and other Hiberno-Latin sources, as McNally showed (1957 pp 108–09 and 117–18). Regarding the theme of the seven gifts exemplifed in the patriarchs, McNally concluded that the attestations of theme in Hiberno-Latin sources (including PS BEDE, COLLECTANEA and the CATACHESIS CELTICA, number *44) "lässt sich, wenn nicht direkt irischer Ursprung, so doch wenigstens Zusammenhang mit irischer Exegese vermuten" (p 109). The linking of the seven seals with the events of Christ's life also occurs in the homilies IN NOMINE DEI SUMMI (number 47), although early Spanish dissemination of this theme is indicated by its occurrence in Apringius, *Tractatus in Apocalypsin*, Ildefonsus of Toledo, *Liber de cognitione baptismi*, and Heterius and Beatus of Liébana, *Epistula aduersus Elipandum* (see Matter, p 121, de Lubac 1959 vol 1 pt 1, p 132; cf. Dobschütz 1912 pp 238–41 for possible patristic sources). Finally, although Matter speaks of "the Spanish connection" of one of the MS families (on the basis of the presence of excerpts from ISIDORE and EUCHERIUS

in the two MSS), and states that "there is no evidence for a Celtic transmission of *De septem sigillis*" (p 137), one of the two MSS of Family A (apparently copied from the other, cf. Matter p 112, citing Bischoff 1960 pp
242–43, especially note 1) is in fact written in an Irish hand (Lambert,
BHM vol 3B, p 399, lists another MS). At the very least, the Irish played
an important role in transmitting the two major themes that make up *De
septem sigillis* (on cultural and literary transmission from Spain to Ireland
see Hillgarth 1961, 1962, and 1965). Frede (*KVS* 1984 p 30) follows Matter:
"zwischen 500 und 633, Spanien."

Cross (1987a pp 19, 82–83) refers to the treatise, as well as to the Irish
examples gathered by McNally, for the theme of the seven gifts exemplified
in the patriarchs in the HOMILIARY OF ST PÈRE DE CHARTRES item 1 (cf numbers 39 and *44). Cross (pp 242–44) prints a close analog for the description in the homily from a Munich MS, Bayerische Staatsbibliothek clm
14311. Dolbeau (1988 p 256) has since shown that this sermon exists in a
collection surviving in several other MSS, including Paris, Bibliothèque
Nationale lat. 2175, from which it had been edited by Dufourcq in 1910.

C. Wright (in a forthcoming study) points out that the theme of the seven
gifts and the patriarchs occurs in *Byrhtferth's Manual* (*ByrM* 1, Crawford,
B20.20.1).

Florilegia and Dialogues

*38. Ps Isidore, Liber numerorum [ANON.Lib.num.I/PS.ISID.]:
RBMA 5174; *CPL* 1193; *ISLMAH* 107; *BCLL* 1254; *KVS* (1984) PS-IS nu I.

MSS—A-S Vers   none.
Quots/Cits   1. ALDH.Metr. 63.15–72: see below.
           2. ? *ByrM* (Crawford, B20.20.1): see below.
Refs   none.

The work is included in the *CPL* among the genuine works of ISIDORE,
but Bischoff (1958 pp 9ff) considered it an Irish production; see also McNally
(1961 pp 314–15), Lapidge and Herren (1979 p 187, note 7), Tristram (1985
pp 32 and 88), and Frede (*KVS* 1984 p 65: "unecht, wohl irisch, 7.Jh").

Lapidge and Herren (1979 p 32; cf. pp 187, notes 4–7 and 190, note 27)
have shown that ALDHELM's treatise on the number seven in the DE METRIS
"is based primarily on the Isidorian or pseudo-Isidorian *Liber Numerorum*."
Although Ehwald (*MGH* AA p xix) noted that Aldhelm drew on other
authors as well, Lapidge and Herren state that "it would be fairer to say
that Aldhelm's work was an elaboration of the *Liber Numerorum* than it would
be to call it a composite work drawing on the *Liber Numerorum* as one of
its sources."

Crawford (GR 5959) cites the *Liber numerorum* at several points for parallels to the treatise on numbers incorporated in *Byrhtferth's Manual* (*ByrM* 1, Crawford, B20.20.1), but states that for this section "the passages quoted can hardly be regarded, perhaps, as the immediate sources used by Byrhtferth" (p 199 note).

39. Ps Isidore, Liber de numeris [ANON.Lib.num.II/PS.ISID.]: RBMA 5157; *CPL* 1193; *ISLMAH* 108; *BCLL* 778; *KVS* (1984) PS-IS nu II.

MSS   none.
Lists   ? Peterborough: ML 13.27.
A-S Vers   none.
Quots/Cits   ? *GenA* (A1.1) 1547–48: see below.
Refs   none.

Despite its author's expressed intention to treat of the "mystical" signification of numbers through twenty-four, the *Liber de numeris* is not really a treatise on number, but rather a compilation of numerical motifs arranged in numerical order, and extends only through the number eight. According to McNally (1957), the work was composed by an Irishman in the circle of the Irish bishop Virgil of Salzburg (d. 784). For a full analysis of the contents, see McNally (1957). The edition in Migne (Bibliography Part I) extends only through the number three. An extract paraphrasing the GELASIAN DECREE is printed by Dobschütz (1912 pp 66–75). An edition is in preparation by Manuel C. Díaz y Díaz. See also PS ISIDORE, DE ORTU ET OBITU PATRUM (*BCLL* 780) for a "sister-work" of the *Liber de numeris* (McNally 1965 p 168; cf. *KVS* 1984 p 66: "von demselben Iren") known in Anglo-Saxon England.

The *Liber de numeris* has been cited by Bazire and Cross (1982) for parallels for numerical themes in several Old English Rogationtide homilies, including the "Seven Joys of Heaven" in *HomS* 34 (*VercHom* 19, B3.2.34; see pp 11–12), *HomS* 38 (*VercHom* 20, B3.2.38; see p 28), *HomS* 42 (B3.2.42; see p 58 and cf. p 119, note 1); and the theme of the three spiritual births in *HomS* 35 (B3.2.35; see pp 68–69).

Cross and Hill (1982) cite the *Liber de numeris* for parallels for several themes in *Solomon and Saturn* (*Sol I*, B5.1), including ADAM OCTIPARTITE and ADAM'S NAME (pp 67–69; cf. Tristram 1975 and C. Wright 1987a 140–44, and see the entry in APOCRYPHA); and the number of bones and veins in the human body (p 125).

Cross (1987a) also cites this work for two themes "which appear to persist in insular texts" (p 82): the Gifts of the Holy Spirit exemplified in the patriarchs, in the HOMILIARY OF ST PÈRE DE CHARTRES item 1 (pp 19, 82–83; but cf. pp 242–43 for a more immediate source; this theme is also in numbers *37 and *44, and in PS BEDE, COLLECTANEA), and the theme of the "Seven Joys of Heaven," in items 89 and 91 (pp 41–42; cf. pp 83, 122, 125, 152–53, 164, 172, 193, and 234, and see numbers *40 and *44). For other examples of the Seven Joys of Heaven theme in Old English, see Hill (GR 3333), C. Wright (1984 pp 62–63), Tristram (1985 p 143) Biggs (1986 pp 39–40), and Lees (1986 p 127). Cross also cites the *Liber de numeris* for the seven sons of Eleazar and Felicitas in the HOMILIARY OF ST PÈRE DE CHARTRES item 47 (pp 36, 84), and for a list based on Prv 6.16–19 in item 91 (pp 42 and 163).

C. Wright (forthcoming in *Cambridge Medieval Celtic Studies*) cites the *Liber de numeris* for examples of numerical themes and apocryphal lore known in Ireland and Anglo-Saxon England, including the conception of the seven heavens (1987a p 129; so too Cross 1986a pp 78–79; for details, see the REFERENCE BIBLE, number 1) and the "Thought, Word, Deed" triad (for the triad see Sims-Williams 1978).

Tristram (1985) cites the *Liber de numeris* in connection with the *Sex aetates mundi* theme in Ireland and Anglo-Saxon England (see especially pp 32 and 88), and edits a portion of the text (pp 294–98).

Biggs (forthcoming in *Traditio*) cites the *Liber de numeris* for an example of the insular theme of the four-fold division of souls in connection with *ChristC* (A3.1; cf. numbers *44 and 45).

According to Lapidge (ML p 80), "that the work was known in late Anglo-Saxon England is clear from the fact that the names of Noah's wife — Percova — and of this three sons' wives — Olla, Olliva, and Ollivana — were interpolated into the Old English poem *Genesis* (lines 1547–8), apparently from this source . . . " (cf. Bammesberger 1984 p 45). The information, however, circulated independently of the *Liber de numeris* (cf. Utley 1941 p 434; McNally 1957 pp 127–28; Tristram 1986 p 120), including in the biblical glosses connected with the school of THEODORE OF CANTERBURY (see Bischoff 1976 p 121) and PS BEDE, IN PENTATEUCHUM COMMENTARII (number *5; see McNally 1969 p 15, and cf. number *3). The *Liber de numeris* need not have been the interpolator's immediate source, though it is certainly a likely source. The names also appear, with slight variation, in other Anglo-Saxon texts: *Solomon and Saturn* (*Sol I*, B5.1; see Cross and Hill 1982 pp 10, 84–87) and *HeptNotes* (B8.1.4.7; see Bischoff 1976 p 121).

*40. Florilegium Frisingense [ANON.Flor.Fris.]: *KVS* (1988) AN Fris.

MSS ? Munich, Bayerische Staatsbibliothek clm 6433: see below.
Lists — Refs none.

The Munich MS (end of the eighth century, Freising; *CLA* 9.1283), was written by the Insular (Northumbrian-trained) scribe Peregrinus (see

Bischoff 1960 pp 61–63, 75; and Kessler 1986 pp 64–77). The editor of the florilegium characterizes it as "eine fast durch und durch von irisch beeinflussten Vorlagen abhängige Sammlung," on the basis of extensive parallels with other Irish works including the LIBER DE NUMERIS (number 39), PREBIARUM (number 42), and the homilies IN NOMINE DEI SUMMI (number 47); see Lehner (Bibliography Part I pp xiii-xxxviii). Frede (*KVS* 1988 pp 22–23) refers to Lehner's characterization of the work but adds: "oder führen die Quellen und das Vorbild DEF [Defensor] eher nach Gallien?" The florilegium includes extracts from PELAGIUS and the grammarian VIRGILIUS MARO. The MS also contains a version of the THREE UTTERANCES SERMON (see under APOCRYPHA).

C. Wright (forthcoming in *Cambridge Medieval Celtic Studies*) cites the florilegium for an example of the Seven Joys of Heaven motif (see number 39 for further examples).

*41. Testimonia diuinae scripturae et patrum [ANON.Test.diu. script.]: *CPL* 385, 1166; *ISLMAH* 145; *KVS* (1988) AN scrip.

MSS ? Munich, Bayerische Staatsbibliothek clm 14096.
Lists — Refs none.

On the Munich MS (from the end of the eighth or the beginning of the ninth century), written by Anglo-Saxon or Irish scribes, see Bischoff (1960 p 229), and Lehner (Bibliography Part I pp 44–48). Bischoff considers the MS "ein Produkt der Berührung keltischer und karolingischer Kultur im westlichen England, in Wales oder Cornwall . . . oder allenfalls in Bretagne zu sein." Lehner distinguishes three phases in the compilation of this work: an original Spanish compilation, including the *Testimonia diuinae scripturae* but with only part of the patristic section; a Redaction with the complete patristic section, from Gaul; and finally a form which incorporated Irish and other material transmitted in the Munich MS. For the connections with Irish texts, including the PROVERBIA GRAECORUM, see Lehner (pp 50–51).

The extracts in Chapter X of this florilegium (*De sobrietate* and *De ebrietate*) occur in other florilegia with Irish connections, including PS BEDE, COLLECTANEA, the Karlsruhe MS Aug. CCLIV, and Munich, Bayerische Staatsbibliothek clm 22053, the Wessobrunner Gebet MS (see McNally 1961 pp 313–14, and C. Wright, forthcoming in *Cambridge Medieval Celtic Studies*). McNally believed this piece "was written in Ireland as early as 700" (p 314). Half of it (*De ebrietate*) appears in an English MS, Cambridge, Corpus Christi College 326: HG 93 (information from J. E. Cross).

42. Prebiarum de multorium exemplaribus [ANON.Preb.mult.exempl.]: *RBMA* 9.9916,3; *BCLL* 777; *KVS* AN ex.

MSS—Refs none.

The *Prebiarum* is a question-and-answer dialogue consisting of miscellaneous motifs, many numerical. McNally (Bibliography Part I pp 158–59) states that it is closely related to the LIBER DE NUMERIS (number 39), and like that work probably originated in the circle of Virgil of Salzburg.

Cross and Hill (1982 p 9) cite the *Prebiarum* for parallels for five items in *Adrian and Ritheus* (*Ad*, B5.2): item 12 on the son who avenged his father in his mother's womb ("the son of the serpent," see pp 137–38); items 26 and 27 on the two feet and four wings of the soul, see pp 149–50; item 38 on the four mute things ("paralleled elsewhere only in COLLECTANEA BEDAE," see pp 154–55); and item 44 on the dearest and most hateful thing ("will," see p 158).

C. Wright (forthcoming in *Cambridge Medieval Celtic Studies*) cites the *Prebiarum* for a parallel for the theme of the three deaths in *HomS* 4 (*VercHom* 9, B3.2.4); cf. number 33 and PS BEDE, COLLECTANEA, which has both the three deaths and the three lives as in *HomS* 4.

Biggs (1986 p 6; cf. Biggs, forthcoming in *Traditio*) cites the *Prebiarum* as one of several Irish analogs (numbers 1, 18, 21, 24, 25, *44, and 45) for the motif of Judgment occuring at midnight in *ChristC* (A3.1).

Cross and Hill (1982 p 9) state that "we may surely assume that the *Prebiarum* is only one representative of its kind." C. Wright (forthcoming in *Cambridge Medieval Celtic Studies*) draws attention to two similar question-and-answer dialogues in Munich, Bayerische Staatsbibliothek clm 19410 and clm 5257, both having extensive parallels with the *Prebiarum* and other Hiberno-Latin texts. These dialogues have versions of the three deaths theme as in *HomS* 4, and of the four mute things as in *Adrian and Ritheus* (*Ad*, B5.2) item 38. Clm 19410 has a sequence of triads (the three ways the devil lures man into false security; three things that lead to hell; three things that lead to heaven; three things not forgiven) parallel to *HomU* 46 (Nap57, B3.4.46); this same sequence occurs also in Munich, Bayerische Staatsbibliothek clm 14364 and clm 22053 (for details, see C. Wright). Clm 19410 also has the Seven Joys of Heaven theme (see number 39) and a variant of the list of virtues of the soul as in *HomM* 13 (*VercHom* 21, B3.5.13) through the HOMILIARY OF ST PÈRE DE CHARTRES item 90; see Szarmach (1986c pp 4–6) and Cross (1987a p 146), who shows that the theme is ultimately from PS BASIL, ADMONITIO AD FILIUM SPIRITUALEM; for ÆLFRIC's translation of this passage see *ÆAdmon* 1 (B1.9.3, pp 38–40). Clm 5257 has the pair of "Thought, Word, Deed" triads discussed by Sims-Williams (1978).

*43. Interrogatio de singulas quaestiones (BN lat. 10616) [ANON.Interr.sing.quaest.]: see Bischoff (1976 number 3); not in *RBMA*.

MSS—Refs none.

This anonymous dialogue between a *Discipulus* and *Magister* begins at fol 94 with selections from ISIDORE, DE NATURA RERUM, but continues at fols 98v–131 with biblical questions. The two-part MS also contains the COMMEMORATIO GENESEOS (number *7). Cross (1987a) notes that "insular writers favoured the question-and-answer form . . . and numbered lists," but declines to identify it as an Irish product "since no Hiberno-Latin scholar has considered it in detail" (p 80). However, McNally (1973 p 192, note 23) refers to the work as "an Irish academic dialogue," and his opinion has been followed by Ó Cróinín (1983 p 146).

Cross (1987a pp 11, 31, and 77–80) cites parallels from this dialogue for several passages in the HOMILIARY OF ST PÈRE DE CHARTRES item 30; see also Dolbeau (1988 pp 256–57).

Homily Collections

*44. Catachesis celtica [ANON.Cat.celt.]: *BCLL* 974; *KVS* AN Wil.

MSS—A-S Vers none.
Quots/Cits ? *HomS* 10 (*BlHom* 3, B3.2.10): see below.
Refs none.

Stancliffe (1982 p 25) describes the *Catachesis* as a compilation "put together from diverse sources, both Irish and Carolingian ones." Rittmueller (1983 pp 201–02) shows that at least one of the supposed Carolingian sources, PASCHASIUS RADBERTUS, was himself drawing on earlier Hiberno-Latin sources used also in the *Catachesis*. Grosjean (1936), and more recently Ó Laoghaire (1987) and McNamara (1989 pp 88–90), have detailed the Irish symptoms and Celtic Latinisms in many of the items in the collection. The MS also contains Rec. III of the DIES DOMINICA (number *4). For an outline of the contents not edited by Wilmart (Bibliography Part I), see Vian (1981/82 pp 353–56). A revision of McNally's typescript edition of the *Catachesis* is under consideration by Leonard Boyle.

The *Catachesis* has been cited for parallels for the portents and events at Christ's nativity in *HomS* 1 (*VercHom* 5, B3.2.1) and *HomU* 10 (*VercHom* 6, B3.4.10) by Willard (1934 pp 229–30) and in detail by Cross (1973; cf. number 18). As Cross later showed (1987a pp 20–21), many of these portents appear in the HOMILIARY OF ST PÈRE DE CHARTRES item 5.

Cross (1972 pp 95–96) also cites the *Catachesis* for a close parallel for the theme of the five likenesses of hell in *HomS* 4 (*VercHom* 9, B3.2.4), concluding that the Latin and Old English are "independent examples of the theme."

C. Wright (1984 pp 56–59, and forthcoming in *Cambridge Medieval Celtic Studies*) shows that the theme of "likenesses" of hell (and heaven) occurs in BISHOP PATRICK, DE TRIBUS HABITACULIS, and in several Irish vernacular sources, including *Apgitir Chrábaid* (cf. Ó Laoghaire 1987 p 157).

Cross (1985a p 233 and 1985b p 121) cites the work for an example of the enumeration of Christ's ten appearances after the Resurrection in *Mart* (B19.bp). This theme, ultimately from AUGUSTINE, DE CONSENSU EVANGELISTARUM, occurs also in Munich, Bayerische Staatsbibliothek clm 6235, the MS containing the PRAEFACIO SECUNDUM MARCUM (number 30) and another Hiberno-Latin commentary on Luke (Bischoff number 29).

Cross (1985b pp 112–13 note 31) cites the *Catachesis celtica* and the CATACHESIS CRACOVIENSIS (number 45), along with several non-Irish sources, as parallels for the list of four manifestations of the Godhead in Christ in *Mart* (B19.p).

Cross (1987a pp 63–64, 66–67, and 90) shows that the HOMILIARY OF ST PÈRE DE CHARTRES items 26 and 27 for Palm Sunday used four pieces from the *Catachesis*, while item 29 "is a variant text" of a fifth piece. Cross concludes that the homiliary "drew on a variant manuscript of the sole extant witness of *Catechesis celtica* in Vat. Reg. lat 49 . . . ." For details, see pp 28–29 for item 26; p 29 for item 27; and p 30 for item 29. Cross also cites the work for two themes "which appear to persist in insular texts" (p 82): the gifts of the Holy Spirit exemplified in the patriarchs, and the Seven Joys of Heaven (see number 39 for details).

Biggs (1986) cites the *Catachesis* as one of several Irish analogs for motifs in *ChristC* (A3.1), including Judgment occurring at midnight (p 6; cf. Biggs, forthcoming in *Traditio*, and numbers 1, 18, 20, 24, 25, 42, and 45) and the angels' fear at Judgment (p 17). Biggs (*Traditio*) also cites the work for the insular theme of the fourfold division of souls (cf numbers 39 and 45) and for the interpretation of the biblical image of the "thief" as the devil.

C. Wright (1988a pp 133–36) cites the *Catachesis*, together with closely parallel comments from the LIBER QUAESTIONUM IN EVANGELIIS (number 21) as a possible source for several passages in *HomS* 10 (*BlHom* 3, B3.2.10); cf. numbers 18, 24–26, 31, and 50).

45. Catachesis Cracoviensis [ANON.Cat.Cracov.]: *RBMA* 9.9494,1; *CPL* 1122; *BCLL* 802; cf. *KVS* An je.

MSS ? Oxford, Bodleian Library Laud Misc. 129 (*SC* 1575): see below.
Lists — Refs none.

The discussion of this collection by David (Bibliography Part I) is based on Cracow, Cathedral Library MS 140 (olim 43; *CLA* 11.1539). Raymond Étaix has since identified four more witnesses: Paris, Bibliothèque Nationale lat. 13408 and 13768; Karlsruhe, Badische Landesbibliothek, Aug. CXCVI; and Orléans, Bibliothèque Municipale 341. Two more partial witnesses are Paris, Bibliothèque Nationale lat. 12021, and the Oxford MS. The Oxford MS (from the first quarter of the ninth century, Main region, written in Anglo-Saxon script; see Coxe 1858–85 fasc 2, col 129) contains part of one homily on the Sermon on the Mount (for another Hiberno-Latin sermon in this MS, see the LINZ HOMILY COLLECTION, number *46). According to Bischoff (1976 p 159, note 124), "although Irish elements can be traced in" the collection, "the language is, to a considerable degree, romanised. In my opinion it is Italian, after 800, not French." See also Frede (*KVS* p 91) on one of the items of the collection: "von einem Iren, Mitte des 8.Jh." An edition of the collection is in preparation by Thomas Amos of the Hill Monastic Microfilm Library.

Cross (1979b p 28, and note 100) notes a passage from the collection that expands the etymology of "Andreas" — "decorus et fortis in corpore et anima" — in a way that corresponds to a phrase in *Mart* (B19.hg).

For parallels for the list of four manifestations of the Godhead in Christ in *Mart* (B19.p), see the CATACHESIS CELTICA (number *44).

Bazire and Cross (1982 p 46) refer to an unpublished passage on the *minora crimina* and *octo principalia vitia* in connection with the distinction between major and minor sins and the purgatorial fire at Judgment in *HomS* 33 (B3.2.33) and *HomS* 44 (B3.2.44), *ÆCHom* II, 45 (B1.2.49), and *HomU* 26 (Nap 29, B.34.26).

Cross (1987a pp 29 and 67), who notes certain "Celtic Latinisms" in the collection, cites a passage from the MS (also found in the CATACHESIS CELTICA, number *44) which is "verbally close" to a passage in the HOMILIARY OF ST PÈRE DE CHARTRES item 26. See also C. Wright (1988a p 134 note 15).

Biggs (forthcoming in *Traditio*) cites homilies in the collection for eschatological motifs in *ChristC* (A3.1), including Judgment occurring at midnight (cf. Biggs 1986 p 6, and numbers 1, 18, 21, 24, 25, 39, 42, and *44) and the Insular theme of the four-fold division of souls at Judgment.

with Frederick M. Biggs

*46. Linz Homily Collection [ANON.Hom.Linz].

MSS   ? Oxford, Bodleian Library Laud Misc. 129 (*SC* 1575): see below.
Lists — Refs   none.

Linz, Bibliothek der Philosophisch-Theologischen Hochschule der Diözese A I/6, fols 71–101 (from the beginning of the ninth century, Bavaria, according to Étaix, citing Bischoff), contains a collection of sermons whose

contents have been analyzed by Plante (1976) and Étaix (1981). Of the thirteen items in this part of the MS, Étaix states that eight "paraissent être
l'oeuvre d'un irlandais établi sur le continent" (p 129; for the incipits and
explicits, see pp 129–30). Étaix edits one of these pieces, a sermon on Mt
7.24–27, from the Linz MS and three other witnesses, including the Oxford MS (from the first quarter of the ninth century, Main region, written
in Anglo-Saxon script; see Coxe 1858–85, fasc 2, col 129), which also contains part of one sermon from the CATACHESIS CRACOVIENSIS (see preceding entry). Étaix suggests Irish authorship on the basis of parallels with
PS JEROME, EXPOSITIO IN QUATUOR EVANGELIORUM (number 18), the VIENNA
COMMENTARY ON LUKE (number 31), and the CATACHESIS CELTICA (number
*44), in addition to the style of the sermon ("particulièrement rocailleux
et heurté," p 111).

C. Wright (forthcoming in *Cambridge Medieval Celtic Studies*) cites a parallel
from a Linz homily for the enumeration of three characteristics of the
Caesarian tax in *HomS* 1 (*VercHom* 5, B3.2.1); cf. number 1.

C. Wright (in a forthcoming study) cites a simile applied to Mary's conception through the Holy Spirit in connection with *Mart* (B19.bm); for details see number 24.

47. Homilies in nomine Dei summi [ANON.Hom.nom.Dei.summi]: BCLL 803; KVS AN McNally.

MSS   ? Vatican, Pal. lat. 220: see below.
Lists—A-S Vers   none.
Quots/Cits HomM 14.2 (B3.5.14.2; ed Luiselli Fadda 169.72–171–83):
ANON.Hom.nom.Dei.summi 141.5–22.
Refs   none.

McNally edited the seven sermons rubricated *in nomine Dei summi* from
a larger collection of homilies in two Vatican MSS, Pal. lat. 212 and 220;
the latter MS (from the first quarter of the tenth century, Middle Rhineland)
is in Anglo-Saxon script. A third MS of the collection, unknown to McNally,
is in East Berlin, Phillipps 1716 (ninth century); see C. Wright (1987a
p 135 and 1987b p 452, note 6), and Cross (1986a p 84).

C. Wright points out that this homily collection "transmits a core of texts
used in some form" in Old English homilies in Oxford, Bodleian Library
Junius 85/86 (C), London, BL Cotton Faustina A.ix (J), and Cambridge,
Corpus Christi College 302 (K). These include the so-called THREE UTTER-
ANCES SERMON, of which three versions exist in Old English, though none
descends directly from the text in this collection (for details on the Three
Utterances sermon, see under APOCRYPHA, MISCELLANEOUS). One of these
Old English versions, *HomM* 5 (Willard, B3.5.5) conflates the Three Ut-

terances exemplum with an excerpt from PS AUGUSTINE, SERMO APP. 251 (see Cross 1982) which appears as the initial item in all three MSS of the Latin homily collection, although it is not one of the sermons McNally edited as Hiberno-Latin (see C. Wright 1987a pp 136–37 and 1987b p 453). Luiselli Fadda (1977 pp 2–3) pointed out that the same Old English homily contains a theme on the food of the soul that appears in the APOCRYPHA PRISCILLIANISTICA (see under APOCRYPHA), but the theme occurs in other contexts, including the homilies In nomine Dei summi. C. Wright (1987b) also shows that a passage contrasting the teachings of God and of the Devil was used in HomM 14.2 (B3.5.14.2), which was in turn adapted by the composite HomS 6 (Ass 14; B3.2.6; 167.102–168.112). Finally, one of the MSS, Pal. lat. 220, also contains Recension III of the Hiberno-Latin DIES DOMINICA (number *4) and an interpolated version of the APOCALYPSE OF THOMAS (see under APOCRYPHA). Wright concludes that "although the Latin collection in the Vatican and Berlin MSS was not itself a direct source for the Old English homilies in C, J, and K, it is an important witness to the kind of florilegium that must have been available to the Old English homilists" (p 453).

To the evidence cited by C. Wright may now be added Cross' statement that PS AUGUSTINE, SERMO 64 (PL 40.1347), a source for passages in the HOMILIARY OF ST PÈRE DE CHARTRES item 20, appears in Pal. lat. 220, fols 33ff, in a variant form "generally much closer in word" than Migne's text (Cross 1987a pp 245–47).

*48. Munich Homily Collection [ANON.Hom.(Mun.6233)]: RBMA 9914–16.

MSS   ? Munich, Bayerische Staatsbibliothek clm 6233: see below.
Lists — Refs   none.

On the Munich MS (second quarter of the eighth century, South Bavarian, with corrections in an Anglo-Saxon hand; CLA 9.1252), which also contains a Hiberno-Latin commentary on Matthew (number 26), see Cross (1987b and 1987a p 10). On the homilies in the MSS see Cross (1987b, and 1987a pp 62–63 and 68–70); Cross states that the collection is "a compilation from diverse areas," including one item from the homiliary of Alanus of Farfa (1987b p 68). However, Cross also argues that "there are 'Irish symptoms' in some of the homilies" (p 10), notably a homily on the Holy Innocents (edited by Cross 1987b) and a homily for the Epiphany (see Cross 1987a pp 69–70). An edition of the homilies in clm 6233, together with the corresponding items in the HOMILIARY OF ST PÈRE DE CHARTRES, is in preparation by Cross and Denis Brearley.

Cross (1987a) cites the sermons in clm 6233 for parallels for passages in several homilies in the HOMILIARY OF ST PÈRE DE CHARTRES, including item 1 on the Holy Innocents (see Cross 1987b, and 1987a pp 23 and 68, and cf. numbers 1, *20, 21, 24, and 50); item 13 on the gifts of the Magi (Cross 1987a pp 69 and 81–82, and cf. numbers 18 and 24); and item 14 on water and wine miracle at Cana and Baptism of Christ (Cross 1987a pp 24, 83–84). Several other sermons in this homiliary represent selections from homilies in clm 6233, including items 43, 45, 46, and 50 (see Cross 1987a pp 34–37), while item 44 has a phrase from the collection (Cross 1987a p 35).

*49. Vatican Homily Collection [ANON.Hom.(Pal.lat.556)]: *KVS* PS-AU Pal.

MSS ? Vatican, Pal. lat. 556: see below.
Lists — Refs none.

A collection of eighteen homilies has been edited from the Vatican MS by S. Teresa (Bibliography Part I), who designates the collection "il florilegio pseudoagostiniano palatino." The Vatican MS (from the beginning of the ninth century), which Bischoff (1977 p 112) assigns to "Deutsch-angelsächsisches Gebiet," is written in Anglo-Saxon script. Among the items several have points of contact with the CATACHESIS CELTICA (number *44; see S. Teresa pp 196 and 204, and cf. Frede, *KVS* p 160).

Wack and Wright (forthcoming) cite a pair of triads in item 4 of the collection (ed. pp 219–20), which occur also in PAULINUS OF AQUILEIA, LIBER EXHORTATIONIS, as a source for an abbreviated version of the THREE UTTERANCES exemplum in Munich, Bayerische Staatsbibliothek clm 28135; this abbreviated Latin version is in turn the source for the Old English version of the exemplum in *HomM* 5 (Willard, B3.5.5; for details, see the entry on the THREE UTTERANCES SERMON under APOCRYPHA, MISCELLANEOUS).

Cross, in the preface to the forthcoming reprint of Bazire and Cross (1982), cites an image in item 17 of the collection (man lives in the world as if in another's house) as a parallel for a passage in *HomS* 31 (B3.2.31).

50. Leabhar Breac Homilies [ANON.Hom.LeabharBreac]: *BCLL* 565.

MSS — Refs none.

Leabhar Breac contains homilies in Irish with interspersed Latin passages, and some items in Latin believed to date back to the eleventh century; for a general study see MacDonncha (1976), and for an outline of the contents, see Tristram (1985 pp 143–45). The Irish portions have been attributed to Maol Iosa Ní Brolcháin (see MacDonncha, and the works by Muireann Ní Bhrolcháin cited by McNamara 1987b p 593 note 107); but for objections to this view, see Tristram (1985 pp 316–17). Rittmueller (1982, 1984, and 1986) examines in detail the homily "In Cena Domini" and its relationship to several Hiberno-Latin commentaries (numbers 1, 21, and 25). In addition to the partial editions by Atkinson and Hogan (Bibliography Part I), two homilies for the Circumcision and Transfiguration have been edited separately by MacDonncha (1983 and 1984). Latin fragments in the body-and-soul homily, omitted by Atkinson, are printed by Gaidoz (1889).

Brown's argument (GR 3391) for the influence on *Elene* (*El*, A2.6) of the (lost) Latin original of the *Leabhar Breac* homilies on the *Invention of the Holy Cross* is discounted by Gradon (GR 3563).

The body-and-soul homily has been cited by Willard (GR 6235, p 93) for an analog of the concept of the garment of the soul in one of the Old English versions of the THREE UTTERANCES SERMON, *HomS* 31 (Willard, B3.2.31; cf. the entry under APOCRYPHA, MISCELLANEOUS).

Menner (GR 4337 p 112) cites a homily (in Irish and Latin) on the Pater Noster as an example of the Pater Noster as a weapon against the devil in connection with the poetic *Solomon and Saturn* (*MSol*, A13).

Hill (GR 3481, p 385) cites an Irish homily, together with a closely parallel passage in an infancy gospel edited by James (1927 p 68), as an example of the motif of cosmic stasis at the birth of Christ in the Old English poem *Descent into Hell* (*Hell*, A3.26).

Cross and Hill (1982 pp 94–95) cite an Irish homily for a parallel for a sequence, ultimately from 4 Esr 5.23–27, listing the "best" plant, bird, water, and tree in *Solomon and Saturn* (*Sol I*, B5.1).

Cross (1986b pp 30–32; cf. Cross 1987a pp 38, 84–86) discusses the story of Michael fighting a dragon in Asia, which occurs in several Latin texts, including the HOMILIARY OF ST PÈRE DE CHARTRES item 55, which Cross also edits (1986b pp 33–35). Cross (1987a p 69) cites another Irish text from the *Leabhar Breac* on the number of Innocents in item 1 (cf. numbers 1, *20, 21, 24, and *48).

C. Wright (1988a pp 130 note 3; 131 note 4; 132 note 8; and 135 note 21) cites the Latin homily on the Temptation for parallels for brief passages in *HomS* 10 (*BlHom* 3, B3.2.10; cf. numbers 18, 21, 24–26, 31, and *44).

Charles D. Wright

HOMILIARIES AND HOMILIES

[Mary Clayton will provide an introduction to the topic, and separate entries on the Latin collections will follow. See, however, HIBERNO-LATIN . . .

HOMILY COLLECTIONS for the anonymous Irish collections. For this *Trial Version*, only the anonymous Old English Homilies are included.]

Anonymous Old English Homilies

A strong tradition of vernacular composition and transmission of homilies and sermons developed in the late Anglo-Saxon period. Within that tradition is the work of a few named writers (ÆLFRIC, Byrhtferth, and WULFSTAN), but a large proportion of the surviving corpus is anonymous. It is not clear how early the vernacular tradition began: some critics have placed many of the surviving Vercelli and Blickling pieces in the ninth century on linguistic and stylistic grounds (see GR 6443 and 6207), while others suggest the end of the tenth century, close to the date of the earliest surviving MSS (see Gatch 1977 pp 4–11). The truth probably lies somewhere between these two extremes.

From the beginning of the tradition as it survives now, writers quoted earlier sermons extensively and often verbatim. One long item in the Vercelli Book (which is palaeographically the earliest surviving MS) has incorporated within it a large part of another item in the same collection. This is a pattern which is repeated throughout the eleventh century as sermon writers quarried existing books for material. The difficulty of establishing a chronology for items recorded only in the eleventh century or later precludes the investigation of indebtedness among them, and this entry is therefore largely confined to the two earlier compositions. These are the Vercelli Homilies (Vercelli, Biblioteca Capitolare CXVII, edited in GR 6200 and Szarmach 1981a), which draw upon the resources of a Canterbury library and which are therefore often quoted in later homilies created from Canterbury books, and the Blickling Homilies (Princeton, Scheide Library 71, edited in GR 6169), which probably represent material that survived in a Mercian library and are therefore not as frequently used in other surviving homilies (see Scragg 1985). It should be noted that it is extremely unlikely that the eleventh-century items cited were drawn directly from extant copies such as those in Vercelli and Blickling, which themselves may be composite (see the comments on VERCELLI HOMILY 21 below).

For a survey of the whole corpus of anonymous homilies in Old English, and for details of possible indebtedness not discussed here, see Scragg 1979. Fuller analysis of the Vercelli items, together with a text of all the relevant Old English material, will appear in the forthcoming EETS edition of the Vercelli Homilies (edited by Scragg).

Vercelli Homily 1 (*HomS* 24).

MSS   1. Vercelli, Biblioteca Capitolare CXVII: HG 941; NRK 394.1.
2. Oxford, Bodleian Library Bodley 340 (*SC* 2404) and 342 (*SC* 2405): HG 569; NRK 309.25.
3. Cambridge, Corpus Christi College 162: HG 50; NRK 38.30.
4. Cambridge, Corpus Christi College 198: HG 64; NRK 48.25.
5. Cambridge, Corpus Christi College 303: NRK 57.15.
Lists—A-S Vers   none.
Quots/Cits   *ÆCHom* II, 14.1 (B1.2.16) 255–65, 303–04, and 346–52: see below.
Refs   none.

Vercelli Homily 1, the first item in the Vercelli Book, is a close rendering of John 18 and 19 with very little homiletic comment. In the Oxford and Cambridge MSS, the same item appears in an extensively revised form, with long additions, although in the standard edition (GR 6200) the main additions are not available because they were intended to appear in an appendix which was never published. (Corpus 303 dates to the twelfth century.) Extracts from the revised version are added to the ÆLFRIC homily in London, BL Cotton Tiberius A.iii (see Godden 1979 pp lv-lvi, and 381–90).

Vercelli Homily 2 (*HomU* 8).

MSS   1. Vercelli, Biblioteca Capitolare CXVII: HG 941; NRK 394.2.
Lists—A-S Vers   none.
Quots/Cits   1. *HomM* 13 (B3.5.13): see below.
2. *HomU* 15 (B3.4.15): see below.
3. *HomU* 32 (B3.4.32): see below.
4. *HomU* 34 (B3.4.34): see below.
Refs   none.

Vercelli Homily 2 is an eschatological piece with a long alliterative passage (Förster prints lines 47–72 as verse in GR 6200). Most of this homily (1–107) is incorporated into VERCELLI HOMILY 21. The version *HomU* 15 in Oxford, Bodleian Library Hatton 115 (edited by Luiselli Fadda 1977 pp 186–211) is a composite homily with one paragraph (114–44) taken from Vercelli 2. Napier homily XL (*HomU* 32; edited in GR 6501) has much of Vercelli Homily 2 added to passages by WULFSTAN. Napier homily XLII (*HomU* 34; edited in GR 6501), contains a translation of ADSO with a conclusion drawn ultimately from this homily.

Vercelli Homily 4 (*HomU* 9).

MSS   1. Vercelli, Biblioteca Capitolare CXVII: HG 941; NRK 394.4.
2. Cambridge, Corpus Christi College 41: HG 39; NRK 32.9.

3. Cambridge, Corpus Christi College 367, Part II: HG 100; NRK 63.10.
Lists—A-S Vers none.
Quots/Cits 1. *HomU* 27 (B3.4.27): see below.
  2. *HomU* 55 (B3.4.55): see below.
Refs none.

Vercelli Homily 4 is also eschatological and has at its heart one of the most dramatic addresses of the soul to the body in Old English literature (see APOCRYPHA, VISIO SANCTI PAULI). It opens, however, with a heavily rhetorical and often conventional exhortation to repentance, parts of which found their way into four composite homilies during the eleventh century: *HomU* 27, which was itself selectively used in the composition of *HomS* 41 (see Scragg 1977), and *HomU* 55, which was drawn upon by the author of *HomU* 26 (see Scragg 1979).

Vercelli Homily 9 (*HomS* 4).

MSS 1. Vercelli, Biblioteca Capitolare CXVII: HG 941; NRK 394.11.
  2. Oxford, Bodleian Library Bodley 340 (*SC* 2404) and 342 (*SC* 2405): HG 569; NRK 309.8.
Lists—A-S Vers none.
Quots/Cits 1. *HomU* 15 (B3.4.15): see below.
  2. *HomU* 35 (B3.4.35): see below.
  3. *HomM* 9 (B3.5.9): see below.
  4. *HomU* 27 (B3.4.27): see below.
  5. *Conf* 1.10.3 (B11.10.3): see below.
Refs none.

Vercelli Homily 9 is another eschatological homily drawing on a variety of Latin sources, some of which have been identified as Hiberno-Latin (see HIBERNO-LATIN . . . HOMILY COLLECTIONS, CATACHESIS CELTICA, number *44). The two surviving copies have slight but significant differences (see the edition in GR 248). The version recorded in the Vercelli Book gave rise to the extracts in the composite pieces *HomM* 9 and *HomU* 27. That recorded in Bodley 340 was drawn on by the compiler of the composite confessional text, *Conf* 1.10.3. A markedly different (and probably earlier) version of Vercelli 9 that has not survived was used by the authors of two distinct items subsumed under the AC designation *HomU* 15, and from this line came two brief (and different) extracts incorporated separately into the two surviving versions of *HomU* 35 (see Scragg 1979; the relationship of the two versions of *HomU* 35 is described in GR 6528, pp 230–32). That the two MS versions of *HomU* 15 constitute two (related) items and not two copies of one (as suggested in AC) is clear from a comparison of the edited texts, Robinson (GR 6229) for that in Cotton Tiberius A.iii, and Luiselli Fadda

1977 for that in Oxford, Bodleian Library Hatton 115, but verbal parallels between them show that they both descend from a version of Vercelli Homily 9 different from that preserved in the Vercelli Book and Bodley 340; for detailed evidence, see my forthcoming edition of the Vercelli Homilies.

Vercelli Homily 10 (*HomS* 40).

MSS 1. Vercelli, Biblioteca Capitolare CXVII: HG 941; NRK 394.12.
  2. Princeton, University Library Library, Scheide Library 71: HG 905; NRK 382.9.
  3. Cambridge, Corpus Christi College 421: HG 198; NRK 69.9.
  4. Cambridge, Corpus Christi College 302: NRK 56.33.
Lists—A-S Vers none.
Quots/Cits 1. *HomS* 7 (B3.2.7): see below.
  2. *HomU* 3 (B3.4.3): see below.
  3. *HomU* 27 (B3.4.27): see below.
  4. ? *HomU* 35 (B3.4.35): see below.
  5. ? *HomU* 15 (B3.4.15): see below.
Refs none.

This popular (to judge from the number of surviving MSS) eschatological homily has three principal Latin sources—PAULINUS OF AQUILEIA, PS AUGUSTINE HOMILY 310, and ISIDORE OF SEVILLE—and consequently can be seen to divide into three parts. Eleventh-century writers utilized these divisions, the author of *HomS* 7 taking the last two (verbatim) to form an independent piece, the author of *HomU* 3 adding only the last to other material to create a new item (edited as number 12 in GR 6219). *HomU* 27 is a composite homily that draws on other Vercelli items (see Scragg 1977). It may also be noticed that an introductory sentence found only in the Vercelli Book version of Vercelli 10 is verbally similar to sentences in *HomU* 35 (both versions) and *HomU* 15 in Oxford, Bodleian Library Hatton 115.

Vercelli Homily 15 (*HomU* 6).

MSS Vercelli, Biblioteca Capitolare CXVII: HG 941; NRK 394.17.
Lists—A-S Vers none.
Quots/Cits *HomS* 6 (B3.2.6): see below.
Refs none.

Vercelli 15 is one of a number of Old English homilies that have as their principal source the APOCALYPSE OF THOMAS (see APOCRYPHA). *HomS* 6 is a composite homily (edited as item 14 in GR 6215) made up entirely of extracts from other surviving vernacular homilies (see Scragg 1979 pp 245–46). Its conclusion is taken from that of Vercelli 15.

Vercelli Homily 19 (*HomS* 34).

MSS   1. Vercelli, Biblioteca Capitolare CXVII: HG 941; NRK 394.24.
     2. Cambridge, Corpus Christi College 162: HG 50; NRK 38.35.
     3. Cambridge, Corpus Christi College 303: NRK 57.43
     4. London, BL Cotton Cleopatra B.xiii: HG 322; NRK 144.6.
Lists — A-S Vers   none.
Quots/Cits   1. *Sol* I (B5.1): see below.
     2. *WCan* 1.2 (B13.1.1): see below.
     3. *HomU* 15 (B3.4.15): see below.
Refs   none.

Vercelli Homilies 19, 20, and 21 are a uniform set prescribed for the three Rogation Days, deriving largely from the HOMILIARY OF ST PÈRE DE CHARTRES (see Cross 1987a, who prints the texts and sources). Probably all three were composed by one writer (a suggestion made in Scragg 1973 p 204, but developed in Szarmach 1978 p 248, denied in Bazire and Cross 1982 p 25, but admitted in Cross 1987a p 126). The appearance of otherwise unique wording, and occasionally consecutive sentences, in more than one of these three pieces is therefore taken as a sign of an author repeating himself, although it is impossible to know in what order the pieces were originally composed. (Fuller consideration of these correspondences will be given in my forthcoming edition of the Vercelli Homilies.)

Vercelli Homily 19 begins with the Trinity and then goes on to a succinct account of the creation of the world, the fall of the angels, and the story of Adam and Eve. The calculation of Adam's life and his time in hell appears in Vercelli 19 and its principle Latin source (see the HOMILIARY OF ST PÈRE DE CHARTRES, and HIBERNO-LATIN . . . BIBLICAL COMMENTARIES, number 1, the REFERENCE BIBLE). The compilation *Solomon and Saturn* has the English in virtually the same wording, where it is unlikely to be drawn independently from the source. A third version in English, in wording even closer to Vercelli 19 than *Solomon and Saturn*, was added as *Notes* 10.3 (B24.10.3) to Oxford, Bodleian Library Hatton 115 in the twelfth century. The probable history is that the sentence was culled from the vernacular homily and preserved in the form of a note like that in Hatton 115 or in a commonplace book. The text falsely associated with WULFSTAN's *Canons of Edgar*, *WCan* 1.2, and the BL Cotton Tiberius A.iii text of *HomU* 15 (variously called "The Devil's Account of the Next World" and "The Theban Legend," see Scragg 1986) are late pieces both of which incorporate sentences from Vercelli 19.

Vercelli Homily 20 (*HomS* 38).

MSS   1. Vercelli, Biblioteca Capitolare CXVII: HG 941; NRK 394.25.
     2. Cambridge, Corpus Christi College 162: HG 50; NRK 38.36.

3. Cambridge, Corpus Christi College 303: NRK 57.44.

Lists—A-S Vers   none.

Quots/Cits HomS 49 (B3.2.49): see below.

Refs none.

As well as compiling Vercelli Homilies 19, 20, and 21, the same anonymous author may be responsible for other surviving pieces. *HomS* 49, edited in GR 5290 as number 2, has a passage in common with Vercelli Homily 20. At the same time, *HomS* 49 was thought by Jost (GR 6528, p 306) to have been written by the same author as *HomS* 13 and *HomS* 16, both of which draw extensively on the HOMILIARY OF ST PÈRE DE CHARTRES used by the author of Vercelli 20 (see the text and sources in Cross 1987a pp 196-231, and a brief discussion of the authorship question at pp 232-35). The precise relations of all of these pieces need further study.

Vercelli Homily 21 (*HomM* 13).

MSS Vercelli, Biblioteca Capitolare CXVII: HG 941; NRK 394.26.

Lists—A-S Vers   none.

Quots/Cits 1. *HomU* 27 (B3.4.27): see below.

 2. *HomU* 12 (B3.4.12): see below.

Refs none.

Vercelli 21 is a composite homily drawing on both Latin sources (see VERCELLI 19) and English ones (see VERCELLI 2). It provided the longest of the extracts from the Vercelli Homilies incorporated in the composite *HomU* 27 (see Scragg 1977). There is also a brief overlap with *HomU* 12 where the Latin source, used elsewhere in Vercelli 21, suggests that *HomU* 12 is the later piece. Cross (1987a pp 149-50) argues that the poem *Exhortation* (A18), which has been regarded as a source for the prose homily (GR 6527, and 6535), might be seen as derived from it.

Blickling Homily 5 (*HomS* 17).

MSS Princeton, University Library, Scheide Library 71: HG 905; NRK 382.5.

Lists—A-S Vers   none.

Quots/Cits HomU 26 (B3.4.26): see below.

Refs none.

This is one of many examples of the conclusion of a homily being abstracted and used for a different piece. Blickling 5 is a Lenten homily. Its conclusion, containing the "Seven Joys" motif found frequently in Old English (see Hill GR 3333), is repeated in the composite *HomU* 26.

Blickling Homily 8 (*HomU* 19).

MSS Princeton, University Library, Scheide Library 71: HG 905; NRK 382.8.
Lists—A-S Vers none.
Quots/Cits HomS 6 (B3.2.6): see below.
Refs none.

Blickling 8 is a powerful eschatological homily which, in a reduced version, forms the longest section of the composite *HomS* 6 (edited as number 14 in GR 6215; see VERCELLI HOMILY 15).

Blickling Homily 10 (*HomU* 20).

MSS Princeton, University Library, Scheide Library 71: HG 905; NRK 382.10.
Lists—A-S Vers none.
Quots/Cits Cambridge, Corpus Christi College 198, item 62 (listed in AC under B3.4.20): see below.
Refs none.

The second half of another Blickling eschatological homily has been added to an ÆLFRIC piece, *ÆAdmon* 3 (B1.9.6), to create a new item.

Junius 86, Item 2 (*HomM* 14).

MSS Oxford, Bodleian Library Junius 86: HG 642; NRK 336.2.
Lists—A-S Vers none.
Quots/Cits HomS 6 (B3.2.6): see below.
Refs none.

The second item in Junius 86 is a late copy of the third of three early pieces used to create the composite *HomS* 6 (see VERCELLI HOMILY 15, and BLICKLING HOMILY 8).

D. G. Scragg

HRABANUS MAURUS: *DS* 13.1-10; Manitius (1911-31) vol 1 pp 288-302.

Hrabanus Maurus (also Rabanus) spent his early years at the monasteries of Fulda and Tours, where he became one of ALCUIN's favorite students.

He was elected abbot of Tours in 822, but about twenty years later he was forced to retire to Petersberg, near Fulda. In 847 he was appointed archbishop of Mainz, where he died in 856. Hrabanus' many writings attempt to help his fellow monks and priests in their normal roles as teachers and preachers. He held the great patristic writers — AUGUSTINE, GREGORY, JEROME, ISIDORE, and BEDE — in high esteem and preferred to extract long passages from their writings to using his own words. His methodology has sometimes caused modern readers to dismiss him as a plagiarizer, with scant consideration of the originality he showed in adapting and arranging his material. More than a thousand MSS survive of his writings, dating from the ninth to the sixteenth century, clearly attesting to his popularity during the Middle Ages. An English summary of his life and career by McCulloh appears in *CCCM* 44; see also Kottje and Zimmermann (1982), and Böhne (1980).

Hrabanus' writings were never as popular in Anglo-Saxon England as they were during the later English Middle Ages. Those works that did become known were introduced during the Benedictine reforms of the tenth century. Generally speaking, it is only the earlier works, themselves the most popular of his writings during the late ninth and tenth centuries, that are attested in England in one form or another, and evidence for knowledge of the later works before the twelfth century is generally slight and circumstantial. One booklist, Ælfwold (ML 5.1), includes a reference to Hrabanus, but does not specify a work. None of his works were ever translated in their entirety (though sections of some were). Gneuss (1978) notes that Dunstan must have been an attentive reader and user of DE LAUDE S. CRUCIS. Bethurum (GR, 6501, p 131) remarks that Wulfstan was "widely read in ninth-century literature, and borrowed . . . from Rabanus (among others)," and recent scholarship has tended to support this view. On the other hand, Hermann's (1972 p 3) contention, that Hrabanus' writings "deeply influenced the Anglo-Saxons," while an attractive one, is difficult to substantiate, if only because Hrabanus himself borrowed so much from his predecessors. One of the chief obstacles to a proper search for Hrabanus' influence is the almost total absence of critical editions.

[For this *Trial Version*, only Hrabanus' didactic works will be discussed.]

De computo [HRAB.MAVR.Comp.].

MSS   1. Exeter, Cathedral Library 3507: HG 258.
        2. London, BL Cotton Vitellius A.xii: HG 398.
        3. Oxford, St John's College 17: HG 683.
Lists   see headnote.

A-S Vers   none.
Quots/Cits   ByrM (B20.20.1): see below.
Refs   none.

According to the dedication, Hrabanus wrote this work in response to questions from a monk named Marcharius; it discusses the divisions of time, and explains how to determine the date of Easter. The Vitellius copy is from Salisbury; it also contains a calendar with some clear Continental associations; see Ker (1976 p 39). According to Ker, the text of *De computo* is derived from the Exeter copy, though not directly. The copy in the St John's MS is actually a summary of part of the work, perhaps by Byrhtferth himself; see Baker (1982 p 126 note 19). Hart (GR 5972 and 6116) has suggested that the MS was copied at Ramsey, and was later sent to Thorney.

Crawford (GR 5959) notes that most of the material in Byrhtferth's *Manual* concerning the division of time (112.6–120.7) is drawn ultimately from Hrabanus' work. Baker (1982 pp 136–37) has shown that the long gloss in the Oxford MS is the immediate source for much of the section.

De disciplina ecclesiastica [HRAB.MAVR.Discip.eccl.].

MSS—A-S Vers   none.
Quots/Cits   ? *WHom* 7 (B2.2.2) 93–95: see below.
Refs   none.

Written for missionary activity, the *De disciplina* treats in simple terms basic tenets of the faith. Bethurum (GR 6503) thinks Wulfstan may echo this work (112.1226.41–43) in his homily on the Creed. The sentence following the one she cites in her note (p 308) may, she thinks, furnish another of Wulfstan's ideas.

De institutione clericorum [HRAB.MAVR.Instit.cler.].

MSS   1. Cambridge, Corpus Christi College 190: HG 59; see below.
    2. Cambridge, Corpus Christi College 265: HG 73; see below.
    3. Cambridge, Pembroke College 25: HG 131; see below.
Lists   Peterborough: ML 13.63.
A-S Vers   *LitBen* 7 (B12.7): see below.
Quots/Cits   WHom 8c (B2.2.5) 59–62: see below.
Refs   none.

This work, intended as an elementary guide to the duties of priests, probably became known in England during the Benedictine reforms of the tenth century. The Corpus MSS 190 and 265 contain extracts from the second book of the *De institutione clericorum*: Fehr (GR 6255, p 338) argues that the extracts were made by ÆLFRIC and sent to WULFSTAN; Bethurum (GR 6522), however, connects MS 190 with Wulfstan; see also Clemoes (GR 6256). Ure (GR 6258) has shown that MS 190 is the source for the prose parts of the Old English *Benedictine Office* (*LitBen* 7, B12.7) ascribed to Wulfstan. A number of passages from *De institutione* were probably known earlier in Anglo-Saxon England through their inclusion in the HOMILIARY OF ST PÈRE DE CHARTRES (see HOMILIARIES), represented by Pembroke 25; Cross (1987a) lists passages drawn from books 2 and 3 in his items 22, 31, 32, 43, 48, and 78–88.

In her note on lines 59–63 of Wulfstan's Homily VIIIc, Bethurum (GR 5503, p 316) notes that Hrabanus' *De institutione* (312.15–26) may underlie the passage. She also suggests that Wulfstan may have known AUGUSTINE's DE DOCTRINA through Hrabanus' resume in book 3 of *De institutione* (GR 6503, p 87 note 2), and she cites this work elsewhere in her edition (see index).

William Schipper

LAURENCE OF NOVARA

Homilia de eleemosyna [LAUR.NOV.Hom.eleem.]: *CPL* 645; *DS* 9.402–04.

MSS   Dublin, Trinity College 174 (B.4.3): HG215.
Lists — Refs   none.

Laurence, a fifth-century bishop of Novara, wrote two homilies or treatises (*CPL*, 644, 645) on penitence and on alms. His work on alms, printed *PL* 66.105–16, appears on fols 99–103v in a MS otherwise containing *passiones*, and sermons on saints; see M. Colker's forthcoming catalog of MSS of Trinity College, Dublin.

J.E. Cross

LAWS

[The entire section will be under the direction of Patrick Wormald.]

Lex Salica [ANON.Lex.Salic.].

MSS—A-S Vers   none.
Quots/Cits   LawAf 1 (B14.4.4) section 9.2: see below.
Refs   none.

The Frankish law code *Lex Salica* is a collection of folk and personal laws in Latin, surviving in six major recensions dating from the reign of Clovis. Frankish kings, ending with Charlemagne, added their own provisions (McKitterick 1980 pp 23–24). Although no known MSS of English origin or provenance survive, circumstantial evidence indicates that the earliest English royal codes, beginning with Æthelberht I of Kent, are indebted to this code, the most authoritative of the Germanic barbaric codes in the sense that at least three recensions emanated from the royal chancery (Wormald 1977 p 108; and McKitterick 1983 p 99).

The evidence is of several types. In the HISTORIA ECCLESIASTICA II.V, BEDE tells us that Æthelberht issued legislation *iuxta exempla Romanorum*, a phrase implying written law codes in Latin as the model. Since there is no trace of Roman law in Æthelberht's legislation, Bede probably had Germanic materials in mind, although these certainly had been developed under Roman influence (Wallace-Hadrill 1962 pp 3–10; and Wallace-Hadrill 1971 pp 32–37). Of Æthelberht's ninety chapters, as many as nineteen are parallel to statements in the *Lex Salica* (Wallace-Hadrill 1971 p 38). Moreover, at least one specialized term surviving in the so-called Malberg (Frankish) glosses to the *Lex Salica—leudes*, which yields the Kentish *leode*—seems to have been borrowed into Æthelberht's code (*LawAbt*, B14.1; section 64), and into Wihtræd's code (*LawWi*, B14.3.2; section 25); on this borrowing see Wallace-Hadrill (1971 p 38), and for information on *leudes* and its Frankish variants, see Rivers (1986 p 226).

Alfred's laws, too, seem to have been influenced by the *Lex Salica*. The list of compensations for injuries in *LawAf1* sections 44–77 bears close resemblance to similar lists contained within the *Lex Salica* (sections 22–23, and 47) and *LawAbt* sections 33–72. More importantly, *LawAf 1* section 9.2 refers to exceptionally large fines for particular offenses, including horse theft and bee theft, which now are to be made equal to fines for all types of theft except kidnapping. These offenses carry the highest fines in the *Lex Salica* (sections 9 and 62) but are not mentioned in any of the surviving Old English laws prior to Alfred's code. Recent studies of Alfred's Continental connections demonstrate the context within which he and his advisers may have been influenced by the *Lex Salica*; see Wallace-Hadrill (1975 pp 212–13), Wormald (1977 pp 132–34), and Nelson (1986).

Mary P. Richards

LITURGY

[The entire section will be under the direction of Richard Pfaff, and based on Helmut Gneuss' "Liturgical Books in Anglo-Saxon England and their Old English Terminology" in Lapidge and Gneuss (1985) 91–141.]

W. Prayers: *CPL* 2015–27; see also AUGUSTINE, BEDE, COLUMBA, EPHRAEM LATINUS, EUGENIUS OF TOLEDO, HILARY OF POITIERS, ISIDORE OF SEVILLE, AURELIUS PRUDENTIUS, RATPERT OF ST GALL, and CAELIUS SEDULIUS.

Latin prayers for private devotion, as opposed to liturgical use, were common in both early and late Anglo-Saxon England. Following this introduction to the evidence for private prayers in general are separate entries for the four early collections, which are most likely to have influenced later Anglo-Saxon literary culture. Not included in this *Trial Version* are entries on certain individual prayers.

In early Anglo-Saxon England, prayers are found in four English anthologies dating from about 750–825: the ROYAL LIBRARY PRAYER BOOK, the BOOK OF NUNNAMINSTER, the HARLEY PRAYER BOOK, and the BOOK OF CERNE. These anthologies, which do not appear to rest on Continental models, might include litanies, hymns, psalms, and extracts from the Gospels on the Passion. The prayers themselves come from a variety of sources, including the liturgy and hagiography. The prayers are sometimes attributed to authors (most frequently to such fathers as AUGUSTINE, JEROME, and GREGORY), but usually they are anonymous. They are addressed to the Trinity, Christ, and God the Father, and less frequently to the Virgin, angels, and saints. In general, the early prayer books reveal Irish or Celtic influence as well as being indebted to the Latin ecclesiastical culture of the continent; see the *BCLL* 1286–99, W. Meyer (1917), and K. Hughes (1970).

There is one devotional miscellany from late Anglo-Saxon England, London, BL Cotton Galba A.xiv (edited by Muir 1988), but most prayers or collections of prayers from this period are found in psalter MSS. The later collections (almost all dating from the eleventh century) borrow prayers drawn from Continental devotional anthologies of the ninth and tenth centuries (see Wilmart 1940 for an edition of representative examples, and Salmon 1976–80 for a repertory of MSS) as well as those from the earlier English anthologies which may have been reintroduced to England from the Continent; see Bestul (1986) for a general discussion. The later collections also occasionally include Old English glosses or translations of Latin prayers.

Psalter collects are short prayers following individual psalms; they may have been used in private devotion. The psalter collects are found in many Continental MSS and exist in three series according to their putative origin. In Anglo-Saxon MSS, the Series Romana is found in Cambridge, Corpus Christi College 272, and London, BL Cotton Galba A.xviii; the Series Hispana is in London, BL Cotton Tiberius C.vi, and BL Stowe 2. Seven collects from the Series Romana are in London, BL Cotton Galba A.xiv; see Brou and Wilmart (1949), and Muir (1988 pp 75–79).

It is possible that the book owned by ALFRED referred to in Asser's *Vita Alfredi* was a devotional anthology, which from the description appears to follow the standard Carolingian form; see Bestul (1986 p 117), and Keynes and Lapidge (1983 p 268).

The influence of Latin devotional prayers on Old English narrative has been examined by Bzdyl (1982) in reference to ÆLFRIC'S LIVES OF SAINTS and CATHOLIC HOMILIES, and to the Old English poems *Andreas* (*And*, A2.1), *Juliana* (*Jul*, A3.5), and *Judith* (*Jud*, A4.2). Hill (1981) suggests the influence of the "lorica" (a Celtic form of prayer for spiritual or physical protection) on the Old English poems *Judith*, *ChristB* (A3.1), *Daniel* (*Dan*, A1.3), *Azarias* (*Az*, A3.3), and *Guthlac A* (*GuthA*, A3.2). The influences postulated by both scholars are general rather than specific. General influence of private prayer on another Old English poem, *Resignation* (*Res*, A3.25), is suggested by Bestul (1977 pp 19–20) and Stanley (GR 1200, p 451). The Old English poem titled *A Prayer* (*Pr*, A28) may also be indebted to this body of material. Bzdyl (1977) traces the sources of Ælfric's Old English devotional prayers (*ÆCHom* II [Prayers], B1.2.50) in Cambridge, University Library Gg.3.28 (NRK p 20, article 94) to prayers in Anglo-Saxon liturgical books and to the Bible.

In addition to London, BL Cotton Galba A.xiv (mentioned above), and the four collections discussed in separate entries below, the other principal collections of private prayers are the following (see also Gneuss 1985 pp 137–39, and Bestul 1986 pp 124–26):

1. Cambridge, Corpus Christi College 391 (Portiforium of Wulfstan): HG 104.
2. London, BL Arundel 60: HG 304.
3. London, BL Arundel 155: HG 306.

4. London, BL Cotton Titus D.xxvi and xxvii: HG 380.
5. London, BL Cotton Vespasian A.i: HG 381.
6. Oxford, Bodleian Library Douce 296 (*SC* 21870): HG 617.
7. Vatican, Reg. Lat. 12 (Bury Psalter): HG 912.

The psalter collects appear in the following MSS:

1. Cambridge, Corpus Christi College 272: HG 77.
2. London, BL Cotton Galba A.xiv: HG 333.
3. London, BL Cotton Galba A.xviii: HG 334.
4. London, BL Cotton Tiberius C.vi: HG 378.
5. London, BL Stowe 2: HG 499.

The following MSS contain Old English prayers with no known Latin sources, or glossed or translated Latin prayers (not included are the Old English versions of the "Pater Noster" [*Lit* 4.1, B12.4.1], the "Bidding Prayer" [*Lit* 4.2, B12.4.2], and the glossed prayers in the *Regularis concordia* [*RegCGl*, C27]):

1. Cambridge, University Library Ll.1.10 (Book of Cerne): HG 28; NRK 27; *LorGl* 2 (C83, and C91.1).
2. Cambridge, University Library Gg.3.28: HG 11; NRK 15; *ÆCHom* II (Prayers; B1.2.50).
3. Cambridge, Corpus Christi College 303: NRK 57; *Lit* 4.8.2 (Först; B12.4.8.2).
4. Cambridge, Corpus Christi College 391 (Portiforium of Wulfstan): HG 104; NRK 67; *Lit* 4.3.1 (Hughes, B12.4.3.1) and *Lit* 4.4.1 (Hughes, B12.4.4.1).
5. Cambridge, Corpus Christi College 421: HG 109; NRK 68; *Lit* 4.8.2 (Först, B12.4.8.2).
6. London, BL Arundel 155: HG 306; NRK 135; *ArPrGl* 1 (C23.1).
7. London, BL Cotton Galba A.xiv: HG 334; NRK 157; *Lit* 4.4.2 (Banks, B12.4.4.2), *Lit* 4.5 (Banks, B12.4.5), *Lit* 4.6 (Birch, B12.4.6), and *OccGl* 91.2 (Ker, C91.2).
8. London, BL Cotton Julius A.ii: HG 336; NRK 159; *Pr* (A28).
9. London, BL Cotton Tiberius A.iii: HG 363; NRK 186; *Conf* 9.3 (B11.9.3), *Lit* 4.3.1 (B12.4.3.1), *Lit* 4.3.2 (Först, B12.4.3.2), and *Lit* 4.3.3 (B12.4.3.3).
10. London, BL Cotton Tiberius C.i: HG 376; NRK 197; *Lit* 4.3.4 (Logeman, B12.4.3.4).
11. London, BL Cotton Vespasian D.xx: HG 395; NRK 212; *Lit* 4.3.5 (Logeman, B12.4.3.5).
12. London, BL Harley 585: HG 421; NRK 231; *LorGl* 1 (C22).
13. London, BL Harley 7653: HG 443; NRK 244; *OccGl* 91.3 (C91.3).

14. London, BL Royal 2 A.xx: HG 450; NRK 248; see the ROYAL LIBRARY PRAYER BOOK.
15. London, BL Royal 2 B.v: HG 451; NRK 249; *Conf* 9.3 (B11.9.3), *Lit* 4.3.1 (B12.4.3.1), *Lit* 4.3.2 (B12.4.3.2), and *Lit* 4.3.3 (B12.4.3.3).
16. London, Lambeth Palace Library 427: HG 518; NRK 280; *Pr* (A28), and *OccGl* 91.4 (C91.4).
17. Oxford, Bodleian Library Bodley 180 (*SC* 2079): NRK 305; *Lit* 4.7 (B12.4.7).
18. Salisbury, Cathedral Library 150: HG 740; NRK 379; *ArPrGl* 3 (Sisam, C23.3).

For further bibliography, see GR 154, 5939, 6250, 6261–74, and 6437.

Royal Library Prayer Book [ANON.Lib.Precum.Royal]: *BCLL* 1278; *CPL* 2018.

MSS London, BL Royal 2 A.xx: HG 450; *CLA* 2.215.
Lists — Refs none.

This MS, from the second half of the eighth century, contains a very early body of devotional prayers, along with extracts from the Gospels, a creed, a litany, the Gloria, canticles, and hymns. Included are the popular hymn of CAELIUS SEDULIUS "A SOLIS ORTUS CARDINE," as well as two metrical prayers, "Me similem cineri" (the prayer begins "O deus aeternae mundo" in its complete version; see *CCSL* 122.445–46, and *CPL* 1373), and "Quam dilecta tui fulgent" (*CCSL* 122.449, and *CPL* 1371b), both of which, according to W. Meyer (1917 pp 614–20), are quite likely BEDE's.

This MS also includes a prayer, "Mane cum surrexero" (found also in the BOOK OF CERNE), a version of which is in the later English collections London, BL Cotton Galba A.xiv and Cambridge, Corpus Christi College 391 (the Portiforium of Wulfstan; edited by A. Hughes 1958–60), but there are Continental analogs as well.

According to NRK (p 318), the Anglo-Saxon glosses in the MS can be dated "probably" to the first quarter of the tenth century.

Book of Nunnaminster [ANON.Lib.precum.Nunnaminster]: *BCLL* 1280.

MSS London, BL Harley 2965: HG 432; *CLA* 2.199.
Lists — Refs none.

This anthology, from the late eighth or early ninth century, begins with the accounts of the Passion of the four evangelists, preceding a collection of private prayers that includes a series organized according to events in the life of Christ, with twenty-five brief prayers devoted to the Passion. As in the BOOK OF CERNE, there is a text of the LORICA OF LAIDCENN; the Nunnaminster version seems to have influenced that found in London, BL Harley 585 (HG 421), of the late tenth or early eleventh century, which has an Old English gloss; see NRK 231, and Herren (1987 pp 4–11). Another prayer also in the Book of Cerne, beginning "Dominator dominus deus omnipotens," is in the eleventh-century collections London, BL Cotton Galba A.xiv, and Cambridge, Corpus Christi College 391 (the Portiforium of Wulfstan). This prayer, often attributed to AUGUSTINE or GREGORY, was disseminated throughout western Europe by the eleventh century. The prayer, "Sancte Michael archangele qui venisti," is found in the Book of Cerne and in the eleventh-century collection in London, BL Arundel 155, where it has a continuous Old English gloss, and in London, BL Arundel 60 (HG 304).

Matter added to the MS shows that it was certainly at Winchester in the tenth century, and probably belonged to ALFRED's queen Ealhswith (d. 909). It is possible that the collection in the Portiforium of Wulfstan, compiled at Winchester, may have been inspired in a general way by it; see Bestul (1986 pp 115–16).

Harley Prayer Book [ANON.Lib.precum.Harley]: *BCLL* 1279.

MSS London, BL Harley 7653: HG 443; *CLA* 2.204.
Lists — Refs none.

The collection is a fragment of seven leaves written in the eighth or ninth century, possibly as a book of private devotions for a woman (see NRK 244). It begins with a litany, and includes the morning prayer, "Mane cum surrexero," also in the BOOK OF CERNE, and the ROYAL PRAYER BOOK. Certain phrases from a petition of the litany appear to have influenced a prayer found in the eleventh-century London MSS, BL Cotton Nero A.ii and BL Cotton Galba A.xiv; see Muir (1988 p 21).

NRK (244) comments that the Old English gloss "is perhaps in the same hand as the glosses" in the Royal Prayer Book, which he dates to the first quarter of the tenth century (p 318).

Book of Cerne [ANON.Lib.precum.Cerne]: *BCLL* 1281; *CPL* 2019.

MSS Cambridge, University Library Ll.1.10: HG 28.
Lists — Refs none.

This large anthology in an early-ninth-century MS includes extracts from the Gospels on the Passion as well as a collection of private prayers. Irish or Celtic influence is shown prominently by the presence of the LORICA of

LAIDCENN MAC BAITH, "Suffragare trinitatis unitas" (*BCLL* 294; and *CPL* 1323, there attributed to GILDAS), a text glossed in Old English in the ninth and tenth centuries. The tenth-century monastic consuetudinary known as the REGULARIS CONCORDIA has prayers used liturgically which are found in the Book of Cerne; see the edition of Symons (1953 p 43). These prayers, however, are also found in Continental MSS, and thus it is not certain that the *Regularis* was directly influenced by the Book of Cerne; see Bestul (1986 pp 114–15). Prayers from the Book of Cerne are found in such eleventh-century English collections as Cambridge, Corpus Christi College MS 391 (the Portiforium of Wulfstan); London, BL Arundel 155; London, BL Cotton Galba A.xiv; London, BL Cotton Titus D.xxvii; and Vatican, Reg. lat. 12 (Bury Psalter). Here again, many of these are found in Carolingian MSS, and thus it cannot be said for certain that the Book of Cerne directly influenced the formation of the later collections. The presence of many Continental analogs in general complicates the issue of influence of the early Anglo-Saxon collections upon the later. Anglo-Saxon or Irish prayers may have travelled to the continent and been reintroduced to England from there, or the compilers of both early and late anthologies may have drawn on a common stock of widely diffused prayers. The best case for the influence of the Book of Cerne, either directly or through lost English intermediaries, is provided by a small group of prayers found in later English collections which seem not to have circulated on the continent. Examples are the prayers "Obsecro te domine," "Rogo te beate Petre," and "O Andreas sancte" (pp 144, 160, and 161), which are found in the Portiforium of Wulfstan in versions textually close to the Book of Cerne; see the edition of A. Hughes (1958–60 pp 9–11), and Bestul (1986 pp 115–16).

The Book of Cerne has a prayer, "Succurre mihi domine antequam moriar" (50), based on ISIDORE OF SEVILLE's SYNONYMA (83.841–42); prayers based on different extracts from the *Synonyma* are in the eleventh-century Bury Psalter, numbers 15 and 18; see Wilmart (1930 pp 207, and 211–12).

Thomas H. Bestul

MEDICAL TEXTS

The surviving medical records in Old English are the oldest in any European language other than Greek and Latin. Sources, therefore, can be found only in Latin works, or in Greek works translated into Latin.

All of the Old English medical texts considered in this article can be found in Cockayne (GR 6370). For general overviews of the subject, see Grattan and Singer (GR 6386), Talbot (1965), Talbot (1967), and Cameron (1983). [For this *Trial Version*, only the entry on Cassius Felix has been included.]

Cassius Felix, De medicina [CASS.FEL.Med.].

MSS—A-S Vers none.
Quots/Cits BEDA.Retract.Act. 28.6-17: CASS.FEL.Med. 122.13-17.
Lists none.

Cassius wrote the *De medicina ex graecis logicae sectae auctoribus liber translatus* in the mid fifth century, and the work was used by later writers, such as ISIDORE OF SEVILLE, and particularly by glossators because Cassius often provides Greek terms for his Latin ones. In commenting on Act 28.8 in his RETRACTIO, BEDE explains dysentery by quoting from this work.

M.L. Cameron

OROSIUS: *ODCC* 1012.
Historiae aduersum paganos [OROS.Hist.adu.pag.]: *CPL* 571.

MSS 1. Düsseldorf, Staatsarchiv HS. Z. 4, Nr 2: HG 820.
    2. Cambridge, Clare College 18 (Kk. 4.5): HG 32.
Lists 1. ? Alcuin: ML 1.3.
    2. ? Worcester II: ML 11.2.
A-S Vers Or (B9.2).
Quots/Cits 1. ALDH.Ped.reg. 167.22: OROS.Hist.adu pag. 63.8-9.
    2. ALDH.Ped.reg. 174.27-75.1: OROS.Hist.adu.pag. 464.16.
    3. BEDA.Hist.eccl.: see below.
    4. BEDA.Comm.Ez.Neh. 1294-302: OROS.Hist.adu.pag. 20.5-21.3.
    5. BEDA.Comm.Gen.: see below.
    6. BEDA.Chron.mai.: see below.
    7. BEDA.Nom.reg.: see below.
    8. ALCVIN.Epist. 397.10-12: OROS.Hist.adu.pag. 544.15- 45.3.
Refs none.

Orosius' *Historiae* achieved great popularity in the Middle Ages, and some 250 MSS, containing all or part of this work, are still in existence. These can be subdivided into a number of clearly defined "families," more than one of which was represented in England by the twelfth century; see Bately (GR 5637) and Bately (1980 pp lv-lx). It is thus somewhat surprising to find that only one copy, written in the second half of the eighth century, possibly in Northumbria, has survived—in the form of fragments in Düsseldorf—from Anglo-Saxon England. The next oldest, the Cambridge MS, dates from the very end of the period.

In addition to the specific quotations and citations noted above, BEDE uses Orosius elsewhere in his work: for lists, see the indices to the EC-CLESIASTICAL HISTORY (p 592), the COMMENTARY ON GENESIS (p 263), the CHRONICA MAIORA (pp 783–84), and the NOMINA REGIONUM ATQUE LOCO-RUM DE ACTIBUS APOSTOLORUM (p 379). ALDHELM may echo Orosius in his prose DE VIRGINITATE (247.15–16; see also Marenbon 1979 pp 77–78) as may ALCUIN in EPISTLE 200 (331.6–7).

There are also Orosius lemmata in the ÉPINAL, ERFURT, LEIDEN, and COR-PUS GLOSSARIES (for Épinal-Erfurt, see Pheifer 1974 pp xlvi-xlvii; for Leiden, see Hessels 1906 pp 38–39; for Corpus, see the discussion in Lindsay 1921b pp 12–14, and Lindsay 1921a passim). As Pheifer (1987) observes, the ar-rangement of the Épinal-Erfurt glosses and the existence of two adjacent runs of entries suggest that these glosses were extracted by the compiler from a MS containing interlinear and possibly also marginal glosses. They also show that Latin texts were being construed in the vernacular when Épinal-Erfurt was compiled in the late seventh century. Bolton (1977a p 390) notes that the commentary by REMIGIUS on BOETHIUS' CONSOLATIO in Cambridge, University Library MS Kk.3.21 (HG 23) includes material probably from Orosius that is not found in the other MSS of this work; see also Bolton (1977b p 47) for a reference to a gloss from Orosius in another Remigius commentary, in Antwerp, Plantin-Moretus Museum 190 (HG 776).

The Old English version (Or) may well have been written in response to the request by King Alfred (d. 899) for translations of those books that are most necessary for all men to know; see Bately (1980 pp lxxxvi-xciii). However, connections between it (or the Latin on which it is based) and Alfred's Boethius (Bo; B9.3.2) are not proven, while the authors of the world history annals in the *Anglo-Saxon Chronicle* made use of Latin authorities other than Orosius. For refutation of the claim that Alfred himself translated Orosius, see Raith (1951), Whitelock (GR 436), Bately (GR 5647), and Liggins (GR 5648). For an Old French poem that seems to have had the Old English version as its source, see Millard (1957 pp 6–18) and Bately (GR 5635).

Cross (1973) shows that the *Historiae* is the ultimate source for some de-tails about portents and events at Christ's birth in VERCELLI HOMILIES 5 and 6 (*HomS* 1, B3.2.1; and *HomU* 10, B3.4.10). For bibliography on the Old English Orosius, see GR 5592–5733, Bately (1979), Bately (1984), and Bately (1986). The Latin text on which Sweet (GR 5597) based the excerpts in his edition of the Old English is close neither to the original nor to the lost MS used by the translator. For a list of known Latin MSS, see Bately and Ross (1961; addenda in progress). For Insular features in a commentary on the early sections of the *Historiae* preserved in Vatican, Reg. lat. 1650, see Lehmann (vol 2 pp 30–31).

Janet M. Bately

PASCHASIUS RADBERTUS: *DS* 12.295–301; *DTC* 13.1628–39; *NCE* 10.1050; *ODCC* 1039. See also RATRAMNUS.

De corpore et sanguine Domini [PASCH.RAD.Corp.sang.Dom.].

MSS 1. London, BL Royal 8.B.xi: HG 474.
2. Salisbury, Cathedral Library: HG 731.
Lists — A-S Vers none.
Quots/Cits ? *ÆCHom* II, 15 (B1.2.18) 159–73: see below.
Refs none.

ÆLFRIC very probably relied on the eucharistic treatise of Paschasius Radbertus — *De corpore et sanguine Domini* — as his source for two lurid miracle stories found in his Easter homily. In the first, the Eucharist appears as an infant being slaughtered by an angel with a knife; in the second, told of GREGORY THE GREAT, the Eucharist is transformed into a bloody finger as Gregory offers it to a woman who harbored doubts about the nature of Christ's true presence in the communion wafer. These two stories are also found, though in reverse order, in chapter xiv of the eucharistic treatise written by Paschasius between 831 and 833 and revised about ten years later. Ælfric's use of Paschasius as a source is open to question: he may have used an altogether different source for the two, and the stories in Paschasius may in fact be the work of a later interpolator.

The story concerning the dismembered infant occurs in the VITAE PATRUM — a fact pointed out by Ælfric — and the story of the doubting woman is found in several early biographies of Gregory. Ælfric may have relied on these earlier sources and independently decided to bring the miracles together. It is more likely, however, that he encountered them already joined in chapter xiv of Paschasius.

Although the text in the *PL* contains both miracle stories, scholars have begun to question whether they were part of the original work. Some have apparently accepted the authenticity of both (e.g. McCracken, in McCracken and Cabaniss 1957 p 92), but the most recent editor of the eucharistic treatise, Beda Paulus (Bibliography Part I), confirms only the story of Gregory and the doubting woman as an authorial addition to the so-called second edition. Relying in part on the work of Sardemann (1877), Paulus relegates the story of the infanticide to a fourth edition that is characterized by a number of non-authorial interpolations (*CCCM* 16.xxxv and 88–89). Roach (1939 pp 22–33) takes a more extreme view and regards both miracle stories as later interpolations. On the whole it seems best to assume that at least one of the miracle stories is authentic and that Ælfric probably found both in a later edition of *De corpore et sanguine Domini*. It is also possible that Ælfric may have encountered the stories circulating together in florilegia or eucharistic treatises closely associated with Paschasius; see Leinbaugh (1986 p 304).

Theodore H. Leinbaugh

PAULINUS OF NOLA: *DS* 12.592–602; *OCD* 791; *ODCC* 1054; *NCE* 11.28–29.

Bishop of Nola (near Naples) and Christian poet of the late fourth and early fifth centuries, Paulinus was a student of AUSONIUS, and corresponded with AMBROSE, AUGUSTINE, RUFINUS, SULPICIUS SEVERUS, and St Martin of Tours, among others. His poems include annual *natalicia* in honor of FELIX NOLANUS (see ACTA SANCTORUM).

Carmina [PAVL.NOL.Carm.]: *CPL* 203.
MSS   1. Leningrad, Public Library Q.v.XIV.1: HG 847; *CLA* 11.1622.
   2. Vatican, Pal. lat. 235: HG 910; *CLA* 1.87.
   3. London, BL Royal 15.B.xix: HG 491.
Lists   1. Æthelwold: ML 4.7.
   2. Peterborough: ML 13.38.
   3. ? Alcuin: ML 1.12.
A-S Vers   none.
Quots/Cits   1. ALDH.Metr. 96.15–16: PAVL.NOL.Carm. XV.1.
   2. BEDA.Art.metr.: see below.
   3. BEDA.Vit.Cuthb.(metr.) 974: PAVL.NOL.Carm. XXVII.645.
   4. BEDA.Comm.Luc. 135, 1360–67: PAVL.NOL.Carm. XXVII.415–20.
   5. ANON.Mir.Nin. 36: PAVL.NOL.Carm.XVIII.24.

6. ANON.Mir.Nin. 364: PAVL.NOL.Carm. XV.43.
7. ANON.Mir.Nin. 439: PAVL.NOL.Carm. XV.275.
8. ANON.Mir.Nin. 502: PAVL.NOL.Carm. XXVII.233.
Refs 1. BEDA.Vit.Fel. 798.6–9.
  2. BEDA.Hist.eccl. V.xxiv.34–35.

A corpus of six poems (in the order 15, 16, 18, 28, 27, and 17) was known to BEDE by the end of the seventh century. Benedict Biscop probably brought the collection from Italy. The two Insular MSS, Vatican and Leningrad, are the only extant MS evidence of this corpus; see Châtelain (1880) and the discussion by T. Brown and Mackay (1988). The tenth-century Royal MS contains *Carmen* 25.1–65 under the rubric "incipit epythalamium a sancto Paulino." However, it is just one among several extracts from various other authors, and the MS is very complex. The English connections of the MS itself are not clear, and it likely that it originated on the continent; the date of its arrival in England is unknown.

The Æthelwold list refers to a "uita sancti felicis metrice," presumably the corpus of six poems; and the Peterborough entry, "vita sancti Felicis uersifice," undoubtely refers to the same MS; see James (GR 123, pp 19–20). The reference in the Alcuin list is not to a specific work.

Bede regularly cites the author by name for his quotations in *De arte metrica* (see *CCSL* 123C.785 for a list of 17 quotations), and in addition to the lines that he quotes in his metrical *Life of Cuthbert* he echoes the work elsewhere (143 and 948). At the beginning of his *Vita S Felicis*, Bede names the source that he adapts and paraphrases and in the list of his works at the end of the ECCLESIASTICAL HISTORY he again acknowledges Paulinus as his source; see Mackay (1976 and, with T. Brown, 1988). His paraphrase of *Carmen* 15 in his MARTYROLOGY clearly comes through his early life of Felix, although Quentin (1908 pp 107–08) suggests a direct relationship. In addition to ALD-HELM's quotation of an entire line in his DE METRIS, he echoes the work in his verse DE VIRGINITATE: in particular, N. Wright (1985) has demonstrated Aldhelm's intense imitation of word, phrase, and thought or image from the short Paulinus corpus in the first 83 lines (the prologue) of this work. Godman (1982, see the index; but see also N. Wright 1985) indicates ALCUIN's possible echoes of Paulinus' work. In addition to the lines quoted in the anonymous *Miracula S. Nyniae*, this work also echoes Paulinus once (449: Carmen XXVII.104).

There is a reference in the twelfth-century Durham booklist (Mynors 1939 p 2) to a "liber Paulini Anglicus" (Raine 1938 p 5; and Becker 1885 p 242); it may refer to an Anglo-Saxon translation of Paulinus, but no MS has been identified.

Thomas W. Mackay

PRISCIAN

Priscian provided his Greek-speaking pupils in early sixth-century Constantinople with a comprehensive account of most aspects of the Latin language in a series of works: the INSTITUTIONES GRAMMATICAE, a monumental reference grammar in eighteen books; the INSTITUTIO DE NOMINE ET PRONOMINE ET VERBO, a concise text which outlines the principal formal categories of the inflecting parts of speech; the PARTITIONES DUODECIM VERSUUM AENEIDOS PRINCIPALIUM, an extended analysis in question-and-answer form of each word in the first line of each of the twelve books of VERGIL's AENEID; *De figuris numerorum*, a guide to terminology relating to numerals; *De metris Terentii*, a short treatise on the metres employed by the comic playwright Terence; and the *Praeexercitamina*, a Latin translation of a Greek rhetorical treatise. I have found no evidence that Anglo-Latin grammarians were familiar with these last three works (*De figuris numerorum* was used by ÆLFRIC in his grammar at second hand only: see EXCERPTA DE PRISCIANO), but such evidence may be forthcoming from borrowings in works on subjects other than grammar. Of doubtful authenticity is the DE ACCENTIBUS, a treatise on the accentuation and prosody of nouns and verbs. These works were not transmitted as a group: the *Institutio de nomine* usually traveled independently, along with other grammars for use at the intermediate level; the *Institutiones grammaticae* either traveled alone (sometimes without its last two books, which in the post-Conquest period were often transmitted separately) or together with the *De accentibus*; and the *De figuris numerorum*, *De metris Terentii* and *Praeexercitamina* formed a small corpus which generally circulated as a unit. In view of these different patterns of transmission — exemplified in Anglo-Saxon England as clearly as on the Continent — it is appropriate to handle these texts separately.

Institutio de nomine et pronomine et verbo [PRISC.Nom. pron.uerb.].

MSS   Worcester, Cathedral Library Q 5: HG 765.
Lists   ? Alcuin: ML 1.16.
A-S Vers   none.
Quots/Cits   1. ALDH.Ped.reg. 174.16–17: PRISC.Nom.pron.uerb. 453.28.
   2. TATWIN.Gramm.: see below.
   3. BONIF.Gramm. III.250 (De uerbo): PRISC.Nom.pron.uerb. 454.8.
Refs   BONIF.Gramm. 44,250.

This work was widely read by the earlier generation of Anglo-Latin grammarians, being one of the only four works (along with DONATUS, ASPER/ASPORIUS, and the first book of ISIDORE's ETYMOLOGIAE) shared by ALDHELM, TATWINE (used throughout), and BONIFACE. Although there is every reason to suppose that it retained its popularity into the later Anglo-Saxon period, direct evidence is scarce for two reasons. First, the practice in booklists and elsewhere of citing works by author's name rather than by title often makes it impossible to tell whether this work or the INSTITU-TIONES GRAMMATICAE was meant, as in Alcuin's list of the books, or rather authors, represented at York. Occasionally, however, the context will provide a clue: Boniface, referring at 44,250 to Priscian's views on verbal nouns, gives us enough information to locate the source of the discussion in the *Institutio de nomine*. Secondly, the widespread distribution of versions of the *Declinationes nominum* and other texts which draw heavily on the *Institutio de nomine* means that the likelihood of indirect borrowing (as in ÆLFRIC's grammar and *Beatus quid est* fol 97v ff.) is high.

Karlsruhe, Badische Landesbibliothek Fragm. Aug. 122 (Passalacqua 1978, number 245; *CLA* 7.1009 and 8.**1009) + Zurich, Staatsarchiv A.G. Nr. XIII (Passalacqua 1978, number 762; *CLA* 7.1009 and 8.**1009; eighth century from an Anglo-Saxon center on the Continent) contains a version of the *Institutio de nomine* which is textually very close to that used by Boniface (Law 1981 p 757). The Worcester MS contains the work on fols 48–64.

One Carolingian commentary on the *Institutio de nomine* is attested in Anglo-Saxon England: REMIGIUS', in London, BL Cotton Domitian I (fols 40–51; HG 326). The opening of this text, as yet unedited in its entirety, was printed by Jeudy (1982) from Amiens, Bibliothèque Municipale 425. See further Jeudy (1972) on the MSS and commentaries.

Institutiones grammaticae [PRISC.Inst.gramm.].

MSS   1. Cambridge, Jesus College 28 (Q.B.11): HG 123; Passalacqua 1978 number 79.

2. Cambridge, Trinity College O.2.51 (1151): HG 192; Passalacqua 1978, number 84.

3. Canterbury, Cathedral Library Add.12719 + Maidstone, Kent County Archives Office, PRC 491a and b: HG 211; Passalacqua 1978, numbers 97 + 344.

Lists   1. ? Alcuin: ML 1.16.

2. ? Worcester: ML 11.18.

A-S Vers   1. ALCUIN.Exc.Prisc.

2. ANON.Oxford, St John's College 17: see below.

Quots/Cits   1. ALDH.Ped.reg.: see below.

2. ALCUIN.Gramm.: see below.

Refs   1. ALCUIN.Gramm.: see below.

2. ANON.Beat. fols 107v, and 110.

This work was little read in England before the later Anglo-Saxon period, being used, it would appear, only by ALDHELM (for a list of borrowings, see *MGH* AA 15.545). It should be noted that despite the large number of parallels listed in the apparatus fontium to BEDE'S DE ORTHOGRAPHIA, Bede did not use the *Institutiones* at all. The evidence at present available suggests that it was popularized on the Continent by ALCUIN: his own grammar makes fairly heavy use of it, he compiled the earliest known collection of excerpts from it (O'Donnell 1976), and the first wave of ninth-century copies spread outwards from his monastery of Tours. What we do not know is where he came into contact with it: did he bring a copy with him from York, or did he first encounter it on the Continent? Another vexed question is the role of the Irish in the introduction of the *Institutiones grammaticae* to Alcuin and to the Continent generally, an issue which might be resolved by a comparison of the readings of the early Irish copy, St Gall 904, with those in (a) Alcuin's excerpts; (b) the early MSS from Tours and the surrounding area; (c) the passages quoted by ninth-century *Scotti peregrini* in Francia: Sedulius Scottus, Murethach, and the anonymous author of the *Ars Laureshamensis*.

The work may be mentioned in two booklists: on the Alcuin list, see above; the Worcester catalog lists "Priscianus maior," which is the name used in some MSS for this work.

Fritzlar, Stiftskirche S. Peter, Schatzkammer s.n. (Passalacqua 1978, number 209; *CLA* 8.1133) + Kassel, Landesbibliothek Philol. Fol. 15 (Passalacqua 1978, number 247; *CLA* 8.1133; eighth century, from an Anglo-Saxon center in Germany) contain fragments of the *Institutiones*.

Alcuin's excerpts (in which he refers often to Priscian; see *PL* 101.859C, 873C, 877C, 880D, 895B, and 896B) heralded a flood of reworked versions of the *Institutiones grammaticae* — florilegia, abbreviations, versions in question-and-answer form — designed to help the student master its content, which often differed from that of DONATUS and the other Late Latin grammarians in both terminology and substance. This process of gradually working through and digesting the *Institutiones grammaticae*, the indispensable preparation for the flowering of speculative grammar in the thirteenth century, is visible in later Anglo-Saxon England in the collection of excerpts from the *Institutiones* in Oxford, St John's College 17 (fols 159v–175; parts of the contents of the manuscript are associated with Byrhtferth; see Baker 1982) and in the anonymous EXCERPTIONES DE PRISCIANO, ÆLFRIC'S principal source for his grammar (Ælfric's references to Priscian — 94,3; 110,4; 129,14; 135,10; 145,3; 205, 12; 262,16; and 263,19 — are to this work). Direct study of the *Institutiones* is attested by the three copies from later Anglo-Saxon England. There are also two references to Priscian in the anonymous unprinted grammar in London, BL Harley 3271 (HG 435).

De accentibus [PRISC.Accent.].

MSS   1. Cambridge, Jesus College 28 (Q.B.11): HG 123; Passalacqua 1978, number 79.
  2. Cambridge, Trinity College O.2.51 (155): HG 192; Passalacqua 1978, number 84.
Lists — Refs   none.

The *De accentibus* often circulated along with the INSTITUTIONES GRAMMAT-ICAE, as in these two MSS. See La Conte (1981) for further MSS of the work.

Partitiones [PRISC.Part.].

MSS   Reims, Bibliothèque Municipale 1097: Passalacqua 1978, number 572.
Lists — Refs   none.

This copy of the *Partitiones* has only recently been recognized as coming from Anglo-Saxon England (Gneuss 1988 p 201). It contains glosses from REMIGIUS' commentary on fols 1–2. See also Gluck (1967) and Jeudy (1971).

V. Law

PROBA

Cento virgilianus [PROBA.Cent.]: *CPL* 1480; *LTK* 2.993 (under "Cento").

MSS — A-S Vers   none.
Quots/Cits   ALDH.Ped.reg. 188.28–31: PROBA.Cent. 569.1.
Refs   none.

Proba's Cento, generally believed to date from the third quarter of the fourth century, is one of the earliest adaptations of Scripture to classical verse form, in this case borrowing verbatim lines and half lines from VIR-GIL's poetry and rearranging them to approximate the scriptural narrative of Genesis, Exodus and several episodes from the New Testament. In the Middle Ages the work was frequently bound with other versifications of Scripture for use in schools, despite its having received severe criticism by JEROME, and denunciation in the GELASIAN DECREE (326). The work is bound with texts known for their use in education, such as ALDHELM's SYMPOSIA and AENIGMATA in Continental MSS Vatican, Reg. lat. 251 and 1666. Ald-helm's citation of the first line of the prologue along with the composer's name suggests first-hand knowledge in Anglo-Saxon England. The Cento is also contained in MS Cambridge, Trinity College O. 7. 7. although this dates from the twelfth century.

Clark and Hatch (1981) present an English translation of the Cento and a discussion of the poet's identity and the work's principal themes. Herzog (1975) examines the Cento's role in the formation of the biblical epic as a literary genre. Contreni (1978) discusses the use of Proba in education on the Continent. Opelt (1964) points to Proba's depiction of Christ as angry lawgiver. This depiction may have influenced subsequent Germanic portrayals of Christ as heroic warrior, e.g. in the *Dream of the Rood* (*Dream*, A2.5).

Daniel Nodes

PRUDENTIUS: *NCE* 11.928–29; *DMA* 10.198–99.

Prudentius, a fourth-century Spanish poet, began writing poetry only late in his life. According to the PRAEFATIO to his works, he was born in 348 and began writing in 405. Since in his poetry he does not seem to be aware of the sack of Rome in 410, he appears to have written all his works, i.e. the CATHEMERINON, the APOTHEOSIS, the HAMARTIGENIA, the PSYCHOMACHIA, the two books of the CONTRA SYMMACHUM, the PERISTEPHANON, and the DITTOCHAEON, in fewer than five years.

The first evidence that Prudentius' works were known in England appears with ALDHELM'S CARMEN DE VIRGINITATE. Though Aldhelm does not mention Prudentius by name, the verbal parallels between their works (see Ehwald 1919 passim, Lapidge and Rosier 1985 p 100, and Wieland 1986 pp 89–90) are too numerous to be explained as mere coincidence. Prudentius seems to have remained popular with the Anglo-Saxons, since later Anglo-Latin writers such as BEDE and ALCUIN both quote from and echo his poems.

The earliest extant Anglo-Saxon MSS containing works by Prudentius were written in France in the late ninth or early tenth century, and were brought to England in the course of the tenth century (Oxford, Bodleian Library Rawlinson C 697: HG 661; and Cambridge, Corpus Christi College 223: HG 70). During the tenth century the English produced their first extant MSS with Prudentian works. Only three contain all the poems: Cambridge, Corpus Christi College 223 (HG 70; the first folio is lost); Durham, Cathedral Library B.IV.9 (HG 246); and Oxford, Bodleian Library Auctarium F.3.6 (HG 537).

The extant Anglo-Saxon MSS contain Latin glosses for all of Prudentius' works, suggesting that his poems were studied in the schools. Old English glosses appear in all poems but the APOTHEOSIS and the DITTOCHAEON. The PSYCHOMACHIA of four MSS is illustrated.

Prudentius' name appears in the Alcuin and Sæwold booklists (ML 1.12, and 8.30), but since no work is specified, they may refer to all, or any, of Prudentius' poems.

Even though Prudentius' works were obviously known and studied in Anglo-Saxon England, they are not explicitly echoed in Old English literature to any great extent. Hermann (1976) argues that the PSYCHOMACHIA influenced certain images in the poetic *Solomon and Saturn* (*MSol*, A13), Cook (GR 3265, p 216) notes a parallel between *ChristC* (A3.1) and CATHEMERI-NON 6, 85ff. (but see Biggs 1986 p 34), and Cherniss (GR 1073) notes that Satan in *Juliana* (A3.5) uses imagery "which calls to mind the imagery of . . . Prudentius' *Psychomachia*" (p 198). Prudentius' influence on Anglo-Saxon literature is strongest in the Anglo-Latin works; his influence on Old English literature seems to be limited to tone and images.

Praefatio [PRVD.Praef.]: *CPL* 1437.

MSS   1. Boulogne, Bibliothèque Municipale 189: HG 805.
    2. Durham, Cathedral Library B.IV.9: HG 246.
    3. Oxford, Bodleian Library Auctarium F.3.6 (*SC* 2666): HG 537.
Lists   see the introduction above.
A-S Vers   see below.
Quots/Cits — Refs   none.

The *Praefatio* gives a brief autobiographical sketch of Prudentius and introduces his poems. It does not seem to be echoed by any Anglo-Latin writer. There are some Old English glosses in the Boulogne MS (see AC C94.1, but the glosses are attributed there to the PSYCHOMACHIA).

Cathemerinon [PRVD.Cath.]: *CPL* 1438.

MSS   1. Boulogne, Bibliothèque Municipale 189: HG 805.
    2. Cambridge, Corpus Christi College 223: HG 70.
    3. Cambridge, Corpus Christi College 391: HG 104.
    4. Durham, Cathedral Library B.III.32: HG 244.
    5. Durham, Cathedral Library B.IV.9: HG 246.
    6. London, BL Additional 37517: HG 291.
    7. London, BL Cotton Vespasian D xii: HG 391.
    8. Oxford, Bodleian Library Auctarium F.3.6 (*SC* 2666): HG 537.
    9. Oxford, Oriel College 3: HG 680.
    10. Rouen, Bibliothèque Municipale 231 (A.44): HG 920.
    11. Vatican, Reg. lat. 338 (folios 64–126): HG 914.

Lists   1. see the introduction above.
    2. Exeter: ML 10.36.
A-S Vers   HyGl 3 (C18.3): see below.
Quots/Cits — Refs   none.

The *Cathemerinon* consists of 12 hymns for daily use; the word itself is coined from the Greek word for "daily." Only MSS 1, 2, 5, 8, and 9 contain the entire work; these MSS also all contain Old English glosses (see AC C94.1, 94.4, 94.5, 94.8, and 94.9 respectively, but the glosses are attributed there to the PSYCHOMACHIA). The others contain only hymns drawn from the work: *Cathemerinon* I.1–8, 81–84, and 97–100 (= hymn 18); *Cathemerinon* II.1–8, 48–49, 52, 57, 59–60, and 67–68 (= hymn 21), and *Cathemerinon* II.25, 93–94, and 96–108 (= hymn 24). MS 6 contains an additional hymn (12a) consisting of *Cathemerinon* VI.125–52 (the numbering of these hymns is Gneuss' in GR 6248). These hymns are part of the New Hymnal and were used in the daily office of monks and clergy from the tenth century onward. Since (aside from 12a) they were translated into Old English in the *Expositio Hymnorum*, they constitute the only extended translations of Prudentian lines into the vernacular.

Echoes of the *Cathemerinon* appear in ALDHELM'S CARMINA ECCLESIASTICA (IV.x.8: *Cathemerinon* III.105), and in his ENIGMATA (XCVI.1: *Cathemerinon* V.48); both are listed in Manitius (1886 p 571). BEDE echoes the work twice in his metrical VITA S. CUTHBERTI (573: *Cathemerinon* V.156; and 970: IV.74).

Apotheosis [PRVD.Apoth.]: *CPL* 1439.

MSS   1. Cambridge, Corpus Christi College 223: HG 70.
    2. Durham, Cathedral Library B.IV.9: HG 246.
    3. Oxford, Bodleian Library Auctarium F.3.6 (*SC* 2666): HG 537.
Lists   see the introduction above.
A-S Vers — Refs   none.

The *Apotheosis* (Greek for "deification") is an argument for the divinity of Christ, in opposition to the pagans and certain heretics. ALDHELM echoes the work twice in his CARMINA ECCLESIASTICA (IV.viii.6: *Apotheosis* 127; and IV.xiii.5: 544); and in his CARMEN DE VIRGINITATE (34: prooem 2; 679: 697; and 851: 127). BEDE may echo *Apotheosis* 74 in his metrical VITA S. CUTHBERTI (13). ALCUIN echoes *Apotheosis* 153 in his VERSUS DE SANCTIS EUBORICENSIS ECCLESIAE (100). Strecker (1922 p 20) argues that the echo of *Apotheosis* 705 in the anonymous *Miracula S. Nyniae* (393) is due to indirect influence. Ehwald lists Aldhelm's *Carmina ecclesiastica* II.7 as echoing *Cathemerinon* IX.1–9; this should be IX.19 (see Manitius 1886 p 571); but *Apotheosis* 602 provides a closer parallel.

Hamartigenia [PRVD.Hamart.]: *CPL* 1440.

MSS   1. Cambridge, Corpus Christi College 223: HG 70.
  2. Cambridge, University Library Gg.5.35: HG 12; see below.
  3. Durham, Cathedral Library B.IV.9: HG 246.
  4. Oxford, Bodleian Library Auctarium F.3.6 (*SC* 2666): HG 537.
Lists   see the introduction above.
A-S Vers   see below.
Quots/Cits   none.
Refs   ALCVIN.off.per.Fer. 544.12–47: PRUD. Hamart.931–66.

The *Hamartigenia* (Greek for "origin of evil") explores the beginnings of sin and evil in this world. The Cambridge University MS contains only lines 931–66, a hymn beginning with "O dee cunctipotens." This is the closing prayer of the *Hamartigenia*, and was used by ALCUIN as an independent prayer in the OFFICIA PER FERIAS; this presumably explains its independent circulation. Old English glosses appear in the Bodleian manuscript (AC C94.8), but they are attributed there to the PSYCHOMACHIA.

ALDHELM echoes the work in his CARMEN DE VIRGINITATE — 1: *Hamartigenia* 281; 103: 524–25; and 2740: 171 — and in his ENIGMATA — LXXVI.1: 340 (see Manitius 1886 p 571). BEDE echoes *Hamartigenia* 537 in his metrical VITA S. CUTHBERTI (709); and ALCUIN 722 in his VERSUS (932).

Psychomachia [PRVD.Psych.]: *CPL* 1441.

MSS   1. Cambridge, Corpus Christi College 23, pt. 1: HG 38.
  2. Cambridge, Corpus Christi College 223: HG 70.
  3. Cambridge, Trinity College O.2.51 (1155), pt. 1: HG 191.
  4. Cambridge, University Library Gg.5.35: HG 12.
  5. Durham, Cathedral Library B.IV.9: HG 246.
  6. London, BL Additional 24199 (folios 2–38): HG 285.
  7. London, BL Cotton Cleopatra C viii (folios 4–37): HG 324.
  8. Munich, Bayerische Staatsbibliothek, clm 29031b: HG 852.
  9. Oxford, Bodleian Library Auctarium F.3.6 (*SC* 2666): HG 537.
  10. Oxford, Bodleian Library Rawlinson C.697 (*SC* 12541): HG 661.
Lists   1. see the introduction above.
  2. Exeter: ML 10.35.
  3. Worcester: ML 11.11.
A-S Vers   see below.
Quots/Cits   1. BEDA.Art.metr. I.xiiii.64: PRVD.Psych. 98.
  2. BEDA.Art.metr. I.xiiii.66: PRVD.Psych. 594.
  3. BEDA.Art.metr. I.xx.9–12: PRVD.Psych. praefatio 1–4.
  4. ANON.Vit.Oswaldi: see below.
Refs   none.

The *Psychomachia* describes the allegorical fight of seven virtues against seven vices; the word is coined from two Greek words meaning "soul" and "battle"; hence it means "battle for" or "in the soul." Without doubt it was the best known of Prudentius' poems in Anglo-Saxon England. It is preserved in more MSS than any other of his works (on the MSS, see Wieland 1987; the Munich MS is a fragment), except for the selections from the CATHEMERINON which became part of the daily office. Old English glosses appear in MSS 1, 2, 4, 7, 8, and 9 (see AC C94.3, 94.4 and Page 1979, 94.2, 94.6, 94.7, and 94.8 respectively).

The *Psychomachia* is quoted and echoed more often than any other Prudentian poem, with echoes in ALDHELM, BEDE, BONIFACE, ALCUIN, and Byrhtferth. The influence of the *Psychomachia* on the section of Aldhelm's CARMEN DE VIRGINITATE usually referred to as "de octo vitiis principalibus" has both been overrated and underestimated: it does not constitute "presque un plagiat de Prudence" as Lavarenne (1948 p 26) claimed, but neither is it true that it was written "Prudentii in Psychomachia exemplo non adscito" (Ehwald *MGH* AA15 p 452). Hermann (1983) is aware "that certain passages reveal the direct dependence of *De octo principalibus vitiis* upon the *Psychomachia*" (p 192), but concentrates on the differences rather than the similarities between the two. Rosier, too, acknowledges the verbal parallels, but asks why Aldhelm did not imitate the *Psychomachia* more closely (Lapidge and Rosier 1985 p 100). Wieland (1986) suggests that Aldhelm wished to turn CASSIAN's COLLATIONES into verse and in doing so used "echoes and overtones of Prudentius' *Psychomachia*" (p 90). The known parallels between the works occur in this section; two are listed in the edition of Aldhelm (*Carmen de uirginitate* 2575: *Psychomachia* 436; and 2882: 736); one (2865: 6) is noted by Rosier in Lapidge and Rosier (1985 p 100); and one (2547: 452) by Wieland (1986 p 89) who also suggests the parallel 2634: 96. One further parallel occurs between Aldhelm's CARMINA ECCLESIASTICA IV.v.1 and *Psychomachia* 467.

There is a verbal parallel between BONIFACE's ENIGMATA 15 and the *Psychomachia* 436, but Boniface probably modeled his line on ALDHELM's CARMEN DE VIRGINITATE 2575, which itself echoes of the *Psychomachia* 436. Dümmler (*MGH* PLAC 1, p 14), and following him Ogilvy (*BKE* p 231) see a parallel between Boniface's *Enigmata* 372 and the *Psychomachia* 161, but the resemblance is slight. BEDE echoes the *Psychomachia* 290 in his metrical VITA S. CUTHBERTI (29). ALCUIN echoes the work in his VERSUS (10: *Psychomachia* 645; 158: 29; 535: 197; 569: 645; 1562: 609). Byrhtferth echoes *Psychomachia* 6 in his *Manual* 16.7 (*ByrM*, B20.20.1), though the editor lists the non-existent "*Psychomachia* vi, 744" as the place of the verbal echo. Lapidge (1988 p 96) notes a parallel between an elegiac couplet attributed to Æthelwold and *Psychomachia* 875. On the use of the *Pyschomachia* 286–90, 769–71, and 785–86 in the *Vita Oswaldi*, see Hermann (1983 pp 189–90).

Peristephanon [PRVD.Peristeph.]: *CPL* 1443.

MSS 1. Boulogne, Bibliothèque Municipale 189: HG 805.
  2. Cambridge, Corpus Christi College 23, pt. 1: HG 38.
  3. Cambridge, Corpus Christi College 223: HG 70.
  4. Durham, Cathedral Library B.IV.9: HG 246.
  5. Oxford, Bodleian Library Auctarium F.3.6 (*SC* 2666): HG 537.
  6. Oxford, Oriel College 3: HG 680.
Lists 1. see introduction above.
  2. Exeter: ML 10.37.
A-S Vers see below.
Quots/Cits none.
Refs BEDA.Vit.Fel. 789.6–16: PRVD.Peristeph. IX.

The *Peristephanon* consists of 14 poems praising various martyrs; the word is derived from the Greek word for "crown." In MS 5 the Passio Romani (= Peristephanon X) is separated from the other poems in the *Peristephanon*. Old English glosses appear in MSS 1, 2, 3, and 5 (see AC C94.1, 94.3, 94.4, and 94.8 respectively, but the glosses are attributed there to the PSYCHOMACHIA).

ALDHELM echoes the *Peristephanon* in his CARMINA ECCLESIASTICA (IV.viii.6: *Peristephanon* X.318; IV.xi.10: III.156; both are listed in Manitius 1886 p 571); his CARMEN DE VIRGINITATE 1952 and 2546 echo *Peristephanon* XIV.55 (Wieland 1986 p 90). BEDE echoes it in his metrical VITA S. CUTHBERTI (723: *Peristephanon* VIII.7; 843: XI.5).

Contra Symmachum [PRVD.Contr.Symm.]: *CPL* 1442.

MSS 1. Boulogne, Bibliothèque Municipale 189: HG 805.
  2. Cambridge, Corpus Christi College 23, pt. 1: HG 38.
  3. Cambridge, Corpus Christi College 223: HG 70.
  4. Durham, Cathedral Library B.IV.9: HG 246.
  5. Oxford, Bodleian Library Auctarium F.3.6 (*SC* 2666): HG 537.
  6. Oxford, Oriel College 3: HG 680.
Lists see introduction above.
A-S Vers see below.
Quots/Cits — Refs none.

The *Contra Symmachum* is an attack against the efforts, led by Symmachus, to revive the Roman pagan religion. MS 2 contains only lines 1–29. Old English glosses occur in MS 1 (see AC C94.1, but the glosses are attributed there to the PSYCHOMACHIA).

The *Contra Symmachum* I.38 is echoed in ALDHELM'S CARMINA ECCLESIASTICA (IV.vi.19) and in the CARMEN DE VIRGINITATE (1173, 1588, and 2059);

the *De uirginitate* (1383) also echoes *Contra Symmachum* II.780; all are listed by Manitius (1886 p 571). BEDE possibly echoes the *Contra Symmachum* in his metrical VITA S. CUTHBERTI (281: *Contra Symmachum* I.192; 585: I.480). AL-CUIN echoes the work in his metrical VITA WILLIBRORDI (IV.12: *Contra Symmachum* II.448) and in his CARMINA (IX.37: *Contra Symmachum* II.1114) — neither is noted in the editions. Byrhtferth echoes *Contra Symmachum* II.477–78 in his *Manual* 8.10 (*ByrM*, B20.20.1).

Dittochaeon [PRVD.Ditt.]: *CPL* 1444.

MSS   1. Cambridge, Corpus Christi College 223: HG 70.
   2. Cambridge, Trinity College O.2.31 (1135): HG 190.
   3. Durham, Cathedral Library B.IV.9: HG 246.
   4. Oxford, Bodleian Library Auctarium F.3.6 (*SC* 2666): HG 537.
   5. Oxford, Oriel College 3: HG 680.
Lists   see introduction above.
A-S Vers   none.
Quots/Cits   ALCVIN.Epist. 26.44: PRVD.Ditt. 3.
Refs   none.

The *Dittochaeon* consists of 48 tetrastichs, the first 24 of which present stories or scenes from the Old Testament, the second 24 from the New Testament; the word is coined from two Greek words meaning "double" and "food," since Christians receive sustenance from both Testaments.

ALDHELM echoes the work in his CARMINA ECCLESIASTICA (IV.ii.2: *Dittochaeon* 190 — see Manitius 1886 p 571). BEDE echoes it in his metrical VITA S. CUTH-BERTI (478: *Dittochaeon* 138).

Epilogus [PRVD.Epil.]: *CPL* 1445.

MSS   1. Boulogne, Bibliothèque Municipale 189: HG 805.
   2. Cambridge, Corpus Christi College 223: HG 70.
   3. Durham, Cathedral Library B.IV.9: HG 246.
   4. Oxford, Bodleian Library Auctarium F.3.6 (*SC* 2666): HG 537.
Lists   see introduction above.
A-S Vers   see below.
Quots/Cits — Refs   none.

In the *Epilogus*, Prudentius prays that God may accept his poems as a suitable gift. Old English glosses appear in MS 1 (see AC C94.1, but the glosses are attributed there to the PSYCHOMACHIA). The *Epilogus* does not seem to be echoed by any Anglo-Saxon writer.

Gernot Wieland

RALPH D'ESCURES

Homily on the Virgin [RALPH.d'Es.Hom.].

MSS   ? Worcester, Cathedral Library F.94.
Lists   none.
A-S Vers   *LS* 22 (B3.3.22).
Quots/Cits — Refs   none.

Ralph d'Escures was Bishop of Rochester (1108–14), and later archbishop of Canterbury (1114–22). His homily on the Virgin Mary appears in Worcester F.94 (fols 1–2v), which is now regarded, with F.93, as a companion volume to Worcester F.92 (HG 763). The F.94 volume includes homilies from PAUL THE DEACON'S HOMILIARY, but has many additions of which this late homily is one. It was translated into Old English in the twelfth century, MS Cotton Vespasian D.XIV, printed by Warner (GR 5292). Max Förster (GR 6222) noted the source of the Old English, and later (1932) refined to take into account Wilmart's (1927) attribution.

The homily, with a prologue, is printed among the works of Anselm (Homily 9) in *PL* 158.644–49 (Bibliography Part I). It also appears without a prologue in *PL* 95.1505–08.

J.E. Cross

RATRAMNUS: *DS* 13.147–53; *DCT* 13.1780–87; and *NCE* 12.93–94.

De corpore et sanguine Domini [RATRAM.CORB.Corp.sang.Dom.].

MSS — A-S Vers   none.
Quots/Cits   *ÆCHom* II, 15 (B1.2.18): see below.
Refs   none.

Ratramnus, a monk from the abbey of Corbie, is best known for his eucharistic treatise *De corpore et sanguine Domini* (written around 850), which challenges the realistic or metabolic interpretation of Christ's presence in the Eucharist put forward by his superior at Corbie, the abbot PASCHASIUS RADBERTUS. Ratramnus makes a distinction between the sacramental and historical body of Christ, arguing that "the bread and the blood that are placed on the altar are placed there as a figure (*in figuram*) or memorial of the death of the Lord" (p 68). This more figurative interpretation of the

Eucharistic presence (*ad modum Ideae*) may be influenced by Platonic thought (see Fahey 1951), and certainly owes much to Augustinian analysis. The treatise is the principal source for ÆLFRIC's Easter homily (B1.2.18), which was noted as early as 1624 by James Ussher, and later in the century by Hopkins (1686). Förster (GR 5300) gives a brief summary of other scholarship on the text, and Leinbaugh (1982 and 1986) surveys the history of the controversy raised by Ælfric's synthesis of the opposing views of Ratramnus and Paschasius.

In a recent general study of Ratramnus, Bouhot (1976) argues that Ælfric had no direct knowledge of Ratramnus (pp 145–46), but his argument does not take into account the precise nature of Ælfric's translations of Ratramnus. Bouhot's assertion that Ælfric and Ratramnus share "resemblances" simply because they share a common subject of interest should be disregarded.

Theodore H. Leinbaugh

SULPICIUS SEVERUS: *CPL* 474–77; *DTC* 14.2759–62; *NCE* 13.787–88.

Sulpicius Severus, who lived between 363 and 420, was a friend of Martin of Tours and PAULINUS OF NOLA, among others, and was a major Christian intellectual in Gaul. His works on Martin not only had immediate popularity, but also had lasting influence on hagiography.

Old English writers used the *Martiniana*, that is the VITA, EPISTULAE, and DIALOGI, to construct their lives of St Martin (among other sources). It would appear that Sulpicius wrote the *Vita* when Martin was still alive, requiring later writers to go beyond the *Vita* for a full, rounded life of the saint from birth to apotheosis. After the individual headnotes, these three works will be treated as together in the discussion. There is no evidence for the use of Sulpicius' other major work, *Chronicorum libri III* (*CPL* 474; *RBMA* 7963), in Anglo-Saxon England; see van Andel (1976).

Vita Martini Turonensis [SVLP.SEV.Vit.Mart.]: *CPL* 475; *BHL* 5610.

MSS   1. Avranches, Bibliothèque Municipale 29: HG 782.
   2. Cambridge, Corpus Christi College 9: HG 36.
   3. Cambridge, Trinity Hall 21: HG 201.
   4. Hereford, Cathedral Library O.vi.11: HG 264.

5. London, BL Add. 40074: HG 296.
6. Vatican, Reg. lat. 489: HG 915.
Lists Peterborough: ML 13.61.
A-S Vers 1. *ÆCHom II* 34 (B1.2.42) 1–221, and 228–38.
    2. *ÆLS* 31 (B1.3.30) 1–649, and 706–844.
    3. *LS* 17 (B3.3.17; ed Szarmach 1981a) 6–(C1–31)–145.
    4. *Mart* (B19.iu).
    5. ALCVIN.Vit.Mart.
    6. ALDH.Pros.uirg. 261–62.
Quots/Cits *LS* 3 (B3.33) 1–10, and 220–39.
Refs *ÆLS* 31 (B1.3.30) 1–9.

Epistulae iii [SVLP.SEV.Epist.]: *CPL* 476; *BHL* 5611–13.

MSS 1. Avranches, Bibliothèque Municipale 29: HG 782.
    2. Cambridge, Corpus Christi College 9: HG 36.
    3. Cambridge, Trinity Hall 21: HG 20.
    4. London, BL Add. 40074: HG 296.
    5. ? Vatican, Reg. lat. 489; HG 915.
Lists none.
A-S Vers 1. *ÆCHom II* 34 (B1.2.42) 270–313.
    2. *ÆLS* 31 (B1.3.30) 845–900, 1306–84.
    3. *LS* 17 (B3.3.17; ed Szarmach 1981a) 146–(C1–128)–77.
    4. ALCVIN.Vit.Mart.
Quots/Cits — Refs none.

Dialogorum Libri iii [SVLP.SEV.Dial.]: *CPL* 477; *BHL* 5614–16.

MSS 1. Cambridge, Corpus Christi College 9: HG 36.
    2. Cambridge, Trinity Hall 21: HG 201.
    3. Hereford Cathedral Library, O.vi.11: HG 264.
    4. London, BL Add. 40074: HG 296.
    5. ? Vatican, Reg. lat. 489: HG 915.
Lists none.
A-S Vers 1. *ÆCHom II* 34 (B1.2.42) 152–54, 221–28, 252–66.
    2. *ÆLS* 31 (B1.3.30) 650–705, 901–1305.
    3. *Mart* (B19.iu).
    4. ALCVIN.Vit.Mart.
Quots/Cits — Refs none.

ÆLFRIC opens his Life of Martin (*ÆLS* 31) with mention of Sulpicius "who wished to write about the miracles and powerful works" Martin did, but Ælfric does not indicate the precise works he himself followed. The Life of Martin is the longest in Ælfric's collection.

Ælfric bases his homiletic treatments of Martin on the *Vita*, which he abridges, *Dialogi II et III*, but he also goes to the *Epistula III*, and GREGORY OF TOURS' HISTORIA FRANCORUM. Gerould (GR 5357) sees conscientiousness and narrative skill in both of Ælfric's treatments, pointing out as well that Ælfric widened the scope of his reading in the years between his two treatments (p 206).

Zettel (1982) argues that Ælfric did not go to the original works of Sulpicius and Gregory of Tours but rather drew on "an intermedate source of edited *Martiniana* closely resembling, if not identical with, that now preserved in the COTTON-CORPUS COLLECTION" (p 26; see LEGENDARIES). Before Zettel scholars (e.g. Gaites 1982) readily assumed that Ælfric creditably or even artfully followed Sulpicius and other sources directly.

The anonymous Old English version found in Vercelli 18 (and also the Blickling Homilies and Oxford, Junius 86) omits the prologue and chapters 1, 4, 6, 9, 11-13, 18-19, and 21-25 of the 27-chapter *Vita*, offering judicious selections from the remaining chapters that omit the ecclesiastical-political struggles of Gaul and retain Martin's campaigns against heathenism. This work also includes material from the *Epistula III*. Szarmach (1978), Gaites (1982), and Dalbey (1984) offer studies on this homily making comparisons with Ælfric.

Martin is remembered in the Old English *Martyrology* on his feast-day, November 11. In addition to material from the *Vita*, this entry draws on one incident from the *Dialogi* III.14.

ALCUIN'S VITA S. MARTINI, only one of four saints' lives attributed to him, draws on Sulpicius' *Vita* and *Dialogi*, while the *Sermo de Transitu Sancti Martini*, coming after the *Vita* in Migne-Frobenius, follows the *Epistula III*. I Deug-Su (1981) compares Alcuin with Sulpicius, noting as well relations with Alcuin's other saints' lives. Chelini (1962) is disappointed by the absence of originality in Alcuin's *Vita*.

In editorial discussions of this entry, Gordon Whatley writes "Phrases and passages of the *Vita Martini* are echoed, without acknowledgment, in BEDE'S prose VITA CUTHBERTI 198.11-12; the anonymous VITA CUTHBERTI 62.15-63.1; FELIX'S VITA GUTHLACI 60.9-15. 162.17-30; ABBO, PASSIO EADMUNDI II.18, IV.3; and WULFSTAN OF WINCHESTER, VITA ÆTHELWOLDI XIX.13."

Paul E. Szarmach

VEGETIUS RENATUS, FLAVIUS: OCD 1110-11.

Epitoma rei militaris [VEGET.epit.].

MSS   1. London, BL Cotton Cleopatra D.i: HG 325.
  2. London, BL Harley 3859: HG 439.
Lists—A-S Vers   none.
Quots/Cits   1. BEDA.Retract.Act. XXVII.33-34.: Veget.epit. 60.15-19.
  2. BEDA.Hist.eccl. 26.6-8: Veget.epit. 26.12-13, 26.20-21.
  3. BEDA.Temp.rat. XXVIII.22-32.: see below.
  4. BEDA.Vit.Cuthb.pr. XVII.16-18.: see below.
  5. ALCVIN.Epist. 415.5.: Veget.epit. 4.4-6, 5.7-8.
Refs   none.

   This work, also known as *De re militari*, is the only ancient Roman military manual to have survived intact, and was composed by Vegetius between 383 and 450 AD.

   BEDE provides the earliest known use of Vegetius by an Anglo-Saxon. He quotes Vegetius (with slight adaptations for sense) in chapter 28 of DE TEMPORUM RATIONE: Vegetius 152.10-16 in lines 22-29 and Vegetius 152.18-153.3 in lines 29-32; later in the same work and again in his prose LIFE OF CUTHBERT, Bede defines the Greek word "rheuma" by drawing on Vegetius' use of the Latin word "aestus" (*Epitoma* 161.1-14; see Jones 1932 p 248, and Colgrave and Mynors 1969 p 214 and note 24). G. Macdonald (1933 p 124) qualifies Jones and suggests a glossary as an alternate source for Bede's definition of "rheuma." Bede also draws on Vegetius in RETRACTATIONES IN ACTUS APOSTOLORUM 27, in his definition of the Greek word "monoxulas." In his ECCLESIASTICAL HISTORY, Bede uses Vegetius in his discussion of Severus, "borrowing a description of a turf wall" (Colgrave and Mynors, 1969, p 26 note); this passage is largely paraphrase, but does contain two direct quotes: lines 6-7 are taken from Vegetius 26.12-13, lines 7-8 from Vegetius 26.20-21 (Jones 1932 p 249).

   ALCUIN also knew Vegetius; in one of his *Epistolae*, Alcuin draws on the preface of *Epitoma rei militaris* in his discussion of Charlemagne (Wallach 1959 pp 50-51 and note). With the exception of one substantial interpolation, Alcuin quotes Vegetius directly, making slight adaptations for sense.

   The most recent complete modern English translation of *Epitoma rei Militaris* is Clarke (1767).

   The most complete contemporary English translation is that of Books I and II by Silhanek (1972). Schoner (1888) is still considered an excellent source for information about Vegetius; more recent studies include Gordon (1974) and Shrader (1979). Lester (1988) contains an useful survey of scholarship on Vegetius and an extensive bibliography.

Deborah Mitchell

VITAE PATRUM

The large body of material that is often loosely referred to in modern scholarship as the *Vitae patrum* was in no sense a single work or even the organized collection that appears in the printed edition of Rosweyde (reprinted in the *PL* 73–74). There is ample evidence that during the Middle Ages the term (often in the form of *Vita* or *Vitas patrum*) was used to refer to almost any work concerned with the lives and sayings of the first monks, the "desert fathers" of Egypt and the Near East. It is true that in time several such texts commonly circulated together; the *Life of Antony*, the *Life of Paul*, and the VERBA SENIORUM are typical examples. But Rosweyde's edition was merely a compilation, and inevitably it imposed a false unity on a number of books that often had their own, quite distinct, textual histories. However, the name itself is found from a very early period, for in the 530s it was mentioned in the BENEDICTINE RULE, and a little later the title was imitated by GREGORY OF TOURS in his own LIBER VITAE PATRUM; see Batlle (1972).

The appeal that such writings must have had to a monastic audience is obvious, for they offered paradigms of conduct in a way that was both arresting and easy to memorize. Certainly their widespread popularity in the Middle Ages cannot be disputed, for there are over 100 complete MSS of the *Verba seniorum* alone dating from the seventh to the fifteenth century, and MSS of selections or of isolated sayings from it are more numerous still. It would in fact be highly surprising if these books had *not* been known to the Anglo-Saxons.

There are, however, some difficulties in establishing the use of the *Vitae patrum* in Anglo-Saxon England that require some comment here. First, as in many other cases, it is quite certain that the early English encountered the work at second hand, by means of intermediate sources. For instance, DEFENSOR OF LIGUGÉ'S LIBER SCINTILLARUM includes over sixty extracts vaguely attributed by the compiler to the *Vitae patrum*, though in fact they are drawn from an extraordinary variety of sources, of which the material now thought of as the *Vitae Patrum* is only one (see Rochais *CCSL* 117). Other examples of the use of such an intermediate source, this time by ALCUIN and ÆLFRIC, are noted below under the *Verba seniorum*. Second, undefined references to the desert fathers do not in themselves constitute evidence of the use of the *Vitae patrum*. Such references abound in Old English and Anglo-Latin literature. For example, in FELIX'S LIFE OF GUTHLAC (see ACTA SANCTORUM), it is reported that the saint was inspired to follow an eremitic life "when he read about the solitary life of monks of former days" (86.13–14), and this detail found its way into the Old English prose life (*LS* 10, B.3.3.10; II.106–10). BEDE gives similar information about the monk Egbert (HISTORIA ECCLESIASTICA 344.19–20), and this too was copied into the Old English homily on St Chad (*LS* 3, B3.3.3; 193–95). Such reports do no more than indicate a general acquaintance by the authors with the biographies of the first monks. They cannot be used to determine which books the authors — let alone the saints — had actually read. (It is, in fact, well-known from other evidence that Felix was greatly influenced by EVAGRIUS' translation of the LIFE OF ANTONY by ATHANASIUS.)

Finally, there is a problem of definition: which books would an Anglo-Saxon audience have understood by the term *Vitae patrum*? Here, at least, the evidence is tolerably clear. Many of the references to the term in the Old English and Anglo-Latin texts are too vague to be of use; however, as Cross (1985a) has shown, in the four instances where Ælfric names the work and extracts an anecdote, the material comes from only one source — the fifth and sixth books of Rosweyde's *Vitae patrum*, the *Verba seniorum*. The only specific evidence that the term could have meant anything *other* in the Anglo-Saxon period is provided by an inscription in Worcester, Cathedral Library F.48, which reads "In nomine Dei summi incipit vita patrum" (fol 49): this inscription stands at the head of a copy of Rosweyde's Book II, the HISTORIA MONACHORUM IN AEGYPTO by RUFINUS OF AQUILEIA.

In what follows, then, it will be assumed that these two books, and these only, were certainly regarded as "Vitae patrum" by the Anglo-Saxons. Hence there will be no discussion of the so-called "vitae maiores," such as the Evagrian *Life of Antony* or JEROME's LIVES OF PAUL, HILARION, and MALCHUS, which Rosweyde prints in Book I of his edition. The only other book that will be dealt with here is the so-called PARADISUS HERACLIDIS, a work whose subject-matter and manner of treatment are so close to those of the HISTORIA MONACHORUM that it deserves to be considered here rather than in an article of its own.

[For this *Trial Version*, only the section on the *Paradisus Heraclidis* has been included.]

Paradisus Heraclidis [ANON.Par.Her.]: *CPG* 6036; *BHL* 6532.

MSS   1. Cambridge, University Library Ff.5.27: HG 10.
       2. Hereford, Cathedral Library P.ii.5: HG 267.
Lists   Peterborough?: ML 13.45.
A-S Vers   none.
Quots/Cits   ANON.Vit.Cuthb.: see below.
Refs   none.

The *Paradisus Heraclidis* is the longer of two Latin translations of the *Lausiac History* of Palladius of Helenopolis, a work which was composed about 419–20 and which contains an autobiographical account of encounters with the desert fathers (see Butler 1898–1904, and for a different view Draguet

1978). This longer translation itself survives in two recensions; the second, a considerably revised and expanded version of the first, is printed in the unsatisfactory edition of Rosweyde (*PL* 74.243-342). The wording of the biblical quotations in the *original* recension suggests that it was composed in Africa some time before the end of the fifth century (see Burkitt in Butler 1898-1904). It is not known who the author was; Rampolla del Tindaro (1905) points out that in some MSS he is identified as a deacon named Paschasius, but this attribution is authoritatively rejected by Batlle (1961). The authorship, place of origin and date of the *revised* recension are all unknown: the Heraclides named in the title is a fifth-century Bishop of Ephesus who is known to have had no connection whatever with the work, either in Greek or Latin.

The two MSS of the *Paradisus* are both from late in the period. According to Bishop (1954) the Cambridge MS was written at Durham late in the eleventh or early in the twelfth century; there is no evidence of the origin or date of its exemplar. The Hereford MS is of unknown origin, but it is a little earlier than the Cambridge MS, though still probably post-Conquest (Sir Roger Mynors, personal communication).

Indications that the work was known earlier in Anglo-Saxon England are slight and far from conclusive. The most suggestive evidence is to be found in two passages in the anonymous LIFE OF CUTHBERT and its successors. The first of these (ANON.Vit.Cuthb. 76.18-78,20) relates how the saint, having unwittingly entertained an angelic visitor, was rewarded by the miraculous gift of three warm loaves. This story was copied into the prose and metrical LIVES OF CUTHBERT by BEDE (prose 176.2-178.22; metrical 180-219), and into ÆLFRIC's homily on the Deposition of Cuthbert (*ÆCHom* II, 10, B1.2.11; 63-73). Miracles of this type are of course extremely common in saints' lives; there are examples in the HISTORIA MONACHORUM (*PL* 21.401 and 431), in the DIALOGUES of SULPICIUS SEVERUS (162.5-163.19), and indeed elsewhere in the anonymous *Life* itself (70.5-25)—the ultimate source being the feeding of Elijah in the desert (III Rg 17.6). However, the *Paradisus* (*PL* 74.341) shares with the Cuthbert story—and against the other version—the number of loaves (three), and may provide in its third person narration, under the guise of the miracle having happened to a lifelong companion of the writer, a source for Bede's comment that the saint would tell such stories "as though they happened to another person."

The second case in the anonymous *Life of Cuthbert*—a description of a vision that the saint had concerning the day and hour of the slaying of King Ecgfrith (122.7-27)—is less convincing. The story was copied by Bede in both his prose and metrical *Lives*, but is not found in Ælfric. Colgrave points out that a similar story is told in the *Paradisus* about Didymus of Alexandria, who saw in a trance the death of Julian the Apostate at the exact moment that the event happened (*PL* 74.254–55), but in his edition of Bede's metrical life, Jaager (610–26) shows that there is an equally similar account in ADAMNAN's *Life of Columba* (I.8), and it is as least as likely that the author of the anonymous *Life of Cuthbert* had access to this as to the *Paradisus*.

Peter Jackson

Bibliography Part I

This part of the bibliography relies on the system designed by Michael Lapidge for this volume and for the *Fontes Anglo-Saxonici*, and published under the title *Abbreviations for Sources and Specification of Standard Editions for Sources* (Binghamton, 1988). Here, however, it includes only the works that appear as entries in this volume. Abbreviations beginning with "ANON" are listed first, and are divided according to the sections in which they appear in the entries; known authors follow.

ACTA SANCTORUM

ANON.Invent.cru. [*BHL* 4169] = ed. Alfred Holder *Inventio Sanctae Crucis* (Leipzig, 1889) 1–13.

ANON.Pas.Dorm.sept. [*BHL* 2316] = ed. P.M. Huber *Beitrag zur Visionsliteratur und Siebenschläferlegende des Mittelalters, I Teil: Text*, Beilage zum Jahresbericht des humanistischen Gymnasiums Metten (1902–03) 39–78.

ANON.Pas.Eul.Barc. [*BHL* 2696] = ed. C. Narbey *Supplément aux Acta Sanctorum pour les Vies de saints de l'époque mérovingienne* 2 vols. (Paris, 1899, 1912) II, 62–64.

ANON.Pas.Eul.Emer. [*BHL* 2700] = ed. Angel Fábrega Grau, *Pasionario Hispanico* 2 vols., Monumenta Hispaniae Sacra: Serie Litúrgica, vol. 6 (Madrid, 1955) II, 68–78.

ANON.Pas.Eust. [*BHL* 2760] = ed. B. Mombritius, *Sanctuarium seu Vitae Sanctorum* 2nd ed., 2 vols. (Paris, 1910) II, 466–73, and 663.

ANON.Pas.Eust.metr. [*BHL* 2767] = ed. H. Varnhargen "Zwei lateinische metrische Versionen der Legende von Placidius-Eustachius II. Eine Version in Hexametern" *Zeitschrift für deutsches Altertum* 25 (1881) 1–25.

ANON.Pas.Fel.II [*BHL* 2857] = ed. B. Mombritius, *Sanctuarium seu Vitae Sanctorum* 2nd ed., 2 vols. (Paris, 1910) I, 550–51, and 671–72.

ANON.Pas.Fel.Tub.N [*BHL* 2894] = ed. H. Delehaye "La passion de S. Félix de Thibiuca" *Analecta Bollandiana* 39 (1921) 241–76.

ANON.Pas.Fel.Tub.V [*BHL* 2895b] = ed. H. Quentin *Les martyrologes historiques du Moyen Âge* (Paris, 1908) 526-27.

ANON.Pas.Julianae [*BHL* 4522/3] = ed. B. Mombritius, *Sanctuarium seu Vitae Sanctorum* 2nd ed., 2 vols. (Paris, 1910) II, 77-80, and 671.

ANON.Vit.Aedw.conf. [*BHL* 2421] = ed. Frank Barlow, *The Life of King Edward who rests at Westminster attributed to a monk of St. Bertin* (London, 1962).

ANON.Vit.Euphros. [*BHL* 2723] = *AS* Feb. 2.537-41.

ANON.Vit.Fel.Rom. [*BHL* 2885] = B. Mombritius, *Sanctuarium seu Vitae Sanctorum* 2nd ed., 2 vols. (Paris, 1910) I, 543-44, and 670.

ANON.Vit.Oswaldi [*BHL* 6374] = ed. J. Raine, *RS* 71.1 (London, 1879) 399-475.

APOCRYPHA

ANON.Act.Andr.Matt. = ed. Franz Blatt, *Die lateinischen Bearbeitungen der Acta Andreae et Matthiae apud Anthropophagos* Beihefte zur Zeitschrift für die neutestamentliche Wissenschaft und die Kunde der älteren Kirche 12 (Giessen, 1930) 33-95.

ANON.Acta.Pet. = ed. R.A. Lipsius in *Acta apostolorum apocrypha* 2 vols., ed. R.A. Lipsius and M. Bonnet (Leipzig, 1891-1903) I, 45-103.

ANON.Adam.comp. = ed. Max Förster, "Adams Erschaffung und Namengebung: ein lateinisches Fragment des s.g. slauischen Henoch" *Archiv für Religionswissenschaft* 11 (1907/08) 479-81.

ANON.Apoc.Mariae = ed. A. Wenger *L'Assomption de la Très Sainte Vierge dans la tradition byzantine du vi^e au xe siècle* Archives de l'Orient chrétien 5 (Paris, 1955) 258-59.

ANON.Apoc.Pris. = *PLS* 2.1508-22.

ANON.Apoc.Thom.Munich.4563 = ed. D.P. Bihlmeyer, "Un texte non interpolé de l'apocalypse de Thomas" *Revue Bénédictine* 28 (1911) 272-74.

ANON.Apoc.Thom.Munich.4585 = ed. Friedrich Wilhelm, *Deutsche Legenden und Legendare* (Leipzig, 1907) 40*-42*.

ANON.Apoc.Thom.Verona.1 = ed. M.R. James, "Notes on Apocrypha" *Journal of Theological Studies* 11 (1910) 289.

ANON.Apoc.Thom.Vienna.16 = ed. J. Bick, *Wiener Palimpseste* Sitzungsberichte der Wiener Akademie der Wissenschaften, philosophisch-historische Klasse 159 (1908) 99.

ANON.Breu.apos. = ed. Leo Cunibert Mohlberg, *Liber Sacramentorum Romanae Aeclesiae ordinis anni circuli* (1960; Rome, 1981) 260-61.

ANON.Enoch = ed. M.R. James, *Apocrypha Anecdota* Texts and Studies 2.3 (Cambridge, 1893) 148.

ANON.Epist.Iac./PS.CLEMENS = ed. B. Rehm, *Die Pseudoklementinen. I Homilien, GCS* 42 (Berlin, 1953) 5–22.

ANON.Epist.Laod. = ed. R. Weber, *Biblia sacra iuxta vulgatam versionem* 2nd ed. (Stuttgart, 1975).

ANON.Epist.Sal. Dom.= ed. Theodor Mommsen, Rufinus' trans of Eusebius' *Ecclesiastical History* I.13 in *Eusebius Werke* 2.1 ed. Eduard Schwartz (Leipzig, 1903) 89–97.

ANON.Epist.Sal.Dom.(BN.12270) = ed. H. Delehaye, "Note sur la légende de la lettre du Christ tombée du ciel" *Académie Royale de Belgique: Bulletin de la classe des lettres* (1899) 181–84.

ANON.Epist.Sal.Dom.(Munich.9950) = ed. H. Delehaye, "Note sur la légende de la lettre du Christ tombée du ciel" *Académie Royale de Belgique: Bulletin de la classe des lettres* (1899) 179–81.

ANON.Epist.Sal.Dom.(Tarragona) = ed. R. Priebsch, *Letter from Heaven* (Oxford, 1936) 34–37.

ANON.Epist.Sal.Dom.(Vienna.1355) = ed. R. Priebsch, "The Chief Sources of Some Anglo-Saxon Homilies," *Otia Merseiana* 1 (1899) 130–34.

ANON.Esdrae.lib.IV = ed. R. Weber, *Biblia sacra iuxta vulgatam versionem* 2nd ed. (Stuttgart, 1975).

ANON.Euang.Nic. = ed. H.C. Kim, *The Gospel of Nicodemus* (Toronto, 1973).

ANON.Euang.Ps.Matt. = ed. C. Tischendorf, *Evangelia Apocrypha* 2nd ed. (Leipzig, 1876) 54–111.

ANON.Hist.Apos./PS.ABD. = ed. J.A. Fabricius, *Codex apocryphus Novi Testamenti* 2nd ed., 2 vols. (Hamburg, 1719) II, 402–742

ANON.Inter.Sal. = no text survives.

ANON.Jamnes = ed. Max Förster, "Das lateinisch-altenglische Fragment der Apokryphe von Jamnes und Mambres" *Archiv für das Studium der neueren Sprachen und Literaturen* 108 (1902) 18–20.

ANON.Jubilees = ed. R.H. Charles, *The Ethiopic Version of the Hebrew Book of Jubilees* Anecdota Oxoniensia, Semitic Series 8 (Oxford, 1895).

ANON.Lib.Antiq./PS.PHILO = ed. Guido Kisch, *Pseudo-Philo's Liber Antiquitatum Biblicarum* (Notre Dame IN, 1949) 109–270.

ANON.Nat.Mariae = ed. Émile Amann, *Le Protévangile de Jacques et ses remaniements latins* (Paris, 1910) 340–64.

ANON.Nom.Apost. = ed. A. Hamilton Thompson and U. Lindlöf *Rituale Ecclesiae Dunelmensis, SS* 140 (London, 1927) 195–97.

ANON.Notit.Apost. = ed. T. Schermann, *Prophetarum vitae fabulosae, indices apostolorum discipulorumque Domini Dorotheo, Epiphanio, Hippolyto aliisque vindicata* (Leipzig, 1907) 212–13.

ANON.Pas.Andr. = ed. M. Bonnet, in *Acta apostolorum apocrypha* 2 vols., ed. R.A. Lipsius and Bonnet (Leipzig, 1891-1903) II.1, 1–37.

ANON.Pas.Bart. = ed. M. Bonnet, in *Acta apostolorum apocrypha* 2 vols., ed. R.A. Lipsius and Bonnet (Leipzig, 1891-1903) II.1, 128-50.

ANON.Pas.Iac.Mai. = ed. Angel Fábrega Grau, *Pasionario Hispanico* 2 vols., Monumenta Hispaniae Sacra: Serie Litúrgica, vol. 6 (Madrid, 1955) II, 111-16.

ANON.Pas.Iac.Min. = ed. Angel Fábrega Grau, *Pasionario Hispanico* 2 vols., Monumenta Hispaniae Sacra: Serie Litúrgica, vol. 6 (Madrid, 1955) II, 100-01.

ANON.Pas.Ioh./PS.MEL. = *PG* 5.1241-50.

ANON.Pas.Marci = ed. B. Mombritius, *Sanctuarium seu Vitae Sanctorum* 2nd ed., 2 vols. (Paris, 1910) II, 173-75.

ANON.Pas.Mattaei = ed. Giuseppe Talamo Atenolfi, *I testi medioevali degli atti di S. Matteo l'evangelista* (Rome, 1958) 58-80.

ANON.Pas.Paul./PS.LINUS = ed. R.A. Lipsius, in *Acta apostolorum apocrypha* 2 vols., ed. Lipsius and Bonnet (Leipzig, 1891-1903) I, 23-44.

ANON.Pas.Pet.Paul./PS.MARCEL = ed. R.A. Lipsius in *Acta Apostolorum Apocrypha*, 2 vols., ed. Lipsius and M. Bonnet (Leipzig, 1891-1903) I, 119-77.

ANON.Pas.Petri = ed. B. Mombritius, *Sanctuarium seu Vitae Sanctorum* 2nd ed., 2 vols. (Paris, 1910) II, 357-65.49.

ANON.Pas.Phil. = ed. B. Mombritius, *Sanctuarium seu Vitae Sanctorum* 2nd ed., 2 vols. (Paris, 1910) II, 385.

ANON.Pas.Sim.Iud. = ed. B. Mombritius, *Sanctuarium seu Vitae Sanctorum* 2nd ed., 2 vols. (Paris, 1910) II, 534-39.

ANON.Pas.Thom. = ed. Klaus Zelzer, *Die alten lateinischen Thomasakten TU* 122 (Berlin, 1977) 3-42.

ANON.Past.Herm.(Gk) = ed. Molly Whittaker, *GCS* 48 (Berlin, 1956).

ANON.Past.Herm.(V) = ed. A. Hilgenfeld, *Hermae Pastor* (Leipzig, 1873).

ANON.Past.Herm.(P) = ed. O. De Gebhardt and A. Harnack, *Patrum Apostolicorum Opera* vol. 3 (Leipzig, 1877).

ANON.Proteuang.Iac. = ed. Émile Amann, *Le Protévangile de Jacques et ses remaniements latins* (Paris, 1910) 179-271.

ANON.Ps.151 = ed. R. Weber, *Biblia sacra iuxta vulgatam versionem* 2nd ed. (Stuttgart, 1975).

ANON.Quaest.Bart.(L) = ed. André Wilmart and E. Tisserant, "Fragments Grecs et Latins de l'Évangile de Barthélemy" *Revue Biblique* 10 (1913) 161-90 and 321-68.

ANON.Quaest.Bart.(C) = ed. Umberto Moricca, "Un nuovo testo dell' 'Evangelo di Bartolomeo'" *Revue Biblique* 30 (1921) 483-516 and 31 (1922) 20-30.

ANON.Recog./PS.CLEMENS = ed. Bernhard Rehm, *Die Pseudoklementinen. II Rekognitionen in Rufins Übersetzung, GCS* 51 (Berlin, 1965) 3-387.

ANON.Res.Christ.Bart. = ed. E. A. Wallis Budge, *Coptic Apocrypha in the Dialect of Upper Egypt* (London, 1913) 1–48 (text) and 179–230 (translation).
ANON.Rev./PS.METH. = ed. Otto Prinz, "Eine frühe abendländische Aktualisierung der lateinischen Übersetzung des Pseudo-Methodios" *Deutsches Archiv für Erforschung des Mittelalters* 41 (1985) 6–17.
ANON.Rev.Esd. = ed. Giovani Mercati, *Nota di Letteratura Biblica e Cristiana Antica* Studi e Testi 5 (Vatican, 1901) 77–79.
ANON.Sibyl. = ed. J. Geffcken, *Die Oracula Sibyllina GCS* 8 (Leipzig, 1902).
ANON.Trans.Mariae.B = ed. Monika Haibach-Reinisch, *Ein neuer "Transitus Mariae" des Pseudo-Melito* (Rome, 1962) 63–87.
ANON.Trans.Mariae.C = ed. André Wilmart, *Analecta Reginensia* Studi e Testi 59 (Vatican, 1933) 325–57.
ANON.Vis.Pauli.(BN.1631) = ed. M.R. James "Visio Pauli" in *Apocrypha Anecdota* Texts and Studies 2.3 (Cambridge, 1893) 11–42.
ANON.Vis.Pauli.(Pal.lat.220) = ed. M.E. Dwyer "An Unstudied Redaction of the *Visio Pauli*" *Manuscripta* 32 (1988) 125–29.
ANON.Vis.Pauli.(StGall.317) = ed. T. Silverstein, *Visio Sancti Pauli* Studies and Documents 4 (London, 1935) 131–47.
ANON.Vis.Pauli.(Vienna.362) = ed. T. Silverstein, *Visio Sancti Pauli* Studies and Documents 4 (London, 1935) 149–52.
ANON.Vit.Adae = ed. W. Meyer, "Vita Adae et Evae" *Abhandlungen der königlich bayerischen Akademie der Wissenschaften, philosophisch-philologische Klasse* 14 (Munich 1878) 221–50.

GRAMMARIANS

ANON.Beat. = unedited. *Beatus quid est* in London, BL Harley 3271, fols 93–117v.

HIBERNO-LATIN AND IRISH-INFLUENCED BIBLICAL COMMENTARIES, FLORILEGIA, AND HOMILY COLLECTIONS

ANON.Arg.psalm./PS.BEDA = *PL* 93.477–1098.
ANON.Breu.psalm./PS.HIER. = *PL* 26.871–1346 (1845 edition, 26.821–1270).

ANON.Cat.celt. = ed. [partial] André Wilmart, *Analecta Reginensia* Studi e Testi 59 (Rome, 1933).
ANON.Cat.Cracov. = ed. [partial] Pierre David, "Un recueil de conférences monastiques irlandaises du VIIIe siècle" *Revue Bénédictine* 49 (1937) 62–89.
ANON.Comm.Apc./PS.HIER. = *PLS* 4.1850–63.
ANON.Comm.Ct.(Marb.Hr2,11) = unedited.
ANON.Comm.Gen.(BN.10457+10616) = unedited.
ANON.Comm.Gen.(Mun.6302) = unedited.
ANON.Comm.Gen.(StGall.908) = unedited.
ANON.Comm.epist.cath.(Karlsr.233) = ed. R.E. McNally, *CCSL* 108B.3–50.
ANON.Comm.Gloss.Matth.(Würzb.61) = ed. [partial] Karl Köberlin, *Eine Würzburger Evangelienhandschrift* (Augsburg, 1891).
ANON.Comm.Luc.(Vien.997) = ed. Joseph Kelly, *CCSL* 108C.1–101.
ANON.Comm.Marc./PS.HIER. = *PL* 30.589–644.
ANON.Comm.Matth.(BN.12021) = unedited.
ANON.Comm.Matth.(Mun.6233) = unedited.
ANON.Comm.Matth.(Vien.940) = unedited.
ANON.Comm.serm.Dom.mont. = ed. Ludwig Bieler and James Carney, "The Lambeth Commentary" *Ériu* 23 (1972) 1–55.
ANON.Dies.dom.(Rec.I-III) = ed. R.E. McNally, *CCSL* 108B.175–86.
ANON.Ecl.tract.psalt. = unedited.
ANON.Expos.epist.cath./PS.HIL.ARELAT. = ed. R.E. McNally, *CCSL* 108B.53–124.
ANON.Expos.Iohan./PS.HIER. = ed. Denis Brearley, "The Expositio Iohannis in Angers BM 275. A Commentary on the Gospel of St John Showing Irish Influence" *Recherches Augustiniennes* 22 (1987) 151–221.
ANON.Expos.Matth./PS.BEDA = *PL* 92.9–132.
ANON.Expos.quat.euang.(Rec. I/PS.HIER.) = *PL* 30.531–90 and 114.861–916.
ANON.Flor.Fris. = ed. Albert Lehner, *CCSL* 108D.3–39.
ANON.Gloss.psalm.(Pal.lat.68) = ed. Martin McNamara, *Glossa in Psalmos. The Hiberno-Latin Gloss on the Psalms of Codex Palatinus Latinus 68* Studi e Testi 310 (Vatican City, 1986).
ANON.Gloss.psalt.South. = unedited.
ANON.Hom.LeabharBreac = ed. [partial] Robert Atkinson, *The Passions and Homilies from the Leabhar Breac* Todd Lecture Series 2 (Dublin, 1887); and Edmund Hogan, *The Irish Nennius from L. na Huidre and Homilies and Legends from Leabhar Breac* Todd Lecture Series 6 (Dublin, 1895).
ANON.Hom.Linz = unedited.
ANON.Hom.(Mun.6233) = unedited.
ANON.Hom.(Pal.lat.556) = ed. Graziano di S. Teresa, "Ramenta patristica 1: Il florilegio pseudoagostiniano palatino" *Ephemerides Carmeliticae* 14 (1963) 195–241.

ANON.Hom.nom.Dei.summi = ed. R.E. McNally, "In Nomine Dei Summi: Seven Hiberno-Latin Sermons" *Traditio* 35 (1979) 121-43.

ANON.Inuent.nom. = ed. M.R. James, "Inventiones Nominum" *Journal of Theological Studies* 4 (1902/03) 218-44.

ANON.Interr.sing.quest. = unedited.

ANON.Lib.num.I/PS.ISID. = *PL* 83.179-200.

ANON.Lib.num.II/PS.ISID. = [partial] *PL* 83.1293-1302.

ANON.Lib.quaest.euang./PS.ALCVIN = unedited.

ANON.Lib.quaest.euang.2/PS.ALCVIN = unedited.

ANON.OIr.Treat.psalt. = ed. Kuno Meyer, *Hibernica Minora, Being a Fragment of an Old-Irish Treatise on the Psalter* Anecdota Oxoniensia, Mediaeval and Modern Series Part 8 (Oxford, 1894).

ANON.Pauc.prob. = unedited.

ANON.Pent.comm.exp.Gen./PS.BEDA = *PL* 91.189-286.

ANON.Praef.Marc. = ed. R.E. McNally, *CCSL* 108B.220-24.

ANON.Preb.mult.exempl. = ed. R.E. McNally, *CCSL* 108B.155-71.

ANON.Quaest.apost. = unedited.

ANON.Quaest.nou.uet.test./PS.ISID. = ed. R.E. McNally, *CCSL* 108B.197-205.

ANON.Sept.sig./PS.ALCVIN = ed. E. Ann Matter "The Pseudo-Alcuinian 'De Septem Sigillis': An Early Latin Apocalypse Exegesis" *Traditio* 36 (1980) 111-37.

ANON.Test.diu.script. = ed. Albert Lehner, *CCSL* 108D.55-127.

LAWS

ANON.Lex.Salic. = ed. K.A. Eckhardt, *MGH* Leges 4.2 (1969).

LITURGY

ANON.Lib.pontif. = ed. L. Duchesne *Le Liber Pontificalis,* 2 vols. (Paris, 1955).

ANON.Lib.precum.Cerne = ed. A.B. Kuypers *The Book of Cerne* (Cambridge, 1902)

ANON.Lib.precum.Harley = ed. F.E. Warren *The Antiphonary of Bangor* HBS 10 (London, 1895).

ANON.Lib.precum.Nunnaminster = ed. W. deG. Birch *An Ancient Manuscript of the Eighth or Ninth Century: Formerly Belonging to St. Mary's Abbey, or Nunnaminster, Winchester* Hampshire Record Society (London, 1889).

ANON.Lib.Precum.Royal = ed. A.B. Kuypers *The Book of Cerne* (Cambridge, 1902) 201–25.

PS BOETHIUS

ANON.Geom.1/PS.BOETH = *PL* 63.1352D–1364 [partial].

VITAE PATRUM

ANON.Par.Her. = ed. C. Butler, *The Lausiac History of Palladius* Texts and Studies 6 (Cambridge, 1898–1904).

AUTHORS

ABBO.Flor.Pass.Eadmund. = ed. M. Winterbottom *Three Lives of English Saints* (Toronto, 1972) 65–87.
ADO.VIENN.Sex.aet.mundi = ed. G.H. Pertz, *MGH* Scriptores 2.317–23.
AIL.Kan.euang. = ed. W. Meyer, "Gildae Oratio rhythmica" *Nachrichten von der Gesellschaft der Wissenschaften zu Göttingen* (1912) 65–66.
ALCVIN.Gramm. = *PL* 101.849–902.
ALCVIN.Off.per.Fer. = *PL* 101.509–612.
ALCVIN.Virt.uit. = *PL* 101.613–38.
ALCVIN.Vit.Mart. = *PL* 101.657–62.
AVG.Confess = ed. L. Verheijen *CCSL* 27.
BEDA.Hist.eccles. = ed. B. Colgrave and R.A.B. Mynors, *Bede's Ecclesiastical History of the English People* (Oxford, 1969).
BEDA.Mart. = ed. J. Dubois and G. Renand, *Édition pratique des Martyrologes de Bède, de l'Anonyme lyonnais et de Florus* (Paris, 1976).
BEDA.Nom.reg. = ed. M.L.W. Laistner, *Nomina regionum atque locorum de actibus apostolorum*, *CCSL* 121.167–78.
BEDA.Orthogr. = ed. C.W. Jones *CCSL* 123A.7–57.
BEDA.Vit. Cuthb.pr. = ed. B. Colgrave, *Two Lives of St. Cuthbert* (Cambridge, 1940; rpt 1985) 141–306.
BEDA.Vit.Cuthb.metr. = ed. W. Jaager, *Bedas Metrische Vita Sancti Cuthberti* Palaestra 198 (Leipzig, 1935).
BOETH.Arith. = ed. G. Friedlein (Leipzig, 1867) 3–173.

BOETH.Cons.Phil. = ed. L. Bieler *CCSL* 94.

BOETH.Mus. = ed. G. Friedlein (Leipzig, 1867) 178–371.

CASS.FEL.Med. = ed. V. Rose *Cassii Felicis De medicina ex graecis logicae sectae auctoribus liber translatus* (Leipzig, 1879).

CYPR.GALL.Carm.rel. = ed. R. Peiper *CSEL* 23.209–11.

CYPR.GALL.Hept. = ed. R. Peiper *CSEL* 23.1–208.

DRACONT.Laud.Dei = ed. F. Vollmer *MGH* AA 14.114–31.

DRACONT.Orest.Trag. = ed. F. Vollmer *MGH* AA 14.197–226.

DRACONT.Romul. = ed. F. Vollmer *MGH* AA 14.132–96.

DRACONT.Satisfact. = ed. F. Vollmer *MGH* AA 14.23–113.

ECGRED.Epist. = ed. Dorothy Whitelock in "Bishop Ecgred, Pehtred and Niall" in *Ireland in Early Mediaeval Europe: Studies in Memory of Kathleen Hughes*, ed. Whitelock, R. McKitterick, and D. Dumville (Cambridge, 1982) 48–49.

FELIX.Vit.Guth. = ed. Bertram Colgrave *Felix's Life of Saint Guthlac* (1956; rpt Cambridge, 1985).

HRAB.MAVR.Comp. = ed. W.M. Stevens *CCCM* 44.199–321.

HRAB.MAVR.Discip.eccl. = *PL* 112.1191–262.

HRAB.MAVR.Instit.cler. = *PL* 107.293–420.

IOS.SCOT.Abbreu.HIER.Comm.Isai. = unedited.

LAIDC.Egl.Mor.Iob = ed. M. Adriaen *CCSL* 145.

LAUR.NOV.Hom.eleem. = *PL* 66.105–116.

MAEL.Comm.euang. = unedited.

OROS.Hist.adu.pag. = ed. K. Zangemeister *CSEL* 5.

PASCH.RAD.Corp.sang.Dom. = ed. B. Paulus *CCCM* 16.1–131.

PAVL.NOL.Carm. = ed. W. Hartel *CSEL* 30.1–338.

PAVLUS.DIAC.NIAPOL.Vit.Maria Aeg. [*BHL* 5415] = *PL* 73.671–90

PRISC.Accent. = *GL* 3.519–28.

PRISC.Inst.gramm. = *GL* 2.1–597 and 3.1–377.

PRISC.Nom.pron.uerb. = *GL* 3.443–56.

PRISC.Part. = *GL* 3.459–515.

PROBA.Cent. = ed. K. Shenkl *CSEL* 16.1, pp. 568–609.

PRVD.Apoth. = ed. M.P. Cunningham *CCSL* 126.73–115.

PRVD.Cath. = ed. M.P. Cunningham *CCSL* 126.3–72.

PRVD.Contr.Symm. = ed. M.P. Cunningham *CCSL* 126.182–250.

PRVD.Ditt. = ed. M.P. Cunningham *CCSL* 126.390–400.

PRVD.Epil. = ed. M.P. Cunningham *CCSL* 126.401–02.

PRVD.Hamart. = ed. M.P. Cunningham *CCSL* 126.116–48.

PRVD.Peristeph. = ed. M.P. Cunningham *CCSL* 126.251–389.

PRVD.Praef. = ed. M.P. Cunningham *CCSL* 126.1–2.

PRVD.Psych. = ed. M.P. Cunningham *CCSL* 126.149–81.

RALPH.D'ES.Hom. = *PL* 158.644–49.

RATRAM.CORB.Corp.sang.Dom. = ed. J.N. Bakhuizen van den Brink (Amsterdam, 1974).

SVLP.SEV.Dial. = ed. K. Halm *CSEL* 1.152-216.

SVLP.SEV.Epist. = ed. K. Halm *CSEL* 1.138-51.

SVLP.SEV.Vit.Mart. = ed. J. Fontaine *SChr* 133-35 (Paris, 1967) I, 248-344.

VEGET.epit. = ed. Carl Lang *Flavi Vegeti Renati Epitoma rei militaris* 2nd ed. (1885; rpt. Stuttgart, 1967).

WVLF.WINT.Vit.Æthelwold. = ed. M. Winterbottom *Three Lives of English Saints* (Toronto, 1972) 33-63.

Bibliography Part II

Acker, Paul "The Going-Out of the Soul in Blickling Homily IV" *English Language Notes* 23.4 (1986) 1–3.

Alexander, J.J.G. and M.T. Gibson eds. *Medieval Learning and Literature: Essays presented to Richard William Hunt* (Oxford, 1976).

Alexander, Paul J. *The Byzantine Apocalyptic Tradition* ed. Dorothy deF. Abrahamse (Berkeley, 1985).

Allen, Michael J.B. and Daniel G. Calder *Sources and Analogues of Old English Poetry: The Major Latin Texts in Translation* (Cambridge, 1976).

Allen, Thomas P. "A Critical Edition of the Old English Gospel of Nicodemus" (Diss. Rice, 1968).

Amann, Émile, ed. *Le Protévangile de Jacques et ses remaniements latins* (Paris, 1910).

Amelli, A. *Miscellanea Cassinense* vol. 1: *Patristica* (Monte Cassino, 1897a).

Amelli, A. *Spicilegium Cassinense* vol. 3.1 (Monte Cassino, 1897b).

Autenrieth, Johanne and Franz Brunhölzl, eds. *Festschrift Bernhard Bischoff* (Stuttgart, 1971).

Avril, François, and Patricia Danz Stirnemann *Manuscrits enluminés d'origine insulaire viie-xxe siècle* Manuscrits enluminés de la Bibliothèque Nationale (Paris, 1987).

Baesecke, Georg *Der Vocabularius Sti. Galli in der angelsächsischen Mission* (Halle, 1933).

Baker, Peter S. "Byrhtferth's *Enchiridion* and the Computus in Oxford, St John's College 17" *Anglo-Saxon England* 10 (1982) 123–42.

Baluzius, S. *Miscellaneorum libri VII, hoc est Collectio veterum monumentorum* 7 vols. (Paris, 1678–1715).

Bammesberger, Alfred "Hidden Glosses in Manuscripts of Old English Poetry" *Anglo-Saxon England* 13 (1984) 43–50.

Bannister, Arthur Thomas *A Descriptive Catalogue of the Manuscripts in the Hereford Cathedral Library* (Hereford, 1927).

Barnard, L. W. "The Shepherd of Hermas in Recent Study" *Heythrop Journal* 9 (1968) 29–36.

Bately, J.M. and D.J.A. Ross "A Check List of Manuscripts of Orosius's *Historiarum adversum Paganos Libri Septem*" *Scriptorium* 15 (1961) 329–34.

Bately, J.M. "The Classical Additions in the Old English Orosius" in Clemoes and Hughes (1971) 237–51.

Bately, J.M. "World History in the Anglo-Saxon Chronicle: Its Sources and Separateness from the Old English Orosius" *Anglo-Saxon England* 8 (1979) 177–94.

Bately, J.M. ed., *The Old English Orosius EETS* SS 6 (Oxford, 1980).

Bately, J.M. *The Literary Prose of King Alfred's Reign: Translation or Transformation?* Old English Newsletter Subsidia 10 (rpt with addenda and corrigenda, Binghamton, 1984); first published King's College London (London, 1980).

Bately, J.M. "Evidence for Knowledge of Latin Literature in Old English" in Szarmach (1986a) pp 35–51.

Bately, J.M. "Those Books that are Most Necessary for All Men to Know: The Classics and late ninth century England, a Reappraisal" in Bernardo and Levin (1990) 45–78.

Bateson, Mary "A Worcester Cathedral Book of Ecclesiastical Collections, Made C. 1000 A.D." *English Historical Review* 10 (1895) 712–31.

Batlle, Columba M. "Contribució a l'estudi de Pascasi de Dumi i la seva versió de *Verba Seniorum*" *Estudis Romànics* 8 (1961) 57–75.

Batlle, Columba M. "'Vetera Nova.' Vorläufige kritische Ausgabe bei Rosweyde fehlender Vätersprüche" in Autenrieth and Brunhölzl (1971) 32–42.

Batlle, Columba M. *Die "Adhortationes Sanctorum Patrum" ("Verba Seniorum" im lateinischen Mittelalter* Beiträge zur Geschichte des alten Mönchtums und des Benediktinerordens 31 (Münster in Westfalen, 1972).

Bauckham, R.J. "The Great Tribulation in the Shepherd of Hermas" *Journal of Theological Studies* ns 25 (1974) 27–40.

Baumler, Ellen B. *Andrew in the City of the Cannibals: A Comparative Study of the Latin, Greek, and Old English Texts* (Diss. Univ of Kansas, 1985).

Bazire, J. and J.E. Cross, eds. *Eleven Old English Rogationtide Homilies* Toronto Old English Series 7 (Toronto, 1982).

Becker, G. *Catalogi Bibliothecarum Antiqui* (Bonn, 1885).

Beeson, Charles Henry *Isidor-Studien* (Munich, 1913).

Bensly, Robert L. and M.R. James *The Fourth Book of Ezra* Texts and Studies 3.2 (Cambridge, 1895) 1–82.

Bernardo, Aldo S. and Saul Levin, eds. *The Classics in the Middle Ages* Medieval and Renaissance Texts and Studies 69 (Binghamton, 1990).

Berschin, Walter "Zur lateinischen und deutschen Juliana-Legende" *Studi Medievali* 3rd ser 14 (1978) 1006–08.

Bestul, Thomas H. "The Old English *Resignation* and the Benedictine Reform" *Neuphilologische Mitteilungen* 78 (1977) 18–23.

Bestul, Thomas H. "Continental Sources of Anglo-Saxon Devotional Writing" in Szarmach (1986a) 103–26.

Beyers, R., ed. *De nativitate Mariae: Kritische Voorstudie en Tekstuitgave* Proefschrift voor het doctoraat in de Wijsbegeerte en Letteren, groep Klassieke Filologie, aan de Katholieke Universiteit Leuven (Antwerp, 1980).

Bibliotheca Phillippica, N.S.: Medieval MSS, Part I. Catalogue of Thirty-Nine Manuscripts of the 9th–16th century (Sotheby & Co., London, 1965).

Bieler, Ludwig "Ireland's Contribution to Northumbrian Culture" in Bonner (1976) 210–18.

Bieler, Ludwig "Corpus Christianorum II" *Scriptorium* 32 (1978a) 69–91.

Bieler, Ludwig "Corpus Christianorum III" *Scriptorium* 32 (1978b) 264–86.

Biggs, Frederick M. *The Sources of Christ III: A Revision of Cook's Notes* Old English Newsletter Subsidia 12 (Binghamton, 1986).

Biggs, Frederick M. "The Passion of Andreas: *Andreas* 1398–1491" *Studies in Philology* 85 (1988) 413–27.

Biggs, Frederick M. "The Fourfold Division of Souls: The Old English 'Christ III' and the Insular Homiletic Tradition" *Traditio* 45 (1989).

Birch, Walter deG., ed. *An Ancient Manuscript of the Eighth or Ninth Century: Formerly Belonging to St. Mary's Abbey, or Nunnaminster, Winchester* Hampshire Record Society (London, 1889).

Birch, Walter deG., ed. *Liber vitae: Register and Martyrology of New Minster and Hyde Abbey Winchester* Hampshire Record Society (London, 1892).

Bischoff, Bernhard "Die lateinischen Übersetzungen und Bearbeitungen aus den Oracula Sibyllina" *Mélanges Joseph De Ghellinck, S.J.* Museum Lessianum, Section Historique 13 (Gembloux, 1951) 121–47; rpt in Bischoff (1966–81) I, 150–71.

Bischoff, Bernhard "Zur Frühgeschichte des mittelalterlichen Chirographum" *Archivalische Zeitschrift* 50/51 (1955) 297–300; rpt in Bischoff (1966–81) I, 118–22.

Bischoff, Bernhard "Eine verschollene Einteilung der Wissenschaften" *Archives d'histoire doctrinale et littéraire du moyen âge* 25 (1958) 5–20; rpt in Bischoff (1966–81) II, 273–88.

Bischoff, Bernhard *Die Südostdeutschen Schreibschulen und Bibliotheken in der Karolingerzeit* vol. 1: *Die Bayrischen Diözesen* (Wiesbaden, 1960).

Bischoff, Bernhard "Die europäische Verbreitung der Werke Isidors von Sevilla" in Díaz y Díaz (1961) 317–44; rpt in Bischoff (1966–81) I, 171–94.

Bischoff, Bernhard *Mittelalterliche Studien* 3 vols. (Stuttgart, 1966–81).

Bischoff, Bernhard "Die Handschrift" in *Der Stuttgarter Bilderpsalter Bibl. fol. 23 Württembergische Landesbibliothek Stuttgart* vol. 2 (Stuttgart, 1968) 15–30.

Bischoff, Bernhard "Turning-Points in the History of Latin Exegesis in the Early Irish Church" trans. Colm O'Grady in McNamara (1976) 74–160; from "Wendepunkte in der Geschichte der lateinischen Exegese im Frühmittelalter" in Bischoff (1966-81) I, 205-73; originally in *Sacris Erudiri* 6 (1954) 189-279.

Bischoff, Bernhard "Lorsch im Spiegel seiner Handschriften" in *Die Reichsabtei Lorsch. Festschrift zum Gedenken an ihre Stiftung 764* 2 vols. ed. Friedrich Knöpp (Darmstadt, 1973-77) II, 7-128.

Bishop, T.A.M. "A Fragment in Northumbrian Uncial" *Scriptorium* 8 (1954) 111-13.

Bishop, T.A.M. "The Corpus Martianus Capella" *Transactions of the Cambridge Bibliographical Society* 4 (1967) 257-75.

Black, M. ed. *Apocalypsis Henochi Graece* (Leiden, 1970).

Bodden, Mary-Catherine *The Old English Finding of the True Cross* (Cambridge, 1987)

Böhne, W. ed. *Hrabanus Maurus und seine Schule: Festschrift der Rabanus-Maurus-Schule* (Fulda, 1980).

Bolton, Diane K. "Remigian Commentaries on the 'Consolation of Philosophy' and their Sources" *Traditio* 33 (1977) 381-94.

Bolton, Diane K. "The Study of the Consolation of Philosophy in Anglo-Saxon England" *Archives d'histoire doctrinale et littéraire du moyen âge* 44 (1978) 33-78.

Bonner, Gerald ed. *Famulus Christi. Essays in Commemoration of the Thirteenth Centenary of the Birth of the Venerable Bede* (London, 1976).

Bonnet, M. *Acta Apostolorum Apocrypha* 2.1 (Leipzig, 1898).

Bouhot, Jean-Paul *Ratramne de Corbie: Histoire littéraire et controverses doctrinales* (Paris, 1976).

Bovon, François, Michel van Esbroeck, et. al. *Les Actes Apocryphes des Apôtres: Christianisme et monde païen* Publications de la Faculté de Théologie de l'Université de Genève 4 (Genève, 1981).

Bower, Calvin M. "Boethius' *De institutione musica*: A Handlist of Manuscripts" *Scriptorium* 42 (1988) 205-51.

Brearley, Denis "The Irish Influences in the *Expositio Iohannis iuxta Hieronimum* in Angers BM 275" *Proceedings of the Irish Biblical Association* 10 (Dublin, 1986) 72-89.

Breen, Aidan "Some Seventh-Century Hiberno-Latin Texts and their Relationships" *Peritia* 3 (1984) 204-14.

Bright, James W., and R. L. Ramsay *Liber Psalmorum: The West-Saxon Psalms, Being the Prose Portion, or the 'First Fifty,' of the so-called Paris Psalter* (Boston, 1907).

Bright, James W. and R. L. Ramsay "Notes on the 'Introductions' of the West-Saxon Psalms" *Journal of Theological Studies* 13 (1912) 520-58.

Brou, Louis and André Wilmart, eds. *The Psalter Collects from the V-VIth Century Sources* HBS 83 (London, 1949).

Brown, George H. *Bede the Venerable* (Boston, 1987).

Brown, Michelle P. "Paris, Bibliothèque Nationale, lat. 10861 and the Scriptorium of Christ Church, Canterbury" *Anglo-Saxon England* 15 (1987) 119-37.

Brown, Peter *The Cult of the Saints* (Chicago, 1981).

Brown, T.J. and T.W. Mackay *Codex Vaticanus Palatinus latinus 235* Corpus Christianorum, Armarium Codicum Insignium 4 (Turnhout, 1988).

Bubnov, Nicolaus, ed. *Gerberti Opera Mathematica* (1899; rpt Hildesheim, 1963).

Bulst, W. "Eine anglo-lateinische Übersetzung aus dem Griechischen um 700" *Zeitschrift für deutsches Altertum* 75 (1938) 105-11.

Burlin, Robert B. and Edward B. Irving, eds. *Old English Studies in Honour of John C. Pope* (Toronto, 1974).

Butler, Cuthbert *The Lausiac History of Palladius*, 2 vols. Texts and Studies 6 (Cambridge, 1898-1904).

Bzdyl, Donald G. "The Sources of Ælfric's Prayers in Cambridge University Library MS. Gg. 3. 28" *Notes and Queries* ns 24 (1977) 98-102.

Bzdyl, Donald G. "Prayer in Old English Narratives" *Medium Ævum* 51 (1982) 135-51.

Caldwell, John "The De Institutione Arithmetica and the De Institutione Musica" in Gibson (1981) 135-54.

Cameron, M.L. "The Sources of Medical Knowledge in Anglo-Saxon England" *Anglo-Saxon England* 11 (1983) 135-55.

Campbell, Jackson J. "To Hell and Back: Latin Tradition and Literary Use of the 'Descensus ad Inferos' in Old English" *Viator* 13 (1982) 107-58.

Campbell, James ed. *The Anglo-Saxons* (Ithaca NY, 1982).

Canal-Sánchez, Jose M. "Antiguas versiónes Latinas del Protoevangelio de Santiago" *Ephemerides Mariologicae* 18 (1968) 431-73.

Carlini, Antonio "La tradizione manoscritta del Pastor di Hermas" in *Papyrus Erzherzog Rainer (Festschrift zum 100-jährigen Bestehen der Papyrussammlung der Österreichischen Nationalbibliothek)* vol. 1: *Textband* (Vienna, 1983) 97-100.

Cerbelaud, Dominique "Le Nom d'Adam et les points cardinaux. Recherches sur un thème patristique" *Vigiliae Christianae* 38 (1984) 285-301.

Chadwick, Henry *Boethius: The Consolations of Music, Logic, Theology, and Philosophy* (Oxford, 1981).

Charlesworth, James H. *The Pseudepigrapha and Modern Research with a Supplement* Septuagint and Cognate Studies 7S (Missoula MT, 1981).

Charlesworth, James H. *The New Testament Apocrypha and Pseudepigrapha: A Guide to Publications, with Excursuses on Apocalypses* with James R. Mueller (Metuchen NJ, 1987).

Chase, Colin "Source Study as a Trick with Mirrors: Annihilation of Meaning in the Old English 'Mary of Egypt'" in Szarmach (1986a) 23-33.

Châtelain, Émile *Notice sur les manuscrits des poésies de S. Paulin de Nole* Bibliothèque des Écoles Françaises d'Athènes et de Rome 14 (Paris, 1880).

Chavasse, Antoine *Le Sacramentaire Gélasien* (Tournai, 1958).

Chelini, J. "Alcuin, Charlemagne et Saint-Martin de Tours" in *Memorial de l'Année Martinienne* (Paris, 1962) 19–50.

Cherchi, Paulo "A Legend from St. Bartholomew's Gospel in the Twelfth-Century" *Revue Biblique* 91 (1984) 212–18.

Clark, J.M. *The Abbey of St Gall as a Centre of Literature and Art* (Cambridge, 1926).

Clark Elizabeth and Diane Hatch *The Golden Bough, the Oaken Cross: The Virgilian Cento of Faltonia Betitia Proba* ed. J. Massey (Chico CA, 1981).

Clarke, J., trans. *Flavius Vegetius Renatus: The Military Institutions of the Romans, in Five Books* (London, 1767).

Clayton, Mary "Ælfric and the Nativity of the Blessed Virgin Mary" *Anglia* 104 (1986a) 286–315.

Clayton, Mary "Blickling Homily XIII Reconsidered" *Leeds Studies in English* 17 (1986b) 25–40.

Clayton, Mary "Delivering the Damned: A Motif in Old English Homiletic Prose" *Medium Ævum* 55 (1986c) 92–102.

Clayton, Mary "The Assumption Homily in CCCC 41" *Notes and Queries* ns 36 (1989) 293–95.

Clayton, Mary *The Cult of the Virgin in Anglo-Saxon England* (Cambridge, 1990).

Clemoes, Peter and Kathleen Hughes eds. *England Before the Conquest* (Cambridge, 1971).

Coccia, Edmondo "La cultura irlandese precarolina: miracolo o mito?" *Studi Medievali* 3rd ser. 8 (1967) 257–420.

Cockayne, O., ed. *Leechdoms, Wortcunning and Starcraft of Early England* 3 vols. *RS* 35 (London, 1864–66).

Coens, Maurice "Aux origins de la Céphalophorie. Un fragment retrouvé d'une ancienne Passion de S. Just" *Analecta Bollandiana* 74 (1956) 86–114.

Cohn, Leopold "An Apocryphal Work Ascribed to Philo of Alexandria" *Jewish Quarterly Review* 10 (1898) 277–332.

Colgrave, Bertram, ed. *Two Lives of Saint Cuthbert* (Cambridge, 1940).

Colgrave, Bertram, ed. *Félix's Life of Saint Guthlac* (London, 1956).

Colgrave, Bertram "The Earliest Saints' Lives Written in England" *Proceedings of the British Academy* 44 (1958) 35–60.

Colgrave, Bertram and R.A.B. Mynors eds. *Bede's Ecclesiastical History of the English People* (Oxford, 1969).

Collett, Katherine Ann Smith "The Gospel of Nicodemus in Anglo-Saxon England" (Diss. Univ. of Pennsylvania, 1981).

Collins, Roger, "Merida and Toledo: 550–585," in *Visigothic Spain: New Approaches* ed. Edward James (Oxford, 1980).

Collins, Rowland L. "Blickling Homily XVI and the Dating of *Beowulf*" in *Medieval Studies Conference, Aachen 1983* ed. Wolf-Dietrich Bald and Horst Weinstock (Frankfurt am Main, 1984) 61–69.

Contreni, John *The Cathedral School of Laon from 850 to 930: Its Manuscripts and Masters* (Munich, 1978).

Courcelle, Pierre *La Consolation de philosophie dans la tradition littéraire* (Paris, 1967).

Courcelle, Pierre *Late Latin Writers and their Greek Sources* trans. H. Wedeck (Cambridge, MA, 1969).

Coxe, H.O. *Catalogus codicum mss. qui in Collegiis aulisque Oxoniensibus hodie adservantur* 2 vols. (Oxford, 1852).

Coxe, H.O. *Catalogi codicum manuscriptorum Bibliothecae Bodleianae. Pars secunda Codices Latinos et Miscellaneos Laudianos complectens* 2 fascicules (Oxford, 1858–85).

Cramp, Rosemary "Schools of Mercian Culture" in *Mercian Studies* ed. A. Dornier (Leicester, 1977) 191–233.

Crombie, F., trans. *The Shepherd of Hermas* Ante-Nicene Fathers vol. 2 (New York, 1905) 9–55.

Cross, J.E. "The Literate Anglo-Saxon: On Sources and Disseminations" *Proceedings of the British Academy* 58 (1972) 67–100.

Cross, J.E. "Portents and Events at Christ's Birth: Comments on Vercelli V and VI and the Old English Martyrology" *Anglo-Saxon England* 2 (1973) 209–20.

Cross, J.E. "Cynewulf's Traditions about the Apostles in *Fates of the Apostles*" *Anglo-Saxon England* 8 (1979a) 163–75.

Cross, J.E. "The Apostles in the *Old English Martyrology*" *Mediaevalia* 5 (1979b) 15–59.

Cross, J.E. "Eulalia of Barcelona" *Notes and Queries* ns 28 (1981a) 482–84.

Cross, J.E. "The Influence of Irish Texts and Traditions on the Old English Martyrology" *Proceedings of the Royal Irish Academy* 81C (1981b) 173–92.

Cross, J.E. "A Doomsday Passage in an Old English Sermon for Lent" *Anglia* 100 (1982) 103–08.

Cross, J.E. "On the Library of the Old English Martyrologist" (1985a) in Lapidge and Gneuss (1985a) 227–49.

Cross, J.E. "The Use of Patristic Homilies in the Old English Martyrology" *Anglo-Saxon England* 14 (1985b) 107–28.

Cross, J.E. "Towards the Identification of Old English Literary Ideas — Old Workings and New Seams" (1986a) in Szarmach (1986a) 77–101.

Cross, J.E. "An Unpublished Story of Michael the Archangel and its Connections" (1986b) in Groos (1986) 23–35.

Cross, J.E. *Cambridge Pembroke College MS 25: A Carolingian Sermonary Used by Anglo-Saxon Preachers* King's College London Medieval Studies 1 (London 1987a).

Cross, J.E. "The Insular Connections of a Sermon for Holy Innocents" (1987b) in Stokes and Burton (1987) 57-70.

Cross, J.E. "Hiberno-Latin Commentaries in Salisbury Manuscripts before 1125 A.D." *Hiberno-Latin Newsletter* 3 (1988).

Cross, J.E. Preface to reprint of Bazire and Cross (1982; forthcoming).

Cross, J.E. and Thomas D. Hill, eds. *The Prose Solomon and Saturn and Adrian and Ritheus* (Toronto, 1982).

Dalbey, Marcia A. "The Good Shepherd and the Soldier of God" *Neuphilologische Mitteilungen* 85 (1984) 422-34.

D'Alverny, Marie-Thérèse "L'Homme comme symbole. Le Microcosme" in *Simboli e Simbologia nell'Alto Medioevo* Settimane di studio del Centro italiano di studi sull'alto Medioevo 23 (Spoleto, 1976) 123-83.

Dando, Marcel "Les Gnostiques d'Égypte, les Priscillianistes d'Espagne et l'Église Primitive d'Irlande" *Cahiers d'Études Cathares* 23 (1972) 3-34.

Daniélou, Jean *The Angels and their Mission* trans. David Heimann (Westminster MD, 1976).

d'Ardenne, S.R.T.O. *Þe Liflade ant te Passiun of Seinte Iuliene* EETS OS 248 (Oxford, 1961) 2-70.

De Bruyne, D. "Fragments retrouvés d'apocryphes priscillianistes" *Revue Bénédictine* 24 (1907) 318-35.

De Bruyne, D. *Préfaces de la Bible latine* (Namur, 1920).

de Gaiffier, Baudouin "Hispana et Lusitana" *Analecta Bollandiana* 77 (1959) 188-217.

de Gaiffier, Baudouin "Le Breviarium Apostolorum (BHL. 652). Tradition manuscrite et oeuvres apparentées" *Analecta Bollandiana* 81 (1963) 89-116.

Delehaye, H. "Les saints du cimitière de Commodille" *Analecta Bollandiana* 16 (1897) 22-23.

Delehaye, H. "Note sur la légende de la lettre du Christ tombée du ciel" *Académie Royale de Belgique: Bulletin de la classe des lettres* (1899).

Delehaye, H. "La Passion de S. Félix de Thibiuca" *Analecta Bollandiana* 39 (1921) 241-76.

Deletant, Dennis "The Sunday Legend" *Revue des études sud-est européennes* 15 (1977) 431-51.

de Lubac, Henri *Exégèse Médiévale. Les quatre sens de l'écriture* Théologie 41, 42, 59; 2 vols. in 4 parts (Paris, 1959-64).

Dempsey, G. T. "Aldhelm of Malmesbury and the Paris Psalter: A Note on the Survival of Antiochene Exegesis" *Journal of Theological Studies* ns 38 (1987) 368-86.

de Santos Otero, Aurelio, ed. and trans. *Los Evangelios Apócrifos* 2nd ed. (Madrid 1963).

Deshman, Robert "The Iconography of the Full-Page Miniatures in the Benedictional of St Æthelwold" (Diss. Princeton, 1970).

Deshman, Robert. "The Leofric Missal and Tenth-Century English Art" *Anglo-Saxon England* 6 (1977) 145–73.

de Smedt, C., J. de Backer, F. van Ortroy, and J. van den Gheyn, eds. "Catalogus codicum hagiographicorum bibliothecae civitatis Carnotensis" *Analecta Bollandiana* 8 (1889) 86–208.

de Strycker, E. *La forme la plus ancienne du Protévangile de Jacques* (Brussels, 1961).

D'Evelyn, Charlotte "The Middle English Metrical Version of the *Revelations* of Methodius; With a Study of the Influence of Methodius in Middle-English Writings" *PMLA* 33 (1918) 135–203.

Díaz y Díaz, Manuel ed. *Isidoriana. Estudios sobre San Isidoro de Sevilla en el XIV centenario de su nacimiento* (León, 1961).

Doane, A.N. *Genesis A: A New Edition* (Madison, 1978).

Dobschütz, Ernst von *Das Decretum Gelasianum TU* 38/4 (Leipzig, 1912).

Dolbeau, François "Du nouveau sur un sermonnaire de Cambridge" *Scriptorium* 42 (1988) 255–57.

Donahue, Charles, ed. *The Testament of Mary: The Gaelic Version of the Dormitio Mariae* Fordham University Studies, Language Series 1 (New York, 1942).

Draguet, René *Les formes syriaques de la matière de l'Histoire lausiaque*, 4 vols., Corpus Scriptorum Christianorum Orientalium 389–90 and 398–99 (Scriptores Syri 169–70 and 173–74; Louvain, 1978).

Dronke, Peter "St Patrick's Reading" *Cambridge Medieval Celtic Studies* 1 (1981) 21–38.

Duchesne, L. ed. *Le Liber Pontificalis* 2nd ed., 2 vols. (Paris, 1955).

Dudley, Louise *The Egyptian Elements in the Legend of the Body and the Soul* (Baltimore, 1911).

Duke, Rachele et al. "A Supplement to *Scriptores Hiberniae Minores* (*CC* 108 B & C)" *Comitatus* 8 (1977) 49–70.

Dumville, David N. "Liturgical Drama and Panegyric Responsory from the Eighth Century?" *Journal of Theological Studies* ns 23 (1972) 374–406.

Dumville, David N. "Biblical Apocrypha and the Early Irish: A Preliminary Investigation" *Proceedings of the Royal Irish Academy* 73C (1973) 299–338.

Dumville, D[avid] N. "Towards an Interpretation of Fís Adamnán" *Studia Celtica* 12/13 (1977/78) 62–77.

Dwyer, M.E. "An Unstudied Redaction of the *Visio Pauli*" *Manuscripta* 32 (1988) 121–38.

Earl, James W. "The Typological Structure of *Andreas*" in *Old English Literature in Context* ed. John D. Niles (Bury S. Edmunds Suffolk, 1980) 66–89.

Étaix, Raymond "Un manuel de pastorale de l'époque carolingienne (Clm 27152)" *Revue Bénédictine* 91 (1981) 105–130.

Evans, J.M. *Paradise Lost and the Genesis Tradition* (Oxford, 1968).

Fábrega Grau, Angel *Pasionario Hispanico* 2 vols., Monumenta Hispaniae Sacra: Serie Litúrgica 6 (Madrid, 1955).

Fahey, John *The Eucharistic Teaching of Ratramn of Corbie* (Mundelein IL, 1951).

Fausbøll, E., ed. *Fifty-Six Fragments* (Copenhagen, 1986).

Fell, John ed. *Lucii Caecilii Firmiani Lactantii De mortibus persecutorum liber* (Oxford, 1680).

Finnegan, Robert Emmett, ed. *Christ and Satan: A Critical Edition* (Waterloo Ontario, 1977).

Fischer, Bonifatius "Bedae de titulis psalmorum liber" in Autenrieth and Brunhölz (1971) 90–110.

Flamion, Josef *Les Actes apocryphes de l'Apôtre André: Les Actes d'André et de Mathias, de Pierre et d'André et les textes apparentés* Recueil de Travaux 33 (Louvain, 1911).

Flower, Robin *Catalogue of Irish Manuscripts in the British Museum* vol. 2 (London, 1926).

Floyer, John Kestell *Catalogue of Manuscripts Preserved in the Chapter Library of Worcester Cathedral* ed. Sidney Graves Hamilton (Oxford, 1906).

Folkerts, Menso *"Boetius" Geometrie II: ein mathematisches Lehrbuch des Mittelalters* (Wiesbaden, 1970).

Folkerts, Menso "The Importance of the Pseudo-Boethian Geometria during the Middle Ages" in Masi (1981) 187–209.

Folkerts, Menso "Die Altercatio in der Geometrie I des Pseudo-Boethius. Ein Beitrag zur Geometrie im mittelalterlichen Quadrivium" in G. Keil (1982) 84–114.

Förster, Max "Adams Erschaffung und Namengebung: ein lateinisches Fragment des s.g. slawischen Henoch" *Archiv für Religionswissenschaft* 11 (1907/08) 477–529.

Förster, Max "Das älteste mittellateinische Gesprächbuchlein" *Romanische Forschungen* 27 (1910) 342–48.

Förster, Max "Abt Raoul d'Escures und der spätae. 'Sermo in festis S. Mariae'" *Archiv für das Studium der neueren Sprachen* 162 (1932) 43–48.

Frede, Hermann Josef *Pelagius, der irische Paulustext, Sedulius Scottus* Aus der Geschichte der lateinischen Bibel 3 (Freiburg, 1961).

Gaidoz, Henri. "Le débat du corps et de l'âme en Irlande" *Revue Celtique* 10 (1889) 463–70.

Gaites, Judith "Ælfric's Longer *Life of St. Martin* and its Latin Sources: A Study in Narrative Technique" *Leeds Studies in English* 13 (1982) 23–41.

García Rodriguez, Carmen *El culto de los santos en la España romana y visigoda* (Madrid, 1966).

Gatch, Milton McC. *Preaching and Theology in Anglo-Saxon England* (Toronto, 1977).

Gatch, Milton McC. and Carl Berkhout, eds. *Anglo-Saxon Scholarship: The First Three Centuries* (Boston, 1982).

Geith, Karl-Ernst *Priester Arnolts Legende von der Heiligen Juliana* (Diss. Freiburg-im-Bresgau, 1965).

Gibson, Margaret, ed. *Boethius: His Life, Thought and Influence* (Oxford, 1981).

Giet, Stanislas *Hermas et les Pasteurs* (Paris, 1963).

Gijsel, Jan "Zu welcher Textfamilie des Pseudo-Matthäus gehört die Quelle von Hrotsvits Maria?" *Classica et Medievalia* 32 (1971-80) 279-88.

Gijsel, Jan "Les 'Évangiles Latins de l'Enfance' de M.R. James" *Analecta Bollandiana* 94 (1976) 289-302.

Gijsel, Jan *Unmittelbare Textüberlieferung des sog. Pseudo-Matthäus* Abhandlungen der Königlichen Akademie der Wissenschaften 43 no 96 (Brussels, 1981).

Glauche, Günter *Schullektüre im Mittelalter: Entstehung und Wandlungen des Lektürkanons bis 1200 nach den Quellen dargestellt* Münchener Beiträge zur Mediävistik und Renaissance-Forschung 5 (Munich, 1970).

Glück, Manfred *Priscians Partitiones und ihre Stellung in der spätantiken Schule* (Hildesheim, 1967).

Glunz, H. H. *History of the Vulgate in England from Alcuin to Roger Bacon* (Cambridge, 1933).

Gneuss, Helmut "Dunstan and Hrabanus" *Anglia* 96 (1978) 136-48.

Gneuss, Helmut "Liturgical Books in Anglo-Saxon England and their Old English Terminology" in Lapidge and Gneuss (1985) 91-141.

Gneuss, Helmut "Eine angelsächsische Köningsliste" in *Scire litteras: Forschungen zum mittelalterlichen Geistesleben* ed. S. Krämer and M. Bernhard. Bayerische Akademie der Wissenschaften, Phil.-Hist. Klasse, Abhandlungen, N.F. 99 (Munich, 1988) 201-09.

Godden, M.R. "Old English Composite Homilies from Winchester" *Anglo-Saxon England* 4 (1975) 57-65.

Godden, M.R. "Ælfric and the Vernacular Prose Tradition" in Szarmach and Huppé (1978) 99-117.

Godden, M.R., ed. *Ælfric's Catholic Homilies: Second Series, Text* EETS SS 5 (London, 1979).

Godman, Peter, ed. *Alcuin: The Bishops, Kings, and Saints of York* (Oxford, 1982).

Gordon, C.D "Vegetius and his Proposed Reforms of the Army" in *Polis and Imperium: Studies in Honour of Edward Togo Salmon* ed. J.A.S. Evans (Toronto, 1974) 35-58.

Gorman, Michael M. "The Encyclopedic Commentary on Genesis Prepared for Charlemagne by Wigbod" *Recherches Augustiniennes* 17 (1982) 173-201.

Grant, Raymond J.S., ed. *Three Homilies from Cambridge, Corpus Christi College 41* (Ottawa, 1982).

Grattan, J.H.G. and C. Singer *Anglo-Saxon Magic and Medicine Illustrated Specially from the Semi-Pagan Text "Lacnunga"* (Oxford, 1952).

Greenfield, Stanley B. and Daniel G. Calder *A New Critical History of Old English Literature* (New York, 1986).

Greenwell, W. ed. *The Pontifical of Egbert, Archbishop of York, A.D. 732-766 SS* 27 (Durham, 1853).

Groos, Arthur "The 'Elder Angel'" in *Guthlac A" Anglia* 101 (1983) 141-46.

Groos, Arthur, et al. eds. *Magister Regis: Studies in Honor of Robert Earl Kaske* (New York, 1986).

Grosjean, Paul. "À propos du manuscrit 49 de la Reine Christine" *Analecta Bollandiana* 54 (1936) 113-36.

Gry, L. *Les Dires Prophétiques d'Esdras (IV Esdras)* 2 vols. (Paris, 1938).

Halford, M.E.B. "The Apocryphal *Vita Adae et Evae*: Some Comments on the Manuscript Tradition" *Neuphilologische Mitteilungen* 82 (1981) 417-27.

Hall, Thomas N. "The Reversal of the Jordan in Vercelli Homily XVI and in Old English Literature" *Traditio* (forthcoming).

Hall, Thomas N. "The Twelve-Fold Division of the Red Sea in Two Old English Prose Texts" *Medium Aevum* (forthcoming).

Hartung, K. *Ein Traktat zur Apokalypse des Apostels Johannes* (Bamberg, 1904).

Healey, Antonette diPaolo *The Old English Vision of St. Paul* Speculum Anniversary Monographs 2 (Cambridge MA, 1978).

Healey, Antonette diPaolo "Anglo-Saxon Use of the Apocryphal Gospel," in Woods and Pelteret (1985) 93-104.

Heffernan, T.J. "An Analysis of the Narrative Motifs in the Legend of St Eustace" *Medievalia et Humanistica* ns 6 (1973) 63-89.

Heimann, Adelheid "Three Illustrations from the Bury St. Edmund Psalter and their Prototypes" *Journal of the Warburg and Courtald Institutes* 29 (1966) 39-46.

Heist, William W. *The Fifteen Signs Before Doomsday* (East Lansing MI, 1952).

Hellholm, David *Das Visionenbuch des Hermas als Apocalypse* vol. 1 Coniectanea Biblica New Testament Series 13/1 (Lund, 1980).

Henderson, George "The Imagery of St Guthlac of Croyland" in *England in the Thirteenth Century Proceedings of the 1984 Harlaxton Symposium* ed. W.M. Ormrod (Dover NH, 1986) 76-94.

Hermann, John P. "The Theme of Spiritual Warfare in the OE Judith" *Philological Quarterly* 55 (1972) 1-9.

Hermann, John P. "The Pater Noster Battle Sequence in *Solomon and Saturn* and the *Psychomachia* of Prudentius" *Neuphilologische Mitteilungen* 77 (1976) 206-10.

Hermann, John P. "Some Varieties of Psychomachia in Old English" *American Benedictine Review* 34 (1983) 74-86 and 188-222.

Herren, Michael W. "Hiberno-Latin Philology: The State of the Question" in *Insular Latin Studies* Papers in Mediaeval Studies 1 ed. Michael Herren (Toronto, 1981) 1-22.

Herren, Michael W., ed. *The Hisperica Famina: II. Related Poems* Studies and Texts 85 (Toronto, 1987).

Herzog, R. *Die Bibelepik der lateinischen Spätantike: Formgeschichte einer erbaulischen Gattung* vol. 1 (Munich, 1975).

Hessels, J.H. ed. *A Late Eighth-Century Latin-Anglo-Saxon Glossary* (Cambridge 1906).

Hill, Thomas D. "Raguel and Ragnel: Notes on the Literary Genealogy of a Devil" *Names* 22 (1974) 145–49.

Hill, Thomas D. "The *Æcerbot* Charm and its Christian User" *Anglo-Saxon England* 6 (1977a) 213–21.

Hill, Thomas D. "A Liturgical Source for *Christ I* 164–213 (Advent Lyric VII)" *Medium Ævum* 46 (1977b) 12–15.

Hill, Thomas D. "The Fall of Satan in the Old English Christ and Satan" *Journal of English and Germanic Philology* 76 (1977c) 315–25.

Hill, Thomas D. "The Middle Way: *Idel-wuldor* and *Egesa* in the Old English Guthlac A" *Review of English Studies* ns 30 (1979) 182–87.

Hill, Thomas D. "Invocation of the Trinity and the Tradition of the *Lorica* in Old English Poetry" *Speculum* 56 (1981) 259–67.

Hill, Thomas D. "Literary History and Old English Poetry: The Case of *Christ I, II,* and *III*" in Szarmach (1986a) 3–22.

Hill, Thomas D. "The Myth of the Ark-born Son of Noe and the West-Saxon Royal Genealogical Tables" *Harvard Theological Review* 80 (1987) 379–83.

Hillgarth, J.N. "The East, Visigothic Spain and the Irish" *Studia Patristica* 4 (Berlin, 1961) 441–56.

Hillgarth, J.N. "Visigothic Spain and Early Christian Ireland" *Proceedings of the Royal Irish Academy* 62C (1962) 167–94.

Hillgarth, J.N. "Old Ireland and Visigothic Spain" in *Old Ireland* ed. R.E. McNally (New York, 1965) 200–27.

Holder-Egger, O., ed. *Vita Willibaldi Episcopi Eichstetensis MGH,* Scriptores 15.1 (1887) 86–106.

Holtz, L. *Donat et la tradition de l'enseignement grammatical: Étude sur l'Ars Donati et sa diffusion (IVe-IXe siècle) et édition critique* (Paris 1981).

Holtz, L. "Les innovations théoriques de la grammaire carolingienne: peu de chose. Pourquoi?" in *L'héritage des grammairiens latins de l'Antiquité aux Lumières* ed. I. Rosier (Paris, 1988) 133–45.

[Hopkins, William] *The Book of Bertram or Ratramnus, Priest and Monk of Corbey, Concerning the Body and Blood of the Lord* (London, 1686).

Huber, P.M. *Die Wanderlegende von den Siebenschläfern: eine literargeschichtliche Untersuchung* (Leipzig, 1910).

Huber, Wolfgang *Heliand und Matthäusexegese* Münchener Germanistische Beiträge 3 (Munich, 1969).

Hughes, Anselm, ed. *The Portiforium of Saint Wulfstan HBS* 90 (Leighton Buzzard, 1958–60).

Hughes, Kathleen "Some Aspects of Irish Influence on Early English Private Prayer" *Studia Celtica* 5 (1970) 48–61.

Hunt, R.W., ed. *Saint Dunstan's Classbook from Glastonbury* Umbrae Codicum Occidentalium 4 (Amsterdam, 1961).

I Deug-Su "L'Opera Agiografica di Alcuino: la *Vita Martini*" *Studi Medievali* 3rd ser 21 (1981) 57–83.

I Deug-Su *L'opera agiografica di Alcuino* Biblioteca degli "Studi Medievali" 13 (Spoleto, 1983).

James, M.R. *Apocrypha Anecdota* Texts and Studies 2.3 (Cambridge, 1893).

James, M.R. *The Western Manuscripts in the Library of Trinity College, Cambridge* 4 vols. (Cambridge, 1900–04).

James, M.R. "Names of Angels in Anglo-Saxon and Other Documents" *Journal of Theological Studies* 11 (1909–10) 569–71.

James, M.R. *A Descriptive Catalogue of the Manuscripts in the Library of Corpus Christi College Cambridge* 2 vols. (Cambridge, 1911–12).

James, M.R. "Irish Apocrypha" *Journal of Theological Studies* 20 (1918–19) 9–16.

James, M.R. *The Lost Apocrypha of the Old Testament* (London, 1920).

James, M.R. *Latin Infancy Gospels* (Cambridge, 1927).

James, M.R. *The Apocryphal New Testament* (1924; corrected edition, Oxford, 1953).

Jenkins, Claude "Bede as Exegete and Theologian" in Thompson (1966) 152–200.

Jeudy, C. "La tradition manuscrite des *Partitiones* de Priscien et la version longue du commentaire de Remi d'Auxerre" *Revue d'histoire des textes* 1 (1971) 123–43.

Jeudy, C. "*L'Institutio de nomine, pronomine et verbo* de Priscien: manuscrits et commentaires médiévaux" *Revue d'histoire des textes* 2 (1972) 73–144.

Jeudy, C. "Un manuscrit de Remi d'Auxerre au debut du IXe siècle" in *Le chanson de geste et le mythe carolingien* Mélanges René Louis 1 (Saint-Père-sous-Vézelay, 1982) 171–75.

Joly, R. *Hermas: Le Pasteur SChr* vol. 53 (Paris, 1958).

Jones, C.W. "Bede and Vegetius" *Classical Review* 46 (1932) 248–49.

Jones, C.W. *Bedae Pseudepigrapha: Scientific Writings Falsely Attributed to Bede* (Ithaca NY, 1939).

Jordan, Louis "Demonic Elements in Anglo-Saxon Iconography" in Szarmach (1986a) 281–317.

Kaestli, Jean-Daniel "Les Principales orientations de la recherche sur les Actes Apocryphes des Apôtres" in Bovon and van Esbroeck (1981) 49–67.

Kaestli, Jean-Daniel. "Où en est l'Étude de l''Évangile de Barthélemy'?" *Revue Biblique* 95 (1988) 5–33.

Keil, Gundolf, ed. *Fachprosa-Studien: Beiträge zur mittelalterlichen Wissenschafts- und Geistesgeschichte* (Berlin, 1982).

Kelly, Joseph F. "Irish Influence in England after the Synod of Whitby: Some New Literary Evidence" *Eire/Ireland* 10 (1975) 35–47.

Kelly, Joseph F. "Augustine in Hiberno-Latin Literature" *Augustinian Studies* 8 (1977) 139–49.

Kelly, Joseph F. "The Originality of Josephus Scottus' Commentary on Isaiah" *Manuscripta* 24 (1980) 176–80.

Kelly, Joseph F. "Frigulus: A Hiberno-Latin Commentator on Matthew" *Revue Bénédictine* 91 (1981a) 363–73.

Kelly, Joseph F. "Hiberno-Latin Exegesis and Exegetes" *Annuale Mediaevale* 22 (1981b) 46–60.

Kelly, Joseph F. "Bede and the Irish Exegetical Tradition on the Apocalypse" *Revue Bénédictine* 92 (1982a) 393–406.

Kelly, Joseph F. "Hiberno-Latin Theology" in *Die Iren und Europa im früheren Mittelalter* 2 vols., ed. Heinz Löwe (Stuttgart, 1982b) I, 549–67.

Kelly, Joseph F. "Early Medieval Irish Exegetical Texts at St. Gall" *Cuyahoga Review* 1 (1983a) 77–87.

Kelly, Joseph F. "The Study of Medieval Ireland" *Old English Newsletter* 16/2 (Spring 1983b) 21–26.

Kelly, Joseph F. "The Venerable Bede and Hiberno-Latin Exegesis" in Szarmach (1986a) 65–76.

Kelly, Joseph F. "Das Bibelwerk: Organization and *Quellenanalyse* of the New Testament Section" in Ní Chatháin and Richter (1987) 113–23.

Kenney, James F. *The Sources for the Early History of Ireland: Ecclesiastical* (1929; New York, 1966).

Ker, N.R. *Medieval Libraries of Great Britain: A List of Surviving Books* 2nd ed Royal Historical Society Guides and Handbooks 3 (London, 1964).

Ker, N.R. "The Beginnings of Salisbury Cathedral Library" in Alexander and Gibson (1976) 23–49.

Kessler, Eva *Die Auszeichnungsschriften in den Freisinger Codices von den Anfängen bis zur karolingischen Erneurung* Denkschriften der Österreichischen Akademie der Wissenschaften, Phil.-Hist. Klasse 188 (Vienna, 1986)

Keynes, Simon and Michael Lapidge *Alfred the Great* (Harmondsworth, 1983).

Kim, H.C., ed. *The Gospel of Nicodemus: Gesta Salvatoris* Toronto Medieval Latin Texts 2 (Toronto, 1973).

Kisch, Guido, ed. *Pseudo-Philo's Liber Antiquitatum Biblicarum* (Notre Dame IN, 1949).

Knust, H. *Geschichte der Legenden der hl. Katharina von Alexandrien und der hl. Maria Aegyptiaca* (Halle 1890).

Kottje, R.J. and H. Zimmermann, eds. *Hrabanus Maurus: Lehrer, Abt und Bischof* Akademie der Wissenschaften und der Literatur Mainz, Abhandlungen der Geistes- und Sozialwissenschaften Klasse, Einzeleröffentlichung 4 (Wiesbaden, 1982).

Kotzor, Günter, ed. *Das altenglische Martyrologium* 2 vols. Bayerische Akademie der Wissenschaften, Phil.-Hist. Klasse, Abhandlungen, N. F. 88/1,2 (Munich, 1981).

Kunze, K. *Studien zur Legende der heiligen Maria Aegyptiaca im deutschen Sprachgebiet* Philologische Studien und Quellen 49 (Berlin, 1969).

Kuypers, A.B., ed. *The Book of Cerne* (Cambridge, 1902).

Lachmann, Karl, F. Blume, and A. Rudorff *Die Schriften der römischen Feldmesser* vol. 1 (1848; rpt Hildesheim, 1967).

La Conte "La tradizione manoscritta del *Liber de accentibus*" *Atti dell'Accademia di Scienze di Torino* 115 (1981) 109–24.

Laistner, M.L.W. "Bede as a Classical and a Patristic Scholar" *Transactions of the Royal Historical Society* 4th ser 16 (1933) 69–94.

Laistner, M.L.W. *Bedae Venerabilis Expositio Actuum Apostolorum et Retractatio* (Cambridge MA, 1939); rpt in *CCSL* 121.3–104.

Laistner, M.L.W. "Some Early Medieval Commentaries on the Old Testament" in *The Intellectual Heritage of the Early Middle Ages* ed. Chester G. Starr (Ithaca NY, 1957) 181–201.

Lapidge, Michael "Aethelwold as Scholar and Teacher" in Yorke (1988) 89–117.

Lapidge, Michael and Helmut Gneuss, eds. *Learning and Literature in Anglo-Saxon England: Studies Presented to Peter Clemoes on the Occasion of his Sixty-fifth Birthday* (Cambridge, 1985).

Lapidge, Michael, and Michael Herren, trans. *Aldhelm: The Prose Works* (Totowa NJ, 1979).

Lapidge, Michael and James Rosier, trans. *Aldhelm: The Poetic Works* (Cambridge, 1985).

Laureys, Marc and Daniel Verhelst "Pseudo-Methodius, *Revelationes*: Textgeschichte und kritische Edition. Ein Leuven-Groninger Forschungsprojekt" in *The Use and Abuse of Eschatology in the Middle Ages* ed. Werner Verbeke, Daniel Verhelst, and Andries Welkenhuysen (Leuven, 1988) 112–36.

Lavarenne, Maurice, ed. *Prudence III: Psychomachie, Contre Symmaque* (Paris, 1948).

Law, V. Review of B. Löfstedt and G.J. Gebauer, eds. *Ars Bonifacii* CCSL 133B in *Studi Medievali* 3rd ser 22 (1981) 752–64.

Law, V. *The Insular Latin Grammarians* (Woodbridge, 1982).

Law, V. "The Study of Latin Grammar in eighth-century Southumbria" *Anglo-Saxon England* 12 (1983) 43–71.

Law, V. "Linguistics in the earlier Middle Ages: The Insular and Carolingian grammarians" *Transactions of the Philological Society* (1985) 171–93.

Law, V. "Late Latin grammars in the early Middle Ages: A Typological History" *Historiographia Linguistica* 13 (1986) 365–80.

Law, V. "Anglo-Saxon England: Ælfric's *Excerptiones de arte grammatica anglice*" *Histoire Epistémologie Langage* 9 (1987) 47–71.

Lazius, W. *Abdiae episcopi Babyloniae Historia certaminis apostolorum* (Basel, 1551).

Lees, Clare A. "The 'Sunday Letter' and the 'Sunday Lists'" *Anglo-Saxon England* 14 (1985a) 129–51.

Lees, Clare A. "The Dissemination of Alcuin's *De Virtutibus et Vitiis Liber* in Old English: A Preliminary Survey" *Leeds Studies in English* ns 16 (1985b) 174–89.

Lees, Clare A. "Theme and Echo in an Anonymous Old English Homily for Easter" *Traditio* 42 (1986) 115–42.

Lehmann, Paul *Mittelalterliche Bibliothekskataloge Deutschlands und der Schweiz* vol. 1 (Munich, 1918).

Lehmann, Paul *Erforschung des Mittelalters* 5 vols. (Stuttgart 1959–62).

Leinbaugh, Theodore H. "Ælfric's Sermo de Sacrificio in Die Pascae: Anglican Polemic in the Sixteenth and Seventeenth Centuries" in Gatch and Berkhout (1982) 51–62.

Leinbaugh, Theodore H. "The Sources for Ælfric's Easter Sermon: The History of the Controversy and a New Source" *Notes and Queries* ns 33 (1986) 294–311.

Lester, Geoffrey *The Earliest English Translation of Vegetius' 'De Re Militari'* Middle English Texts 21, ed. M. Görlach and O.S. Pickering (Heidelberg, 1988).

Lightfoot, J.B. *Saint Paul's Epistles to the Colossians and to Philemon: A Revised Text* (1879; rpt Grand Rapids MI, 1959).

Lindsay, W.M. ed. *The Corpus Glossary* (Cambridge, 1921a).

Lindsay, W.M. ed. *The Corpus, Épinal, Erfurt and Leyden Glossaries* Publications of the Philological Society 8 (Oxford 1921b).

Lindström, Bengt "The Old English Translation of Alcuin's *Liber de Virtutibus et Vitiis*" *Studia Neophilologica* 60 (1988) 23–35.

Lolos, Anastasios, ed. *Die Apokalypse des Ps. Methodios* Beiträge zur klassischen Philologie 83 (Meisenheim am Glan, 1976).

Lo Menzo Rapisarda, G. *Commentarius in Apocalypsin* (Catania, 1967).

Lowe, E.A. "The Vatican MS of the Gelasian Sacramentary and its Supplement at Paris" *Journal of Theological Studies* 27 (1925–26) 357–73.

Luiselli Fadda, Anna Maria "'De descensu Christi ad inferos': una inedita omelia anglosassone" *Studi Medievali* 3rd ser 13 (1972) 989–1011.

Luiselli Fadda, Anna Maria "Una inedita traduzione anglosassone della *Visio Pauli* (MS Junius 85, ff 3r–11v)" *Studi Medievali* 3rd ser 15 (1974) 482–95.

Luiselli Fadda, Anna Maria *Nuove omelie anglosassone della rinascenza benedettina* Filologia germanica, Testi e Studi 1 (Florence, 1977).

MacDonald, Dennis R. "The *Acts of Andrew and Matthias* and the *Acts of Andrew*" in MacDonald (1986) 9–26 and 35–39.

MacDonald, Dennis R. *The Apocryphal Acts of Apostles* Semeia 38 (1986).

Macdonald, George "Bede and Vegetius" *Classical Review* 47 (1933) 124.

Mac Donncha, Frederic "Medieval Irish Homilies" in McNamara (1976) 59–71.

Mac Donncha, Frederic "Don Tarmchrutta—An 11th-Century Homily on the Transfiguration" *Collectanea Hibernica* 25 (1983) 7–11.

Mac Donncha, Frederic "Imdibe Crist—An 11th-Century Homily on the Circumcision of Christ" *Collectanea Hibernica* 26 (1984) 7–12.

Mackay, Thomas "Bede's Hagiographical Method: His Knowledge and Use of Paulinus of Nola" in Bonner (1976) 77–92.

Mac Niocaill, Gearó id "Na Seacht Neamha" *Éigse* 8 (1956) 239–41.

Madan, Falconer, H.H.E. Craster, and R.W. Hunt *A Summary Catalogue of Western Manuscripts in the Bodleian Library at Oxford* (Oxford, 1895–1953).

Magennis, H. "On the sources of the non-Aelfrician Lives in the Old English *Lives of the Saints*, with Reference to the Cotton-Corpus Legendary" *Notes and Queries* ns 32 (1985) 292–99.

Magennis, H. "Contrasting features in the non-Aelfrician Lives in the Old English *Lives of the Saints*" *Anglia* 104 (1986) 316–48.

Magennis, H. "The Anonymous Old English *Legend of the Seven Sleepers* and its Sources," *Leeds Studies in English* (forthcoming).

Magennis, H. "What Aelfric Did to the Legend of the Seven Sleepers" (forthcoming).

Manitius, Max "Zu Aldhelm und Baeda" *Sitzungsberichte der Österreichischen Akademie der Wissenschaften. Phil.-Hist. Klasse* 112 (1886) 535–634.

Manitius, Max *Geschichte der lateinischen Literatur des Mittelalters* 3 vols. in Handbuch der klassischen Altertum-Wissenschaft 9 (Munich 1911–31).

Marenbon, John "Les Sources du vocabulaire d'Aldhelm" *Bulletin du Cange* 41 (1979) 75–90.

Masi, Michael, ed. *Boethius and the Liberal Arts: A Collection of Essays* (Bern, 1981).

Masi, Michael *Boethian Number Theory: A Translation of the De Institutione Arithmetica* Studies in Classical Antiquity 6 (Amsterdam, 1983).

Matter, E. Ann "The 'Revelatio Esdrae' in Latin and English Traditions" *Revue Bénédictine* 92 (1982) 376–92.

Mazzini, Innocenzo "Il codice Urbinate 486 e la versione Palatina del Pastore de Erma" *Prometheus* 6 (1980) 181–89.

Mazzini, Innocenzo, and E. Lorenzini "Il Pastore di Erma: due versioni latine o due antologie di versioni?" *Civiltà classica e cristiana* 2 (1981) 45–86.

McCracken, George and Allen Cabaniss, eds. *Early Medieval Theology* The Library of Christian Classics 9 (Philadelphia, 1957).

McGurk, Patrick *Latin Gospel Books from A.D. 400 to A.D. 800* (Paris-Bruxelles, 1961).

McKitterick, Rosamond "Some Carolingian Law-Books and their Functions" in Tierney and Lineham (1980) 13-27.

McKitterick, Rosamond *The Frankish Kingdoms under the Carolingians, 751-897* (London, 1983).

McNally, R.E. *Der irische Liber de Numeris; Eine Quellenanalyse des pseudo-isidorischen Liber de numeris* (published Inaugural – Diss. Munich, 1957).

McNally, R.E. *The Bible in the Early Middle Ages* Woodstock Papers 4 (Westminster MD, 1959).

McNally, R.E. "Isidorian Pseudepigrapha" in Díaz y Díaz (1961) pp 305-26.

McNally, R.E. "'Christus' in the Pseudo-Isidorian 'Liber de ortu et obitu patriarcharum'" *Traditio* 21 (1965) 167-83.

McNally, R.E. "The Imagination and Early Irish Biblical Exegesis" *Annuale Mediaevale* 10 (1969) 5-27.

McNally, R.E. "The Three Holy Kings in Early Irish Latin Writing" in *Kyriakon. Festschrift Johannes Quasten* 2 vols., ed. Patrick Granfield and Josef Jungmann (Münster, 1970) II, 667-90.

McNally, R.E. "The Evangelists in the Hiberno-Latin Tradition" in Autenrieth and Brunhölzl (1971) 111-22.

McNally, R.E., ed. *Scriptores Hiberniae Minores Pars I CCSL* 108B (Turnhout, 1973).

McNally, R.E. "'In Nomine Dei Summi': Seven Hiberno-Latin Sermons" *Traditio* 35 (1979) 121-43.

McNamara, Martin "A Plea for Hiberno-Latin Biblical Studies" *Irish Theological Quarterly* 39 (1972) 337-53.

McNamara, Martin "Psalter Text and Psalter Study in the Early Irish Church (A.D. 600-1200)" *Proceedings of the Royal Irish Academy* 73C (1973a) 201-98.

McNamara, Martin "Hiberno-Latin Biblical Studies: I An Addendum" *Irish Theological Studies* 40 (1973b) 364-67.

McNamara, Martin "Hiberno-Latin Biblical Studies: II An Irish Abbreviation of St Gregory the Great on the Book of Job" *Irish Theological Studies* 40 (1973c) 367-70.

McNamara, Martin *The Apocrypha in the Irish Church* (Dublin, 1975).

McNamara, Martin, ed. *Biblical Studies: The Medieval Irish Contribution* (Dublin, 1976).

McNamara, Martin "Ireland and Northumbria as Illustrated by a Vatican Manuscript" *Thought* 54 (1979) 274-90.

McNamara, Martin "Early Irish Exegesis. Some Facts and Tendencies" *Proceedings of the Irish Biblical Association* 8 (Dublin, 1984a) 57-96.

McNamara, Martin "Tradition and Creativity in Early Irish Psalter Study" in Ní Chatháin and Richter (1984b).

McNamara, Martin *Glossa in Psalmos. The Hiberno-Latin Gloss on the Psalms of Codex Palatinus Latinus 68* Studi e Testi 310 (Vatican, 1986).

McNamara, Martin "Plan and Source Analysis of Das Bibelwerk, Old Testament" (1987a) in Ní Chatháin and Richter (1987) 84–112.

McNamara, Martin "The Inverted Eucharistic Formula *Conversio Corporis Christi in Panem et Sanguinis in Vinum*: The Exegetical and Liturgical Background in Irish Usage" *Proceedings of the Royal Irish Academy* 87C (1987b) 573–93.

McNamara, Martin "Hiberno-Latin Bulletin" *Proceedings of the Irish Biblical Association* 12 (Dublin, 1989) 86–95.

Meaney, A.L. "Variant Versions of Old English Medical Remedies and the Compilation of Bald's *Leechbook*" *Anglo-Saxon England* 13 (1985) 235–68.

Mearns, James *The Canticles of the Christian Church Eastern and Western in Early and Medieval Times* (Cambridge, 1914).

Mellinkoff, Ruth "Cain's Monstrous Progeny in Beowulf: Part I Noachic Tradition" *Anglo-Saxon England* 8 (1979) 143–62.

Mellinkoff, Ruth "Cain's Monstrous Progeny in Beowulf: Part II Postdiluvian Survival" *Anglo-Saxon England* 9 (1981) 183–97.

Meyer, Kuno *Hibernica Minora, Being a Fragment of an Old-Irish Treatise on the Psalter* Anecdota Oxoniensia, Mediaeval and Modern Series 8 (Oxford, 1894).

Meyer, Paul "Notice du MS. Rawlinson Poetry 241 (Oxford)" *Romania* 29 (1900) 1–84.

Meyer, Wilhelm "Poetische Nachlese aus dem sogenannten Book of Cerne in Cambridge und aus dem Londoner Codex Regius 2 A.XX" *Nachrichten von der Königlichen Gesellschaft der Wissenschaften zu Göttingen,* Phil.-Hist. Klasse 1 (Berlin, 1917) 597–625.

Michel, Paul, and Alexander Schwarz *Unz in obanentig. Aus der Werkstatt der karolingischen Exegeten Alcuin, Erkanbert und Otfrid von Weissenburg* Studien zur Germanistik, Anglistik und Komparatistik 79 (Bonn, 1978).

Milik, J.T. *The Books of Enoch: Aramaic Fragments of Qumrân Cave 4* with the collaboration of Matthew Black (Oxford, 1976).

Millard, Galia ed. *Calendre, Les Empereors de Rome* (Ann Arbor, 1957).

Mombritius, B. *Sanctuarium seu Vitae Sanctorum* 2nd ed., 2 vols. (Paris, 1910).

Monteverdi, A. "I testi della leggenda di S. Eustachio" *Studi Medievali* 3 (1908–11) 393–498.

Morrell, Minnie Cate *A Manual of Old English Biblical Materials* (Knoxville, 1965).

Moussy, Claude and Colette Camus, eds. *Dracontius oeuvres: Tome 1, Louanges de Dieu, livres 1 et 2* (Paris, 1985).

Muir, Bernard, ed. *A Pre-Conquest English Prayer-Book HBS* 103 (Woodbridge, 1988).

Mynors, R.A.B. *Durham Cathedral Manuscripts* (Oxford, 1939).

Nausea, F. *Anonymi Philalethi Eusebiani in vitas, miracula passionesque apostolorum rhapsodiae* (Cologne, 1531).

Nelson, Janet L. "'A King Across the Sea': Alfred in Continental Perspective" *Transactions of the Royal Historical Society* 5th ser., 36 (1986) 45-68.

Ní Chatháin, Próinséas and Michael Richter, eds. *Irland und Europa. Die Kirche im Frühmittelalter* (Stuttgart, 1984).

Ní Chatháin, Próinséas and Michael Richter, eds. *Irland und die Christenheit. Bibelstudien und Mission* (Stuttgart, 1987).

Ó Ceallaigh, G.C. "Dating the Commentaries of Nicodemus" *Harvard Theological Review* 61 (1963) 21-58.

Ó Cróinín, Dáibhí Review of McNamara (1975) *Éigse* 16 (1976) 348-56.

Ó Cróinín, Dáibhí, ed. *The Irish Sex Aetates Mundi* (Dublin, 1983).

O'Donnell, J. R. "Alcuin's *Priscian*" in O'Meara and Naumann (1976) 222-35.

O'Keeffe, Katherine O'Brien "The Use of Bede's Writings on Genesis in Alcuin's Interrogationes" *Sacris Erudiri* 23 (1978/79) 463-83.

Ó Laoghaire, Diarmuid. "Irish Elements in the Catechesis Celtica" in Ní Chatháin and Richter (1987) 146-64.

O'Meara, J.J. and B. Naumann, eds. *Latin Script and Letters A.D. 400-900* (Leiden, 1976).

Omont, H. "Notice du manuscrit Nouv. Acq. Lat. 763 de la Bibliothèque Nationale contenant plusieurs anciens glossaires grecs et latins" in *Notices et Extraits des manuscrits latins de la Bibliothèque Nationale et autres bibliothèques* 38 (1906) 341-96.

Ó Néill, Pádraig (Patrick P. O'Neill) "Airbertach Mac Cosse's Poem on the Psalter" *Éigse* 27 (1977) 19-46.

Ó Néill, Pádraig (Patrick P. O'Neill) "The Old Irish Treatise on the Psalter and its Hiberno-Latin Background" *Ériu* 30 (1979) 148-64.

Ó Néill, Pádraig (Patrick P. O'Neill) "The Old English Introductions to the Prose Psalms of the Paris Psalter: Sources, Structure, and Composition" in *Eight Anglo-Saxon Studies* Texts and Studies, 1981 [*Studies in Philology* 78 (1981)] 20-38.

Opelt, I. "Der zürnende Christus im Cento der Proba," *Jahrbuch für Antike und Christentum* 7 (1964), 106-16.

Osiek, Carolyn "The Genre and Function of the Shepherd of Hermas" *Semeia* 36 (1986) 113-21.

Pächt, Otto "A Cycle of English Frescoes in Spain" *Burlington Magazine* 103 (1961) 166-75.

Page, R.I. "More Old English Scratched Glosses" *Anglia* 97 (1979) 27-45.

Parkes, M.B. "A Note on MS Vatican, Bibl. Apost., lat. 3363" Gibson (1981) 425-27.

Passalacqua, M. *I codici di Prisciano* (Rome, 1978).

Pheifer, J.D. ed. *Old English Glosses in the Épinal-Erfurt Glossary* (Oxford 1974).

Pheifer, J.D. "Early Anglo-Saxon glossaries and the school of Canterbury" *Anglo-Saxon England* 17 (1987) 17-44.

Philippart, Guy "Fragments palimpsestes Latins du Vindobonensis 563 (Ve siècle?)" *Analecta Bollandiana* 90 (1972) 391-411.

Plante, Julian G. "Catalogue of Manuscripts in the 'Bibliothek der Phil.-Theol.-Hochschule der Diözese Linz'" *Traditio* 32 (1976) 427-74.

Plummer, C. *Baedae Historia Ecclesiastica gentis Angelorum: Venerabilis Baedae opera historica* 2 vols. (Oxford, 1896).

Prescott, A. "The Structure of English Pre-Conquest Benedictionals" *British Library Journal* 13 (1987) 118-58.

Price, Jocelyn G. "The Liflade of Seinte Iuliene and Hagiographic Convention" *Medievalia et Humanistica* ns 14 (1986) 37-58.

Priebsch, R. "John Audelay's Poem on the Observance of Sunday and its Source" in *An English Miscellany Presented to Dr. Furnivall in Honour of his Seventy-Fifth Birthday* (Oxford, 1901) 397-407.

Priebsch, R. *Letter from Heaven* (Oxford, 1936).

Prieur, Jean-Marc "Response" in MacDonald (1986) 27-33.

Prinz, Otto "Eine frühe abendländische Aktualisierung der lateinischen Übersetzung des Pseudo-Methodios" *Deutsches Archiv für Erforschung des Mittelalters* 41 (1985) 1-23.

Quentin, H. *Les martyrologes historiques du Moyen Âge* (Paris, 1908).

Raine, James *Catalogi veteres librorum ecclesiae cathedralis Dunelm SS* 7 (London 1938).

Raith, Josef *Untersuchungen zum englischen Aspekt, I: Grundsätzliches Altenglisch* (Munich 1951).

Rampolla del Tindaro, M. Sancta Melania Giuniore, Senatrice Romana. Documenti Contemporanei e Note (Rome, 1905).

Ramsay, Robert L. "Theodore of Mopsuestia and St. Columban on the Psalms" *Zeitschrift für celtische Philologie* 8 (1912a) 421-51.

Ramsay, Robert L. "Theodore of Mopsuestia in England and Ireland" *Zeitschrift für celtische Philologie* 8 (1912b) 452-97.

Rehm, Bernhard *Die Pseudoklementinen. II Rekognitionen in Rufins Übersetzung* GCS 51 (Berlin, 1965).

Reinsch, Robert *Die Pseudo-Evangelien von Jesu und Maria's Kindheit in der romanischen und germanischen Literatur* (Halle, 1879).

Remly, Lynn L. "Salome in England: A Note on 'Vercelli Homily X'" *Vetera Christianorum* 11 (1974) 121-23.

Reynolds, Roger "Unity and Diversity in Carolingian Canon Law Collections: The Case of the *Collectio Hibernensis* and its Derivatives" in *Carolingian Essays* ed. Uta-Renate Blumenthal (Washington DC, 1983) 99–135.

Riggenbach, Eduard D. *Historische Studien zum Hebräerbrief* vol. 1: *Die ältesten lateinischen Kommentare zum Hebräerbrief* Forschungen zur Geschichte des neutestamentlichen Kanons 8/1 (Leipzig, 1907).

Rittmueller, Jean "The Hiberno-Latin Background of the Matthew Commentary of Maél-Brigte Ua Maéluanaig" *Proceedings of the Harvard Celtic Colloquium* 1 (1981) 1–8.

Rittmueller, Jean "The Hiberno-Latin Background of the Leabhar Breac Homily 'In Cena Domini'" *Proceedings of the Harvard Celtic Colloquium* 2 (1982) 1–10.

Rittmueller, Jean "The Gospel Commentary of Máel Brigte Ua Máeluanaig and its Hiberno-Latin Background" *Peritia* 2 (1983) 185–214.

Rittmueller, Jean "Postscript to the Gospels of Máel Brigte" *Peritia* 3 (1984) 215–18.

Rittmueller, Jean "The Text Tradition of the Hiberno-Latin Liber questionum in euangeliis" *Hiberno-Latin Newsletter* 1/1 (Fall, 1986) 6 [summary of conference paper].

Rivers, Theodore John, trans., *Laws of the Salian and Ripuarian Franks* (New York, 1986).

Rivière, Ernest M. "La Lettre du Christ tombée du ciel" *Revue des questions historiques* ns 35 (1906) 600–05.

Roach, William "Eucharistic Tradition in the *Perlesvaus*" *Zeitschrift für romanische Philologie* 59 (1939) 10–56.

Roberts [Crawford], Jane *Guthlac: An edition of the Old English Prose Life, together with the Poems in the Exeter Book* (Diss. Oxford, 1967).

Roberts, Jane, ed. *The Guthlac Poems of the Exeter Book* (Oxford 1979).

Roberts, Jane "The Old English Prose Translation of Felix's *Vita sancti Guthlaci*" in Szarmach (1986b) 363–79.

Roberts, Jane "Guthlac A: Sources and Source Hunting" in *Medieval Studies Presented to George Kane* ed. E. D. Kennedy, R. Waldron, and J.S. Wittig (Wolfeboro NH, 1988) 1–18.

Roberts, Michael. *Biblical Epic and Rhetorical Paraphrase in Late Antiquity* (Liverpool, 1985).

Rochais, H.-M. "Le *Liber de Virtutibus et Vitiis* d'Alcuin" *Revue Mabillon* 41 (1951) 77–86.

Rodríguez, C. García, *El culto de los santos en la España romaña y visigoda* (Madrid 1966).

Röhricht, Reinhold "Ein 'Brief Christi'" *Zeitschrift für Kirchengeschichte* 11 (1890) 436–42.

Romano, D. *Studi Draconziani* (Palermo, 1959).

Sackur, Ernst *Sibyllinische Texte und Forschungen: Pseudomethodius, Adso und die Tiburtinische Sibylle* (1898; Turin, 1963).

Salmon, Pierre "Livrets de prières de l'époque Carolingienne" *Revue Bénédictine* 86 (1976) 218–34; and 90 (1980) 147–49.

Sardemann, F. *Der theologische Lehrgehalt der Schriften des Paschasius Radbertus* (Marburg, 1877).

Sawyer, P.H. and I.N. Wood eds. *Early Medieval Kingship* (Leeds, 1977).

Schenkl, H. *Bibliotheca patrum latinorum britannica* (rpt Hildesheim, 1969) from the Sitzungsberichte der kaiserlichen Akademie der Wissenschaften in Wien, philosophisch-historische Klasse 121 (1890), 123 (1891), 124 (1891), 126 (1892), 127 (1892), 131 (1894), 133 (1896), 136 (1897), 137 (1898), 139 (1898), 143 (1901), 150 (1905), and 157 (1908).

Schermann, T. *Prophetarum vitae fabulosae, indices apostolorum discipulorumque Domini Dorotheo, Epiphanio, Hippolyto aliisque vindicata* (Leipzig, 1907).

Schönbach, Anton E. *Über einige Evangelienkommentare des Mittelalters* Sitzungsberichte der kaiserlichen Akademie der Wissenschaften in Wien, phil.-hist. Klasse 146/4 (Vienna, 1903).

Schoner, C. *Studien zu Vegetius* (Erlangen, 1888).

Scragg, D.G. "The Compilation of the Vercelli Book" *Anglo-Saxon England* 2 (1973) 189–207.

Scragg, D.G. "Wulfstan Homily XXX: Its Sources, its Relationship to the Vercelli Book, and its Style" *Anglo-Saxon England* 6 (1977) 197–211.

Scragg, D.G. "The Corpus of Vernacular Homilies and Prose Saints' Lives Before Ælfric" *Anglo-Saxon England* 8 (1979) 223–77.

Scragg, D.G. "The Homilies of the Blickling Manuscript" in Lapidge and Gneuss (1985) 299–316.

Scragg, D.G. "'The Devil's Account of the Next World' Revisited" *American Notes and Queries* ns 24 (1986) 107–10.

Seymour, St. John D. "The Seven Heavens in Irish Literature" *Zeitschrift für celtische Philologie* 14 (1923) 18–30.

Seymour, St. John D. "The Vision of Adamnan" *Proceedings of the Royal Irish Academy* 37C (1927) 304–12.

Seymour, St. John D. *Irish Visions of the Other-World* (London, 1930).

Shrader, C.R. "A Handlist of Extant Manuscripts containing the *De Re Militari* of Flavius Vegetius Renatus" *Scriptorium* 33 (1979) 280–305.

Siegmund, A. *Die Überlieferung der griechischen christlichen Literatur in der lateinischen Kirche bis zum zwölften Jahrhundert* Abhandlungen der Bayerischen Benediktiner-Akademie 5 (Munich 1949).

Silhanek, D.K. "Vegetius' *Epitoma*, Books I and II: A Translation and Commentary" (Diss. New York University, 1972).

Silverstein, Theodore *The Visio Sancti Pauli: The History of the Apocalypse in Latin, together with Nine Texts* Studies and Documents 4 (London, 1935).

Silverstein, Theodore "The Vision of St. Paul: New Links and Patterns in the Western Tradition" *Archives d'histoire doctrinale et littéraire du Moyen Âge* 34 (1959) 199–248.

Silverstein, Theodore "The Date of the 'Apocalypse of Paul'" *Medieval Studies* 14 (1962) 335–48.

Silverstein, Theodore "The Graz and Zürich Apocalypse of Saint Paul: An Independent Medieval Witness to the Greek" in Alexander and Gibson (1976) 166–80.

Silverstein, Theodore, Review of Healey (1978) in *Medium Ævum* 50 (1981) 120–22.

Sims-Williams, Patrick "Thought, Word and Deed: An Irish Triad" *Ériu* 29 (1978) 78–111.

Sims-Williams, Patrick "An Unpublished Seventh- or Eighth-Century Anglo-Latin Letter in Boulogne-sur-Mer MS 74 (82)" *Medium Aevum* 48 (1979) 1–22.

Snyder, Graydon F., trans. *The Shepherd of Hermas* The Apostolic Fathers, ed. Robert M. Grant vol. 6 (Camden NJ, 1968).

Souter, Alexander *The Earliest Latin Commentaries on the Epistles of St. Paul* (Oxford, 1927).

Stancliffe, Clare "Early 'Irish' Biblical Exegesis" *TU* 115 [*Studia Patristica* 12] (Berlin, 1975) 361–70.

Stancliffe, Clare "Red, White and Blue Martyrdom" in Whitelock, McKitterick and Dumville (1982) 21–46.

Stanley, E.G., ed. *Continuations and Beginnings* (London, 1966).

Stevenson, Jane "Ascent through the Heavens, from Egypt to Ireland" *Cambridge Medieval Celtic Studies* 4 (1982) 21–35.

Stokes, Myra and T.L. Burton, eds. *Medieval Literature and Antiquities: Studies in Honour of Basil Cottle* (Cambridge, 1987) 57–70.

Stokes, Whitley, and J. Strachan *Thesaurus Palaeohibernicus* 2 vols. (1901–03; rpt Dublin, 1975).

Stone, Michael E. "The Metamorphosis of Ezra: Jewish Apocalypse and Medieval Vision" *Journal of Theological Studies* NS 33 (1982) 1–18.

Strecker, Karl "Zu den Quellen für das Leben des Hl. Ninian" *Neues Archiv der Gesellschaft für ältere deutsche Geschichtskunde* 43 (1922) 1–26.

Symons, Thomas, ed. *Regularis Concordia* (New York, 1953).

Szarmach, Paul E. "The Vercelli Homilies: Style and Structure" in Szarmach and Huppé (1978) 241–67.

Szarmach, Paul E., ed. *Vercelli Homilies IX-XXIII* Toronto Old English Series 5 (Toronto, 1981a).

Szarmach, Paul E. "A Preliminary Handlist of Manuscripts Containing Alcuin's *Liber de Virtutibus et Vitiis*" *Manuscripta* 25 (1981b) 131–40.

Szarmach, Paul E., ed. with Virginia Darrow Oggins *Sources of Anglo-*

Saxon Culture Studies in Medieval Culture 20 (Kalamazoo, 1986a).

Szarmach, Paul E., ed. *Studies in Earlier Old English Prose* (Albany, 1986b).

Szarmach, Paul E. "Two Notes on the Vercelli Homilies" *English Language Notes* 24 (1986c) 3–7.

Szarmach, Paul E. "The Latin Tradition of Alcuin's *Liber de Virtutibus et Vitiis*, cap. xxvii-xxxv, with Special Reference to Vercelli Homily XX" *Mediaevalia* 12 (1989 for 1986) 13–41.

Szarmach, Paul E. and Bernard F. Huppé, eds. *The Old English Homily and its Backgrounds* (Albany, 1978).

Szittya, Penn "The Living Stone and the Patriarchs: Typological Imagery in *Andreas*, Lines 706–810" *Journal of English and Germanic Philology* 72 (1973) 167–74.

Talbot, C.H. "Some Notes on Anglo-Saxon Medicine" *Medical History* 9 (1965) 156–69.

Talbot, C.H. *Medicine in Medieval England* (London, 1967).

Therel, M.L. *A l'origine du decor du portail occidental de Notre-Dame de Senlis: la triomphe de la Vierge-Église* (Paris, 1984).

Thompson, A. Hamilton, ed. *Bede His Life, Times, and Writings* (1932; rpt New York, 1966).

Thomson, R. M. "The Library of Bury St Edmunds Abbey in the Eleventh and Twelfth Centuries" *Speculum* 47 (1972) 617–45.

Tierney, Brian, and Peter Lineham, eds. *Authority and Power* (Cambridge, 1980).

Tischendorf, C. *Acta Apostolorum Apocrypha* (Leipzig, 1851).

Tischendorf, C. *Apocalypses Apocryphae* (Leipzig, 1866).

Tischendorf, C. *Evangelia Apocrypha* 2nd ed. (Leipzig, 1876).

Torkar, Roland, ed. *Eine Altenglischen Übersetzung von Alcuins de Virtute et Vitiis, Kap. 20* Texte und Untersuchungen zur Englischen Philologie 7 (Munich, 1981).

Traube, Ludwig *Karolingische Dichtungen* Schriften zur germanischen Philologie 1 (Berlin, 1888).

Tristram, Hildegard L.C. "Der 'homo octipartitus' in der irischen und altenglischen Literatur" *Zeitschrift für celtische Philologie* 34 (1975) 119–53.

Tristram, Hildegard L.C. *Sex aetates mundi. Die Weltzeitalter bei den Angelsachsen und den Iren* (Heidelberg, 1985).

Troncarelli, Fabio *Tradizione perdute: La "Consolatio Philosophiae" nell'alto medioevo* Medioevo e umanesimo 42 (Padua, 1981).

Turner, Cuthbert Hamilton *Early Worcester MSS* (Oxford, 1916).

Turville-Petre, J. "Translations of a Lost Penitential Homily" *Traditio* 19 (1963) 51–78.

Ullmann, Walter "The Significance of the *Epistola Clementis* in the Pseudo-Clementines" *Journal of Theological Studies* ns 11 (1960) 295–317.

Ussher, James *An Answer to a Challenge Made by a Jesuite in Ireland* (Dublin, 1624).

Utley, F. Lee. "The One Hundred and Three Names of Noah's Wife" *Speculum* 16 (1941) 426-52.

van Andel, G.K. *The Christian Concept of History in the Chronicle of Sulpicius Severus* (Amsterdam, 1976).

Vattioni, F. "Frammento latino del Vangelo di Giacomo" *Augustinianum* 17 (1977) 505-09.

Verhelst, D. "La préhistoire des conceptions d'Adson concernant l'Antichrist" *Recherches de Théologie ancienne et médiévale* 40 (1973) 52-103.

Vian, Giovanni Maria. "Le catechesi celtiche pubblicate da André Wilmart" *Romano-Barbarica* 6 (1981/82) 345-59.

Vollmann, Benedikt *Studien zum Priszillianismus* (St. Ottilien, 1965).

Wack, Mary F., and Charles D. Wright. "A New Latin Source for the Old English 'Three Utterances' Exemplum" (forthcoming in *Anglo-Saxon England*).

Waite, Gregory G. "The Vocabulary of the Old English Version of Bede's *Historia Ecclesiastica*" (Diss. University of Toronto). *Dissertation Abstracts International* 46A (1985) 1276.

Waldman, Glenys A. *The Wessobrun Prayer Manuscript, Clm 22053: A Transliteration, Translation and Study of Parallels* (Diss. Univ. of Pennsylvania, 1975).

Walker, Alexander *Apocryphal Gospels, Acts, and Revelations* Ante-Nicene Christian Library 16 (Edinburgh, 1873).

Wallace-Hadrill, J.M. *The Long-Haired Kings* (London, 1962).

Wallace-Hadrill, J.M. *Early Germanic Kingship in England and on the Continent* (Oxford, 1971).

Wallace-Hadrill, J.M. *Early Medieval History* (Oxford, 1975).

Wallach, Luitpold *Alcuin and Charlemagne: Studies in Carolingian History and Literature* (Ithaca NY, 1959).

Walsh, Marie Michelle "The Baptismal Flood in the Old English 'Andreas': Liturgical and Typological Depths" *Traditio* 33 (1977) 137-58.

Walsh, Marie Michelle "St. Andrew in Anglo-Saxon England: The Evolution of the Apocryphal Hero" *Annuale Mediaevale* 20 (1981) 97-122.

Walsh, Maura "Some Remarks on Cummian's Paschal Letter and the Commentary on Mark Ascribed to Cummian" in Ní Chatháin and Richter (1987) 216-29.

Walsh, Maura, and Dáibhí Ó Cróinín *Cummian's Letter De Controversia Paschali and the De Ratione Conputandi* Studies and Texts 86 (Toronto, 1988).

Warner, George F. and Julius P. Gilson *British Museum. Catalogue of Western Manuscripts in the Old Royal and King's Collections* 4 vols. (London, 1921).

Watson, Andrew G. *Medieval Libraries of Great Britain: A List of Surviving Books. Supplement to the Second Edition* Royal Historical Society Guides and Handbooks 15 (London, 1987).

Weber, Robert ed. *Le Psautier Romain* (Rome, 1953).

Wenger, A. *L'Assomption de la Très Sainte Vierge dans la tradition byzantine du vie au xe siècle* Archives de l'Orient chrétien 5 (Paris, 1955).

Wenisch, F. *Spezifisch anglisches Wortgut in den nordhumbrischen Interlinearglossierungen des Lukasevangeliums*, Anglistische Forschungen 132 (Heidelberg, 1979).

White, Alison. "Boethius in the Medieval Quadrivium" in Gibson (1981) 162–205.

Whitelock, Dorothy "The Prose of Alfred's Reign" in Stanley (1966) 67–103.

Whitelock, Dorothy "Bishop Ecgred, Pehtred and Niall" in Whitelock, McKitterick and Dumville (1982) 47–68.

Whitelock, Dorothy, Rosamond McKitterick, and David Dumville eds. *Ireland in Early Mediaeval Europe* (Cambridge, 1982).

Wieland, Gernot R. "The Glossed Manuscript: Classbook or Library Book?" *Anglo-Saxon England* 14 (1985) 153–73.

Wieland, Gernot R. "Aldhelm's *De Octo Vitiis Principalibus* and Prudentius' *Psychomachia*" *Medium Ævum* 55 (1986) 85–92.

Wieland, Gernot R. "The Anglo-Saxon Manuscripts of Prudentius's *Psychomachia*" *Anglo-Saxon England* 16 (1987) 213–31.

Willard, R. Review of Förster (GR 6200) in *Speculum* 9 (1934) 225–31.

Willard, R. "The Testament of Mary: The Irish Account of the Death of the Virgin" *Recherches de Théologie ancienne et médiévale* 9 (1937) 341–64.

Willard, R. "La ville d'Agathe? Note sur le Transitus Mariae C" *Échos d'Orient* 38 (1939) 5–28.

Wilmart, A. "Les homélies attribuées a S. Ansleme," *Archives d'histoire doctrinale et littéraire du Moyen Âge* 2 (1927) 5–29 and 339–41.

Wilmart, A. "The Prayers of the Bury Psalter" *Downside Review* 48 (1930) 198–216.

Wilmart, A., ed. *Codices Reginenses Latini* 2 vols. (Vatican, 1937–45).

Wilmart, A., ed. *Precum libelli quattuor ævi karolini* (Rome, 1940).

Wilson, H.A. ed. *The Calendar of St. Willibrord HBS* 55 (London, 1918).

Wittig, Joseph S. "King Alfred's Boethius and its Latin sources: A Reconsideration" *Anglo-Saxon England* 11 (1983) 157–98

Woods, J. Douglas and David A.E. Pelteret, eds. *The Anglo-Saxons: Synthesis and Achievement* (Waterloo, Ontario, 1985).

Woolley, R. M., ed. *The Canterbury Benedictional HBS* 51 (London, 1917).

Wormald, Patrick "*Lex Scripta* and *Verbum Regis*: Legislation and Germanic Kingship, from Euric to Cnut" in Sawyer and Wood (1977) 105–38.

Wright, Charles D. "Irish and Anglo-Saxon Literary Culture: Insular Christian Traditions in Vercelli Homily IX and the Theban Anchorite Legend" (Diss. Cornell, 1984).

Wright, Charles D. "Apocryphal Lore and Insular Tradition in St Gall, Stiftsbibliothek MS 908" in Ní Chatháin and Richter (1987a) 124–45.

Wright, Charles D. "*Docet Deus, Docet Diabolus*: A Hiberno-Latin Theme in an Old English Body-and-Soul Homily" *Notes and Queries* ns 34 (1987b) 451-53.

Wright, Charles D. "Blickling Homily III on the Temptations in the Desert" *Anglia* 106 (1988a) 130-37.

Wright, Charles D. Review of *BCLL* in *Envoi: A Review Journal of Medieval Literature* 1 (1988b) 227-31.

Wright, Charles D. "The Pledge of the Soul: A Judgment Theme in Old English Homiletic Literature and Cynewulf's *Elene*" *Neuphilologische Mitteilungen* (forthcoming).

Wright, Charles D. "The Irish 'Enumerative Style' in Old English Homiletic Literature, Especially Vercelli Homily IX" *Cambridge Medieval Celtic Studies* 18 (Winter, 1989) 27-74.

Wright, Neil "Imitation of the Poems of Paulinus of Nola in Early Anglo-Latin Verse" *Peritia* 4 (1985) 134-51.

Wright, William, *Contributions to the Apocryphal Literature of the New Testament, Collected and Edited from Syriac Manuscripts in the British Museum* (London, 1865).

Yorke, Barbara, ed. *Bishop Aethelwold: His Career and Influence* (Woodbridge, 1988).

Zelzer, Klaus *Die alten lateinischen Thomasakten* TU 122 (Berlin, 1977).

Zettel, Patrick H. "Ælfric's Hagiographic Sources and the Legendary Preserved in B.L. MS Cotton Nero E i + CCCC MS 9 and other Manuscripts" (Diss. Oxford, 1979).

Zettel, Patrick H. "Saints' Lives in Old English: Latin Manuscripts and Vernacular Accounts: Ælfric" *Peritia* 1 (1982) 17-37.

Appendix A:
Martyrology

References to the Old English *Martyrology* are to a modified version of the system in the *MCOE*, and so require some comment here. Rather than dividing the material according to the six MSS (as the Toronto Dictionary has done), references in this volume assume a division according to the individual entries in the edition of Günter Kotzor, *Das altenglische Martyrologium* 2 vols. (Munich, 1981; the text appears in volume 2). This system, designed by Donald Scragg for the *Fontes Anglo-Saxonici* and changed slightly to conform to the style of the present volume, assigns a letter, or letters for each entry; in order to avoid ambiguity, "l" and "o" are avoided in all cases; "i," "v," and "x" are not used alone; and "ii," "iv," and "ix" have been excluded.

B19.a	*Mart*	25 December
	The Birth of Christ	
B19.b	*Mart*	25 December
	St Anastasia	
B19.c	*Mart*	25 December
	St Eugenia	
B19.d	*Mart*	26 December
	St Stephen	
B19.e	*Mart*	27 December
	St John the Evangelist	
B19.f	*Mart*	28 December
	The Holy Innocents	
B19.g	*Mart*	31 December
	Pope Silvester I	
B19.h	*Mart*	31 December
	St Columba	
B19.j	*Mart*	
	The beginning of January	
B19.k	*Mart*	1 January

	Octave of Christ and St Mary (Circumcision of Christ)	
B19.m	*Mart*	3 January
	Pope Anteros	
B19.n	*Mart*	5 January
	St Emiliana	
B19.p	*Mart*	6 January
	Epiphany, Baptism of Christ etc.	
B19.q	*Mart*	6 January
	St Julian, Basilissa	
B19.r	*Mart*	6 January
	Pope Telesphorus	
B19.s	*Mart*	9 January
	St Pega	
B19.t	*Mart*	10 January
	St Paul the Hermit	
B19.u	*Mart*	12 January
	St Benedict Biscop	
B19.w	*Mart*	13 January
	St Hilary of Poitiers	
B19.y	*Mart*	14 January
	St Felix	
B19.z	*Mart*	16 January
	Pope Marcellus	
B19.aa	*Mart*	16 January
	St Fursa	
B19.ab	*Mart*	17 January
	St Anthony the Hermit	
B19.ac	*Mart*	17 January
	St Speusippus, Eleusippus, Meleusippus	
B19.ad	*Mart*	18 January
	St Prisca; Consecration of St Peter's Church	
B19.ae	*Mart*	19 January
	St Ananias, Petrus etc.	
B19.af	*Mart*	20 January
	St Sebastian	
B19.ag	*Mart*	20 January
	Pope Fabian	
B19.ah	*Mart*	20 January

	St Marius, Martha, Audifax, Abacuc	
B19.ai	*Mart*	21 January
	St Agnes	
B19.aj	*Mart*	22 January
	St Vincent	
B19.ak	*Mart*	22 January
	St Anastasius	
B19.am	*Mart*	23 January
	St Emerentiana	
B19.an	*Mart*	24 January
	St Babylas etc.	
B19.ap	*Mart*	25 January
	The Conversion of St Paul	
B19.aq	*Mart*	27? February
	Discovery of the head of St John the Baptist; the end of February	
B19.ar	*Mart*	
	The beginning of March	
B19.as	*Mart*	2 March
	St Chad	
B19.at	*Mart*	4 March
	St Adrian, Natalia	
B19.au	*Mart*	7 March
	St Perpetua, Felicity	
B19.av	*Mart*	7 March
	St Eastorwine	
B19.aw	*Mart*	9 March
	Forty Soldiers of Sebastea	
B19.ax	*Mart*	12 March
	Pope Gregory the Great	
B19.ay	*Mart*	13 March
	St Macedonius, Patricia, Modesta	
B19.az	*Mart*	17 March
	St Patrick	
B19.ba	*Mart*	18 March
	The First Day of Creation	
B19.bb	*Mart*	19 March
	The Second Day of Creation	
B19.bc	*Mart*	19 March

	St Gregory Nazianzen	
B19.bd	*Mart*	20 March
	The Third Day of Creation	
B19.be	*Mart*	20 March
	St Cuthbert	
B19.bf	*Mart*	21 March
	The Fourth Day of Creation	
B19.bg	*Mart*	21 March
	St Benedict of Nursia	
B19.bh	*Mart*	22 March
	The Fifth Day of Creation	
B19.bi	*Mart*	23 March
	The Sixth Day of Creation, Adam and Eve	
B19.bj	*Mart*	23 March
	St Theodoret	
B19.bk	*Mart*	24 March
	The Seventh Day of Creation	
B19.bm	*Mart*	25 March
	Annunciation Day; Crucifixion	
B19.bn	*Mart*	26 March
	Christ's Descent into Hell	
B19.bp	*Mart*	27 March
	Resurrection; the end of March	
B19.bq	*Mart*	
	The beginning of April	
B19.br	*Mart*	3 April
	St Agape, Chionia, (Irene)	
B19.bs	*Mart*	5 April
	St Ambrose of Milan	
B19.bt	*Mart*	5 April
	St Irene	
B19.bu	*Mart*	9 April
	Seven Women at Sirmium	
B19.bv	*Mart*	11 April
	St Guthlac	
B19.bw	*Mart*	14 April
	St Valer(ia)nus, Tiburtius, Maximus	
B19.bx	*Mart*	18 April

	St Eleutherius, Antia	
B19.by	*Mart*	21 April
	St Æthelwald	
B19.bz	*Mart*	23 April
	St George	
B19.ca	*Mart*	24 April
	St Wilfrid	
B19.cb	*Mart*	25 April
	Rogation Day	
B19.cc	*Mart*	25 April
	St Mark	
B19.cd	*Mart*	27 April
	St Alexandr(i)a	
B19.ce	*Mart*	28 April
	St Vitalis	
B19.cf	*Mart*	28 April
	St Christopher; the end of April	
B19.cg	*Mart*	
	The beginning of May	
B19.ch	*Mart*	1 May
	St Philip	
B19.ci	*Mart*	2 May
	St Athanasius	
B19.cj	*Mart*	3 May
	Pope Alexander I, St Eventius, Theodulus	
B19.ck	*Mart*	3 May
	The Discovery of the Holy Cross	
B19.cm	*Mart*	
	Rogation Days	
B19.cn	*Mart*	5 May
	The Ascension of Christ	
B19.cp	*Mart*	6 May
	St Eadberht	
B19.cq	*Mart*	7 May
	St John of Beverley	
B19.cr	*Mart*	8 May
	Discovery of St Michael's Church	
B19.cs	*Mart*	8 May

	St Victor Maurus	
B19.ct	*Mart*	9 May
	The beginning of Summer	
B19.cu	*Mart*	10 May
	St Gordianus, Calepodius	
B19.cv	*Mart*	12 May
	St Pancras	
B19.cw	*Mart*	14 May
	St Victor, Corona	
B19.cx	*Mart*	15 May
	Pentecost	
B19.cy	*Mart*	18 May
	Pope John I	
B19.cz	*Mart*	20 May
	St Basilla	
B19.da	*Mart*	25 May
	Pope Urban I	
B19.db	*Mart*	26 May
	St Augustine of Canterbury	
B19.dc	*Mart*	29 May
	St Sisinnius, Matyrrius, Alexander	
B19.dd	*Mart*	31 May
	St Petronilla; the end of May	
B19.de	*Mart*	
	The beginning of June	
B19.df	*Mart*	1 June
	St Priscus, Nicomedes	
B19.dg	*Mart*	2 June
	St Erasmus	
B19.dh	*Mart*	2 June
	St Marcellinus, Peter	
B19.di	*Mart*	2 June
	St Artemius, Candida, Paulina	
B19.dj	*Mart*	9 June
	St Columba of Iona	
B19.dk	*Mart*	10 June
	St Barnabas	
B19.dm	*Mart*	15 June
	St Vitus, Modestus	
B19.dn	*Mart*	16 June

	St Ferreolus, Ferrucio	
B19.dp	*Mart*	17 June
	St Nicander, Blastus	
B19.dq	*Mart*	18 June
	St Mark, Marcellian	
B19.dr	*Mart*	19 June
	St Gervase, Protase	
B19.ds	*Mart*	22 June
	St James the Less	
B19.dt	*Mart*	22 June
	St Alban	
B19.du	*Mart*	23 June
	St Æthelthryth	
B19.dv	*Mart*	24 June
	The Birth of St John the Baptist	
B19.dw	*Mart*	24 June
	Summer Solstice	
B19.dx	*Mart*	25 June
	St Luc(e)ia, Auceia	
B19.dy	*Mart*	26 June
	St John and Paul	
B19.dz	*Mart*	29 June
	St Peter and St Paul	
B19.ea	*Mart*	29 June
	St Cassius	
B19.eb	*Mart*	30 June
	St Martial; the end of June	
B19.ec	*Mart*	
	The beginning of July	
B19.ed	*Mart*	2 July
	St Processus, Martinianus	
B19.ee	*Mart*	4 July
	St Zoe	
B19.ef	*Mart*	6 July
	Octave of Peter and Paul	
B19.eg	*Mart*	6 July
	St Tranquillinus	
B19.eh	*Mart*	7 July
	St Procopius	
B19.ei	*Mart*	7 July
	St Marina	

B19.ej	*Mart*	10 July
	The Seven Brothers	
B19.ek	*Mart*	10 July
	St Anatolia, Audax	
B19.em	*Mart*	10 July
	St Rufina, Secunda	
B19.en	*Mart*	14 July
	St Phocas	
B19.ep	*Mart*	15 July
	St Cyricus, Julitta	
B19.eq	*Mart*	17 July
	St Speratus and the Scillitan Martyrs	
B19.er	*Mart*	18 July
	St Symphorosa and her Seven Sons	
B19.es	*Mart*	19 July
	St Christina	
B19.et	*Mart*	19 July
	St Arsenius	
B19.eu	*Mart*	21 July
	St Victor of Marseilles etc.	
B19.ev	*Mart*	22 July
	St Mary Magdalen	
B19.ew	*Mart*	22 July
	St Apollinaris	
B19.ex	*Mart*	25 July
	St James the Greater	
B19.ey	*Mart*	27 July
	St Simeon Stylites	
B19.ez	*Mart*	28 July
	St Nazarius, Celsus	
B19.fa	*Mart*	29 July
	St Lupus	
B19.fb	*Mart*	30 July
	St Abdo, Sennes; the end of July	
B19.fc	*Mart*	
	The beginning of August	
B19.fd	*Mart*	1 August
	The Machabees	
B19.fe	*Mart*	1 August

	St Germanus	
B19.ff	*Mart*	1 August
	St Eusebius of Vercelli	
B19.fg	*Mart*	2 August
	Pope Stephen I	
B19.fh	*Mart*	2 August
	St Theodota and her Three Sons	
B19.fi	*Mart*	3 August
	Discovery of the Body of St Stephen	
B19.fj	*Mart*	5 August
	St Oswald	
B19.fk	*Mart*	6 August
	Pope Sixtus II	
B19.fm	*Mart*	7 August
	St Donatus, Hilarinus	
B19.fn	*Mart*	8 August
	St Afra, Hilaria etc.	
B19.fp	*Mart*	9 August
	St Romanus	
B19.fq	*Mart*	10 August
	St Lawrence	
B19.fr	*Mart*	11 August
	St Tiburtius	
B19.fs	*Mart*	12 August
	St Eupl(i)us	
B19.ft	*Mart*	13 August
	St Hippolytus	
B19.fu	*Mart*	13 August
	St Cassian	
B19.fv	*Mart*	15 August
	Assumption of the Virgin Mary	
B19.fw	*Mart*	17 August
	St Mamas	
B19.fx	*Mart*	18 August
	St Agapitus	
B19.fy	*Mart*	19 August
	St Magnus	
B19.fz	*Mart*	22 August
	St Symphorian	

B19.ga	*Mart*	22 August
	St Timothy	
B19.gb	*Mart*	25 August
	St Bartholomew	
B19.gc	*Mart*	25 August
	St Genesius the Comedian	
B19.gd	*Mart*	26 August
	St Irenaeus, Abundius	
B19.ge	*Mart*	27 August
	St Rufus	
B19.gf	*Mart*	28 August
	St Hermes	
B19.gg	*Mart*	28 August
	St Augustine of Hippo	
B19.gh	*Mart*	29 August
	The Death of St John the Baptist	
B19.gi	*Mart*	29 August
	St Sabina	
B19.gj	*Mart*	30 August
	St Felix of Thibuca etc.	
B19.gk	*Mart*	31 August
	St Aidan; the end of August	
B19.gm	*Mart*	
	The beginning of September	
B19.gn	*Mart*	1 September
	St Priscus	
B19.gp	*Mart*	2 September
	St Antoninus	
B19.gq	*Mart*	3 September
	St Aristion, Paternianus, Felicianus	
B19.gr	*Mart*	4 September
	St Marcellus	
B19.gs	*Mart*	5 September
	St Quintus	
B19.gt	*Mart*	5 September
	St Bertinus	
B19.gu	*Mart*	7 September
	St Sinotus	
B19.gv	*Mart*	8 September
	The Birth of St Mary	

B19.gw	*Mart*	8 September
	St Omer	
B19.gx	*Mart*	11 September
	St Protus, Hyacinth	
B19.gy	*Mart*	14 September
	Pope Cornelius etc.	
B19.gz	*Mart*	14 September
	St Cyprian	
B19.ha	*Mart*	15 September
	St Valerian	
B19.hb	*Mart*	15 September
	St Mamilian	
B19.hc	*Mart*	16 September
	St Euphemia	
B19.hd	*Mart*	19 September
	St Januarius etc.	
B19.he	*Mart*	20 September
	St Fausta, Evilasius	
B19.hf	*Mart*	21 September
	St Matthew	
B19.hg	*Mart*	22 September
	St Maurice and the Theban Legion	
B19.hh	*Mart*	23 September
	St Sosius	
B19.hi	*Mart*	23 September
	St Thecla	
B19.hj	*Mart*	24 September
	The Conception of St John the Baptist	
B19.hk	*Mart*	24 September
	St Andochius, Thyrsus, Felix	
B19.hm	*Mart*	25 September
	St Ceolfrith	
B19.hn	*Mart*	26 September
	St Justina, Cyprian	
B19.hp	*Mart*	27 September
	St Cosmas, Damian	
B19.hq	*Mart*	29 September
	The Consecration of St Michael's Church	
B19.hr	*Mart*	30 September

	St Jerome; the end of September	
B19.hs	*Mart*	
	The beginning of October	
B19.ht	*Mart*	3 October
	The Two Hewalds	
B19.hu	*Mart*	7 October
	Pope Mark	
B19.hv	*Mart*	8 October
	St Dionysius, Rusticus, Eleutherius	
B19.hw	*Mart*	11 October
	St Æthelburh	
B19.hx	*Mart*	14 October
	Pope Callistus I	
B19.hy	*Mart*	15 October
	St Lupulus	
B19.hz	*Mart*	18 October
	St Luke	
B19.ia	*Mart*	18 October
	St Tryphonia	
B19.ib	*Mart*	18 October
	St Justus	
B19.ic	*Mart*	19 October
	St Pelagia	
B19.id	*Mart*	21 October
	St Hilarion	
B19.ie	*Mart*	22 October
	St Genesius	
B19.if	*Mart*	24 October
	Sixteen Soldiers	
B19.ig	*Mart*	26 October
	St Cedd	
B19.ih	*Mart*	28 October
	St Simon, Thaddeus	
B19.ij	*Mart*	28 October
	St Cyrilla	
B19.ik	*Mart*	31 October
	St Quentin; the end of October	
B19.im	*Mart*	
	The beginning of November	

B19.in	*Mart*	1 November
	All Saints	
B19.ip	*Mart*	1 November
	St Caesarius	
B19.iq	*Mart*	1 November
	St Benignus	
B19.ir	*Mart*	6 November
	St Winnoc	
B19.is	*Mart*	7 November
	The beginning of Winter	
B19.it	*Mart*	8 November
	The Four Crowned Ones	
B19.iu	*Mart*	11 November
	St Martin of Tours	
B19.iw	*Mart*	11 November
	St Mennas, Heliodorus	
B19.iy	*Mart*	15 November
	St Milus, Senneus	
B19.iz	*Mart*	17 November
	St Hild	
B19.ja	*Mart*	22 November
	St Cecilia	
B19.jb	*Mart*	23 November
	Pope Clement I	
B19.jc	*Mart*	23 November
	St Felicity	
B19.jd	*Mart*	24 November
	St Chrysogonus	
B19.je	*Mart*	28 November
	St Saturninus	
B19.jf	*Mart*	28 November
	St Chrysanthus, Daria	
B19.jg	*Mart*	30 November
	St Andrew; the end of November	
B19.jh	*Mart*	
	The beginning of December	
B19.ji	*Mart*	10 December
	St Eulalia	
B19.jj	*Mart*	13 December
	St Lucy	
B19.jk	*Mart*	13 December

	St Ursicinus	
B19.jm	*Mart*	14 December
	St Higebald	
B19.jn	*Mart*	21 December
	St Thomas	

Appendix B:
Projected Entries
and Contributors List

(ed. note: current as of October 25, 1989)

xxx = crosslist
inv. = invited

Abbo of Fleury	
Abbo of Saint-Germain-des-Pres	J.E. Cross/A. Brown
De accipitribus custodiendis (see Alfred)	xxx
Acta Sanctorum	G. Whatley + multi alii: H. Magennis, F. Biggs, J. Hill etc. [organized by saints]
Adalbero of Laon	D. Dew
Adalbert (see *Speculum Gregorii*)	xxx
Ado of Vienne	D. Nodes
Adomnan	F. Biggs
Adrevald of Fleury (see *Acta Sanctorum*)	xxx
Adso of Montier-en-Der	F. Biggs
Ælfric	M. Godden
Ælfric Bata	P. Lendinara
Ænigmata	D. Johnson
Aesop	
Æthelweard (see Chronicles)	xxx
Æthelwold	
Aethicus Ister	D. Dew
Æthilwulf	
Aetna (see pseudo-Vergil)	xxx
Agathobolus	
Agroecius (see Grammatical Writings)	xxx
Alaric	D. Ganz
Alcuin	D. Bullough, with

	P. Szarmach,
	V. Law, F. Biggs,
	T. Mackay
pseudo-Alcuin	P. Szarmach
Aldhelm	M. Lapidge
pseudo-Aldhelm	M. Lapidge
Alexander of Tralles (see Medical Writings)	xxx
pseudo-Alexander	J. Romm
Historia Alexandri	J. Romm
Alfred	M. Godden (inv.)
Amalarius of Metz	J.E. Cross
Ambrose	L. Swift
pseudo-Ambrose	L. Swift (inv.)
Ambrosiaster	
Ambrosius Autpertus	F. Biggs
Ammianus Marcellinus	T. Mackay
pseudo-Anatolius (see Computistical Writings)	xxx
Andreas Orator (see *Anthologia Latina*)	xxx
Antiphonaries	R. Pfaff et al.
Anonymous Bobiensis (see Grammatical Writings)	xxx
Anthologia Latina	J. McGowan
Antidotaria (see Medical Writings)	xxx
In Apocalypsin	F. Biggs
Apocalypsis Pauli (see Apocrypha)	xxx
Apocrypha	(F. Biggs, A. Healey, T. Hall, et multi alii)
Apollonius of Tyre	P. Szarmach
Apponius	M. Clayton
Apuleius	T.D. Hill
pseudo-Apuleius (see Medical Writings)	xxx
Sphera Apulei (see Magical Writings)	xxx
Apuleius Platonicus (Barbarus) (see Medical Writings)	xxx
Arator	G. Wieland
Aratea (see Computistical Writings)	xxx
De argumentis lunae (see Computistical Writings)	xxx
Aristobulus	
Aristotle	
Grammar (see Grammatical Writings)	xxx

Arnobius	J. Ericksen
Asper/Asporius (see Grammatical Writings)	xxx
Asser	S. Hauer
Athanasius	
pseudo-Athanasius	
Audax (see Grammatical Writings)	xxx
Hymnus Audomaropolitanus (see *Hisperica Famina*)	xxx
Scriptores historiae Augustae	
Augustine	J. Kelly with J. Cavadini
pseudo-Augustine	
Regulae (see Grammatical Writings)	xxx
Augustinus Hibernicus	C. Wright
Aurea gemma	M. Boudreau
Ausonius	T. Hall
De ave Phoenice	
Avianus	
Alcimus Avitus	J.R. Hall
Avitus Bracarensis (see Lucianus Presbyter)	xxx

Bachiarius	J. Ericksen
Expositio baptisterii	
Barontus of Pistoia (see *Visio Baronti*)	xxx
Basil	W. Stoneman
pseudo-Basil	J.E. Cross
Bede	G. Brown
pseudo-Bede	G. Brown
OE Bede (*Old English Version of Bede's Ecclesiastical History of the English People*)	E. Cooney
Belisarius Scholasticus	T. Hall
Benedict of Aniane	H. Sauer
Benedict of Nursia	
Beowulf	T.D. Hill
Bestiary (see *Physiologus*)	xxx
Bible	T.D. Hill
Boethius	J. Wittig
pseudo-Boethius	J. Wittig
Boniface	
Aenigmata	D. Johnson
pseudo-Boniface V	

Caecilius Cyprianus
Caelius Aurelianus
Caesar
Caesarius of Arles   J. Trahern
pseudo-Caesarius
Calcidius
pseudo-Callisthenes (see Julius Valerius)   xxx
Calpurnius Siculus
Cambridge Songs   J. Ziolkowski
In Cantica Canticorum   T. Jones
Martianus Capella (see Martianus)   xxx
Caper
Capreolus of Carthage
Carolingian Commentaries (see Grammati-
    cal Writings)   xxx
Cassian   D. Nodes
Cassiodorus   J. Halporn
Cassius Felix (see Medical Writings)   xxx
Catalina (see pseudo-Cicero)   xxx
Cato
Dionysius Cato (see *Disticha Catonis*)   xxx
M. Porcius Cato   L. Melazzo
Charisius (see Grammatical Writings)   xxx
Charms (see Magical Writings)   xxx
Chirius Fortunatianus   D. Sprunger
Chorus (see Macrobius)   xxx .
Chrodegang of Metz
Chromatius of Aquileia   T. Jones
Chronicles   J. Bately
Chrysostom
pseudo-Chrysostom
Cicero   T. Mackay
pseudo-Cicero
Cincius
Claudian   R. Babcock
Claudius of Turin   J. Cross
Cledonius (see Grammatical Writings)   xxx
Clement of Alexandria
pseudo-Clemens Romanus (see
    APOCRYPHA, *Acts of Peter*)   xxx
Coelestinus I
Collectanea Bedae   T.D. Hill

Collectars	R. Pfaff et al.
Colloquies	P. Lendinara
Versus in Colmannum	
Coloniensis Prologus	
Columbanus	F. Biggs
Columella	
Commendatio Animae	C.B. Tkacz
Computistical Writings	P. Baker
Concilia	
Council of Aachen	J. Cross
Consentius (see Grammatical Writings)	xxx
Constantius Lugdunensis	
Coronation Rites	R. Pfaff et al.
Cosmas Indicopleustes	D. Dew
Aethicus Cosmographius (see Aethicus Ister)	xxx
Crux (see *Acta Sanctorum*)	xxx
Cummian	
Curtius Rufus	
Cyprian	
pseudo-Cyprian	
Cyprianus Gallus	D. Nodes
Caecilius Cyprianus (see Caecilius Cyprianus)	xxx
Cyril	
pseudo-Cyril	
Damasus	
Declinationes Nominum (see Grammatical Writings)	xxx
Defensor of Ligugé	P. Pulsiano
Dialogus philosophi cuiusdam et christiani	
Didymus the Blind	T. Mackay
Didymus	
pseudo-Diocles	
Diomedes (see Gramamtical Writings)	xxx
Dionysius of Alexandria	L. Melazzo
pseudo-Dionysius Areopagus	
Dionysius Exiguus (see Computistical Writings)	xxx
pseudo-Dionysius Exiguus (see Computistical Writings)	xxx
Dionysii Successor	L. Melazzo

Dionysius Thrax
Dioscorides
Disticha Catonis   M. Twomey
De divisione temporum (see Computistical
  Writings)   xxx
Donatus (see Grammatical Writings)   xxx
Tiberius Claudius Donatus
Dositheus   L. Melazzo
pseudo-Dositheus (hermeneumata)   P. Lendinara
Dracontius   D. Nodes
Dunchad (see Martianus Capella)   xxx
Dungalus Reclusus   D. Dew
De duodecim abusivis saeculi   T.D. Hill

Eadmer   J. Cross
In ecclesiasten expositio
In ecclesiastica disciplina (see Legal Writings)   xxx
Ecclesiastical Institutes (see Legal Writings)   xxx
Elenchi
Elias III (see Medical Writings)   xxx
pseudo-Eligius   D. Sprunger
Elucidarium (see Honorius of Autun)   M. Twomey
Ennius
Ennodius
Liber Enoch (see Apocrypha)   xxx
Ephemeris (see Computistical Writings)   xxx
Ephraem Latinus   F. Biggs
pseudo-Ephraem   F. Biggs
Epiphanius   T. Hall
Epiphanius Cypri   T. Hall
Eresius (see Medical Writings)   xxx
Ethicus Cosmographus (see Aethicus Ister)   xxx
De Eucharista   R. Pfaff et al.
Eucherius   J. Ericksen
pseudo-Eucherius   J. Ericksen
Eugenius of Toledo
Eusebius Pamphilus
Eutropius   T. Mackay
Eutyches (see Grammatical Writings)   xxx
Eutycius of Constantinople   M. Boudreau
Evagrius (see Athanasius in *Acta Sanctorum*)   xxx
Evax (see Lapidaries)   xxx

Evodius (see Augustine, *Epistulae*)	xxx
Excerptiones de Prisciano (see Grammatical Writings)	xxx
Exorcism (see Liturgical Texts)	xxx
pseudo-Ezra (see Apocrypha)	xxx
Faustus of Riez	D. Nodes
Felix I	
Felix	
Fermes	P. Wallace
Ferrandus	
De festivitatibus anni	R. Pfaff
Festus	
Florus	
Florus of Lyons	D. Nodes
Folcard	
Chirius Fortunatianus (see Grammatical Writings)	xxx
Venantius Fortunatus	P. Lendinara
Francus Anonymous	
Freculf of Lisieux	
Frithegod of Canterbury	
Fulbert of Chartres	R. Pfaff/J. Cross
Fulgentius Ferrandus	H. Sauer
Fulgentius the Mythographer	H. Sauer
Fulgentius of Ruspe	D. Nodes
Galen (see Medical Writings)	xxx
Gallus	
Titus Gallus	
Gaudentius of Brescia	J. Cross
Gelasian Decree (see Apocrypha)	F. Biggs
Aulus Gellius	
OS Genesis (see Old Saxon Genesis)	xxx
Gennadius of Marseilles	
Germanic Sources	
Germanicus	
Gesta Cnutonis	R. Pfaff
Gildas	D. Dumville (M. Lapidge)
Glossaries	J. Pheifer
Goliardic Verse (see Cambridge Songs)	xxx

Gospel of Nicodemus (see Apocrypha)   xxx
De litteris Graecorum
Grammatical Writings   V. Law
Greek Texts
Gregorius Illiberitanus
Gregorius Nazianzenus
Gregory the Great   M. McC. Gatch
Gregory of Tours   T.D. Hill

Halitgar of Cambrai (see Penitentials)   xxx
Harmony of the Gospels
Haymo of Auxerre   F. Biggs
Hegesippus   J.R. Hall
Pseudo-Hegesippus   J.R. Hall
Heliand   S. Deskis
Helperic of Auxerre (see Computistical
   Writings)   xxx
Helvidius
Heraclides Eremita (see *Acta Sanctorum*)   xxx
Herbarius (see Medical Writings)   xxx
Heriman (see Computistical Writings)   xxx
Hermas (see *Apocrypha*)   xxx
Hiberno-Latin Biblical Commentaries   C. Wright
Q. Julius Hilarianus
Hilarius Ignotus   T. Jones
Hilarius Papa   T. Jones
Hilary of Poitiers
Hildebertus of Lavardin   T. Hall
Hilduin of Saint-Denis (see *Acta Sanctorum*)   xxx
Hincmar of Rheims
Hippocrates (see Medical Writings)   xxx
pseudo-Hippocrates   xxx
Hisperica Famina   M. Herren
Historia Brittonum   D. Dumville
Historia de ligno crucis   T. Hall
Hogeri Musica (see Musical Writings)   xxx
Homer (see Greek Texts)   xxx
Homiliaries   M. Clayton
Anonymous OE Homilies   D. Scragg
Homiliae in Apocalypsin XVIII   F. Biggs
Honorius of Autun   M. Twomey
Horace   T. Mackay

Horus (see Macrobius)	xxx
Hrabanus Maurus	W. Schipper
Hucbald of Saint-Amand	
De Humoribus (see Medical Writings)	xxx
Hwætberht	
Hyginus	
Hymnaries	G. Wieland
Hymni (see Hymnaries)	xxx
Hymnum dicat turba fratrum (see Hymnaries)	xxx
Idatius Clarus	
Ildefonsus	D. Sprunger
Innocent I	R. Pfaff
Inventio S. Crucis (see *Acta Sanctorum*)	xxx
Irish Biblical Commentaries (see Hiberno-Latin Commentaries)	xxx
Isidore of Seville	M. Herren
pseudo-Isidore (see Hiberno-Latin Biblical Commentaries)	xxx
Isidorus Junior	
Ivo of Chartres	J.E. Cross
Jannes and Mambres (see Apocrypha)	xxx
Jerome	T. Amos
pseudo-Jerome	
Ars	V. Law
Epistola Hieronimi de nominibus pedum	V. Law
Jesse of Amiens	J.E. Cross
Joca Monachorum	T.D. Hill
Johannes Archicantor (see Musical Writings)	xxx
Johannes Constanopolitanea Antistes (see Chrysostom)	xxx
Johannes Diaconus (see Johannes Levita)	xxx
Johannes Eremita	
Johannes Foldensis	
Johannes Levita (see *Acta Sanctorum*)	xxx
Johannes Lydus	
Johannes Maxentius	
Johannes Scottus	
Johannes Subdiaconus (see *Acta Sanctorum*)	xxx
John Scottus Eriugena	

Homily on the Prologue to the Gospel of John	J. Cross
Jonas of Orléans	C. Gravis
Jordanes	
Josephus	J.R. Hall
Jovinianus	
In Judicum	
Julian of Eclanum	T. Mackay
Julianus Pomerius	P. Pulsiano
Julian of Toledo	F. Biggs et alii
Julius Africanus	
Julius I	
Junianius Justinus	
Junillus Africanus	
Justinian	
Justinus	T. Mackay
Juvenal	
Juvencus	C. Springer
pseudo-Juvencus (see Cyprianus Gallus)	xxx
Lactantius	G. Wieland
Lantbert	
Lantfred of Winchester	
Laidcenn mac Baith (see Hiberno-Latin Biblical Commentaries)	xxx
Lapidaries	P. Kitson (inv.)
Lateran Council (see *Concilia*)	xxx
Latin Verse	
Laurence of Novara	J. Cross
Expositiones lectionum	
Legal Writings	P. Wormald, M. Richards
Pope Leo I	
Leontius (see *Acta Sanctorum*)	xxx
Leporius Gallicanus	
In Leviticum	
Lex Salica (see Legal Writings)	xxx
Lex Romana Visigothorum (see Legal Writings)	xxx
Liber de computo (see Computistical Writings)	xxx
Liber episcopus	
Liber monstrorum	J. Friedman
Liber pontificalis	
Liturgical Writings	R. Pfaff
Livy	

Evangelii sec. Lucam vetus argumentum
Lucan
Lucian
Lucifer Calaritanus
Lucilius
Lucretius
Ludovicus Imperator

Macedonius (see Augustine, *Epistulae*)   xxx
Macer (see Odo of Meung in Medical
   Writings)   xxx
Macrobius   W. Wetherbee
Magical Writings   D. Dew
—Charms   D. Dew
De acerbissimis malis
Mallius
pseudo-Manfred (see Computistical
   Writings)   xxx
Manilius
Mappa Mundi   J. Friedman
Marcellinus Comes
Marcellus of Bordeaux
Marianus Scottus   D. Dew
Marius Aventicus
Marius Victorinus (see Cicero, *de inventione*)   xxx
Maro Poeta
Martial
Martianus Capella   W. Wetherbee
Martin of Braga   P. Szarmach
Martyrology   J. E. Cross
Marvels of the East   J. Friedman
Maternus (see Firmicinus Maternus)   xxx
In Matthaeum (see Hiberno-Latin Commen-
   taries)   xxx
pseudo-Matthew (see Apocrypha)   xxx
Maximianus
Maximus of Turin   F. Biggs
Medical Writings   L. Cameron
pseudo-Melito (see Apocrypha)   xxx
Mellitus (see Apocrypha)   xxx
De mensuris et ponderibus   T. Hall
pseudo-Methodius   M. Twomey

Milo of Saint-Amand
De mirabilibus orientis (see Marvels of the
   East) xxx
Miracula
Liber miraculorum
Expositio Missae R. Pfaff et al.
Morinus (pseudo)
Musical Writings

Nennius (see *Historia Brittonum*) xxx
Nicetas Remesianensis (see Pseudo-
   Ambrose, *De lapsu virginis consecretae*) xxx
Gospel of Nicodemus (see Apocrypha) xxx
Nonius Marcellus

Julius Obsequens
Odo of Cluny T. Hall/J. Cross
Odo of Meung (see Medical Writings) xxx
Ohtloh (see *Acta Sanctorum*)
Old English Bede E. Cooney
Old Saxon Genesis S. Deskis
Ordinals of Christ T. Hall
Ordines Romani R. Pfaff et al.
Oribasius (see Medical Writings) xxx
Origen D. Nodes
pseudo-Origen
Orosius J. Bately
pseudo-Orosius
Ovid

pseudo-Pachomius (see *Acta Sanctorum*) xxx
Pacuvius (see Grammatical Writings) xxx
Palaemon (see Grammatical Writings) xxx
Palladius Helenopolitanus P. Jackson
Papias D. Sprunger
Parsing Grammars (see Grammatical
   Writings) xxx
Paschal
Paschasinus Lillybitanus
Paschasius Diaconus T. Jones
Paschasius Radbertus of Corbie T. Leinbaugh
Paschasius Subdiaconus (see *Acta Sanctorum*) xxx

Passio Christi (see Liturgical Writings)	xxx
Passio Johannis (see Apocrypha)	xxx
Paterius	
Patrick of Dublin, Bishop	J. Cross
Paul of Aegina (see Medical Writings)	xxx
Pauli et Senecae epistolae (see Apocrypha)	xxx
Paul the Deacon	J. Cross
Paulinus of Nola	T. Mackay
Paulinus of Périgueux	
Paulus Quaestor	
De peccatorum vindictis	C. Wright
Pelagius	D. Dumville (inv.)
Penitentials	A. Frantzen
Persius	
Petosiris (see Magical Writings)	xxx
Petrus Chrysologus	D. Sprunger
Petrus Petricoriensis	
Philippus presbyter	M. Boudreau
Philo Judaeus	T. Mackay
Phocas (see Grammatical Writings)	xxx
Junius Phylargyrius	
Physiologus	F. Biggs
Pirmin	J. Hill
Pliny	
apud grammaticos	V. Law
Polemius Silvius (see Computistical Writings)	xxx
Polycarp	
Julianus Pomerius	
Pompeius (see Grammatical Writings)	xxx
Pompeius Trogus	T. Mackay
Optatianus Porphyrius	
Porphyry	
Possidius	
Posthumianus (see Gallus in *Acta Sanctorum*)	xxx
Potamius	
Praedestinatus	
Prayers	T. Bestul
Primasius	T. Mackay
Priscian (see Grammatical Writings)	xxx
Proba	D. Nodes
Probus (see Grammatical Writings)	xxx

Valerius Probus (?)
Proclus
Prognostica   R. Bremmer
Propertius
Prosper of Aquitaine   J.E. Cross
Proterius
Proverbia Graecorum   C. Wright
In Proverbiis expositio
Proviso futurarum rerum (see Julian of Toledo)   xxx
Prudentius   G. Wieland
Scholia in Psalmos (see *Hiberno-Latin . . . Com-*
mentaries)
Psalters   R. Pfaff et al.
Psalterium hieronymi sec. Hebraeos
Expositio super Psalterium
Sermo super quosdam Psalmos
Punifius (see Medical Writings)   xxx

Quintilian   M. Boudreau
Quintus Serenus (see Medical Writings)   xxx
Quodvultdeus   T. Hall

Ralph d'Escures   J. Cross
De ratione embolismorum (see Computistical
  Writings)   xxx
Ratramnus of Corbie   T. Leinbaugh
Ravenna Annals
Regino of Prum   P. Szarmach
Regularis Concordia   J. Hill
Remigius of Auxerre
Rituals   R. Pfaff et al.
Romana Computatio (see Computistical
  Writings)   xxx
Rubisca auctore Olimbriano (see *Hisperica Famina*) xxx
Rufinus   P. Jackson

Sabellus
Sacramentaries   R. Pfaff et al.
Sallust
Solomon and Saturn   T.D. Hill
Salonius   J. Ericksen
Taius Samuel (see Taio)   xxx

Caelius Sedulius	C. Springer
Seneca	P. Szarmach
pseudo-Seneca	P. Szarmach
Septem mirabilibus mundi (see pseudo-Bede)	xxx
Sergius (see Grammatical Writings)	xxx
Servius	D. Ganz
Sulpicius Severus	P. Szarmach
Sextus	
Sextus Placitus (see Medical Writings)	xxx
Sibylla (see Apocrypha)	xxx
Apollinaris Sidonius	
Sigillum S. Mariae	
De xii signis zocdiaci (see Computistical Writings)	xxx
Actus Silvestri (see *Acta Sanctorum*)	xxx
Sisebutus	
Smaragdus	J. Hill
Solinus (see *Aenigmata*)	xxx
Speculum Augustini	J.E. Cross
Speculum Gregorii	J.E. Cross
Sophronius	
Statius	
Stephen of Ripon	
Successor Dionysii (see Dionysii Successor)	
Suetonius	
Sulpicius Severus	xxx
Sylloge	
Sylloge Turonensis (see *Sylloge*)	xxx
Symphosius	D. Johnson
Synaxarium of Constantinople	
Tacitus	
Taio	
Tatwine	D. Johnson
De ratione temporum (see Computistical Writings)	xxx
Terence	
Tertullian	
Theodore of Canterbury	
Theodore of Mopsuestia	T. Mackay
Theodoret	
Theodorus Priscianus	

Mallius Theodorus
Theodotus Ancyrae
Theodulf of Orleans
Theodulus Presbyter
Theophili Actus   M. Clayton
Theophilus of Alexandria
pseudo-Theophilus
Theotbaldus Italicus
Thucydides
Tibullus
De s. Trinitate
Turcius Rufus Asterius
Tyconius   T. Mackay

De ratione unciarum
Usuard

Valerius
Julius Valerius
Valerius Maximus
Valerius Probus
Varro (see Grammatical Writings)   xxx
Vegetius   D. Mitchell
Veleius Longus   D. Mitchell
Ventorum Nomina (see Computistical Writings)   xxx
Verba seniorum (see *Vitae Patrum*)   xxx
Vergil
pseudo-Vergil
C. Julius Victor   D. Nodes
Victor of Capua
Cl. Marius Victor
Marius Victorinus
Victorinus of Pettau   F. Biggs
Victorinus Poeta
Maximus Victorinus
St. Victorinus
Victorius of Aquitaine
Vigilius Thapsensis
Vincentius Lerinensis
Vindicianis   R. Bremmer
Vindicta Salvatoris   T. Hall

Virgilius Maro Grammaticus (see Grammatical Writings)	xxx
Virgilius Salisburgensis (see Aethicus Ister)	xxx
Visio Baronti	T. Hall
Visio Pauli (see Apocypha)	xxx
Vitae Patrum	P. Jackson
Vitruvius	D. Mitchell
Wærferth of Worcester	C. Gravis
Wulfstan of Winchester	
Wulfstan of York	M. Richards

Appendix C:
SASLC Acta Sanctorum
List of Saints

Below is a preliminary list of saints' lives and hagiographical works known to the Anglo-Saxons up to A.D. 1100, identified where possible by *BHL* number [*Bibliotheca hagiographica latina*, 1st ed. & 1911 *Supplément* only; information from *Supplementum novum*, ed. H. Fros (Brussels 1986), not yet incorporated]. Cross references to other *saints* (SS.) refer to the other entries in *Acta sanctorum*; cross references to *authors* may refer to actual or projected main entries in *SASLC*, where the work in question is discussed. Other brief references to authors may indicate when a vernacular treatment of a saint's life or passion derives from a larger work, such as Bede's *Ecclesiastical History*, and not from an independent hagiographical text.

The compiler, E. Gordon Whatley [English Department, Queens College, City University of New York, Flushing, NY 11367–0904, USA] would be grateful for information about any other hagiographical works that should be included. The project is ongoing.

ABDON & Sennen, passio: *BHL* 6. See also SS. AGAPITUS & Felicissimus, SIXTUS & Laurentius & Hippolytus, LAURENTIUS, ROMANUS.

ABRAHAM & Maria, vita: *BHL* 12.

ABUNDIUS. See S. IRENAEUS.

ACHATIUS (ACACIUS) & soc. (10,000), passio: *BHL* 20. See also ANASTASIUS BIBLIOTHECARIUS.

ADRIANUS (HADRIANUS) Nicom., passio: *BHL* 3744.

AEGIDIUS, vita: *BHL* 93–95.

ÆTHELREDUS & Æthelbertus mm., passio (auct. Byrhtferth Ram.): *BHL* 2643. See BYRHTFERTH; see also S. MILDREDA.

ÆTHELWALDUS erem., ?vita/narratio (lost): *BHL* none.

ÆTHELWOLDUS Winton. ep., vita: *BHL* 2646, 2647. See ÆLFRIC (*BHL* 2646), and WULFSTANUS Wint. (*BHL* 2647).

AFRA & SOC., passio: *BHL* 108-09, 111.

AGAPE & Chione & Irene, passio: *BHL* 118. See also SS. ANASTASIA, CHRYSOGONUS, THEODOTA.

AGAPITUS Praen., passio: *BHL* 125.

AGATHA, passio: *BHL* 133-4.

AGNES, passio (auct. Ps.-Ambrosius): *BHL* 156. Also in PRUDENTIUS, PERISTEPHANON 14, *BHL* 159.

AICHARDUS, vita (lost): *BHL* 181.

AIDUS ep. (Aidan), vita: *BHL* 190. From BEDA HIST. ECCLES.

ALBANUS, passio: *BHL* 211a. Also from BEDA HIST. ECCLES., *BHL* 206-10.

ALBINUS Andeg., vita: *BHL* 234. See VENANTIUS FORTUNATUS.

ALEXANDER & SOC., passio: *BHL* 266.

ALEXANDRIA, passio: *BHL* 3363, 3379. See S. GEORGIUS.

ALEXIUS Edess., vita: *BHL* 286.

AMALBERGA, vita: *BHL* 323.

AMANDUS, vita: *BHL* 332 (auct. Baudemundus), *BHL* 333 (auct. Milo). See BAUDEMUNDUS; MILO.

AMBROSIUS, vita (auct. Paulus Mediolanus): *BHL* 377.

AMOS (AMMON) Nitria., vita: *BHL* 6524. See also VITAE PATRUM.

ANANIAS & Petrus & Septem Milites, passio: *BHL* 397?

ANASTASIA, passio: *BHL* 401. See also SS. AGAPE & SOC., CHRYSOGONUS, THEODOTA.

ANASTASIUS, passio: *BHL* 408 & 410b, 412.

ANATOLIA, passio: *BHL* 417, 418.

ANDOCHIUS & Thyrsus & Felix, passio: *BHL* 424. See also S. BENIGNUS.

ANDREAS, passio: *BHL* 428. See APOCRYPHA, PASSIO ANDREAE.

ANIANUS, vita: *BHL* 473.

ANNA. BHL?

ANTONINUS Apamea, passio: *BHL* 568-9, 572-3.

ANTONIUS, vita: *BHL* 609. See ATHANASIUS, EVAGRIUS.

APOLLINARIS Rav., passio: *BHL* 623.

APOLLONIUS (APOLLO) ab., vita: *BHL* 646 [= *BHL* 6524, cap. 7]. See also VITAE PATRUM.

ARSENIUS. *BHL* 6527. See also VITAE PATRUM.

ARTEMIUS (ARTHEMIUS.) See SS. MARCELLINUS & Petrus & soc.

ASCLA, passio: *BHL* 722.

ATHANASIUS, vita: *BHL* 728-30. See also EUSEBIUS/RUFINUS, HIST. ECCL.

AUDOENUS (Ouen), vita: *BHL* 750; vita metrica (lost; auct. Frithegodus).

AUDOMARUS, vita: *BHL* 765. See also SS. BERTINUS & WINNOCUS.

AUGUSTINUS Cant., vita: *BHL* 1:124. From BEDA HIST. ECCLES.

AUGUSTINUS Hippo., vita (auct. Possidius): *BHL* 785.

BABYLAS, passio: *BHL* 889-891.

BARONTUS, visio: *BHL* 997.

BARTHOLOMEUS, passio: *BHL* 1002. See APOCRYPHA, PASSIO BARTHOLOMAEI.

BASILIDES & SOC., passio: *BHL* 1018–20.

BASILISSA, passio: *BHL* 4529–32. See SS. JULIANUS & BASILISSA & SOC.

BASILIUS, vita (auct. Ps.-Amphilocus, interp. Euphemius): *BHL* 1022–3. See also ANASTASIUS BIBLIOTHECARIUS, RUFINUS.

BASILLA, passio. See S. EUGENIA & SOC.

BATHILDIS (BALTHILDIS) reg., vita: *BHL* 905.

BEDA presb., vita: *BHL* 1069. See also CUTHBERTUS, EP. DE OBITU BEDAE.

BENEDICTUS Bisc. ab., vita. See BEDA, HISTORIA ABBATUM (*BHL* 8968).

BENEDICTUS Bisc. ab., homilia: *BHL* 1101. See BEDA?

BENEDICTUS Nurs., vita: *BHL* 1102. See GREGORIUS MAGN., DIALOGI 2.

BENEDICTUS Nurs., miracula (auct. Adrevaldus Flor.): *BHL* 1123.

BENEDICTUS Nurs., sermo (auct. Odo Cluniac.). See ODO CLUNIAC.

BENEDICTUS Nurs., & Scholastica, translatio: *BHL* 1117.

BENIGNUS, passio: *BHL* 1153.

BERTINUS, vita: *BHL* 763. See SS. AUDOMARUS, WINNOCUS.

BLANDINA & SOC., narratio: *BHL* 6839 (passio Photini). From EUSEBIUS/RUFINUS, HIST. ECCLES.

BLASTUS, ?passio: *BHL* ?

BONIFATIUS m. Tars., passio: *BHL* 1413.

BRIGIDA, vita (auct. Cogitosus): *BHL* 1457.

BRITIUS (BRICCIUS), vita: *BHL* 1452. See GREGORIUS TURON.

CAECILIA, passio: *BHL* 1495.

CAESARIUS, passio: *BHL* 1511.

CALEPODIUS, passio. See S. CALLISTUS.

CALLISTUS & Calepodius & soc., passio: *BHL* 1523.

CASSIANUS Aug. ep., vita: *BHL* 1632, 1633.

CASSIANUS Ludimagister, passio; *BHL* 1626.

CASSIUS ep. Narn., narratio: *BHL* 1:248.

CEADDA ep. (Chad), narratio: *BHL* 1:258. From BEDA, HIST. ECCLES.

CEOLFRIDUS ab., vita: *BHL* 1726. See also BEDA, HISTORIA ABBATUM (*BHL* 1726 recently attributed to Bede himself).

CHIONE. See S. AGAPE & SOC.

CHRISTINA, passio: *BHL* 1748b, 1751, 1756.

CHRISTOPHER, passio: *BHL* 1764, 1766.

CHRYSANTHUS & Daria, passio: *BHL* 1787. CHRYSOGONUS, passio: *BHL* 1795. See also S. ANASTASIA & SOC.

CIRYCUS & Iulitta, passio: *BHL* 1802-07.

CLEMENS pap., passio: *BHL* 1848, 1855, 1857.

COLUMBA Hien. From BEDA, HIST. ECCLES.

COLUMBA Sen., passio: *BHL* 1892-94.

CONON, passio: *BHL* 1912.

CONSTANTINA Filia Constantini imp., narrationes: *BHL* 156-7, 3236- 38. See SS. GALLICANUS, IOHANNES & PAULUS; see also S. AGNES.

CORNELIUS, passio: *BHL* 1958.

CORONATI QUATTUOR. See SYMPHORIANUS.

COSMAS & Damianus, passio: *BHL* 1967–70.

CRISPINUS & Crispinianus, passio: *BHL* 1990.

CUTHBERTUS, vita: *BHL* 2019; historia: *BHL* 2024–5. See also BEDA, VITA CUTHB. METR. (*BHL* 2020), VITA CUTHB. PROS. (*BHL* 2021), and HIST. ECCLES.

CYPRIANUS & Justina & soc. Nicomed., passio: *BHL* 2047–48, 2050–51?

CYPRIANUS Carth., passio/acta: *BHL* 2038–39; *BHL* 2041 (auct. Pontus diaconus).

CYRILLA. See SS. SIXTUS & LAURENTIUS & SOC.

DIONISIUS ep., passio: *BHL* 2175. See HILDUINUS; also FORTUNATUS?

DOMITILLA (FLAVIA) & SOC., passio: *BHL* 6066.

DONATUS Aret., passio: *BHL* 2289.

DORMIENTES (SEPTEM), passio: *BHL* 2316. See also GREGORIUS TURON., PASSIO DORM. SEPT.; also in *Glor. mart.*

DUNSTANUS, vita: *BHL* 2342 (auct. "B"). See ADELARDUS BLANDIN. for *BHL* 2343 (MS London Gray's Inn 3).

EADBERHT Lindisf. ep., narratio. From BEDA *vita Cuthb. pros.*

EDBURGA Wint. (Nunnaminster & Pershore), vita (lost): *BHL* none (cf. *BHL* 2385).

EDITHA (EADGITHA) Wilton., OE miracle (lost): *BHL* none (cf. *BHL* 2388).

EDMUNDUS rex & m., passio: *BHL* 2392. See ABBO FLOR.

EDUARDUS, rex & m., passio (lost); miracula (lost): *BHL* none (cf. *BHL* 2418).

EGWINUS Wigorn. ep., vita: *BHL* 2432. See BYRHTFERTH?

ELEUTHERIUS & Anthia, passio: *BHL* 2451.

ELIGIUS ep., vita: *BHL* 2477.

EMERENTIANA, passio: *BHL* 156 (?2527). See S. AGNES.

EOSTERWINUS ab., vita. See BEDA, HISTORIA ABBATUM.

ERASMUS ep., passio: *BHL* 2578–82.

ERKENWALDUS, vita (lost): *BHL* none (cf. *BHL* 1:391, BEDA, HIST. ECCLES.).

ETHELBURGA Berecingensis ab., vita/miracula (lost): *BHL* none (cf. *BHL* 1:396, BEDA, HIST. ECCLES.).

ETHELDREDA abb., vita, miracula, hymnus: *BHL* 2632–3 (BEDA HIST. EC-CLES); OE vita (lost).

EUGENIA & soc., passio: *BHL* 2666, 2667–8.

EULALIA Barcinone, passio: *BHL* 2696.

EULALIA Emeritae, passio: *BHL* 2700. See also PRUDENTIUS, PERISTEPHA-NON 3.

EUPHEMIA, passio: *BHL* 2708.

EUPHRAXIA (EUPHRASIA), vita: *BHL* 2718.

EUPHROSYNA, vita: *BHL* 2723.

EUPLUS (EUPLIUS), passio: *BHL* 2729.

EUSEBIUS Romae presb., passio: *BHL* 2740.

EUSEBIUS Vercelli ep., passio: *BHL* 2748–9.

EUSTACHIUS, passio: *BHL* 2760; passio metrica: *BHL* 2767.

EUSTOCHIUM, epistola (cf. *BHL* 1:416). See HIERONIMUS, ep. 22.

EUTYCHES & Victorinus & Maro, passio: *BHL* 6064 (also 2789).

EXALTATIO SANCTAE CRUCIS, historia: *BHL* 4178. See also INVENTIO S. CRUCIS.

FAUSTA & Evilasii, passio: *BHL* 2833.

FELICITAS & 7 filiis, passio: *BHL* 2853.

FELIX II pap., passio: *BHL* 2857.

FELIX Nolanus presb., vita. See BEDA, PAULINUS NOLAN.

FELIX Romae presb. (Felix in Pincis), passio: *BHL* 2885.

FELIX Tubzacensis, passio: *BHL* 2894–95b.

FERREOLUS & Ferrucio, Vesontione, passio: *BHL* 2903.

FIRMINUS Ambianensis, passio: *BHL* 3002.

FRUCTUOSUS Tarroconensis & soc., passio : *BHL* 3200. See also PRUDEN-
TIUS, PERISTEPHANON 6.

FURSEUS, vita: *BHL* 3209–10.

FUSCIANUS & soc, passio: *BHL* 3226.

GALLICANUS, passio: *BHL* 3236 & 3238. See also SS. IOHANNES & Paulus;
CONSTANTINA.

GAUGERICUS, vita: *BHL* 3287.

GENESIUS Arlatensis, passio: *BHL* 3304, 3307.

GENESIUS Romae, passio: *BHL* 3320.

GENOVEFA, vita: *BHL* 3336.

GEORGIUS, passio: *BHL* 3363/3379, 3373–74.

GERMANUS Autisiodorensis, vita (auct. Constantius Lugd.): *BHL* 3453.

GERMANUS Parisiensis, vita: *BHL* 3468. See VENANTIUS FORTUNATUS.

GERVASIUS & Protasius, inventio/passio: *BHL* 3514. See also AMBROSIUS (ep. 22 = *BHL* 3513).

GETULIUS, passio: *BHL* 3524.

GISLENUS, vita: *BHL* 3552-7?

GORDIANUS & EPIMACHUS, passio: *BHL* 3612.

GREGORIUS Magnus, pap., vita: *BHL*. See also PAULUS DIACONUS (WARNEFRIDUS), *BHL* 3639; IOHANNES DIACONUS, *BHL* 3641.

GREGORIUS Nazienzenus, vita. From EUSEBIUS/RUFINUS, HIST. ECCLES.

GUTHLACUS, vita (auct. Felix): *BHL* 3723.

HERMES, passio: *BHL* 266 (cf. 3853-4). See also SS. ALEXANDER & SOC.

HIERONYMUS presb., vita: *BHL* 3869.

HILARION Erem., vita. See HIERONYMUS, *BHL* 3879.

HILARIUS Pict., vita. See VENANTIUS FORTUNATUS, *BHL* 3885.

HILDA, vita (lost): *BHL* 1:583. Also from BEDA, HIST. ECCLES.

HIPPOLYTUS Romae presb., passio: *BHL* 3961. See SS. SIXTUS, LAURENTIUS & HIPPOLYTUS; see also PRUDENTIUS, PERISTEPHANON 11.

HUGBERHTUS Leodiensis, vita. See JONAS of Orléans, *BHL* 3994.

HWAETBERHTUS ab., vita. See BEDA, HISTORIA ABBATUM.

HYACINTHUS & Protus, passio: *BHL* 2666. See SS. EUGENIA & Soc. for MSS.

HYANCINTHUS in Portu Romano, passio: *BHL* 4053.

IACOBUS MAJOR ap., passio: *BHL* 4057. See APOCRYPHA, PASSIO IACOB. MAJ.

IACOBUS MINOR ap., passio: *BHL* 4089, 4094. See APOCRYPHA, PASSIO IACOB. MIN.

IANUARIUS & SOSIUS & SOC., passio: *BHL* 4116-7, 4124-5, 4132.

IESUS CHRISTUS, IMAGO BERYTENSIS, sermo: *BHL* 4230. See PS-ATHAN-
ASIUS/ANASTASIUS BIBLIOTHECARIUS.

INDRACTUS, ?OE passio (lost): *BHL* 1:633.

INVENTIO SANCTAE CRUCIS, historia: *BHL* 4169, 4171.

IOHANNES & Paulus, passio: *BHL* 3236, 3238. See also SS. CONSTANTINA,
GALLICANUS, HILARINUS

IOHANNES BAPT., inventio (capitis). See DIONYSIUS EXIGUUS, *BHL* 4290-91.
See also MARCELLINUS COMES, Chron.

IOHANNES Eleemosyinarius, vita: *BHL* 4388-9. See ANASTASIUS BIB-
LIOTHECARIUS.

IOHANNES Evang. ap., acta/passio: *BHL* 4320, 4321. See APOCRYPHA, PS-
MELLITUS. PASSIO IOHANNIS EVANG.

IRENEUS & Abundius, passio. See SS. SIXTUS, LAURENTIUS & HIPPOLYTUS.

IULIANUS Cenomanensis, lectiones: *BHL*?

JUDOCUS, vita: *BHL* 4504.

JULIANA, passio: *BHL* 4522/4523.

JULIANUS & Basilissa, passio: *BHL* 4529-32.

JUSTUS Bellov., passio: *BHL* 4590.

KENELMUS, passio (lost, auct. Wlwinus?).

KIARANUS (Clonmac. or Sagir.), vita: *BHL* 4654-5 (Clonmac.) or *BHL*
4657-8 (Sagir.).

LANDBERTUS, vita: *BHL* 4677.

LAURENTIUS, passio: *BHL* 4752, 4753. See SS. SIXTUS, LAURENTIUS, & HIP-
POLYTUS; also PRUDENTIUS, PERISTEPHANON 2.

LEODEGARIUS, passio/vita: *BHL* 4853.

LEONARDUS Nobiliacensis, vita, miracula: *BHL* 4862, 4863-?

LONGINUS, passio: *BHL* 4965.

LUCAS evang., laudatio: *BHL* 4973, 4976d. Also in ISIDORUS, DE ORTU ET OBITU PATRUM; also PS.ISIDORUS, DE ORTU.

LUCEIA (LUCIA) Romae, passio: *BHL* 4980.

LUCIA & GEMINIANUS, passio: *BHL* 4985.

LUCIA Syracusis, passio: *BHL* 4992.

LUCIANUS, passio: *BHL* 5010.

LUCIANUS & MARCIANUS, passio: *BHL* 5015.

LUPUS Trecensis, vita: *BHL* 5087.

MACEDONIUS & Patricia & Modesta. *BHL* none.

MACHUTUS, vita (auct. Bili): *BHL* 5116.

MALCHUS, vita. See HIERONYMUS, *BHL* 5190.

MAMAS (Mammes), passio: *BHL* 5192-4.

MAMILIANUS ep. Panorm. *BHL* 5204d?

MARCELLINUS & PETRUS, passio: *BHL* 5231.

MARCELLUS Cabillon., passio: *BHL* 5245-6?

MARCELLUS pap., passio: *BHL* 5234-35.

MARCUS evang.& ap., passio: *BHL* 5276, 5279. See APOCRYPHA, PASSIO MARCI.

MARGARETA (MARINA), passio: *BHL* 5303, 5306.

MARIA Aegypt., vita: *BHL* 5415.

MARIA MAGDALENA, sermo. See ODO of Cluny, *BHL* 5439.

MARIA MERETRIX. See ss. ABRAHAM & Maria.

MARIAE B.V. ASSUMPTIO, epistola/acta (Ps.-Hieronymus, ep. 9 = PASCHASIUS RADBERTUS, EP.PAUL.EUST.): *BHL* 5355d. See also s. EUSTOCHIUM; PASCHASIUS RADBERTUS.

MARIAE NATIVITAS, evangelium apoc.; sermo de nativitate Mariae. See APOCRYPHA, GOSPEL OF PS-MATTHEW; PROTO-EVANGELIUM OF JAMES.

MARII & MARTHAE & SOC., passio: *BHL* 5543. See also s. VALENTINUS Interamn. & s. VALENTINUS Rom.

MARINUS puer, passio: *BHL* 5538.

MARTIALIS Lemovicensis, vita: *BHL* 5561?

MARTINA, passio: *BHL* 5588.

MARTINUS Tur., vita. See SULPICIUS SEVERUS, *BHL* 5610; ALCVINUS, *BHL* 5625-6.

MARTINUS Tur., epistolae. See SULPICIUS SEVERUS, *BHL* 5611-13.

MARTINUS Tur., miracula: *BHL* 5619-23. See also GREGORIUS TUR.

MARTINUS Tur., dialogi. See SULPICIUS SEVERUS, *BHL* 5614-16.

MARTINUS Tur., inscriptio: *BHL* none.

MARTINUS Tur., notae: *BHL* none.

MARTINUS Tur. (Ps.-Martinus), confessio: *BHL* none. See HILARIUS PICT.?

MATTHEUS ap., passio. See APOCRYPHA, PASSIO MATTHEI.

MAURITIUS & Soc., passio: *BHL* 5743; passio metrica (auct. Walafrido): *BHL* 5750? See also WALAFRIDUS?

MAURUS, vita: *BHL* 5773.

MAXIMUS, Severa, Flavianus & soc. *BHL* 5857d-e.

MEDARDUS, vita. See VENANTIUS FORTUNATUS, *BHL* 5864-65.

MENNAS Aegypt., passio: *BHL* 5921.

MICHAELIS archang., ?apparitio: *BHL* 5948–49.

MILDREDA abb., life (OE); translatio: *BHL* 5961. See also ss. AETHELREDUS & Æthelbertus; s. SEXBURGA.

MILUS & SENNEUS. *BHL* none?

NARCISSUS Hierosolimytanus ep., vita. From EUSEBIUS/RUFINUS, HIST. ECCLES.

NAZARIUS & CELSUS, passio: *BHL* 6039–41.

NEOTUS, vita (lost): *BHL* none (cf. 2:882); OE life.

NEREUS & ACHILLEUS, passio: *BHL* 6058, 6060–66, 6059.

NICANDER & SOC., ?passio: *BHL* 6070–73.

NICHOLAS Mir., vita: *BHL* 6104–06, 6108 (in CCCC 9 only?). See IOHANNES LEVITA (John the deacon).

NICHOLAS Mir., miracula: *BHL* 6133, 6150–56, 6160–61, 6163–65, 6172, 6174.

NICHOLAS Mir. ep., translatio (auct. Iohannes Barensis): *BHL* 6190.

NICOMEDES, passio: *BHL* 6062. See ss. NEREUS & ACHILLEUS.

NINIANUS (Ninian), miracula (metr.): *BHL* ?

OSWALDUS Ebor. ep., vita: *BHL* 6374. See BYRHTFERTH.

OSWALDUS Nord. rex: *BHL* 2:919. From BEDA, HIST. ECCLES.

PANCRATIUS, passio: *BHL* 6423.

PANTALEON, passio: *BHL* 6437.

PATRICIUS, confessio, epistola: *BHL* 6492–3.

PATROCLUS Trecensis, passio: *BHL* 6520.

PAULINUS Ebor. ep.: *BHL* 2:951. From BEDA, HIST. ECCLES.

PAULUS Erem., vita: *BHL* 6596. See HIERONYMUS.

PAULUS. ap., passio: *BHL* 6570. See APOCRYPHA, PS. LINUS, PASSIO PAULI.

PEGA. See S. GUTHLACUS.

PELAGIA paen., vita (auct. Iac. Diacon., interpr. Eustochius): *BHL* 6605–09.

PERPETUA & Felicitas, passio: *BHL* 6633–35.

PETRONILLA & FELICULA, passio: *BHL* 6061. See SS. NEREUS & ACHILLEUS.

PETRUS ap., passio: *BHL* 6664. See APOCRYPHA, PASSIO PETRI.

PHILIBERTUS (FILIBERTUS), vita: *BHL* 6806.

PHILIPPUS ap., passio: *BHL* 6814/15. See APOCRYPHA, PASSIO PHILIPPI.

PHOCAS Sinop., passio: *BHL* 6838.

PIATO, passio: *BHL* 6845.

POLYCARPUS, passio ("epistula Eccles. Smyrnensis"): *BHL* 6870.

POTITUS, passio: *BHL* 6908.

PRAXEDIS, vita: *BHL* 6920. See also S. PUDENTIANA.

PRIMUS & Felicianus, passio: *BHL* 6922.

PRISCA, passio: *BHL* 6926/6926b?

PROCESSUS & Martinianus, passio: *BHL* 6947.

PROCOPIUS Caes., passio: *BHL* 6949.

PUDENTIANA, passio: *BHL* 6991. See also S. PRAXEDIS.

QUADRAGINTA MARTYRES ("SEBASTENI"), passio: *BHL* 7538.

QUADRAGINTASEX MARTYRES. See SS. SIXTUS, LAURENTIUS & HIPPOLYTUS.

QUATTUOR CORONATI. See S. SYMPHORIANUS & SOC.

QUINTINUS, passio: *BHL* 6999/7000.

QUINTUS. *BHL* none.

REMIGIUS, vita, translatio, miracula (auct. Hincmar.): *BHL* 7152–59. See
HINCMAR REM.

RICHARIUS, vita (auct. Alcuin.): *BHL* 7224. See ALCVINUS.

ROMANUS Rom. miles. See SS. SIXTUS, LAURENTIUS & HIPPOLYTUS.

RUFINA & Secunda, passio: *BHL* 7359.

RUFINUS & Valerius, passio: *BHL* 7374. See PASCHASIUS RADBERTUS.

RUMWALDUS infans, vita: *BHL* 7385.

SABINA (SAVINA) Trecis, vita: *BHL* 7408.

SABINA Romae, passio: *BHL* 7407. See also S. SERAPIA.

SABINUS Spoleti, passio: *BHL* 7451.

SALVIUS ep. Valencen., passio: *BHL* 7472.

SATURNINUS & Sisinnus Rom., passio: *BHL* 5234, 7493.

SATURNINUS Tolos. passio: *BHL* 749?

SCILLITANI, passio: *BHL* 7531 & ?

SEBASTENI (MARTYRES/MILITES XL), passio: *BHL* 7538, 7539.

SEBASTIANUS & soc., passio (auct. Ps.-Ambrosius): *BHL* 7543.

SERAPIA, passio: *BHL* 7586. See also S. SABINA Rom.

SERGIUS & Bacchus, passio: *BHL* 7599.

SERVATIUS ep., sermo: *BHL* 7614. See RADBODUS (of Utrecht).

SEXBURGA, vita (OE): *BHL* none (cf. *BHL* 7693).

SIGFRIDUS ab., vita. See BEDA, HISTORIA ABBATUM.

SILVESTER pap., gesta/actus: *BHL* 7725-37, 7739.

SIMON & IUDAS (THADDEUS) app., passio: *BHL* 7749-51. See APOCRYPHA, PASSIO SIMONIS ET IUDAE.

SIMPLICIUS & Faustina & Beatrix, passio: *BHL* 7790.

SISINNIUS & Martyrius & Alexander, passio: *BHL* 7794?.

SIXTUS & LAURENTIUS & HIPPOLYTUS, passio: *BHL* 7801; 6884, 6, 4754, 3961. See also SS. ABDON & Sennen; PRUDENTIUS, PERISTEPHANON 2, 9.

SPEUSIPPUS & Soc. (TERGEMINI), passio: *BHL* 7828, 7829 (auct. Warnaharius).

STEPHANUS pap., passio: *BHL* 7845/46.

STEPHANUS protom., inventio (auct. Lucianus, interpr. Avitus); homilia: *BHL* 7854. Also AUGUSTINUS HIP., DE CIV. DEI 22.

SULPICIUS Bitur., vita: *BHL* 7928.

SWITHUNUS, miracula, translatio: *BHL* 7944-5 (auct. Lantfredus Winton.), 7947 (auct. Wvlfstanus Winton.). See also WULFSTANUS Winton.

SYMEON stylita, vita: *BHL* 7956-8?

SYMPHORIANUS & Claudius & soc. (Quattuor Coronati), passio: *BHL* 1837.

SYMPHORIANUS AUGUSTUD. *BHL* 7967-69.

SYMPHOROSA & Filiis, passio (auct. Ps.-Julius Africanus): *BHL* 7971.

THAIS, vita: *BHL* 8012/13.

THECLA, passio: *BHL* 8020a, 8024.

THEODORA & Didymus, passio: *BHL* 8072.

THEODORETUS *BHL* 8074-76.

THEODORUS Amas., passio: *BHL* 8077.

THEODOSIA, passio: *BHL* 8090-91.

THEODOTA & filii, passio: *BHL* 8093, 8096. See also SS. ANASTIASIA, AGAPE & SOC., CHRYSOGONUS.

THEOGENES, passio: *BHL* 8107.

THEOPHILUS Adan., vita/actus (auct. Paulus Diac.): *BHL* 8121.

THOMAS ap. *BHL* 8436-? See APOCRYPHA, PASSIO THOMAE.

THYRSUS & Leucius & soc., passio: *BHL* 8280.

TIMOTHEUS Rom. See S. SILVESTER.

TORPES Pisan., passio: *BHL* 8307.

TRUDO Hasbania (Trond), vita (auct. Donatus diac.): *BHL* 8321.

TRYPHON, passio: *BHL* 8338.

URSICINUS medicus. See S. VITALIS Rav.

VALENTINUS Interamnensis (Terni), passio : *BHL* 8460.

VALENTINUS Romae, passio. See SS. MARIUS, MARTHA & SOC.

VALERIANUS Trenorchii, passio: *BHL* 8488.

VEDASTUS Atrebatensis ep., vita: *BHL* 8506/8508. See ALCVINVS.

VICTOR & Corona, passio: *BHL* 8559, 8561.

VICTOR Massil., passio: *BHL* 8569-72.

VICTOR Mediol., passio: *BHL* 8580.

VICTORIA Rom., passio: *BHL* 8591. See also S. ANATOLIA.

VINCENTIUS Caes., passio: *BHL* 8628, 8630/31, 8634.

VITALIS Rav., passio: *BHL* 8700? See also ss. GERVASIUS & Protasius.

VITUS & Modestus & Crescentia, passio: *BHL* 8712.

WALERICUS, vita: *BHL* 8762.

WANDREGISILUS, vita: *BHL* 8805.

WERBURGA, vita (lost): *BHL* none; cf. *BHL* 8855.

WIGSTANUS (WISTANUS), ?passio (lost): *BHL* 2:1295.

WILFRIDUS, vita (auct. Eddius Stephanus): *BHL* 8889. Also BEDA, HIST. EC-CLES.; and see FRITHEGODUS.

WINNOCUS, vita: *BHL* 8952. See also ss. AUDOMARUS & BERTINUS.

WULFSTANUS Wigorn., lost OE life (auct. Coleman). Cf. *BHL* 8756 (William of Malmesbury, *Vita Wulfstani*).

ZOE Rom. See s. SEBASTIANUS.